Lecture Notes in Computer Science 4126

Commenced Publication in 1973
Founding and Former Series Editors:
Gerhard Goos, Juris Hartmanis, and Jan van Leeuwen

T0192565

Pedro Barahona   François Bry
Enrico Franconi   Nicola Henze
Ulrike Sattler (Eds.)

Reasoning Web

Second International Summer School 2006
Lisbon, Portugal, September 4-8, 2006
Tutorial Lectures

 Springer

Volume Editors

Pedro Barahona
Universidade Nova de Lisboa
2829-516 Caparica, Portugal
E-mail: pb@di.fct.unl.pt

François Bry
University of Munich
D-80538 München,Germany
E-mail: bry@pms.ifi.lmu.de

Enrico Franconi
Free University of Bozen–Bolzano,
1-39100 Bozen-Bolzano, Italy
E-mail: franconi@inf.unibz.it

Nicola Henze
University of Hannover
D-30167 Hannover, Germany
E-mail: henze@kbs.uni-hannover.de

Ulrike Sattler
University of Manchester
Manchester, UK
E-mail: sattler@cs.man.ac.uk

Library of Congress Control Number: 2006931476

CR Subject Classification (1998): H.4, H.3, C.2, H.5, J.1, K.4, K.6, I.2.11

LNCS Sublibrary: SL 3 – Information Systems and Application, incl. Internet/Web
and HCI

ISSN   0302-9743
ISBN-10   3-540-38409-X Springer Berlin Heidelberg New York
ISBN-13   978-3-540-38409-0 Springer Berlin Heidelberg New York

Springer is a part of Springer Science+Business Media

springer.com

© Springer-Verlag Berlin Heidelberg 2006

Typesetting: Camera-ready by author, data conversion by Scientific Publishing Services, Chennai, India
Printed on acid-free paper   SPIN: 11837787   06/3142   5 4 3 2 1 0

Preface

This volume contains the lecture notes of the Summer School "Reasoning Web 2006" (http://reasoningweb.org), which took place on September 4-6, 2006 in Lisbon and was hosted by the New University of Lisbon (Universidade Nova de Lisboa).

Like the first "Reasoning Web" Summer School (cf. LNCS 3564), which took place in 2005, the Summer School "Reasoning Web 2006" was organized by the Network of Excellence REWERSE, "Reasoning on the Web with Rules and Semantics" (http://rewerse.net), its member "Centre of Artificial Intelligence (CENTRIA)" at the New University of Lisbon being responsible for the local organization.

Reasoning is one of the central issues in Semantic Web research and development. Indeed, the Semantic Web aims at enhancing today's Web with semantics-carrying "meta-data" and reasoning methods. The Semantic Web is a very active field of research and development, which involves both academia and industry.

The "Reasoning Web" Summer Schools provide a yearly forum for presenting and discussing recent developments in the "Semantic Web" field. They have a specical focus on *applied reasoning* and on *applications.* They are primarily, but not only, intended for young researchers, especially PhD students and young professionals involved in research and/or development in the "Semantic Web" field.

The programme of the Summer School "Reasoning Web 2006" cover the following issues:

- Semantic Web Query Languages
- Semantic Web Rules and Ontologies
- Bioinformatics and Medical Ontologies
- Industrial Aspects

Semantic Web Query Languages. Query languages are expected to become as important on the Web and on the Semantic Web as they already are in data-bases. Indeed, many practical applications on today's Web, and many of the Semantic Web applications that are expected to emerge, can be seen as information systems. Query languages ease the retrieval of data from complex databases or information systems. Query languages for the Web and the Semantic Web are an active area of research: in April 2006 the query language SPARQL, a query language for the Resource Description Framework RDF, attained the status of a "W3C Candidate Recommendation" (cf. http://www.w3.org/TR/rdf-sparql-query/); since 2004 a plethora of approaches to querying RDF have been proposed. The Summer School "Reasoning Web 2006" paid a tribute to this by including in its programme firstly a presentation of SPARQL by Bijan Parsia, a member of the "W3C RDF Data Access Working Group" which develops SPARQL, and secondly a comparative overview by Tim Furche,

Benedikt Linse, Dimitris Plexousakis, Georg Gottlob, and myself of selected query languages for RDF. This overview deepens and completes a first comparison presented at the Summer School "ReasoningWeb 2005", which considered almost all query languages proposed for RDF but in a more superficial manner.

Semantic Web Rules and Ontologies. Rule-based formalisms currently receive considerable attention from Semantic Web researchers and developers: The W3C, for example, launched in November 2005 a "Rule Interchange Format (RIF)" Working Group (cf. `http://www.w3.org/2005/rules/`) and many researchers are now investigating how rule-based reasoning can be applied with XML, RDF, and/or OWL data. The Summer School "Reasoning Web 2006" therefore offered four complementary lectures on the subject. Two of them, given by Riccardo Rosati and by Thomas Eiter, Giovambattista Ianni, Axel Polleres, Roman Schindlauer, and Hans Tompits, respectively presented recent approaches to rule-based reasoning with ontologies. A further lecture by Silvie Spreeuwenberg and Rik Gerrits was devoted to discussing the commonalities and the differences of "Business Rules" and "Semantic Web Rules". A fourth and last lecture on rule-based formalisms for the Semantic Web by Uwe Aßmann, Jendrik Johannes, Jakob Henriksson, and Ilie Savga showed how modern software composition methods can be applied to Semantic Web rule languages.

Bioinformatics and Medical Ontologies. Bioinformatics and Medicine are a premier application field of Semantic Web methods. For this reason, Semantic Web researchers and developers can learn much from Semantic Web applications in these fields. The Summer School "Reasoning Web 2006" therefore offered three complementary lectures on Bioinformatics and Medical Ontologies: A first lecture by Alan Rector and Jeremy Rogers introduced the representation of medical concepts in the GALEN ontology; a second lecture by Michael Schroeder and Patrick Lambrix described a basis for a "Semantic Web for the Life Sciences", and a third lecture by Ludwig Krippahl was devoted to the integration of Web data in the prediction of the' structures and functions of proteins.

Industrial Aspects. Finally, the Summer School "Reasoning Web 2006" offered a lecture by Alain Léger, Johannes Heinecke, Lyndon J.B. Nixon, Pavel Shvaiko, Jean Charlet, Paola Hobson, and François Goasdoué on an industrial perspective of the Semantic Web.

Many persons contributed towards making the Summer School "Reasoning Web 2006" possible: First and foremost, the above mentioned lecturers; second the local organizers, in particular Carlos Viegas Damásio from the New University of Lisbon; and finally the programme committee consisting of Pedro Barahona, New University of Lisbon, Enrico Franconi, Free University of Bozen-Bolzano, Nicola Henze, University of Hannover, and Ulrike Sattler, University of Manchester, who all helped me in selecting the Summer School lectures and assessing their quality. Ulrike Sattler deserves a special mention for having collected the lecture notes and prepared this book. I would also like to mention Jan

Małuszyński from the University of Linköping, and Norbert Eisinger from the University of Munich, coordinator and deputy coordinator of the REWERSE Working Group "Education and Training" on behalf of which the "Reasoning Web" Summer Schools are run.

I thank all of them warmly for their work, their dedication, and also for their lasting patience, which, I am afraid, was tried again and again during the eight months leading up to the summer school.

June 2006   François Bry

Organization

Programme Committee

Pedro Barahona	New University of Lisbon (Portugal)
François Bry	University of Munich (Germany), chair
Enrico Franconi	Free University of Bozen-Bolzano (Italy)
Nicola Henze	University of Hannover (Germany)
Ulrike Sattler	University of Manchester (UK)

Local Organisation

Carlos Viegas Damásio   New University of Lisbon (Portugal)

Sponsoring Institutions

The Reasoning Web 2006 Summer School is supported by the following organisations:

Fundação para a Ciência e a Tecnologia, Ministério da Ciência e Ensino Superior, Portugal.

Faculdade de Ciências e Tecnologia da Universidade Nova de Lisboa, Portugal.

Network of Excellence *REWERSE*,
http://rewerse.net

Table of Contents

Industrial Aspects

RDF Querying:
Language Constructs and Evaluation Methods Compared

Tim Furche[1], Benedikt Linse[1], François Bry[1],
Dimitris Plexousakis[2,3], and Georg Gottlob[4]

[1] Institute for Informatics, University of Munich,
Oettingenstraße 67, 80538 München, Germany
http://www.pms.ifi.lmu.de/
[2] Department of Computer Science, University of Crete
Vassilika Vouton, P.O. Box 1385, GR 711 10 Heraklion, Crete, Greece
http://www.ics.forth.gr/isl/people/people_individual.jsp?Person_ID=5
[3] Information Systems Laboratory, Institute of Computer Science, FORTH
Vassilika Vouton, P.O. Box 1385, GR 711 10 Heraklion, Crete, Greece
[4] Oxford University Computing Laboratory,
Wolfson Building, Parks Road, Oxford, OX1 3QD, England
http://web.comlab.ox.ac.uk/oucl/people/georg.gottlob.html

Abstract. This article is firstly an introduction into query languages for the Semantic Web, secondly an in-depth comparison of the languages introduced. Only RDF query languages are considered because, as of the writing of this paper, query languages for other Semantic Web data modeling formalisms, especially OWL, are still an open research issue, and only a very small number of, furthermore incomplete, proposals for querying Semantic Web data modeled after other formalisms than RDF exist. The limitation to a few RDF query languages is motivated both by the objective of an in-depth comparison of the languages addressed and by space limitations. During the three years before the writing of this article, more than three dozen proposals for RDF query languages have been published! Not only such a large number, but also the often immature nature of the proposals makes the focus on few, but representative languages a necessary condition for a non-trivial comparison.

For this article, the following RDF query languages have been, admittedly subjectively, selected: Firstly, the "relational" or "pattern-based" query languages SPARQL, RQL, TRIPLE, and Xcerpt; secondly the reactive rule query language Algae; thirdly and last the "navigational access" query language Versa. Although subjective, this choice is arguably a good coverage of the diverse language paradigms considered for querying RDF data. It is the authors' hope and expectation, that this comparison will motivate and trigger further similar studies, thus completing the present article and overcoming its limitation.

P. Barahona et al. (Eds.): Reasoning Web 2006, LNCS 4126, pp. 1–52, 2006.
© Springer-Verlag Berlin Heidelberg 2006

1   Introduction

Query Answering on the Semantic Web

Query answering is as central to the Semantic Web as it is to the conventional Web. Indeed, the Web as well as the emerging Semantic Web can be seen as information systems; and query answering is an essential functionality of any information system.

The Semantic Web is a research and development endeavor aiming at overcoming limitations of today's Web. It has has been described as follows by W3C founder Tim Berners-Lee, Jim Hendler, and Ora Lassila:

> "The Semantic Web will bring structure to the meaningful content of Web pages, creating an environment where software agents roaming from page to page can readily carry out sophisticated tasks for users." [16]

In the Semantic Web, conventional Web data (usually represented in (X)HTML or other XML formats) is enriched by meta-data (represented, e.g., in RDF, Topic Maps, OWL) specifying the "meaning" of other data and allowing Web-based systems to take advantage of "intelligent" reasoning capabilities.

Query answering on the Semantic Web might be seen as more complex than querying on the conventional Web because the "meaning" conveyed by meta-data has to be properly "understood" and processed. In particular, query languages for RDF may convey RDF/S's semantics as expressed, e.g., by RDF type triples.

Focus of this Article

This article is

1. an introduction into query languages for the Semantic Web;
2. an in-depth comparison of the languages introduced along prominent language constructs and concepts.

Only RDF query languages are considered in this article. The reason for this is, that as of the writing of this paper, query languages for other Semantic Web data modeling formalisms, especially OWL, still are an open research issue, and only a very small number of, furthermore incomplete, proposals for querying Semantic Web data modeled after other formalisms than RDF are known.

Furthermore, only a few RDF query languages are considered in this article. This limitation is motivated both by the objective of an in-depth comparison of the languages addressed and by space limitations. During the three years before the writing of this article, more than three dozen proposals for RDF query languages have been published! Not only such a large number, but also the often immature nature of the proposals makes the focus on few, but representative languages a necessary condition for a non-trivial comparison.

In the spirit of a practical introduction into these query languages, we have taken an example-centered approach. We believe that this is advantageous to the reader to quickly gain an impression of the language and constructs. Furthermore, a more formal treatment of the languages is impeded by the lack of (published) formal semantics. In Section 5, however, different semantics for interesting language constructs are addressed and compared in select cases.

This article builds upon and complements the survey [5] of Semantic Web query languages co-authored in 2005 by some of the authors of the present article.[1] While the focus of the 2005 survey has been a complete, but therefore necessarily somewhat shallow coverage of Semantic Web query languages, including on the one hand query languages for Topic Maps and on the other hand all known "dialectal" variations of RDF query languages. In contrast, the present article is focused on an in-depth comparison of a few selected RDF query languages that the authors consider representative. Although building upon the survey [5], this article is self-contained.

At least the first part, of the article is mostly of an introductory nature. We believe, however, that also researchers and scientists already acquainted with RDF query languages can benefit from the presented material. This applies particularly to the comparison of language constructs and evaluation methods in the second part. We hope that the direct comparisons reveal choices that language designers face when deciding which constructs to support in which way, and that language users face when deciding which languages are suitable for their particular needs.

Language Selection and Order

This article aims at introducing from the perspective of the authors interesting and representative selection of query languages proposed for RDF:

- Firstly, the "relational" or "pattern-based" query languages SPARQL, RQL, TRIPLE, and Xcerpt (with its visual "twin" visXcerpt).
- Secondly, the "reactive rule" query language Algae.
- Thirdly, the "navigational access" query language Versa.

Although incomplete and admittedly subjective, this choice can be seen as a good coverage of the diverse language paradigms considered for querying RDF data.

It is the authors' hope and expectation that this comparison will motivate further similar studies that complete the present article and overcome its limitation. It is also the authors' hope that this article will provide Semantic Web practitioners and researchers alike with a good introduction into query answering on the Semantic Web even though it does not address all query languages proposed for the Semantic Web.

Structure of this Article

The following three questions are at the heart of this article and give it its structure:

---

[1] Sections 2 and 3 are shortend versions of corresponding sections of [5].

1. what are the core *paradigms* of each query language,
2. what *language constructs* do different languages offer to solve tasks such as path traversal, optional selection, or grouping,
3. how are they *realized*?

In Section 2, the RDF/S data model, a running example, the RDF/S semantics and serialization formats are introduced. Section 3 begins by presenting a categorization of Semantic Web queries and sample queries for each category. Subsequently, in Section 4 the RDF query languages selected are introduced—grouped according to their families, i.e., "relational" or "pattern-based", "reactive rule" and "navigational access". For each language considered, some of the sample queries are formulated. For the sake of conciseness and simplicity, not all sample queries are expressed in each language considered. In Section 5 a summary and comparison of language features observable and desirable for RDF query languages is given. Section 6 examines evaluation methods of Semantic Web queries. Section 7 concludes this survey.

2   A Brief Introduction to RDF and RDFS

2.1   Data Model

RDF [10, 59] data are sets of "triples" or "statements" of the form *(Subject, Property, Object)*. RDF data are commonly seen as directed graphs the nodes of which are statement's subjects and objects and the arcs of which correspond to statement's properties, i.e., an arc relates a statement's subject with the statement's object. Properties are also called "predicates". Nodes (i.e., subjects and objects) are either

1. labeled by URIs describing Web resources,
2. or labeled by literals, i.e., scalar data such as strings or numbers,
3. or are unlabeled and called anonymous or "blank nodes".

Blank nodes are commonly used to group or "aggregate" properties. Specific properties are predefined in the RDF and RDFS recommendations [21, 53, 59, 69], e.g., rdf:type for specifying the type of resources, rdfs:subClassOf for specifying class-subclass relationships between subjects/objects, and rdfs:subPropertyOf for specifying property-subproperty relationships between properties. Furthermore, RDFS has "meta-classes", e.g., rdfs:Class, the class of all classes, and rdf:Property, the class of all properties.[2]

RDFS [21] allows one to define so-called "RDF Schemas" or "ontologies", similar to object-oriented data models. The inheritance model of RDFS exhibits the following peculiarities:

1. resources can be classified in different classes that are not related in the class hierarchy,

---

[2] This survey tries to use self-explanatory prefixes for namespaces where possible.

2. the class hierarchy can be cyclic so that all classes on the cycle are "subclass equivalent",
3. properties are first-class objects, and
4. RDF does not describe which properties can be associated with a class, but instead the domain and range of a property.

Based on an RDFS schema, "inference rules" can be specified, for instance the transitivity of the class hierarchy, or the type of an untyped resource that has a property associated with a known domain.

RDF can be *serialized* in various formats, the most frequently used being (RDF/) XML. Early approaches to RDF serialization have raised considerable criticism due to their complexity. As a consequence, a surprisingly large number of RDF serializations have been proposed, cf. [26] for a detailed survey.

2.2   Running Example: Classification-Based Book Recommender

In the following, queries in a simple book recommender system describing various properties and relationships between books are considered as running examples.[3] The recommender system describes properties of and relationships between books. It consists of a hierarchy (or *ontology*) of the book categories Writing, Novel, Essay, Historical_Novel, and Historical_Essay, and two books *The First Man in Rome* (a Historical_Novel authored by *Colleen McCullough*) and *Bellum Civile* (a Historical_Essay authored by *Julius Caesar* and *Aulus Hirtius*, and translated by *J.M. Carter*). Figure 1 depicts these data as a (simplified) RDF graph [21, 59, 63]. Note in particular that a Historical_Novel is both, a Novel and an Essay, and that books may optionally have translators, as is the case for *Bellum Civile*.

The simple ontology in the book recommender system only makes use of the subsumption (or "is-a-kind-of") relation rdfs:subClassOf and the instance (or "is-a") relation rdf:type. This simple and small ontology is sufficient to illustrate the most important aspects of RDF query languages.

The RDF representation of the sample data refers to the "simple datatypes" of XML Schema [17] for scalar data: Book titles and authors' names are "strings", (untyped or typed as xsd:string), publication years of books are "Gregorian years", xsd:gYear. The sample data are assumed to be accessible at the URI http://example.org/books#. Where useful, e.g, when referencing the vocabulary defined in the ontology part of the data, this URL is associated with the prefix books.

Representation of the Sample Data in RDF. The RDF representation of the book recommender system directly corresponds to the simplified RDF graph in Fig. 1. It is given here in the *Turtle* serialization [7].

```
@prefix rdf:  <http://www.w3.org/1999/02/22-rdf-syntax-ns#> .
@prefix rdfs: <http://www.w3.org/2000/01/rdf-schema#> .
```

---

[3] The same example is used in [5].

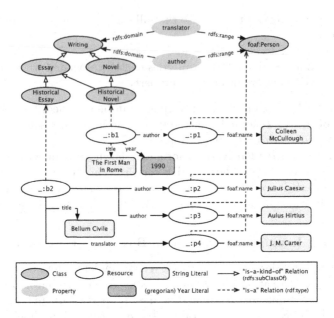

Fig. 1. Sample Data: representation as a (simplified) RDF graph

```
@prefix xsd:  <http://www.w3.org/2001/XMLSchema#> .
@prefix foaf: <http://xmlns.org/foaf/0.1/> .
:Writing a rdfs:Class ;   rdfs:label "Novel" .
:Novel   a rdfs:Class ;   rdfs:label "Novel" ;
        rdfs:subClassOf :Writing .
:Essay   a rdfs:Class ;   rdfs:label "Essay" ;
        rdfs:subClassOf :Writing .
:Historical_Essay a rdfs:Class ;
        rdfs:label "Historical Essay"; rdfs:subClassOf :Essay.
:Historical_Novel a rdfs:Class ;
        rdfs:label "Historical Novel" ;
        rdfs:subClassOf :Novel ;        rdfs:subClassOf :Essay .
:author   a rdf:Property ;
        rdfs:domain :Writing ;          rdfs:range foaf:Person .
:translator a rdf:Property ;
        rdfs:domain :Writing ;          rdfs:range foaf:Person .
_:b1      a :Historical_Novel ;
        :title "The First Man in Rome" ;
        :year  "1990"^^xsd:gYear ;
        :author [foaf:name "Colleen McCullough"] .
_:b2      a :Historical_Essay ;
        :title "Bellum Civile" ;
        :author [foaf:name "Julius Caesar"] ;
        :author [foaf:name "Aulus Hirtius"] ;
        :translator [foaf:name "J. M. Carter"] .
```

Books, authors, and translators are represented by blank nodes without identifiers, or with temporary identifiers indicated by the prefix "_:".

2.3   Semantics

The meaning of RDF data (e.g., what means "book"?) cannot be fully understood by applications and is interpreted in different ways also by human readers. Naturally, it depends on social, cultural, temporal and other types of context information. However, RDF/S allow to specify part of the semantics of applications (e.g., "a book might have an author").

As is common practice for *declarative* languages, the semantics of RDF/S is specified in terms of a model theory [39, 53]. RDF applications should be able to derive information using the inference rules for basic RDF, while only schema-aware applications are expected to take into account information provided by RDFS inference rules.

3   Sample Queries

The RDF query languages considered in this article are illustrated and illustrated using five different types of queries against the sample data.[4] This categorization is inspired by [67] and [34].

Selection queries simply retrieve parts of the data based on its content, structure, or position. The first query is thus:

Query 1. *"Select all* Essays *together with their* authors *(i.e. author items and corresponding names)"*

Extraction queries extract substructures, and can be considered as a special form of Selection Queries returning not only explicitly queried resources or statements, but entire subgraphs.

Query 2. *"Select all data items with any relation to the book titled 'Bellum Civile'."*

Reduction queries: Some queries are more concisely expressed by specifying what parts of the data *not* to include in the answer:

Query 3. *"Select all data items except ontology information and translators from the book recommender system."*

Restructuring queries: In Web applications, it is often desirable to *restructure* data, possibly into different formats or serializations. For example, the contents of the book recommender system could be restructured to an (X)HTML representation for viewing in a browser, or derived data could be created, like inverting the relation author:

---

[4] Again, these queries are mostly the same as in [5].

Query 4. *"Invert the relation* author *(from a book to an author) into a relation* authored *(from an author to a book)."*

In particular, RDF requires restructuring for *reification*, i.e. expressing "statements about statements". When reifying, a statement is replaced by four new statements specifying the subject, predicate, and object of the old statement. For example, the statement *"Julius Caesar is author of Bellum Civile"* is reified by the four statements *"X is a statement"*, *"X has subject Julius Caesar"*, *"X has predicate author"*, and *"X has object Bellum Civile"*.

Aggregation queries: Restructuring the data also includes *aggregating* several data items into one new data item. As Web data usually consists of tree- or graph-structured data that goes beyond flat relations, we distinguish between *value aggregation* working only on the values (like SQL's $\max(\cdot)$, $\text{sum}(\cdot)$, ...) and *structural aggregation* working also on structural elements (like "how many nodes"). Query 5 uses the $\max(\cdot)$ value aggregation, while Query 6 uses structural aggregation:

Query 5. *"Return the last year in which an author with name 'Julius Caesar' published something."*

Query 6. *"Return each of the subclasses of 'Writing', together with the average number of authors per publication of that subclass."*

Combination and inference queries: It is often necessary to *combine* information that is not explicitly connected, like information from different sources or substructures. Such queries are useful with ontologies that often specify that names declared at different places are synonymous:

Query 7. *"Combine the information about the book titled 'The Civil War' and authored by 'Julius Caesar' with the information about the book with identifier* bellum_civile*."*

Combination queries are related to inference, because inference refers to combining data, as illustrated by the following example: If the books entitled 'Bellum Civile' and 'The Civil War' are the same book, and 'if 'Julius Caesar' is an author of 'Bellum Civile', then 'Julius Caesar' is also an author of 'The Civil War'. *Inference queries* e.g. compute transitive closures of relations like the RDFS subClassOf relation:

Query 8. *"Return the transitive closure of the* subClassOf *relation."*

Not all inference queries are combination queries, as the following example illustrates:

Query 9. *"Return the co-author relation between two persons that stand in author relationships with the same book."*

Some query languages have closure operators applicable to any relation, while other query languages have closure operators only for certain, predefined relations, e.g., the RDFS subClassOf relation. Some query languages support *general recursion*, making it possible and easy to express the transitive closure of every relation.

4   The RDF Query Language Families

In this survey, we focus on three groups of RDF query languages differing in what the authors perceive as central paradigms of the languages:[5] Languages following the relational or pattern-based paradigm use selection constructs similar to selection-projection-join (SPJ) queries. Though they share a common query core, the languages in this group vary quite noticeably, some extending SPJ queries very conservatively, others going well beyond with novel constructs aiming to adequately support the specifics of RDF. The second group is set apart by the use of reactive rules but otherwise shares some commonality with the first group. The final group is more distinctly separated by preferring navigational access and path expressions over patterns.

Figure 2 may serve as orientation through the "language zoo" discussed in this chapter and includes also "dialects" and variants that are only briefly mentioned in the following.

4.1   The Relational Query Languages SPARQL, RQL, TRIPLE, and Xcerpt

The SPARQL Family. *SPARQL* [84] is a query language that has already reached candidate recommendation status at the W3C, and is on a good way to become *the* W3C recommendation for RDF querying. It has its roots in *SquishQL* [76] and *RDQL* [91].

Querying RDF data with languages in the SPARQL family amounts to matching graph patterns that are given as sets of triples of subjects, predicates and objects. These triples are usually connected to form graphs by means of joins expressed using several occurrences of the same variable. SPARQL uses the Turtle [7] serialization format for RDF as basis for its own triple syntax. It inherits certain syntactic shorthands from Turtle: e.g., *predicate-object lists* allow several statements to share the same subject without repeating the subject. Pairs of predicates and objects following the subject are separated by colons. *Object lists* are shorthands for several statements sharing both the subject and the predicate, the objects being separated by commas.

Solutions to SPARQL (or SquishQL or RDQL) queries are given in the form of result sets, for which also an XML format has been specified [9]. In SPARQL, result sets are sets of mappings from the variables occurring within the query to nodes of the queried data. Although RDQL and SquishQL are predecessors of SPARQL, this section presents realizations of the sample queries only in SPARQL. The formulation in the other members of the SPARQL family are very similar though some of the queries use features only recently added and not available in RDQL and SquishQL.

In SPARQL, Query 1 is expressed as follows.

```
PREFIX books: <http://example.org/books#>
PREFIX rdf: <http://www.w3.org/1999/02/22-rdf-syntax-ns#>
```

---

[5] See [5] for a more comprehensive survey of Semantic Web query languages.

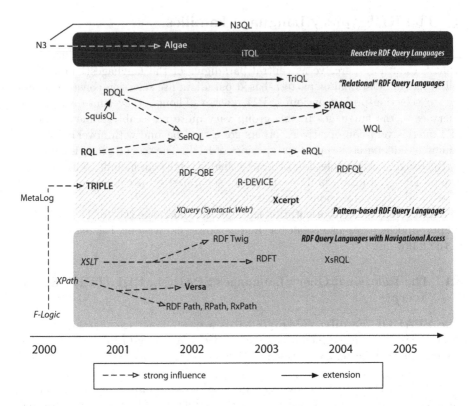

Fig. 2. Chronological Overview of RDF Query Languages (in **bold** typeface: languages covered in this survey; in *italic* typeface: non-RDF (mostly XML) query languages with proposals/extensions for querying RDF; MetaLog's unique approach to RDF querying based on a natural language interface defies classification in this framework); N3QL is not classified due to incomplete description

```
SELECT  ?essay ?author ?authorName
FROM    <http://example.org/books>
WHERE   { ?essay rdf:type books:Essay .
          ?essay books:author ?author .
          ?author books:name ?authorName . }
```

The WHERE clause specifies the graph pattern to match using variables to select data. Variables are recognized by either ? or $ prefix. Triples are connected to graph patterns using "." (colon). The FROM clause specifies the URL (or some other identifier) of the data to be queried and the SELECT clause the result variables.

Extraction queries like Query 2 can only be approximately expressed in all members of the SPARQL family, because recursive traversals of the data are not possible. Thus one cannot extract all information relevant to a particular resource. Collecting all outgoing edges of a node together with the directly linked objects of these predicates is possible and is showcased in the sample code below.

As can be seen, SPARQL does not syntactically differentiate between variables for predicates and for resources, as opposed to RQL discussed below. Also the extraction of information occurring at a fixed distance from the resource representing the book named "Bellum Civile" is possible by adding further statements to the query below.

```
PREFIX books: <http://example.org/books#>
SELECT ?property ?propertyValue
FROM   <http://example.org/books>
WHERE  {?essay books:title "Bellum Civile" .
        ?essay ?property ?propertyValue . }
```

Another way to approximate extraction queries are SPARQL's DESCRIBE queries that allow the retrieval of "descriptions" for resources. The exact extent of such a "description" is not defined in [84], but concise bounded descriptions [96] are referenced as a reasonable choice. These represent a form of predefined extraction query that returns all immediate properties for a resource as well as the immediate properties of all blank nodes that are reachable from the resource to be described without other named resources in between.

The FILTER keyword is used in SPARQL to eliminate result sets which evaluate to false when substituted in the boolean expressions given in the body of the FILTER clause. A query that finds the persons that have authored a book with title "Bellum Civile" can be expressed in SPARQL as follows:

```
PREFIX books: <http://example.org/books#>
SELECT ?person
FROM   <http://example.org/books>
WHERE  { ?book books:author ?person .
         ?book books:title ?title .
         FILTER (?title = 'Bellum Civile') }
```

The three queries mentioned above are also expressible in SPARQL's predecessors SquishQL and RDQL with a slightly different syntax but almost identical structure. SPARQL and its relatives do not support RDF/S inferencing, which means that among other tasks, querying all resources of type books:Writing of the example data above would not return any results, because there are no resources which are directly associated with books:Writing via an rdf:type property. If the SPARQL family provided support for inferencing, the resources represented by the blank nodes _:b1 and _:b2 in the serialization in Section 2.2 could be returned as results to the query in compliance with the rule RDFS9 of the RDFS semantics. One can argue that RDF/S and OWL reasoning should not be a task of the query language, but should be provided by an underlying black box reasoner. Given such a reasoner that transparently provides the full RDFS entailment graph, i.e., the closure graph under the RDF/S inference rules, the languages of the SPARQL family can very well answer queries such as the one just mentioned.

There are several other characteristics and also limitations of the members of the SPARQL family, which deserve to be mentioned:

- Queries cannot be composed or nested.
- Negation can only be used in FILTER clauses (they are called AND-clauses in SquishQL and RDQL), but not in WHERE clauses, i.e., triple patterns can only occur positively.
- Due to the lack of recursion, members of the SPARQL family cannot express certain kinds of inference queries such as 8 and extraction queries (as has been mentioned above).

SPARQL being a descendant of RDQL and SquishQL, it provides some additional features, that go beyond the queries mentioned above and which are not included in RDQL and SquishQL. Among these new features are:

- The construction, using CONSTRUCT clauses, of new RDF graphs with data from the RDF graph queried. Just as the query patterns, the construct patterns are specified as sets of triples with variables serving as placeholders. Naturally, all variables appearing within the construct pattern must also appear within the query.
- The possiblity to return, using DESCRIBE clauses, "descriptions" of the resources matching the query part. The exact meaning of "description" is left undefined, cf. [96] for a proposal.
- The specification of OPTIONAL triple or graph query patterns, i.e., data that should contribute to an answer if present in the queried data, but whose absence does not prevent from returning an answer. A corollary of is the ability of SPARQL to test for absence of triples (i.e., negation-as-failure). E.g., finding all books which do not have a translator is achieved by using the OPTIONAL keyword and a FILTER expression requiring that the optional variable is *not* bound included in the optional query part:
```
PREFIX   books: <http://example.org/books#>
PREFIX   rdf: <http://www.w3.org/1999/02/22-rdf-syntax-ns#>
SELECT   ?writing
FROM     <http://example.org/books>
WHERE    { ?writing books:author _:Author .
             OPTIONAL { ?writing books:translator ?translator } .
             FILTER (!bound(?translator)) }
```
- The expression of disjunctions of queries with the keyword UNION.
- Querying named graphs. First introduced in TriQL [18], another variant of RDQL, named graphs allow the scoping of triples and triple patterns: A query is evaluated not against a single set of triples but rather against a set of such sets each associated with a name (in form of a URI). The FROM NAMED clause can limit the matching of the triple pattern in the associated WHERE to the graphs with the specified names.

In contrast to other RDF query languages, SPARQL supports four different *query result forms*, which vary in the type of results returned. Only queries formulated using CONSTRUCT or DESCRIBE are closed in the sense that the results are RDF graphs just as the queried data. Queries using ASK return a boolean value and is used to find out whether a query pattern matches with the data. The SELECT query pattern is used to collect variable bindings from query patterns just as in SquishQL and RDQL.

The CONSTRUCT clause provides a straightforward enhancement over mere collection of variable bindings. Following the CONSTRUCT keyword, a result template is specified, which is an RDF graph that contains some or all of the variables from the query pattern in the WHERE-clause. For each match of the query pattern with the queried data, the result template is filled with the corresponding variable bindings, and the resulting RDF graph is included in the answer graph. However, CONSTRUCT patterns are rather limited missing, e.g., any ability for grouping (and thus can not construct new RDF containers or collections).

Using the CONSTRUCT clause, restructuring and non-recursive inference queries can be expressed in SPARQL. Query 4 can be expressed in SPARQL as follows:

```
PREFIX     books: <http://example.org/books#>
CONSTRUCT {?y books:authored ?x}
FROM       <http://example.org/books>
WHERE      {?x books:author ?y}
```

and Query 9 by

```
PREFIX     books: <http://example.org/books#>
CONSTRUCT {?x books:co-author ?y}
FROM       <http://example.org/books>
WHERE      { ?book books:author ?x .
             ?book books:author ?y .
             FILTER (?x != ?y) }
```

One of SPARQL's design principles is that queries should be easily derivable from RDF graphs. Thus, any RDF graph can be included in the WHERE-clause of a SPARQL query in Turtle [7] syntax. A further result of this design principle is that blank nodes are allowed to appear within query patterns. It must be emphasized that blank nodes in query patterns are not required to match with blank nodes of the data to be queried, but are mere syntactical sugar for existentially quantified variables.[6]

Besides query result forms, SPARQL provides the *solution modifiers* DISTINCT, ORDER BY, LIMIT, and OFFSET. DISTINCT eliminates duplicates in the sets of variable bindings, LIMIT specifies an upper bound for the number of solutions, OFFSET is used to omit the first n solutions of the solution sequence, and ORDER BY allows to order the solution sequence ascending or descending according to one or more variable bindings or according to a function.

[84] contains a formal semantics for SPARQL. For details on SPARQL's semantics refer to [84] and to the tutorial on SPARQL in this volume [81]. The latter, in particular, motivates the, at a first glance, slightly odd definition of SPARQL's semantics.

---

[6] See http://lists.w3.org/Archives/Public/public-rdf-dawg-comments/2006Jan/0073-.html for a discussion about blank nodes in SPARQL queries.

The RQL Family. Under "RQL family", we group the languages *RQL* [57] and *SeRQL* [22]. Common to these languages is that they support combining data and schema querying. In the case of RQL, the RDF data model deviates slightly from the standard data model for RDF and RDFS: (1) cycles in the subsumption hierarchy are forbidden, and (2) for each property, both a domain and a range must be defined. These restrictions ensure a clear separation of the three abstraction layers of RDF and RDFS: (1) data, i.e. description of resources such as persons, XML documents, etc., (2) schemas, i.e. classifications for such resources, and (3) meta-schemas specifying meta-classes such as rdfs:Class, the class of all classes, and rdf:Property the class of all properties. They make possible a flexible type system tailored to the specificities of RDF and RDFS.

In the following discussion we concentrate on **RQL**, the "RDF Query Language", that has been developed at ICS-FORTH [31, 54, 55, 56, 57]. Its most distinguishing feature is a strong support for typing as well as a more complete set of advanced language operators such as set operations, aggregation, container construction and access than in most other RDF query languages.

SeRQL aims to be a more accessible derivate of RQL. Therefore several syntactic shorthands (e.g., object-property and object lists and optional expressions, all three later adopted in SPARQL) are introduced for common query situations. Also SeRQL drops built-in support for typing beyond literals, presumably under the impression that the multitude of language constructs provided in RQL makes the language too complex. The same reasoning applies for advanced query constructs such as set operations, universal quantification, aggregations, etc.

Another derivate of RQL is eRQL, a radical simplification of RQL based mostly on a keyword-based interface. It is the expressed goal of the authors of eRQL to provide a *"Google-like query language but also with the capacity to profit of the additional information given by the RDF data"*.[7] The resulting language is, unsurprisingly, of rather limited expressiveness and can not express most of the sample queries.

Basic schema queries. A salient feature of RQL is the use of the types from RDFS schemas. The query subClassOf(books:Writing) returns the sub-classes of the class books:Writing[8]. A similar query, using subPropertyOf instead of sub-ClassOf, returns the sub-properties of a property. The following three queries returns the domain ($C1) and range ($C2) of the property author defined at the URI named books. The prefix $ indicates "class variable", i.e., a variable ranging on schema classes. It can be expressed in RQL in three different manners:

1. using class variables:
   ```
   SELECT $C1, $C2  FROM {$C1}books:author{$C2}
   USING  NAMESPACE books = &http://example.org/books#
   ```

2. using a *type constraint*:
   ```
   SELECT C1, C2  FROM Class{C1}, Class{C2}, {;C1}books:author{;C2}
   USING  NAMESPACE books = &http://example.org/books#
   ```

---

[7] http://www.dbis.informatik.uni-frankfurt.de/~tolle/RDF/eRQL/
[8] Assuming: USING NAMESPACE books = &http://example.org/books-rdfs#

3. without class variables or type constraints:
```
SELECT C1, C2  FROM subClassOf(domain(book:author)){C1},
                    subClassOf(range(books:author)){C2}
USING  NAMESPACE books = &http://example.org/books#
```

While the first two queries return exactly the same result—namely the domain and range of the books:author-property and all possible combinations of their subclasses—the third query does not include the domain and range of books:author itself but only the combinations of their subclasses. There is another subtle difference: the first two queries should only return class combinations for which actual statements exist, the third should also return class combination where no actual statement for that combination exists.

The query topclass(books:Historical_Essay) returns the top of the subsumption hierarchy, i.e., books:Writing, cf. Figure 1. Similar constructs for querying the leaves of the subsumption hierarchy or the nearest common ancestor of the two classes are available. Moreover, RQL has "property variables" that are prefixed by @ and which can be used to query RDF properties (just as classes can be queried using class variables). The following query, with property variables prefixed by @ returns the properties, together with their actual ranges, that can be assigned to resources classified as books:Writing:

```
SELECT @P, $V  FROM {;books:Writing}@P{$V}
USING  NAMESPACE books = &http://example.org/books#
```

Combining these facilities, Query 8 is expressible in RQL as follows:
```
SELECT X, Y  FROM Class{X}, subClassOf(X){Y}.
```

Data queries. With RQL, data can be retrieved by its types or by navigating to the appropriate position in the RDF graph. Restrictions can be expressed using filters. Classes, as well as properties, can be queried for their (direct and indirect, i.e., inferred) extent. The query books:Writing returns the resources classified as books:Writing or as one of its sub-classes. This query can also be expressed as follows: SELECT X FROM books:Writing{X}. Prefixing the variable X with ^ in the previous queries, yields queries returning only resources directly classified as books:Writing, i.e., for which a statement $(X, \text{rdf:type}, \text{books:Writing})$ exists. The extent of a property can be similarly retrieved. The query ^books:author returns the pairs of resources X, Y that are in the books:author relation, i.e., for which a statement $(X, \text{books:author}, Y)$ exists. RQL offers extended dot notation as used in OQL [29], for navigation in data and schema graphs. This is convenient for expressing Query 1:

```
SELECT X, Y, Z FROM {X;books:Essay}books:author{Y}.books:authorName{Z}
USING  NAMESPACE books = &http://example.org/books#
```

The data selected by an RDF query can be restricted with a WHERE clause:

```
SELECT X, Y FROM {X;books:Essay}books:author.books:authorName{Y},
                 {X}books:title{T}
WHERE  T = "Bellum Civile"
USING  NAMESPACE books = &http://example.org/books#
```

Mixed schema and data queries. With RQL, access to data and schema can be combined in all manners, e.g., the expression X;books:Essay restricts bindings for variable X to resources with type books:Essay. Types are often useful for filtering, but type information can also be interesting on their own, e.g., to return a "description" of a resource understood as its schema:

```
SELECT $C, ( SELECT @P, Y  FROM {Z ; ^$D} ^@P {Y}
             WHERE  Z = X and $D = $C )
FROM   ^$C {X}, {X}books:title{T}  WHERE T = "Bellum Civile"
USING  NAMESPACE books = &http://example.org/books#
```

This query returns the classes under which the resource with title "Bellum Civile" is directly classified; ^$C{X} finds the classes under which the resource X is directly classified.

Further features of RQL are not discussed here, e.g., support for containers, aggregation, and schema discovery. Although RQL has no concept of "view", its extension RVL [66] gives a facility for specifying views.

RQL has been criticized for its large number of features and choice of syntactic constructs (like the prefixes ^ for calls and @ for property variables), which resulted in the simplifications SeRQL and eRQL of RDF. On the other hand, RQL is far more expressive than most other RDF query languages, especially those of the SPARQL family. Most queries of Section 3, except those queries referring to the transitive closures of arbitrary relations, can be expressed in RQL.

Query 1 is already given in RQL above. Query 2 cannot be expressed in RQL exactly, since RQL has no means to select "everything related to some resource". However, a modified version of this query, where a resource is described by its schema, is also given above. Reduction queries, e.g. Query 3, can often be concisely expressed in RQL, in particular if types are available:

```
SELECT S, @P, O
FROM   (Resources minus (SELECT T FROM {B}books:translator{T})){S},
       (Resources minus (SELECT T FROM {B}books:translator{T})){O},
       {S}@P{O}
USING  NAMESPACE books = &http://example.org/books#
```

An implementation of the restructuring Query 4 is given above in the extension RVL of RQL. RQL is convenient for expressing aggregation queries, e.g., Query 5:

```
max(SELECT Y
    FROM   {B;books:Writing}books:author.books:authorName{A},
           {B}books:pubYear{Y}
    WHERE  A = "Julius Caesar")
```

Inference queries that do not need recursion, e.g., Query 9, can be expressed in RQL as follows:

```
SELECT A1, A2  FROM {Z}books:author{A1}, {Z}books:author{A2}
WHERE  A1 != A2
USING  NAMESPACE books = &http://example.org/books#
```

In RQL's extension RVL, an expression of Query 9 can actually create new statements as follows:

```
CREATE NAMESPACE mybooks = &http://example.org/books-rdfs-extension#
VIEW   mybooks:co-author(A1, A2)
FROM   {Z}books:author{A1}, {Z}books:author{A2}  WHERE A1 != A2
USING  NAMESPACE books = &http://example.org/books#
```

A formal semantics for RQL has been defined together with the language, e.g., in [57].

TRIPLE. [51, 92, 93] is a rule-based query, inference, and transformation language for RDF. TRIPLE is based upon ideas published in [40]. TRIPLE's syntax is close to F-Logic [58]. F-Logic is convenient for querying semi-structured data, e.g., XML and RDF, as it facilitates describing schema-less or irregular data [64]. Other approaches to querying XML and/or RDF based on F-Logic are XPathLog [75] and the ontology management platform Ontobroker[9]. TRIPLE has been designed to address two weaknesses of previous approaches to querying RDF: (1) Predefined constructs expressing RDFS' semantics that restrain a query language's extensibility, and (2) lack of formal semantics.

Instead of predefined RDFS-related language constructs, TRIPLE offers Horn logic rules (in F-Logic syntax) [58]. Using TRIPLE rules, one can implement features of, e.g., RDFS. Where Horn logic is not sufficient, as is the case of OWL, TRIPLE is designed to be extended by external modules implementing, e.g., an OWL reasoner. Thanks to its foundations in Horn logic, TRIPLE can inherit much of Logic Programming's formal semantics. Referring to, e.g., a representation of UML in RDF [60, 61], the authors of TRIPLE claim in [93] that TRIPLE is well-suited to query non-RDF meta-data. This can be questioned, especially if, in spite of [44], one considers the rather awkward mappings of Topic Maps into RDF proposed so far.

TRIPLE differs from Horn logic and Logic Programming as follows [93]:

- TRIPLE supports resources identified by URIs.
- RDF statements are represented in TRIPLE by slots, allowing the grouping and nesting of statements; like in F-Logic, Path expressions inspired from [43] can be used for traversing several properties.
- TRIPLE provides concise support for reified statements. Reified statements are expressed in TRIPLE enclosed in angle brackets, e.g.:
  ```
  Julius\_Caesar[believes-><Junius\_Brutus[friend-of -> Julius\_Caesar]>]
  ```

---

[9] http://www.ontoprise.de/products/ontobroker

- TRIPLE has a notion of module allowing specification of the 'model' in which a statement, or an atom, is true. 'Models' are identified by URIs that can prefix statement or atom using @.
- TRIPLE requires an explicit quantification of all variables.

Query 1 can be approximated as follows:

```
rdf    := 'http://www.w3.org/1999/02/22-rdf-syntax-ns#'.
books := 'http://example.org/books#'.
booksModel := 'http://example.org/books'.
FORALL B, A, AN  result(B, A, AN) <-
     B[rdf:type -> books:Essay;
        books:author -> A[books:authorName -> AN]]@booksModel.
```

This query selects only resources directly classified as books:Essay. Query 1 is properly expressed below.

TRIPLE's rules give rise to specify properties of RDF. [93] gives the following implementation of a part of RDFS's semantics:

```
rdf    := 'http://www.w3.org/1999/02/22-rdf-syntax-ns#'.
rdfs   := 'http://www.w3.org/2000/01/rdf-schema#'.
type   := rdf:type.
subPropertyOf := rdfs:subPropertyOf.
subClassOf    := rdfs:subClassOf.

FORALL Mdl @rdfschema(Mdl) {
  transitive(subPropertyOf).
  transitive(subClassOf).
  FORALL O,P,V O[P->V] <-
             O[P->V]@Mdl.
  FORALL O,P,V O[P->V] <-
             EXISTS S S[subPropertyOf->P] AND O[S->V].
  FORALL O,P,V O[P->V] <-
             transitive(P) AND EXISTS W (O[P->W] AND W[P->V]).
  FORALL O,T   O[type->T] <-
             EXISTS S (S[subClassOf->T] AND O[type->S]).
}
```

Inference from range and domain restrictions of properties are not implemented by the rule given above. This is no limitation of TRIPLE, though, as they can be realized by the following additional rules:

```
FORALL S,T  S[type-$>$T] <-
            EXISTS P, O (S[P-$>$O] AND P[rdfs:domain-$>$T]).
FORALL O,T  O[type->T] <-
            EXISTS P, S (S[P-$>$O] AND P[rdfs:range-$>$T]).
```

With the rules given above, the approximation of Query 1 given above only needs to be modified so as to express the 'model' it is evaluated against: instead of @booksModel, @rdfschema(booksModel) should be used, i.e., the original 'model' should be extended with the above-mentioned rules implementing RDFS' semantics. Most queries of Section 3 can be expressed in TRIPLE. Aggregation queries cannot be expressed in TRIPLE, for the language does not support aggregation.

[93] specifies an RDF, and therefore XML, syntax for a fragment of TRIPLE. By relying on translations to RDF, one can query data in different formalisms with TRIPLE, e.g., RDF, Topic Maps, and UML. This, however, might lead to rather awkward queries. Some aspects of RDF, viz. containers, collections, and blank nodes, are not supported by TRIPLE.

Xcerpt. Xcerpt [13, 24, 88, 89], cf. http://xcerpt.org, is a language for querying both data on the "standard Web" (e.g., XML and HTML data) and data on the Semantic Web (e.g., RDF, Topic Maps data). Therefore the approach of querying an XML serialization of Semantic Web data is feasible in Xcerpt, but it is not as natural as directly querying the RDF data. Xcerpt uses common language constructs for querying data in several different formats and is therefore very useful for authoring applications that combine all kinds of Web data. This survey focuses on applying Xcerpt to querying RDF data, but querying XML and Topic Maps with Xcerpt is quite similar (cf. [5]).

Three features of Xcerpt are particularly convenient for querying RDF data. (**1**) Xcerpt's pattern-based incomplete queries are convenient for collecting related resources in the neighbourhood of some given resources and to express traversals of RDF graphs of indefinite lengths. (**2**) Xcerpt chaining of (possibly recursive rules) is convenient for expressing RDFS's semantics, e.g., the transitive closure of the subClassOf relation, as well as all kinds of graph traversals. (**3**) Xcerpt's optional construct is convenient for collecting properties of resources.

All nine queries from Section 3 can be expressed in Xcerpt. The following Xcerpt programs show solutions for the queries against the RDF serialization from Section 2.

[19] proposes two views on RDF data: as in most other RDF query languages as plain triples with explicit joins for structure traversal and as a proper graph.

On the plain triple view, Query 1 can be expressed in Xcerpt as follows:

```
DECLARE ns-prefix rdf = "http://www.w3.org/1999/02/22-rdf-syntax-ns#"
        ns-prefix books = "http://example.org/books#"

GOAL
  result [
    all essay [
      id [ var Essay ],
      all author [
        id [ var Author ],
        all name [ var AuthorName ]
    ] ] ]
FROM
  and(
    RDFS-TRIPLE [
      var Essay:uri{}, "rdf:type":uri{}, "books:Essay":uri{} ],
```

```
RDF-TRIPLE [
  var Essay:uri{}, "books:author":uri{}, var Author:uri{} ],
RDF-TRIPLE [
  var Author:uri{}, "books:authorName":uri{}, var AuthorName ] )
END
```

Using the prefixes declared in line 1 and 2, the query pattern (between FROM and END) is a conjunction of tree queries against the RDF triples represented in the predicate RDF-TRIPLE. Notice that the first conjunct actually uses RDFS-TRIPLE. This view of the RDF data contains all basic triples plus the ones entailed by the RDFS semantics [53] (cf. [19] for a detailed description). Using RDFS-TRIPLE instead of RDF-TRIPLE ensures that also resources actually classified in a sub-class of books:Essay are returned. Xcerpt's approach to RDF querying shares with [86] the ability to construct *arbitrary* XML as in this rule.

On Xcerpt's graph view of RDF, the same query can be expressed as follows:

```
DECLARE ns-prefix rdf = "http://www.w3.org/1999/02/22-rdf-syntax-ns#"
        ns-prefix books = "http://example.org/books#"

GOAL
  result [
    all essay [
      id [ var Essay ],
      all author [
        id [ var Author ],
        all name [ var AuthorName ]
      ] ] ]
FROM
  RDFS-GRAPH {{
    var Essay:uri {{
      rdf:type {{ "books:Essay":uri {{ }} }},
      books:author {{
        var Author:uri {{
          books:name {{ var AuthorName }}
        }}
      }}
    }} }} }}
END
```

The RDF graph view is represented in the RDF-GRAPH predicate. Here, the RDFS-GRAPH view is used that extends RDF-GRAPH just like RDFS-TRIPLE extends RDF-TRIPLE. Triples are represented similar to striped RDF/XML: each resource is a direct child element in RDF-GRAPH with a sub-element for each statement with that resource as object. The sub-element is labeled with the URI of the predicate and contains the object of the statement. As Xcerpt's data model is a rooted *graph* (possibly containing cycles) this can be represented without duplication of resources.

In contrast to the previous query no conjunction is used but rather a nested pattern that naturally reflects the structure of the RDF graph with the exception that labeled edges are represented as nodes with edges to the elements representing their source and sink.

Xcerpt rules are convenient for making the language "RDF serialization transparent". For each RDF serialization, a set of rules expresses a translation from or into that serialization. However, the rules for parsing RDF/XML [10], the official XML serialization, are very complex and lengthy due to the high degree of flexibility RDF/XML allows. They can be found in [19], similar functions for parsing RDF/XML in XQuery are described in [87]. The following rules parse RDF data serialized in the RXR (Regular XML RDF) format [4], a far simpler and more regular RDF serialization.

The following rule extracts all triples from an RXR document. Since different types (such as URI, blank node, or literal) of subjects and objects of RDF triples are represented differently in RXR, the conversion of the RXR representation into the plain triples is performed in separate rules, see [19].

```
DECLARE ns-prefix rxr = "http://ilrt.org/discovery/2004/03/rxr/"

CONSTRUCT
  RDF-TRIPLE[
    var Subject, var Predicate:uri{}, var Object ]
FROM
  and[
    rxr:graph {{
      rxr:triple {
        var S as rxr:subject{{}},
        rxr:predicate{ attributes{ rxr:uri{ var Predicate } } },
        var O as rxr:object{{}}
      }
    }},
    RXR-RDFNODE[ var S, var Subject ],
    RXR-RDFNODE[ var O, var Object ]
  ]
END
```

Querying RDF data with Xcerpt is the subject of ongoing investigation [19].

A visual language, called *visXcerpt* [11, 12], has been conceived as a visual rendering of textual Xcerpt programs, making it possible to freely switch during programming between the visual and textual view, or rendering, of a program.

A formal semantics of Xcerpt has been published in [88]. Static type checking methods have been developed for Xcerpt [25, 98] that are based on seeing tree grammars in their various disguises, e.g., DTD, XML Schema, RelaxNG, as definitions of abstract data type. Recent work [28, 90] on Xcerpt focuses on efficient evaluation of Xcerpt's high-level constructs.

There is quite a number of other query languages that fall into this group but can not be covered here for space reasons (for further details see [5]). Further investigaton of such languages might start with R-DEVICE [6], RDF-QBE [85], and RDFQL [1].

4.2 The Reactive Rule Query Language Algae

Algae[10] is an RDF query language developed as part of the W3C Annotea project
(http://www.w3.org/2001/Annotea/) aiming at enhancing Web pages with semantic annotations, expressed in RDF and collected from 'annotation servers',
as Web pages are browsed. Algae is based on two concepts: (1) "Actions" are the
directives ask, assert, and fwrule that determine whether an expression is used
to query the RDF data, insert data into the graph, or to specify ECA[11]-like
rules. (2) Answers to Algae queries are bindings for query variables as well as
triples from the RDF graph as "proofs" of the answer. Algae queries can be composed. Syntactically, Algae is based on the RDF syntax N-triples [46], a subset
of the N3 [14] notation for RDF. This subset excludes specifically N3 rules or
queries as used in the N3QL proposal [15]. Algae extends the N-triple syntax
with the above mentioned "actions" and with so-called "constraints", written
between curly brackets, that specify further arithmetic or string comparisons to
be fulfilled by the data retrieved.

Query 1 can be expressed as follows:

```
ns rdf   = <http://www.w3.org/1999/02/22-rdf-syntax-ns#>
ns books = <http://example.org/books#>
read <http://example.org/books> ()
ask (    ?essay  rdf:type          <http://example.org/books#Essay> .
         ?essay  books:author      ?author .
         ?author books:authorName ?authorName )
collect( ?essay, ?author, ?authorName )
```

This query becomes more interesting if we are not only interested in the titles
of essays written by "Julius Caesar" but also want the translators of such books
returned, if there are any:

```
ns rdf   = <http://www.w3.org/1999/02/22-rdf-syntax-ns#>
ns books = <http://example.org/books#>
read <http://example.org/books> ()
ask (    ?essay rdf:type           <http://example.org/books#Essay> .
         ?essay books:author       ?author .
         ?author books:authorName  ''Julius Caesar'' .
         ?essay books:title        ?title .
         ~?essay books:translator ?translator .
     )
collect( ?title, ?translatorName )
```

Note ~ used to declare 'translator' an optional. This query returns the answer
given in Table 1.

Query 2 and Query 4 cannot be expressed in Algae due to the lack of closure,
recursion, and negation. Queries 5 and 6 cannot be expressed in Algae due to
the lack of aggregation operators. All other queries can be expressed in Algae,
most of them requiring 'extended action directives' [82].

---

[10] Also called "Algae2". This survey follows [83] and retains the name "Algae".

[11] ECA stands for event-condition-action.

Table 1. Answer to Query 1

?title	?translator	*Proof*
"Bellum Civile"	"J. M. Carter"	`_:1 rdf:type <http://exam...ks-rdfs#Essay>.`
		`_:1 books:author _:2.`
		`_:2 books:authorName ''Julius Caesar''.`
		`_:1 books:title ''Bellum Civile''.`
		`_:1 books:translator ''J. M. Carter''.`

No formal semantics has been published for Algae.

Algae is not the only RDF query language that provides reactive rules: iTQL [2] is used in the Kowari Metastore and provides querying, update, and transaction management functionality, for details see [5]. iTQL is also one of the few RDF query languages with a form of unrestricted closure path expressions (thanks to the trans function). RUL [65], the RDF update language, provides update expressions on top of RQL.

4.3   The Navigational Access Query Language Versa

Developed as part of the Python-based *4Suite* XML and RDF toolkit[12], **Versa** [77, 78, 79] is a query language for RDF inspired, but significantly different from XPath[33, 45]. Versa can be used in lieu of XPath in the XSLT version of 4Suite. Like the Syntactic Web Approach, TreeHugger, and RDF Twig, Versa is aligned with XML. Like XPath, Versa can be extended by externally defined functions. Versa's authors claim that Versa is easier to learn than RDF query languages inspired from SQL.

Versa has constructs for a *forward traversal* of one or more RDF properties, e.g., `all() - books:author -> *` selects those resources that are author of other resources. Instead of the wildcard `*`, string-based restrictions can be expressed. Using Versa's forward traversal operators, Query 1 can be expressed as follows:

```
distribute(type(books:Essay), ".",
    "distribute(.-books:author->*, ".", ".-books:authorName->*)")
```

The function distribute() returns a list of lists containing the result of the second, third, ... argument evaluated starting from each of the resources selected by the first argument. As in XPath, . denotes the current node.

Versa has a *Forward filter* for selecting the subject of a statement, e.g., `type(books:Essay) |- books:title -> eq("Bellum Civile")` returns the essays entitled "Bellum Civile". Versa has also constructs for a *backward traversal* (but no backward filter), e.g., the essays titled "Bellum Civile" are returned by

---

[12] http://4suite.org/

```
(books:Essay <- rdf:type - *) |- books:title -> eq("Bellum Gallicum").
```

Versa's function traverse serves to traverse paths of arbitrary length, e.g., the following query returns all sub-classes of books:Writing:

```
traverse(books:Writing, rdf:subClassOf, vtrav:inverse, vtrav:transitive)
```

Similarly, Versa's function filter provides a general filter, e.g., all essays entitled "Bellum Gallicum" having a translator named "J. M. Carter" are returned by the following query:

```
filter(books:Essay <- rdf:type - *,
  ". - books:title -> eq('Bellum Gallicum')",
    ". - books:translator -> books:translatorName -> eq('J. M. Carter')"
```

Selection and extraction queries can be easily implemented in Versa, although the selection of related items is not very convenient, as the above implementation of Query 1 demonstrates. In contrast to most RDF query languages, Versa allows the extraction of RDF subgraphs of arbitrary sizes, as required by Query 2. Reduction queries can be expressed in Versa, e.g., using negation or set difference. Query 3 can be implemented in Versa as follows:

```
difference(all(),
  union(type(rdfs:Class),
        union(type(rdf:Property,
              all() <- books:translator - *))
      )
  )
```

Restructuring, combination, and inference queries cannot be expressed in Versa, as the result of a Versa query is always a list (possibly a list of lists). However, Query 4 and 9 can be approximated in Versa as follows:

```
distribute(all(), ". - books:author -> *", ". - books:author -> *")
```

Answers to this query include "Julius Caesar" (as if he would be a co-author of himself !). This does not seem to be avoidable with Versa. Versa also provides several aggregation functions. Query 5 can be expressed as follows in Versa:

```
max(filter(all(),
      ". - books:author -> books:authorName -> eq('Julius Caesar')"
      )
    - books:year -> *)
```

Query 6 can be implemented in Versa using the function length as follows:

```
distribute(traverse(books:Writing, rdf:subClassOf,
                    vtrav:inverse,vtrav:transitive),
          ".",
          "max(length((. <- rdf:type *) - books:author -> *))"
          )
```

No formal semantics has been published for Versa.

Aside from Versa, most RDF query languages that fall into this group are derivatives of XPath or XSLT or are at least very similar to these XML query languages, for details once more refer to [5]. There are a few proposals for XPath-style RDF path languages (RDF Path [80], RPath [74], RxPath [94]), however all proposals are very limited in expressiveness and often immature. [86, 87] suggests the use of XQuery for querying RDF, TreeHugger [95] and RDF Twig [97] do the same for XSLT (1.0), the latter two relying on external functions for preprocessing the RDF data. RDFT [38] suggests an RDF template language in the style of XSLT, as does [62]. Both approaches seem to have been abandoned.

This section has introduced a number of RDF query languages divided in three groups. For an overview of the discussed languages and their relations, refer again to Figure 2. The following two sections relate the introduced languages comparing their approaches to selection, construction, evaluation, etc.

5 Language Constructs Compared

The previous section establishes a basic understanding of interesting exemplars of RDF query languages. This broad overview of languages is complemented in this section with a close look at specific language concepts and constructs. For instance, selecting optional data is essential for RDF, since all properties are optional by default. However, different languages provide quite different means to handle such data. All these language constructs are compared over several of the languages from the previous section as appropriate to show the range of solutions for the particular need.

For the purpose of this section, the constructs are divided in three classes: selection, construction, and procedural abstraction or view definition.

5.1 Selection

The basic functionality of any query language is selection, i.e., the ability to characterize subsets of the queried data that match the user's query intent. In relational databases where the schema of the data is well-known, such characterizations are often based on few attributes of the sought-for data items and possibly a small number of relations with other data items. On semi-structured data such as XML or RDF, selection becomes more centered around the position of the sought-for data items within the structure of the queried data. Some RDF (and most XML) query languages therefore provide not just selection based on attribute value, but richer selection constructs.

Triple Patterns vs. Path expressions

Triple patterns. The basic form of selection construct is a triple pattern that corresponds to a relational selection-(projection-)join query. A triple pattern consists of a conjunction of one or more triples, that are just like data triples but may additionally be extended with query constructs such as variables. SPARQL uses triple patterns in Turtle syntax. E.g.,

```
?essay books:title "Bellum Civile"
```

selects the resources with "Bellum Civile" as value of the books:title property. This basic form of a triple pattern is like a selection operation from the relational algebra. If variables occur in several triples in the same triple pattern, that pattern becomes a selection-(projection-)join query[13], e.g.,

```
?essay books:author ?author.
?author foaf:name "Julius Caesar"
```

Joins expressed, e.g., through multiple occurrences of the same variable in the same pattern query are even more prevalent in RDF than in usual relational queries. This is partially due to the binary nature of RDF properties. Furthermore, one often needs to "traverse" several intermediary nodes in the RDF graph to select the actually used data items.

Specifying such traversals in a succinct way has been considered not only in the context of RDF, but also in the context of relational (GEM [100]), object-oriented ([43]) and XML ([33]) data. The most successful and for semi-structured and XML query languages widely accepted construct for specifying structure traversal are **path expressions**. Essentially, they allow the omission of variables for intermediary nodes that are just used to "reach" the target nodes. E.g., the above SPARQL query can also be written as

```
?essay books:author [foaf:name "Julius Caesar"].
```

which uses the ability of SPARQL's syntax to omit blank nodes (i.e., existentially quantified variables) in queries and is tantamount to a path expression. RQL specifically introduces path expressions with a syntax similar to OQL's dot notation:

```
{Essay}books:author.foaf:name{A}.
```

Path Expressions. Path expressions constructs can be classified along their intended use and expressiveness in three classes:

1. *Basic path expressions* are only abbreviations for triple patterns as seen in SPARQL or RQL. They allow only the specification of fixed length traversals, i.e., the traversed path in the *data* is of same length as the path expression. These path expressions are not more expressive than triple patterns (and therefore SPJ queries), but are nevertheless encountered in several query languages as "syntactic sugar". Examples of query languages with only basic path expressions are GEM [100], OQL [29], SPARQL [84], and RQL [84].
2. *Unrestricted closure path expressions* are a common class of path expressions that adds to the basic path expressions the ability to traverse arbitrary-length paths. XPath path expressions (disregarding XPath predicates for the moment) fall into this category with closure axes such as descendant. This type of path expressions is very common in XML query languages

---

[13] Triple pattern queries as discussed here and used, e.g., in SPARQL have more or less the same expressiveness and evaluation complexity as relational SPJ-queries.

(e.g., XML-QL [41], Quilt [30], XPath and all XML query languages based on XPath). It is also used in the RDF query language iTQL[2]. Its expressiveness is indeed higher than that of basic triple patterns (SPJ queries). It can be realized in languages that provide only triple patterns but additionally (at least linear) recursive views. SQL-99 is an example of a language that provides no closure path expressions but linear recursion and thus can emulate (unrestricted) closure path expressions. For RDF, there are few query languages that fall into this class since RDF has, in contrast to XML, no dominating hierarchical relation but many relations of equal importance. This makes unrestricted closure often too unrestrictive for interesting queries.

3. Therefore, several RDF query languages provide *generalized or regular path expressions*. Here, full regular expression syntax including repetition and alternative is provided on top of path expressions. E.g., a*.((b|c).e)+ traverses all paths of arbitrary many a properties followed by at least one repetition of either a b or a c in each case followed by an e. Such regular path expressions are provided, e.g., by Versa's traverse operator, Xcerpt's qualified descendant, or the XPath extension with conditional axes [71]. The latter work showed that regular path expressions are even more expressive than unrestricted closure path expressions and a path language like XPath becomes indeed first-order complete with the addition of regular path expressions. Nevertheless, direct language support is not only justified by the ease of use for the query author but also by complexity results, e.g., in [70] that show that regular path expressions do not affect the complexity of a query language such as XPath and can be evaluated in polynomial time w.r.t. data and query size. Simulation of regular path expressions using triple patterns (SPJ queries) and recursive views is possible but the resulting queries become excruciatingly complex even for simple regular path expressions.

Summarizing, path expressions provide convenient means to specify structural constraints in RDF queries and are therefore supported by a large number of RDF query languages. However, surprisingly many RDF query languages ignore (unrestricted or regular) closure path expressions. This is surprising as these path expressions make query authoring (they allow avoiding recursive views) easier and can be implemented efficiently as research on these constructs for XML query languages has shown. In particular, unrestricted closure path expressions can be implemented nearly as efficiently as basic path expressions using, e.g., tree labeling schemes [48] or closure indices.

Closure Subgraph Extraction. Closely related to (regular or unrestricted) closure path expressions, is the issue of subgraph extraction: Since schema and extent of RDF data are often, at best, only vaguely known, extracting interesting portions of the data whose extent is not known statically (i.e., at query authoring or compilation time) becomes an often encountered problem: E.g., given information about authors and books, extract all information on one book, e.g., for export into a bibliography management application or for styled display on a Web site.

It should be immediately clear, that closure subgraph extraction is easily achieved in languages providing (regular or unrestricted) closure path expressions. Regular path expressions are probably needed in the case of RDF to define a reasonable subgraph, e.g., by traversing only certain relations, traversing only a certain number of times, or stopping at resources with certain characteristics.

What about languages with only triple patterns and/or basic path expressions such as SPARQL, RQL, or RDQL? Some of these languages, e.g., RQL, provide built-in closure for certain fixed, predefined relations, cf. Section 5.1. SPARQL provides one specialized language construct, DESCRIBE, that is intended to return relevant and representative information about resources, e.g., in the style of concise bounded descriptions [96] where a resource is described by its immediate properties and the immediate properties of all blank nodes reachable from the resource without other named resources in between. The intuition here is that further information about the latter blank nodes can not be retrieved in further queries to the RDF data as they are not addressable from outside. The SPARQL specifications, however, does not require DESCRIBE to return concise bounded descriptions but leaves the extent of the returned information up to the implementation. Nevertheless, DESCRIBE is the only construct in SPARQL that approximates closure subgraph extraction.

Schema-aware Selection. The discussion of closure path expressions could not be complete without looking at one common way of reducing closure path expressions to basic expressions: It is assumed that closure is only relevant for a few, predefined relations such as rdfs:subClassOf which are known to be transitive. For these, the implementation transparently provides the closure.

This is just one of the effects when RDF query languages provide schema-aware (in this case RDFS-aware) selection. An RDF query language may elect to match the query not against the bare data graph but against the entailment graph according to some set of entailment rules, e.g., the RDFS entailment rules. E.g., RQL provides support for the specific entailment rules of RDFS with some exceptions (acyclic subsumption hierarchy, only part of the axiomatic triples are included). The latter exception is, in fact, needed to guarantee that query answer are always finite, as the RDFS entailment rules in [53] include one axiomatic triple for each integer i to handle rdf:_i properties. Query languages must, in this case, opt for a reasonable restriction, e.g., to include only axiomatic triples for integers $i \leq m$ with m the maximum size of a container in the data.

TRIPLE [93] takes schema-aware querying a step further by providing means to parameterize a query with a "model" containing the rules to use for computing the entailment graph against which the query is to be matched. This allows the treatment of different schema languages in the same query framework.

Similarly, schema-awareness can be achieved in any RDF query language with (recursive) views by providing a collection of rules implementing the schema entailment rules. Xcerpt chooses this approach, as it makes schema access transparent for the query author. However, languages like Xcerpt and Versa that provide regular path expressions allow the query author also to specify queries with ad-hoc schema-awareness in the queries, e.g., by using a closure path expression like `(rdfs:subClassOf)+` instead of just `rdfs:subClassOf`.

None of these approaches forces the entailment graph ever to be materialized. Rather, it may be lazily (i.e., in a goal-driven backward-chaining manner) computed, partially materialized, or fully materialized depending on the needs of the implementation and the query.

Optional Selection and Disjunctions. So far, we have considered pure conjunctive queries only. Disjunction or equivalent union constructs allow the query author to collect data items with different characteristics in one query. E.g., to find "colleagues" of a researcher from an RDF graph containing bibliography and conference information, one might choose to select co-authors, as well as co-editors, and members in the same program committee. On RDF data, disjunctive queries are far more common place than on relational data since all RDF properties are by default optional. Many queries have a core of properties that have to be defined for the sought-for data items but also include additional properties (often labeling properties or properties relating the data items to "further" information such as Web sites) that should be reported if they are defined for the sought-for data items but that may also be absent. E.g., the following SPARQL query returns pairs of books and translators for books that have translators and just books otherwise. If one considers the results of a query as a table with null values, the translator column is null in the latter case.

```
SELECT   ?writing, ?translator
WHERE    { ?writing a books:Essay .
         OPTIONAL { ?writing books:translator ?translator } }
```

Such optional selection eases the burden both on the query author and the query processor considerably in contrast to a disjunctive or union query which has to duplicate the non-optional part:

```
SELECT   ?writing, ?translator
WHERE    { ?writing a books:Essay .
           ?writing books:translator ?translator }
         UNION
         { ?writing a books:Essay }
```

Furthermore, the latter is not actually equivalent as it returns also for writings X with translators one result tuple $(X, \texttt{null})$. Indeed, this points to the question of the precise semantics of an optional selection operator. One can observe that the answer to this question is not the same for different RDF (or XML) query languages. The main difference between the offered semantics in languages such as SPARQL, Xcerpt, or XQuery lies in the treatment of multiple optional query parts with dependencies. E.g., in the expression $A \wedge \mathsf{optional}(B) \wedge \mathsf{optional}(C)$ the same variable V may occur in both B and C. In this case, if we just go forward and use the B part to determine bindings for V those bindings may be incompatible with C, i.e., prevent the matching of C. The way this case of multiple interdependent optionals is handled allows to differentiate the following four semantics for optional selection constructs:

1. *Independent optionals:* Interdependencies between optional clauses is disregarded by imposing some order on the evaluation of optional clauses. SPARQL, e.g., uses the order of optional clauses in the query: The following query selects essays together with translators and, if that translator is also an author, also the author name.

   ```
   SELECT   ?writing, ?person, ?name
   WHERE    { ?writing a books:Essay .
            OPTIONAL { ?writing books:translator ?person }
            OPTIONAL { ?writing books:author ?person .
                       ?person foaf:name ?name } }
   ```

   If we change the order of the two optional parts, the semantics of the query changes: select all essays together with authors and author names (if there are any). The second optional becomes superfluous, as it only checks whether the binding of ?person is also a translator of the same essay but whether the check fails does not affect the outcome of the query.

   It should be obvious that this semantics for interdependent optionals is equivalent to allowing only a single optional clause per conjunction that may in turn contain other optional clauses. Therefore, the above query could also be written as follows:

   ```
   SELECT   ?writing, ?person, ?name
   WHERE    { ?writing a books:Essay .
            OPTIONAL { ?writing books:translator ?person
               OPTIONAL { ?writing books:author ?person .
                          ?person foaf:name ?name }
            } }
   ```

   This observation, however, only applies if the optional clauses are interdependent. If they are not interdependent multiple optional clauses in the same conjunction differ from the case where they are nested.

   Algae seems to employ the same optional semantics as SPARQL, though the language specification is rather vague at that point.

2. *Maximized optionals:* Another form of optional semantics considers any order of optionals: In the example it would return the union of the orders, i.e., either first binding translators than checking whether they are also authors or first binding authors and author names then checking whether they are also translators. This is more involved than the above form and assigns different semantics to adjunct optionals vs. nested optionals. The advantage of this semantics is that it is equivalent to a rewriting of optional to disjunctions with negated clauses: $A \land \mathsf{optional}(B) \land \mathsf{optional}(C)$ is equivalent to $(A \land \mathsf{not}(B) \land \mathsf{not}(C)) \lor (A \land \mathsf{not}(B) \land C) \lor (A \land B \land \mathsf{not}(C) \lor (A \land B \land C)$. This semantics ensures that the maximal number of optionals for a certain (partial) variable assignment is used. This semantics has been introduces in Xcerpt.

3. *All-or-nothing optional:* A rare case of optional semantics is the "all-or-nothing" semantics where either all optional clauses are consistent with a certain variable assignment or all optional variables are left unbound. This semantics can be achieved in SPARQL and Xcerpt using a single optional clause instead of multiple independent ones.

RDF Specificities. Following the look at general issues for query languages in the specific context of RDF, this section closes the discussion of selection constructs with a consideration of selection constructs for RDF specificities such as blank nodes, collections, reified statements etc. RDF query languages should support these specificities in some way (possibly only as syntactic sugar) to be considered adequate to the RDF data model.

Blank Nodes. Among the considered specificities, blank nodes are the only ones that introduce new challenges for the query language. For matching, blank nodes are just like any other resource, but obviously do not match if a URI is specified in the query. However, for result construction blank nodes have to be considered specifically, see Section 5.2.

Collections and Containers are RDF's constructs to represent sets, sequences, and similar structures. The difference between containers and collections lies in the fact that containers are always open (i.e., new members may be added through additional RDF statements) and collections may be closed. Both containers and collections are merely vocabulary and representational conventions but do not extend the data model. I.e., a sequence container $\langle A, B, C \rangle$ is reduced to the triples

```
_:1 rdf:type rdf:Sequence
_:1 rdf:_1   A
_:1 rdf:_2   B
_:1 rdf:_3   C
```

Similarly, collections are reduced to binary relations of rdf:first and rdf:last:

```
_:1 rdf:first A
_:1 rdf:rest   _:2
_:2 rdf:first B
_:2 rdf:rest   _:3
_:3 rdf:first C
_:3 rdf:rest rdf:nil
```

However, these reductions result in lengthy and hard to understand triple patterns. Furthermore, querying directly on these representations proves challenging in many RDF query languages. Consider the simple query intent for selecting all members of a container or collection C. This query cannot be expressed in most RDF query languages if C is a collection, as it requires an arbitrary-length traversal of rdf:first and rdf:last edges (or direct support of collections) neither of which most RDF query languages provide including SPARQL. In languages with regular path expressions such as Versa or Xcerpt this query can be expressed as C `rdf:first.(rdf:rest.rdf:first)*` R with R selecting the contained resources. In the case of containers, an RDF query language either needs direct support or some support for regular expressions over property URIs. SPARQL, e.g., can express the query as

```
SELECT    ?contained_resource
WHERE     { ?C ?P ?contained_resource .
          FILTER(regex(str(?P),
            "http://www.w3.org/1999/02/22-rdf-syntax-ns#_\d+")) }
```

where the regular expression \d+ stands for one or more digits.

RQL is one of the few RDF query languages that provide specific constructs for querying membership in containers and even position in ordered containers. E.g., the above query can simply be expressed as R in C, selecting all resources R in the container C. Though RQL does not yet consider collections, this addition should be straightforward.

Reification. Reified statements are another example for a modeling construct that is reduced to several triples but is often convenient to query without requiring the author to perform the reduction by hand. Indeed, some RDF query languages such as SeRQL [22] and TRIPLE [93] provide specific syntax for reified statements, that allows reified statements to be queried with the same syntax as normal statements. SeRQL simply encloses a triple pattern in curly braces to indicate reification.

5.2   Construction

Where the previous section has focused on how RDF query languages select data from the underlying RDF graph, this section looks at the reporting of the selected data including construction of new data.

Graph Construction vs. Selection-only. Surprisingly many RDF query languages are not closed, i.e., their result is not again RDF but often simply sets or sequences of tuples representing alternative variable assignments. Examples of such languages are RDQL [91] and Versa. SPARQL provides both just variable assignments using the SELECT keyword and some limited form of graph construction using the CONSTRUCT keyword which, however, falls short of even the most simple grouping tasks.

Even when considering only variable selection **blank nodes** in results are an interesting challenge for RDF query languages. Blank nodes can not be identified from outside thus any "internal" identifier for a blank node returned as part of a result provides at best existential information (i.e., there is a node that fulfills a query). This makes grouping and aggregation even more important than in relational queries. All the more surprising is the lackluster support for these well-established language features in RDF query languages. RQL is one of the few languages providing aggregation including grouping by sub-queries: The following query selects all resources authored by "Julius Caesar" together with the count of their properties.

```
SELECT R, count(SELECT @P FROM {R @P }
FROM   {R}books:author{A}
WHERE  A = "Julius Caesar"
```

The languages in the SPARQL family mostly lack any form of aggregation thus requiring, e.g., post-processing of query results to solve such queries.

Graph Construction. A basic requirement for any query language is closure, i.e., the ability to construct data in the same data model as the queried data. In the case of RDF query languages, quite a number of languages focus on selection only, e.g., Versa and RDQL. Others, such as SPARQL provide graph construction but only the most basic form. Most notably, SPARQL omits any form of **grouping** which severely limits the sort of graphs that can be constructed.

The basic form of graph construction in SPARQL is

```
CONSTRUCT { ?R ?P ?O }
WHERE     { ?R books:author "Julius Caesar". ?R ?P ?O }
```

Constructing a graph with one triple for each property of all resources with author "Julius Caesar". Indeed, SPARQL's constructions are just triple patterns again generating one instance of the triple pattern for each variable assignment produced by the query.

In particular, this means that blank nodes in construct patterns are instantiated once for each variable assignment. There is no way that triples for different variable assignments "share" blank nodes.

Collections and containers. This separate handling of constructed instances prevents any form of **grouping** including the construction of **containers** and **collections**, for both of which some form of grouping is needed. Thus, it is impossible to answer simple queries such as "put the names of hotels for each city in a container/collection" or link each city and all its inhabitants to a common (blank) node. What SPARQL lacks is a proper "identity invention" facility, cf. [3].

RQL provides specialized constructs for constructing collections and containers and allows arbitrary grouping using nested queries, but also lacks proper treatment of blank nodes in construction.

Minimal Result Graphs. In addition to the support of blank nodes for grouping properties, blank nodes pose another challenge for graph construction in RDF query languages: Naively, one might generate one result instance for each blank node in the variable assignments. However, in many cases this leads to unnecessary large result graphs.

E.g., consider the assignment set $\{(R \rightarrow \text{http://w3.org/}, P \rightarrow \text{director}, O \rightarrow \text{"Tim Berners-Lee"}), (R \rightarrow \text{http://w3.org/}, P \rightarrow \text{director}, O \rightarrow \_:1)\}$. Then the above SPARQL query constructs a graph containing two statements, one stating that the W3C has director "Tim Berners-Lee" and one stating that the W3C has some (unknown or unspecified) creator. However, the second statement is entailed by the first one and therefore superfluous. A **minimal** result graph would only retain those blank nodes that are not "compatible" and thus entailed by the other resources in the graph.

Conditional construction. When constructing a result graph, the shape of the graph is often closely linked to the variable assignments. This goes, again, beyond mere instantiation of variables at predefined positions. E.g., one might only want to include a subgraph if a certain optional variable is bound. This ability of a query language is referred to as conditional construction. One can essentially distinguish three forms of conditional construction:

1. *Unscoped optional construction* is used, e.g., in SPARQL: A triple containing optional variables is only included if bindings for all optional variables are provided in the current variable assignment. The drawback of this approach is that it does not allow the existence of a binding for an optional variable to have effect beyond triples using that variable. E.g., it is not possible to add the statement that a resource is (of type) translated if a translator exists.
2. *Scoped optional construction* allows this sort of queries by providing an explicit optional construction construct (e.g., optional in Xcerpt construct terms) with a scope. In RDF, this scope is usually a set of triples that are to be included if a binding for the optional variable is present. In contrast to the first case, not all of these triples have to contain the optional variable.
3. *Full conditional construction* finally uses conditional constructs such as if ...then or case with arbitrary boolean expressions over the query variables. E.g., one might want to add the triple `?P rdf:type my:Teen` for persons with `?Age` between 12 and 18 and the triple `?P rdf:type my:Adult` for older persons.

Notice, that all three forms can be expressed if the query language allows disjunction to span selection and construction as is the case in most rule-based query languages such as Xcerpt, Algae, or Triple. In SPARQL, however, disjunction is limited to selection (i.e., WHERE clauses) thus making (2) and (3) inexpressible in SPARQL.

Construction of XML Results. If one looks at the RDF data access use cases [35] and considers often cited usage for RDF query languages, the need for a bridge between RDF queries and XML processing becomes evident. Some languages address this by integrating RDF and XML querying, e.g., Xcerpt or approaches such as [87]. Such languages become versatile in the sense of [27].

Most RDF query languages, however, do not consider the intertwining of XML and RDF queries. Still, the need for at least a means to deliver XML as result of an RDF query is evident. SPARQL, e.g., defines a static schema for representing answers in XML, cf. [9]. Such a static schema can then serve for further processing by means of XML query languages or other processing tools.

5.3   Procedural Abstraction

This section closes with a brief look at procedural abstraction mechanisms for RDF query languages. Procedural abstraction in form of database views or rules is a common feature of both programming and expressive query languages. For the Semantic Web to succeed, an efficient rule layer to implement large scale reasoning tasks is essential. Separating querying and (rule) reasoning, however, is often infeasible, in particular if the extent of the queried data depends on the reasoning and is not known a priori (as is the case, e.g., in crawling RDF queries).

In addition, rules or views are useful for the query author for all the reasons traditional procedural abstraction has become commonplace in programming languages (separation of concern, reuse, etc.).

Therefore, quite a number of RDF query languages provide some form of rules or views. TRIPLE and Xcerpt, e.g., use deductive rules similar to Logic Programming or Datalog, Algae uses production rules, cf. Section 6 on the evaluation of these different rule paradigms.

Both, TRIPLE and Xcerpt use rules to provide *transparent RDFS-aware selection* as discussed above in Section 5.1, but also allow the user to define their own rules expressing, e.g., application semantics already on the query layer.

A further important use for rules is the integration and mediation of heterogeneous data. The data may differ in format, schema, or just representation, if the schema is flexible as most RDFS schemata. In these cases, rules can ease data integration, e.g., if mappings between the different schemata are provided in some form, cf. [89]. They can also perform data normalization transparent to the query user, i.e., allow the user to query representational variants without considering all these variants in each query anew.

6   Query Evaluation

Methods for RDF query evaluation differ in several aspects:

- RDF data may be stored in memory or on disk.
- Query evaluation may be distributed over a network of collaborating nodes, or it may be local.
- RDF triples may include provenance information. In this case, they are called quadruples (s, p, o, c) of subject, predicate, object and so-called *context information*. Alternatively, the provenance information may be associated with entire subgraphs rather than with triples.
- RDF graphs can be stored as decomposed triples or quadruples in a relational database engine, as documents on a file system, or as entire graphs in an object oriented or semi-structured database. The type and schema of the storage have a high influence on the efficiency of query processing.
- Queries may either consist of single RDF statements with variables substituted for any combination of subject, predicate and object (e.g. (?X, foaf:knows, ?Y)), or they may consist of conjunctions of such statements, then referred to as *conjunctive queries*. In the latter case, multiple occurrences of the same variable are evaluated by joins and allow querying graph patterns.

In this article we mainly focus on non-distributed answering of RDF queries on large RDF repositories stored on disk. Both querying graphs with and without provenance information are discussed, and different storage methods are examined. Both single statement queries and conjunctive queries consisting of multiple RDF statements are considered.

6.1   Storage of RDF Data

The first issue highlighted in the field of query evaluation is data storage: a closer look is taken at three alternative approaches to storing RDF data. First, light is shed on the use of the Berkeley database for storing RDF in the Jena framework, second several proposed methods for using relational database engines for RDF storage are reproduced, and third approaches for deploying object oriented and object relational databases for RDF storage are described. Taking into account their widespread use, it is not surprising that the greatest number of suggestions and implementations of RDF storage is based upon relational database engines. In each of the sections, the impact of the choice of the storage method on query evaluation is highlighted.

RDF Storage in Berkeley Databases. According to the directory of the Free Software Foundation[14], the Berkeley Database is

> [..] an embedded database system. Its access methods include B+tree, Extended Linear Hashing, fixed and variable-length records, and Persistent Queues. Berkeley DB provides full transactional support, database recovery, online backups, and separate access to locking, logging and shared memory caching subsystems. [..]

The initial database back-end for the Jena RDF framework [47] supports both relational database back-ends and the Berkeley database. The relational database schema for storing RDF statements in Jena1 (the first version of Jena) is very efficient in space, because it does not contain any redundant information. In contrast, each RDF statement is stored three times in the Berkeley database – using all of subject, predicate and object as hash-keys. According to [99] the redundant storage yields a significant enhancement of query performance, and from this experience the authors of Jena decided to not fully normalize the relational database schema for Jena2 (the second version of the Jena RDF Framework). Besides Jena, also the Redland RDF Application Framework [8], rdfDB and RDFStore make use of the Berkeley database.

Storage of RDF at the aid of Relational Database Engines. The majority of suggestions for permanently storing RDF data concern relational database engines.

RDF storage in Jena1 and Jena2 The most straight-forward approach to storing RDF in a relational DBS is to create a single table with the columns subject,

---
[14] http://directory.fsf.org/

predicate and object, containing all statements of the RDF graph. In order to save space, the relational database schema of Jena1 differs from this simplistic approach in that the schema is normalized to contain each resource and literal only once. Therefore a *resource table* and a *literals table* are introduced, containing a column for a short primary key, and a column for resources and literals, respectively. The subjects, predicates and objects of the statement table refer to these keys.

Although this schema is very efficient in space, retrieving the subject, object and predicate of a statement already requires three joins between the *statement table*, the *resource table* and the *literals table*. Therefore the relational database back-end of Jena2 [99] stores literals and resources directly in the *statements table* unless they supersede a configurable maximum size. As a result, short URLs may be stored multiple times in order to avoid joins, but large URLs are only stored once in order to save space. There are several other optimizations that have been incorporated into Jena2:

- *Multiple tables for different graphs.* RDF applications may wish to store data which is seldom accessed together in different tables, and data which is often queried together in the same tables. "The use of multiple statement tables may improve performance and caching" [99, Section 3.1].
- *Property tables.* In RDF graphs, there are usually sets of statements with the same subject that occur frequently together. An example would be the properties `foaf:name`, `foaf:nick`, `foaf:knows`, etc. of the FOAF vocabulary. So as to provide efficient access to these *common statement patterns*, they are stored in special *property tables*. For each common statement pattern, one property table is provided, and common statement patterns may be automatically detected in RDF Graphs.
- *Reified statements tables.* In Jena1 reified statements are not stored in their reified form (which would require four ordinary statements for one reified statement), but in the statements table with two extra columns – one of them indicating whether the statement is reified, and the other containing the statement identifier. Since also reified statements constitute common access patterns, Jena2 stores reified statements in property tables.

Storage of RDF data in 3store 3store [50] is a C-library developed at the University of Southampton with a MySQL database back-end. It is intended for very large RDF databases and is being tested with over 30 million RDF triples holding knowledge about authors, publications and institutions in UK Computer Science research. The database schema employed is very similar to that of Jena1. It consists of a statements table, and a table for resources and literals. As in Jena1, literals and resources are not directly stored in the statements table. Instead a portion of their MD5 hash values are stored as 64-bit foreign keys in the statements table. The use of the hash function for literals and URIs and the storage in extra tables guarantee lower overall space of the database, few string comparisons, and a uniform length of the records in the statements table, "an optimization which benefits the MySQL database engine" [50, Section

4.3]. Although the probability of hash collisions is very low (10^{-10} for $5 \cdot 10^8$ resources), hash collisions are detected and reported at assertion time. [50] does not mention how hash collisions are corrected. Hash collisions among homonymous literals and URIs are averted by splitting the hash space into two equally large parts, one for literals, the other for URIs.

The most recent version of 3store [49] allows the formulation of queries in SPARQL, which supports the concept of named graphs. Therefore, the statements table contains an additional row which indicates the graph that the statement belongs to (triples with such provenance information are often called *quads*. Besides the statements table, and the tables for literals and URIs, 3store also stores the languages and data types of literals in special tables.

RDF Storage in Sesame Sesame is an RDF database with support for Schema inferencing and querying using the SeRQL query language. By introducing an additional *Storage and Inference Layer* (SAIL) between the RDF storage system and the applications accessing the data, Sesame is designed to support a wide variety of different storage possibilities. In [23] an implementation of SAIL in the open source databases PostgreSQL and MySQL is presented.

The PostgreSQL database schema makes use of transitive sub-table relations, which are a special PostgreSQL feature, to model RDFS' property and class subsumption hierarchies. A table holding instances of a class C_1 which is a subclass of class C_2 inherits from the table for C_2 – in other words it is declared as a sub-table of C_2. A query issued on the contents of table C_2 is also evaluated on the entries of table C_1. As Jena1 and 3store, Sesame stores resource URIs and literal values only once to save space. An important difference between Sesame RDF storage and the solutions discussed so far is that statements are not stored in a single statements table consisting of subject, property and object. Instead, an extra table is created for each property and class which is used in the RDF graph. Since this procedure requires the insertion of new tables to the schema when RDF statements are added which use properties or classes which have not appeared in the RDF graph so far, we call these kinds of schemas *dynamic schemas* as opposed to *static schemas* as used in 3store and Jena. An RDF graph with FOAF data would thus include tables `foaf:knows` containing all pairs of person URIs for persons knowing each other, tables `foaf:name`, `foaf:nick` for storing ordinary names and nick names, etc. are created. For each class used in the RDF schema, tables such as `foaf:Person`, `foaf:Document`, etc. Data about the schema is stored in special tables `rdfs:Class`, `rdfs:Property`, `rdfs:domain`, `rdfs:range`, etc. A performance comparison with a *static* PostgreSQL schema has shown, that schemas with a single statement table are faster when inserting or updating data from the RDF graph. Especially the insertion of new `rdfs:subClassOf` statements is expensive, since it requires rebuilding the parts of the subclass-hierarchy modeled by PostgreSQL sub-tables. On the other hand, the authors of [23] expect querying to be faster in the *dynamic* database schema.

The alternative MySQL implementation of the Sesame *Storage and Inference Layer* uses a static database schema. This schema is significantly more

complex than the static schemes of 3store and Jena in that it contains tables
dedicated to holding the predefined RDF/S properties `rdfs:subPropertyOf`,
`rdfs:subClassOf`, `rdf:type`, etc. Although not explicitly mentioned in [23],
administering this schema information in separate tables enhances the performance of RQL schema queries such as `subClassOf(Artist)`. The fact that RQL
is a language that explicitly supports the straightforward formulation of schema
queries, and that the other storage engines are coupled with languages with lower
support for schema queries may be an explanation for the different database
schemas employed.

RDF Storage in RDFSuite RDFSuite is a set of tools for querying, validating and
storing RDF data. It natively supports the RQL query language. In this paragraph, its storage system is briefly examined. RDFSuite uses the PostrgreSQL
DBS for storing RDF data, and its schema is a dynamic schema resembling
the PostgreSQL schema of Sesame. Sub-table relationships are used to implement `subClassOf` and `subPropertyOf`-relationships among classes and properties. Since RQL provides syntactic means specifically geared to querying RDF
Schema, such queries must be evaluated quickly. Therefore, the schema information is kept in separate tables such as `subProperty`, `subClass`, `Property`, `Class`
and `Type`. In contrast to the schemas described above, Namespaces are stored
in a separate `Namespace` table in order to save space. This namespace table is
referenced from the other tables. A database is built from an RDF-description
using a two phase algorithm: In the first phase, properties and classes occurring within the RDF data are extracted, and from this information the database
schema is constructed. In the second phase this schema is populated with the
instance data from the RDF file.

Path Based Storage of RDF Data Matono et al. [73] point out that storing
RDF graphs as decomposed sets of triples is efficient for evaluating single statement queries, but is inefficient for *path based queries*. Whereas in single statement queries one or two items of *subject, predicate* and *object* are omitted,
path based queries as defined in [73] are finite sequences of arcs $(v_0, v_1), (v_1, v_2),$
$\ldots, (v_{k-1}, v_k)$ from a source node v_0 to the destination v_k. Answering path based
queries of length k at the aid of a single statement table requires $k - 1$ joins over
the table. So as to improve performance, Matono et al. suggest the following
procedure:

– The RDF graph to be queried is separated into five subgraphs named CI,
   PI, T, DR, G containing the class hierarchy (`rdfs:subClassOf` statements),
   the hierarchy amongst properties (`rdfs:subPropertyOf`), type information
   (`rdf:type`), domain and range information of properties and all remaining
   statements, respectively. Only the paths occurring within G are explicitly
   saved within an appropriate relational table. For the hierarchical subgraphs
   CI and PI an interval numbering scheme is applied in order to efficiently
   answer queries concerning their transitive closures. Since the subgraphs T
   and DR are flat, it does not make sense to extract paths from them.

- For each resource r in the graph G all paths starting at any root node of G and ending at r are saved. In order to be able to efficiently deal with path based queries that start with a wild card (e.g. "give me all titles of books authored by someone"), path expressions are saved in reverse order. Moreover, only the names of the predicates are reflected within the path expressions, whereas node names are omitted. An example path expressions saved in the database would thus be `'#title<#author`. The relational table containing the path expressions consists of two columns, one holding path identifiers, and the other holding path expressions such as the one given above. In a *resource table*, resources are associated with paths that end at this resource.
- Path queries are evaluated by concatenating their predicate names in reverse order and subsequently comparing the resulting string with the path expressions stored in the path expressions table.

The authors of [73] present a performance comparison with the Jena2 framework which suggests that for path queries of length greater than 3, path based storage of RDF data allows significantly faster query processing. For queries of length 1 and 2, Jena2 performed better. The *resource table* associating resources with path identifiers is significantly larger than the actual number of resources, especially in the case of deep and densely interwoven graphs. A further issue not addressed within [73] are path queries that do not start with wildcard nodes (e.g. "Find all titles of books and their authors"). Since the stored paths only contain predicates and no node identifiers, answering such queries still requires joins over the statements table.

RDF Storage in Object Databases. In [20] Bönström et al. propose to directly store RDF graphs modeled in an object oriented programming language in an object oriented database (OODB). They compare the performance of all kinds of queries including schema and hybrid queries expressed in RQL on top of the OODBS Fastobjects with the performance of the same queries on top of the relational MySQL database back-end of Sesame. Due to the similarity of RQL and OQL, RQL queries can be straightforwardly translated to OQL. All resources (URIs for nodes and predicates as well as literals) are represented as objects, and the statements of the RDF graphs are stored in the OODB as "an object/reference structure". The performance comparisons conducted in [20] suggest that directly storing an RDF graph in an OODB system considerably speeds up query evaluation, especially for schema and hybrid queries. Performance comparisons with the PostgreSQL back-end of Sesame and other RDF storage systems mentioned above have not been mentioned in the article.

Index Structures for RDF. The approaches considered so far use standard database management systems (OODBS and RDBS) or standard libraries (Berkeley DB) to efficiently store and retrieve RDF data on disk. However, some research has already been carried out on developing index structures specifically aimed at RDF. In [72] Matono et al. propose to use suffix arrays to efficiently find paths in RDF graphs. In [52] index structures for RDF statements with context information (also called RDF quads or RDF triples with provenance information). In this section, both of these approaches are briefly reviewed and discussed.

Indexing RDF and RDF Schema with Suffix Arrays Suffix Arrays [68] are index structures used to search for a pattern P of length p in a larger string M of length m. All suffixes of M are sorted in lexicographical order, and the suffix array is efficiently stored as the string M and a sequence of *indexing points* $p_1, \ldots, p_m$ where $p_i, 1 \le i \le m$ is the position of the ith suffix (in lexicographical order) in the original string m. Suffix arrays allow to find all instances of P in M in $O(p \cdot log m)$.

Matono et al. propose to extract all paths from an acyclic RDF graph that start at root nodes (nodes without incoming edges) and end at leaf nodes (nodes without outgoing edges) and to represent them as strings by concatenating their labels (or identifiers for their labels). The alphabet Σ of these strings is thus the set of resource URIs and literal values of the Graph. They define the notion of suffix arrays for directed acyclic graphs as a list of indexing points $(pa_1, po_1), \ldots, (pa_l, po_l)$ where pa_i denotes the path that the ith suffix (in lexicographical order) appears in, and po_i denotes the position within pa_i. Paths within the queried RDF graph matching a particular path query can be found by performing binary searches on the suffix array.

In order to cope with schema queries efficiently, Matono et al. divide the RDF graph into several subgraphs according to the type of predicates, see [72] for details. Performance evaluations presented in [68] indicate that depending on the type of path queries, the proposed indexing scheme speeds up query execution by a factor in between two and nine.

Index Structures for RDF Quadruples Web applications processing data from several different resources usually are interested in tracing where the information originated from in order to judge its trustworthiness. Furthermore, it is often desirable to perform substring searches on large amounts of Semantic Web data. While RDF storage systems making use of the Berkeley database get by with three hashes for the efficient look-up of triples for two given items of the triple, [52] suggest index structures for efficiently searching for substrings (*keyword index*) within resource and literal values and for looking up quadruples (*quad indexes*) based on any combination of subject, predicate, object and context information.

Since resources and literals are referenced from both the keyword index and from the quad indexes, nodes in the RDF graph are mapped to shorter object identifiers which are stored in the indexes instead. Substring matches are determined by using an inverted index on all words appearing as tokens within the queried RDF graph. The inverted index allows to look up lists of object identifiers of resources that a given word appears in and also provides occurrence counts for the words that can be used to optimize the join order of conjunctive queries.

The quad indexes allow to efficiently look up RDF quadruples matching a given query quadruple in which some of the four entries may be omitted. Query quadruples such as (?:rdf:type:?:http//example.com/stmts.rdf), which finds all rdf:type statements originating from the context http//example.com/ stmts.rdf, can be categorized into $2^4 = 16$ access patterns, depending on which of the four elements of the quadruple are given. A naive implementation would construct 16 indexes to allow the efficient evaluation of queries falling in any of the 16 categories, but Harth et al. show that by taking advantage of prefix queries in B+-trees, only 6 "combined" indexes suffice for this purpose.

6.2   Schema- and Reasoning-Aware RDF Querying

As has been pointed out in Section 4, RDF languages can be distinguished by the fact whether they provide constructs taking advantage of RDF/S and OWL reasoning. While the major part of languages does not provide direct means of finding e.g. all subclasses of a given class, or all instances of a class, others do provide such features (e.g. RQL).[15] But also the languages of the SPARQL family do not reject the RDF/S semantics, but simply maintain that the computation of derived facts should be provided by an underlying graph model (e.g., by pre-materialization or on-the-fly construction performed by the storage layer). Therefore, an overview over several approaches of implementing especially the RDF/S semantics are given in this section.

One step in this direction that has already been discussed in Section 6.1, is the use of dynamic relational database schemes containing tables for each defined rdfs:Class holding all the instances of the class. This allows to efficiently retrieve all instances of a given class. Additionally, the use of sub-table relationships within database schemes allows the implementation of the rdfs9 inference rule as defined in [53]. Other RDF/S inference rules have not been covered so far. There are mainly three approaches that deal with the implementation of the RDF/S semantics:

- *Labeling schemes* can help to implement the RDF/S entailment rules concerning the rdfs:subClassOf and rdfs:subPropertyOf relationships, and any other relationship that is defined to be transitive.
- *Precomputation of derived facts (forward chaining).* Forward chaining can be used to precompute implied RDF statements, not contained in the original RDF graph that are derived from any of the RDF/S rules or even from user-defined rules. This approach trades memory space for execution time, and is especially useful, if the queried graph and its schema information are stable and if the number of queries issued on the graph is high. Note, however, that this approach requires that RDF triples and therefore the Web sites involved are known beforehand. Indeed, this computation model is not suitable for *crawler queries* where the extent of the data is extended at query time.

---

[15] Note that none of the examined languages provides constructs for taking advantage of OWL semantics. However, some research on how to combine query languages with OWL reasoners has already been carried out.

However, since many RDF query languages including SPARQL and RDQL do not support such queries the computation model is relevant for RDF querying.

- *Backward chaining.* Like forward chaining, backward chaining can be used to implement any kind of rules including all RDF/S entailment rules. Backward chaining is preferred when the underlying graph changes frequently, and when the the number of queries is low. Xcerpt uses backward chaining in combination with simulation unification to evaluate programs. The evaluation of Xcerpt is not treated in this article for the sake of brevity, cf. [28, 90].

Labeling Schemes for RDF/S Reasoning. Christophides et al. advocate the use of labeling schemes in conjunction with relational database storage of RDF graphs for "avoiding costly transitive closure computations over voluminous class hierarchies"[32] in Semantic Web data bases such as the Open Directory Portal. The use of labeling schemes reportedly results in a decrease in query execution time for transitive closure computations of 3-4 orders of magnitude compared to evaluating such queries on a dynamic relational database scheme such as the one described in [55].

In [32] three types of labeling schemes are compared with respect to their suitability for supporting ancestor/descendant (which is a more general form of subclass queries), adjacent/sibling, and nearest common ancestor queries. Some of the results concerning the use of these labeling schemes for both hierarchical subsumption relationships and those structured as directed acyclic graphs (DAGs) are recapitulated here and an example is given in Figure 3.

- *Bitvector schemes* assign bitvectors of length n (n is the number of nodes within a DAG to be represented by the scheme) to the nodes. The ith node in the DAG has a 1 bit at the ith position, and a 1 bit at the position k, if the kth node is one of its ancestors. All other positions within its bitvector are 0. Bitvector schemes allow subsumption checking in constant time (the length of the bitvectors is assumed to be constant), but finding all ancestors, descendants or siblings can only be achieved in $O(n)$. Additionally, the size of the bitvector must be adjusted, when new classes are added to a class hierarchy, making this method inappropriate for class hierarchies in the presence of dynamic updates. As Figure 3 shows, the bitvector scheme can be naturally extended to account for multiple inheritance among RDF classes.
- *Prefix schemes* assign labels to nodes within a class hierarchy (or DAGs in general), such that for each node N and an arbitrary ancestor A the label of A is a prefix of the label of N. Probably the most known representative of prefix schemes is the Dewey Decimal Encoding (DDE). A major advantage of prefix schemes is their support for dynamic updates. New sibling nodes can be added as long as the total number of siblings does not exceed the size of the alphabet chosen (in the figure the alphabet is $\Sigma = \{1, \ldots, 9\}$). The major disadvantage is the inflationary label size for class hierarchies

which are not tree-shaped: Each non-spanning-tree edge in Figure 3 causes the node it originates from and all of its descendants to inherit the label of the node the non-spanning-tree edge points at.

- *Interval schemes* assign lower and upper bounds to nodes, such that for a node N and an arbitrary ancestor A, the interval of N is contained within the interval of A, and for two sibling nodes the intervals are disjoint.In the interval based labeling scheme of Agraval et al., the label of a node v is composed of a pair of numbers $(min(v), post(v))$ where $post(v)$ is the post-order number of the node and $min(v)$ is the minimal post-order number of the descendants of v. As shown in Figure 3, the labeling scheme by Agrawal et al. can also be extended to handle DAGs. In contrast to the downward propagation of labels in the prefix schemes, labels are propagated upwards when non-spanning-tree edges are to be reflected (e.g. the node `ex:d` inherits the label of the node `ex:g` because there is a non-spanning-tree edge from `ex:g` to `ex:d`. The top node `ex:a` does not need to inherit the label `[1,1]` of `ex:g`, since `[1,1]` is already included in the interval `[1,7]` of `ex:a`.

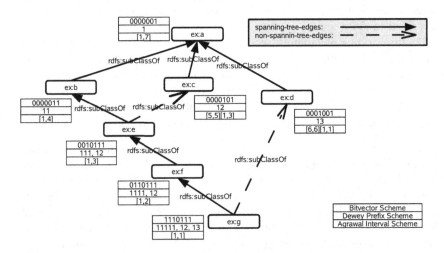

Fig. 3. Labeling schemes for DAG sub-class hierarchies

Note that all of the above labeling schemes cannot be used to represent cycles in the subsumption graph. An alternative labeling scheme for graphs with cycles is the 2-hop labeling [36].

Forward Chaining. The most apparent approach to calculating the transitive closure of `rdfs:subPropertyOf` and `rdfs:subClassOf` relationships and other implied RDF statements derivable by inference rules is the following: The body of a rule is instantiated with facts from the knowledge base, such that it becomes true (if possible) and the instantiated head of the rule is added to the knowledge base if it is a new fact. In this way, each of the rules is applied to the knowledge base in turn, until a complete run over the rules does not produce any new derived statements. Once that the application of all rules does not produce any new statements, one can be sure that all implied RDF/S statements have been added to the knowledge base.

Let F be the number of facts, R the number of rules and C the average number of conditions within the head of the rules. Then the maximum number of comparisons between facts and conditions for one loop over the rules is $R * F^C$. The overall complexity additionally depends on the number of loops that need to be performed. Several proposals for improving runtime behavior can be thought of:

- Applying the rules to the entire knowledge base in each round is not necessary. It suffices to consider only those instantiations of the inference rules that make use of a *new* fact – that means a fact that has been added after the last application of the rule. In doing so, the specific semantics of RDF blank nodes should be considered.
- If the body of an inference rule could almost be completely instantiated in one round, the information about the successfully instantiated part gets lost before the rule is reconsidered. By remembering partial instantiations of rule bodies one can treat space for time.
- Especially in the case that rules are complex, the bodies of different rules may share common parts of the condition. In the naive algorithm these sub-conditions are evaluated once for each rule.

Note, that forward chaining might be difficult to realize if the Web sites involved and thus the RDF facts are not all known before hand as is the case, e.g., with crawler queries.

CWM and Pychinko CWM[16] (an acronym for Closed World Machine) is a Python command line tool for RDF documents that can – amongst other things – convert between different formats (currently the serializations Notation3, RDF/-XML and NTriples are supported) and store triples in a queryable database. The more interesting feature of CWM for this section is its ability to do forward chaining. Given the following rule and data, CWM will infer that :`Frank`, :`Bob`, and :`Sam` are :`Male` (the shorthand a represents an `rdf:type` property).

```
{ ?x :son ?y } => { ?y a :Male }.

:Mary :son :Frank, :Bob, :Sam.
```

Since CWM does not employ any optimization techniques for forward chaining, it does not perform very well on large sets of assertions and rules. The authors of Pychinko[17], a CWM clone, improved the performance of CWM by implementing the RETE-algorithm [42].

---

[16] http://infomesh.net/2001/cwm/
[17] http://www.mindswap.org/~katz/pychinko/

The RETE-Algorithm The RETE-algorithm was conceived by Charles Forgy at Carnegie Mellon University in 1979, and formed the basis for new developments in the ambit of expert systems. Its core idea is to (1) merge (parts of) the antecedents of rules if they are the same, to (2) memorize possibly partial instantiations of antecedents of rules, and to only consider new facts within each loop over the set of rules. The data structure at the core of the RETE algorithm is a network computed from the antecedents of the rules. An example of this data structure for RDF/S entailment rules and some RDF/S statements is given in Figure 4. The network reflects the RDF/S inference rules `rdfs9` and `rdfs11` and contains two kinds of nodes: α-nodes representing simple conditions and β-nodes representing conjunctions over α-nodes. The α-nodes are populated with matching facts from the knowledge base (an RDF graph), and beta nodes are populated if a conjunction of simple conditions becomes true. The set of initially known facts is given at the top right of Figure 4. Note that although `rdfs9` and `rdfs11` are very simple entailment rules, the principles of the RETE algorithm already allow for some optimizations. Both rules share a common antecedent (the node `rdfs:subClassOf(X,Y)`), and partial instantiations of rules are memorized (e.g. the instantiation (`ex:mammal, ex:animal`), which will help to derive additional implied RDF statements in the next loop).

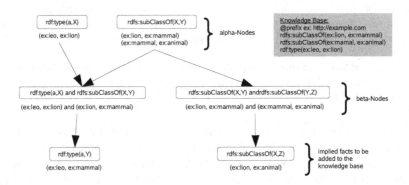

Fig. 4. Memorization of partially instantiated antecedents and combination of rule antecedents in RETE algorithm

As Figure 4 shows, the new facts `rdf:type(ex:leo, ex:mammal)` and `rdfs:subClassOf(ex:lion,ex:animal)` can be inferred. Adding these new facts to the knowledge base as in Figure 5 shows that the amount of comparisons to be performed is low: The derived facts must only be compared with the two α-nodes, and trigger one new instantiation for each α-node and a new instantiation for the left β-node, such that the last implied statement `rdf:type(ex:leo, ex:animal)` can be derived. Note that also the removal of facts (RDF statements) from the knowledge base (the RDF graph) can be efficiently handled by the RETE-algorithm in the same way as the addition of new facts.

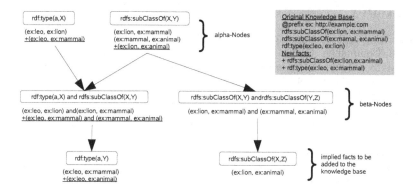

Fig. 5. Addition of new facts to the rete decision tree

Although the optimizations of the RETE algorithm have a greater impact for a large number of rules with complex antecedents, its implementation in Pychinko allegedly yields a five-fold performance increase. Therefore its application to larger and more involved rules for Semantic Web reasoning seems to be promising.

7   Conclusion

Although this survey only considers a (subjectively chosen) subset of the RDF query languages proposed so far, it makes quite clear that the research community has not yet settled on a dominant paradigm to querying Semantic Web data and that this field of research is changing quite quickly. Language constructs and approaches to querying RDF differ both in their availability (e.g. regular path expressions) and also in their exact semantics (e.g. the optional construct). The widespread use of the query languages within Semantic Web projects, which will most probably take place within the upcoming years, will allow to judge the real-world utility of the presented approaches and constructs and will ultimately establish the most usable amongst them.

This article presents some interesting methods for accelerating RDF query evaluation. With the amount of available Semantic Web data increasing exponentially, evaluation methods, efficient storage and retrieval and index structures specifically aimed at RDF become more important for realizing any of the proposed languages.

Acknowledgments

This research has been funded by the European Commission and by the Swiss Federal Office for Education and Science within the 6th Framework Programme project REWERSE number 506779 (cf. http://rewerse.net).

Bibliography

[1] RDFQL Database Command Reference. Online only, 2004.

[2] iTQL Commands. Online only, 2004.

[3] S. Abiteboul and P. C. Kanellakis. Object Identity as a Query Language Primitive. *Journal of the ACM*, 45(5):798–842, 1998.

[4] D. Backett. Modernising Semantic Web Markup. In *Proc. XML Europe*, April 2004.

[5] J. Bailey, F. Bry, T. Furche, and S. Schaffert. Web and Semantic Web Query Languages: A Survey. In J. Maluszinsky and N. Eisinger, editors, *Reasoning Web Summer School 2005*, pages 35–133. Springer-Verlag, LNCS 3564, 2005.

[6] N. Bassiliades and I. Vlahavas. Capturing RDF Descriptive Semantics in an Object Oriented Knowledge Base System. In *Proc. International Word Wide Web Conference*, May 2003.

[7] D. Beckett. *Turtle - Terse RDF Triple Language*, February 2004.

[8] D. Beckett. The Design and Implementation of the Redland RDF Application Framework. 2001.

[9] D. Beckett and J. Broekstra. *SPARQL Query Results XML Format*. W3C, 2006.

[10] D. Beckett and B. McBride. *RDF/XML Syntax Specification (Revised)*. W3C, 2004. URL http://www.w3.org/TR/rdf-syntax-grammar/.

[11] S. Berger, F. Bry, and S. Schaffert. A Visual Language for Web Querying and Reasoning. In *Proc. Workshop on Principles and Practice of Semantic Web Reasoning*, LNCS 2901. Springer-Verlag, December 2003.

[12] S. Berger, F. Bry, S. Schaffert, and C. Wieser. Xcerpt and visXcerpt: From Pattern-Based to Visual Querying of XML and Semistructured Data. In *Proc. Int. Conf. on Very Large Databases*, 2003.

[13] S. Berger, F. Bry, O. Bolzer, T. Furche, S. Schaffert, and C. Wieser. Xcerpt and visXcerpt: Twin Query Languages for the Semantic Web. In *Proc. Int. Semantic Web Conf.*, 11 2004. I4 I3.

[14] T. Berners-Lee. Notation 3, an RDF language for the Semantic Web. Online only, 2004.

[15] T. Berners-Lee. N3QL—RDF Data Query Language. Online only, 2004.

[16] T. Berners-Lee, J. Hendler, and O. Lassila. The Semantic Web—A new form of Web content that is meaningful to computers will unleash a revolution of new possibilities. *Scientific American*, 2001.

[17] P. Biron and A. Malhotra. *XML Schema Part 2: Datatypes*. W3C, 2001. URL http://www.w3.org/TR/xmlschema-2/.

[18] C. Bizer. TriQL—A Query Language for Named Graphs. Online only, 2004.

[19] O. Bolzer. Towards Data-Integration on the Semantic Web: Querying RDF with Xcerpt. Diplomarbeit/Master thesis, University of Munich, 2 2005. URL http://www.pms.ifi.lmu.de/publikationen#DA_Oliver.Bolzer.

[20] V. Bönström, A. Hinze, and H. Schweppe. Storing rdf as a graph. In *LA-WEB*, pages 27–36. IEEE Computer Society, 2003.

[21] D. Brickley, R. Guha, and B. McBride. *RDF Vocabulary Description Language 1.0: RDF Schema*. W3C, 2004. URL http://www.w3.org/TR/rdf-schema/.

[22] J. Broekstra and A. Kampman. SeRQL: A Second Generation RDF Query Language. In *Proc. SWAD-Europe Workshop on Semantic Web Storage and Retrieval*, 2003.

[23] J. Broekstra, A. Kampman, and F. Harmelen. Sesame: A Generic Architecture for Storing and Querying RDF and RDF Schema. In *Proc. International Semantic Web Conference*, 2002.

[24] F. Bry and S. Schaffert. The XML Query Language Xcerpt: Design Principles, Examples, and Semantics. In *Proc. Int. Workshop on Web and Databases*,
volume 2593 of *LNCS*. Springer-Verlag, 2002.

[25] F. Bry, W. Drabent, and J. Maluszynski. On Subtyping of Tree-structured
Data A Polynomial Approach. In *Proc. Workshop on Principles and Practice of
Semantic Web Reasoning, St. Malo, France*, volume 3208 of *LNCS*. REWERSE,
Springer-Verlag, 9 2004. I4 I3.

[26] F. Bry, T. Furche, L. Badea, C. Koch, S. Schaffert, and S. Berger. Identification of Design Principles for a (Semantic) Web Query Language. Deliverable
I4-D1, REWERSE, 2004. URL http://rewerse.net/publications/index.
html#REWERSE-DEL-2004-I4-D2.

[27] F. Bry, T. Furche, L. Badea, C. Koch, S. Schaffert, and S. Berger. Querying
the Web Reconsidered: Design Principles for Versatile Web Query Languages.
Journal of Semantic Web and Information Systems, 1(2), 2005. I4.

[28] F. Bry, A. Schroeder, T. Furche, and B. Linse. Efficient Evaluation of n-ary
Queries over Trees and Graphs. Submitted for publication, 2006.

[29] R. G. G. Cattell, D. K. Barry, M. Berler, J. Eastman, D. Jordan, C. Russell,
O. Schadow, T. Stanienda, and F. Velez, editors. *Object Data Standard: ODMG
3.0*. Morgan Kaufmann, 2000.

[30] D. Chamberlin, J. Robie, and D. Florescu. Quilt: An XML Query Language for
Heterogeneous Data Sources. In *Proc. Workshop on Web and Databases*, 2000.

[31] V. Christophides, D. Plexousakis, G. Karvounarakis, and S. Alexaki. Declarative
Languages for Querying Portal Catalogs. In *Proc. DELOS Workshop: Information Seeking, Searching and Querying in Digital Libraries*, 2000.

[32] V. Christophides, D. Plexousakis, M. Scholl, and S. Tourtounis. On Labeling
Schemes for the Semantic Web. In *WWW*, pages 544–555, 2003.

[33] J. Clark and S. DeRose. *XML Path Language (XPath) Version 1.0*. W3C, 1999.

[34] K. Clark. *RDF Data Access Use Cases and Requirements*. W3C, 2004.

[35] K. G. Clark. RDF Data Access Use Cases and Requirements. Working draft,
W3C, 10 2004.

[36] E. Cohen, E. Halperin, H. Kaplan, and U. Zwick. Reachability and distance
queries via 2-hop labels. *SIAM J. Comput.*, 32(5):1338–1355, 2003.

[37] I. F. Cruz, V. Kashyap, S. Decker, and R. Eckstein, editors. *Proceedings of
SWDB'03, The first International Workshop on Semantic Web and Databases,
Co-located with VLDB 2003, Humboldt-Universität, Berlin, Germany, September
7-8, 2003*, 2003.

[38] I. Davis. RDF Template Language 1.0. Online only, September 2003.

[39] J. de Bruijn, E. Franconi, and S. Tessaris. Logical Reconstruction of RDF and
Ontology Languages. In *Workshop on Principles and Practice of Semantic Web
Reasoning*, volume 3703 of *LNCS*. Springer-Verlag, 2005.

[40] S. Decker, D. Brickley, J. Saarela, and J. Angele. A Query and Inference Service
for RDF. In *Proc. W3C QL'98 – Query Languages 1998*, December 1998.

[41] A. Deutsch, M. Fernandez, D. Florescu, A. Levy, and D. Suciu. XML-QL: A
Query Language for XML. In *Proc. W3C QL'98 – Query Languages 1998*. W3C,
1998.

[42] C. L. Forgy. *On the efficient implementation of production systems*. PhD thesis,
1979.

[43] J. Frohn, G. Lausen, and H. Uphoff. Access to Objects by Path Expressions and
Rules. In *Proc. International Conference on Very Large Databases*, 1994.

[44] L. M. Garshol. Living with Topic Maps and RDF. Online only, 2003.

[45] G. Gottlob, C. Koch, and R. Pichler. Efficient Algorithms for Processing XPath Queries. *ACM Transactions on Database Systems*, 30(2):444–491, 2005.

[46] J. Grant and D. Backett. *RDF Test Cases*. W3C, February 2004.

[47] H. L. S. W. R. Group. Jena – A Semantic Web Framework for Java. Online only, 2004.

[48] T. Grust, M. V. Keulen, and J. Teubner. Accelerating XPath Evaluation in any RDBMS. *ACM Transactions on Database Systems*, 29(1):91–131, 2004.

[49] S. Harris. SPARQL query processing with conventional relational database systems, 2005.

[50] S. Harris and N. Gibbins. 3store: Efficient Bulk RDF Storage. In *Proc. International Workshop on Practical and Scalable Semantic Systems*, 2003.

[51] A. Harth. Triple Tutorial. Online only, 2004.

[52] A. Harth and S. Decker. Optimized Index Structures for Querying RDF from the Web, 2005.

[53] P. Hayes and B. McBride. *RDF Semantics*. W3C, 2004. URL http://www.w3.org/TR/rdf-mt/.

[54] G. Karvounarakis, V. Christophides, D. Plexousakis, and S. Alexaki. Querying RDF Descriptions for Community Web Portals. In *Proc. Journees Bases de Donnees Avancees*, 2001.

[55] G. Karvounarakis, S. Alexaki, V. Christophides, D. Plexousakis, and M. Scholl. RQL: A Declarative Query Language for RDF. In *Proc. International World Wide Web Conference*, May 2002.

[56] G. Karvounarakis, A. Magkanaraki, S. Alexaki, V. Christophides, D. Plexousakis, M. Scholl, and K. Tolle. Querying the Semantic Web with RQL. *Computer Networks and ISDN Systems Journal*, 42(5):617–640, August 2003.

[57] G. Karvounarakis, A. Magkanaraki, S. Alexaki, V. Christophides, D. Plexousakis, M. Scholl, and K. Tolle. RQL: A Functional Query Language for RDF. In P. Gray, P. King, and A. Poulovassilis, editors, *The Functional Approach to Data Management*, chapter 18, pages 435–465. Springer-Verlag, 2004.

[58] M. Kifer, G. Lausen, and J. Wu. Logical Foundations of Object Oriented and Frame Based Languages. *Journal of ACM*, 42:741–843, 1995.

[59] G. Klyne, J. Carroll, and B. McBride. *Resource Description Framework (RDF): Concepts and Abstract Syntax*. W3C, 2004. URL http://www.w3.org/TR/rdf-conc epts/.

[60] M. Lacher and S. Decker. On the Integration of Topic Maps and RDF Data. In *Proc. Extreme Markup Languages*, 2001.

[61] M. Lacher and S. Decker. RDF, Topic Maps, and the Semantic Web. *Markup Languages: Theory and Practice*, 3(3):313–331, December 2001.

[62] Langdale Consultants. Nexus Query Language. Online only, 2000.

[63] O. Lassila and R. Swick. *Resource Description Framework (RDF) Model and Syntax Specification*. W3C, 1999. URL http://www.w3.org/TR/1999/REC-rdf-syntax-19990222/.

[64] B. Ludäscher, R. Himmeroeder, G. Lausen, W. May, and C. Schlepphorst. Managing Semistructured Data with FLORID: A Deductive Object-oriented Perspective. *Information Systems*, 23(8):1–25, 1998.

[65] M. Magiridou, S. Sahtouris, V. Christophides, and M. Koubarakis. Rul: A declarative update language for rdf. In *Proceedings Int'l. Semantic Web Conf. (ISWC)*, 2005.

[66] A. Magkanaraki, V. Tannen, V. Christophides, and D. Plexousakis. Viewing the Semantic Web Through RVL Lenses. In *Proc. International Semantic Web Conference*, October 2003.

[67] D. Maier. Database Desiderata for an XML Query Language. In *Proc. W3C QL'98 – Query Languages 1998*, December 1998.

[68] U. Manber and G. Myers. Suffix Arrays: A New Method for On-Line String Searches. In *SODA*, pages 319–327, 1990.

[69] F. Manola, E. Miller, and B. McBride. *RDF Primer*. W3C, 2004. URL http://www.w3.org/TR/rdf-primer/.

[70] M. Marx. Conditional XPath, the First Order Complete XPath Dialect. In *Proc. ACM Symposium on Principles of Database Systems*, pages 13–22. ACM, 6 2004.

[71] M. Marx. XPath with Conditional Axis Relations. In *Proc. Extending Database Technology*, 2004.

[72] A. Matono, T. Amagasa, M. Yoshikawa, and S. Uemura. An indexing scheme for rdf and rdf schema based on suffix arrays. In [37], pages 151–168.

[73] A. Matono, T. Amagasa, M. Yoshikawa, and S. Uemura. A Path-based Relational RDF Database. 2005.

[74] K. Matsuyama, M. Kraus, K. Kitagawa, and N. Saito. A Path-Based RDF Query Language for CC/PP and UAProf. In *Proc. IEEE Conference on Pervasive Computing and Communications Workshops*, 2004.

[75] W. May. XPath-Logic and XPathLog: A Logic-Programming Style XML Data Manipulation Language. *Theory and Practice of Logic Programming*, 3(4):499–526, 2004.

[76] L. Miller, A. Seaborne, and A. Reggiori. Three Implementations of SquishQL, a Simple RDF Query Language. In *Proc. International Semantic Web Conference*, June 2002.

[77] U. Ogbuji. Versa by example. Online only, 2004.

[78] U. Ogbuji. Thinking XML: Basic XML and RDF techniques for knowledge management: Part 6: RDF Query using Versa. Online only, April 2002.

[79] M. Olson and U. Ogbuji. Versa Specification. Online only, 2003.

[80] S. Palmer. Pondering RDF Path. Online only, 2003.

[81] B. Parsia. Querying the web with sparql. In P. Barahona, F. Bry, E. Franconi, U. Sattler, and N. Henze, editors, *Reasoning Web, Second Int'l. Summer School 2006, Tutorial Lectures*. Springer-Verlag, 2006.

[82] E. Prud'hommeaux. Algae Extension for Rules. Online only, 2004.

[83] E. Prud'hommeaux. Algae RDF Query Language. Online only, 2004.

[84] E. Prud'hommeaux and A. Seaborne. SPARQL Query Language for RDF. Working draft, W3C, 4 2006.

[85] D. Reynolds. RDF-QBE: a Semantic Web Building Block. Technical Report HPL-2002-327, HP Labs, 2002.

[86] J. Robie. The Syntactic Web: Syntax and Semantics on the Web. In *Proc. XML Conference and Exposition*, December 2001.

[87] J. Robie, L. M. Garshol, S. Newcomb, M. Fuchs, L. Miller, D. Brickley, V. Christophides, and G. Karvounarakis. The Syntactic Web: Syntax and Semantics on the Web. *Markup Languages: Theory and Practice*, 3(4):411–440, 2001.

[88] S. Schaffert. *Xcerpt: A Rule-Based Query and Transformation Language for the Web*. Dissertation/Ph.D. thesis, University of Munich, 2004. URL http://www.pms.ifi.lmu.de/publikationen/#PMS-DISS-2004-1.

[89] S. Schaffert and F. Bry. Querying the Web Reconsidered: A Practical Introduction to Xcerpt. In *Proc. Extreme Markup Languages*, August 2004.

[90] A. Schroeder. An Algebra and Optimization Techniques for Simulation Unification. Diplomarbeit/Master thesis, Institute for Informatics, University of Munich, 2005. URL http://www.pms.ifi.lmu.de/publikationen#DA_Andreas.Schroeder.

[91] A. Seaborne. RDQL – A Query Language for RDF. Online only, January 2004.

[92] M. Sintek and S. Decker. TRIPLE—An RDF Query, Inference, and Transformation Language. In *Proc. Deductive Database and Knowledge Management*, October 2001.

[93] M. Sintek and S. Decker. TRIPLE—A Query, Inference, and Transformation Language for the Semantic Web. In *Proc. International Semantic Web Conference*, June 2002.

[94] A. Souzis. RxPath Specification Proposal. Online only, 2004.

[95] D. Steer. TreeHugger 1.0 Introduction. Online only, 2003.

[96] P. Stickler. CBD—Concise Bounded Description. Online only, 2004.

[97] N. Walsh. RDF Twig: accessing RDF graphs in XSLT. In *Proc. Extreme Markup Languages*, 2003.

[98] A. Wilk and W. Drabent. On Types for XML Query Language Xcerpt. In *Proc. Workshop on Principles and Practice of Semantic Web Reasoning*, LNCS 2901. Springer-Verlag, 2003.

[99] K. Wilkinson, C. Sayers, H. Kuno, and D. Reynolds. Efficient RDF Storage and Retrieval in Jena, 2003.

[100] C. Zaniolo. The Database Language GEM. In *Proc. ACM SIGMOD Conf.*, 1983.

Querying the Web with SPARQL

Bijan Parsia

University of Manchester

1 SPARQL Background

Consider the following two conceptions of the Semantic Web:

- A web of (logic based) knowledge representations.
- A web of (semi-)structured data.

In both conceptions, the common factor (the web) imposes certain requirements: extremely variable scalability (from a home page to community sites to
sites that encompass a significant fraction of the web), rapid evolution, radical
distribution, arbitrary interconnection and aggregation, and very little validation or other means of control. The demands of the web are forcing both the
knowledge representation (KR) and the database communities to stretch their
understanding and technology in different ways. While implementation techniques require revamping to deal with web scale, finding the right level and
sort of expressiveness is even more critical. The web doesn't just need bigger
databases, it needs "better" ones. The rise of semi-structured data, especially in
the form of XML and associated languages, is driven by the success of HTML
as a data representation language as well as its many failures. The amount of
data that has been created or converted to HTML is staggering. HTML allows
novices to publish all sorts of information quite easily while also supporting complex information structures (for example, see the typical site map of a large site).
However, HTML is lacking in a number of ways, especially in the management,
evolution, integration, and repurposing of data. HTML, especially in common
use, has (at least) three fundamental problems: malformed or misused constructs,
a heavy presentation orientation, and a lack of needed expressivity. These problems stem from aspects of HTML (and associated software like the browser)
that, we believe, contributed to its success. Browsers were very permissive in
their parsing and rendering of HTML, which lowered the barrier to producing
pages. Various presentation features in HTML made it an attractive platform
for publishing information from software manuals to dictionaries to newspapers
with ads. HTML's core simplicity requires a lack of expressivity, which makes
it easier to learn (and to learn to "abuse"). More significantly, by pushing the
balance of expressivity (and thus complexity) toward the presentation aspects of
the language, it was relatively neutral toward content of different sorts. Consider
the effect of requiring a specialized content language to be developed before one
could publish, say, a recipe. Either the user would have to develop their own

P. Barahona et al. (Eds.): Reasoning Web 2006, LNCS 4126, pp. 53–67, 2006.

language (a difficult task in itself), or find a suitable one if it exists. Both paths are strongly inhibitory.

While these "problems" arguably helped the web to grow, they make managing, reusing, or evolving data difficult, as can be seen by the move away from websites based on collections of HTML files toward database backed websites, and, more generally, to "content management systems". More recently, under the "Web 2.0" moniker (for public, community-oriented sites) and with the rise of Web Services (primarily for business interaction), there has been an increase in the reuse of web published information across organizational boundaries in complex ways. This increase has been enabled by the use of XML to overcome exactly the three problems listed above: XML insists on well formedness and strongly discourages permissive parsers — if there is a mismatched tag, most parsers reject the document hard and fast. XML has no inherent presentation semantics, and, pragmatically, presentation has been handled either by transformation to HTML or by Cascading Style Sheets (CSS). Finally, XML is a metalanguage for defining markup languages, so, at the very least, users can develop languages specific to their representational task. On the other hand, XML based languages retain some of the flexibility of HTML: well-formedness is a very minimal constraint on XML documents, so in the worst case, one can jumble arbitrary tags together and process the data *ad hocly*. Schemas are all out of band and generally allow for a great deal of flexibility in the structure. Finally, the query and transformation languages (XPath, XQuery, and XSLT) reflect and exploit the base flexibility of XML: they do not require complete structuring of the data, they can impose constraints in an as needed and as possible basis, and they incorporate a strong navigational model[2].

While XML has been criticized by the semi-structured data community for its tree, rather than graph, orientation[5] among other things, its wide adoption and strong infrastructure make it a difficult behemoth to ignore, and make it silly to do so. However, XML technologies are firmly rooted in a datastructure view of the world, and thus not particularly suitable for logic based knowledge representation[1]. For example, XQuery, while admirably declarative, is a fairly standard functional programming language (with some twists in the type system, XML Schema, to deal with tree structured data), and typical XML tasks such as validation, transformation, and (database like) query focus on the structural, or syntactic, aspects of an XML fragment. Thus, in order to *represent* some aspect of the world, one must design all aspects of the representation, generally leaving many aspects implicit.[1] Of course, one could use XML as the

---

[1] "In a nut-shell (and somewhat exaggerated), the difference between knowledge-based programming (which processes knowledge) and classical programming (which processes data) can be formulated as follows. In classical programming, one designs specialized programs that are tailored to a specific application problem. The knowledge about the problem description and the application domain is implicitly represented in the structure of the program, and must thus be acquired by the programmer. In knowledge-based programming, the knowledge about the application domain is represented explicitly ... ideally, the preocessing can be done with the help of general ... problem solving methods."[1].

syntax of a knowledge representation language and, in a sense, that is what RDF, RDFS, and OWL do. However, RDF is an inexpressive enough logic that it is ambiguous as to whether it is a knowledge representation language or a data language (see section 3.2 for more discussion). When you add that people often use (or misuse) RDF as competitor to XML, then the picture gets even more murky.

In any information based application, whether a database driven web application or an AI planning system interacting with a theorem prover, there needs to be an effective interface between the information and information management part of the system, and the rest. In database management literature, this interface is often in the form of a specialized language called a *data manipulation language*, which includes facilities for retrieving, structuring, adding, modifying, and deleting information in the database. Of these, perhaps the most prominent is the retrieval aspect, that is, the *query language*. For XML, the most common query language is XPath which uses a navigational retrieval model. For the Semantic Web languages RDF(S) and OWL, there are a plethora of languages available, but the W3C is in the process of standardizing one, called SPARQL (an acronym expanding to SPARQL Protocol and RDF Query Language). While SPARQL technically includes both a query language and a protocol for (typically remote) access of Semantic Web data, development of the protocol greatly lags behind that of the query language. Thus, we shall focus on the query language, and hereafter use "SPARQL" to refer to the query language.

Historically, RDF query languages were primarily of two sorts: navigational, "path"-like languages and relational, SQL-like languages. Of the former, there are two prominent members: Versa[2] and the Wilbur Query Language[3], though they remain little used, with only one implementation each. SQL-like languages are widespread, with RDQL[4] being the most popular. RDQL is the starting point of SPARQL, though during development SPARQL acquired a new syntax for graph patterns based on Turtle[5] and features from other SQL-like RDF query languages, most notably, SeRQL[6], were added.

2   RDF

Here we present an abbreviated overview of the RDF abstract syntax, conceptual model, and semantics. The reader will find it helpful to review the relevant specifications: *RDF: Concepts and Abstract Syntax*[7], and *RDF Semantics*[8], in particular sections 0, 1, and 2. The concrete syntax used in this paper is Turtle, which is also the core graph syntax is SPARQL.

---

[2] http://uche.ogbuji.net/tech/rdf/versa/
[3] http://wilbur-rdf.sourceforge.net/2004/05/11-comparison.shtml
[4] http://www.w3.org/Submission/RDQL/
[5] http://www.dajobe.org/2004/01/turtle/
[6] http://www.openrdf.org/doc/sesame/users/ch06.html
[7] http://www.w3.org/TR/rdf-concepts/
[8] http://www.w3.org/TR/rdf-mt/

2.1 Syntax

RDF documents describe *graphs*, which are collections of *triples*. Triples are understood as assertions, that is, as true or false indicative sentences. Each triple, as the name indicates, consists of three parts, a subject, predicate, and object. Each "slot" of a triple can be filled with an RDF term, though there are syntactic restrictions on where certain terms can appear. The canonical RDF term is the Uniform Resource Identifier, or URI (recently supplanted with International Resource Indentifiers, IRIs, which are constructed from a much wider character set). URIs can be the subject, predicate, or object of a triple and correspond either to a singular term (that is, as the name of an individual) when the subject or object, or to a two place relation when the predicate. In plain RDF, there is not a significant distinction between a predicate and other URI terms, so it is convenient to think of a triple as *reified* into a three place predicate (call it 'rdf', or 'triple').

Objects can also be data values (in RDF jargon these are called "literals"). There are two basic sorts of literal, plain literals and typed literals. Literals fundamentally consist of two parts, a *lexical form* and a *value*. The lexical form is always a Unicode string and it is expressed the syntax of the literal. For plain literals, the lexical form and the value are identical (perhaps modulo encoding or whitespace), and plain literals may have a language tag as well. Typed literals all have a third part, a *datatype URI*[9] which determines the range of admissible values and the mapping from the lexical form into the value space. For example, consider the following typed literals:

Example 1. **Value Identical Typed Literals**
"1"^^<http://www.w3.org/2001/XMLSchema#integer>
"01"^^<http://www.w3.org/2001/XMLSchema#integer>

These literals have identical datatype URIs and values, but their lexical forms are distinct. Certain SPARQL test functions will treat these literals as identical. There is one predefined datatype in RDF [10] for XML content.

So far, the possible RDF graphs we have described are all *ground*, that is, they contain no variables of any sort. Ground graphs are similar to XML Infosets without type information (that is, the abstract datastructures corresponding to well formed XML documents) — they are very similar to a standard database. Standard database techniques (i.e., model checking) suffice to deal with them. However, RDF throws a twist into the mix: so-called *blank nodes* (commonly known as *BNodes*). BNodes may appear only in subject and object positions, and correspond to existentially quantified variables. The BNode quantifier for a particular graph occurs outside the entire graph, thus all such variables have a single, graph-global, scope.

---

[9] It is somewhat characteristc of RDF that certain syntactic concerns are mixed with semantic ones. In this case, instead of the notion of a *type* being fundamental, it is the type's *identifier* that is primary. Part of this is due to the desire to compose specifications (and the things they specified) via standard Web mechanisms.

[10] Named by the URI: http://www.w3.org/1999/02/22-rdf-syntax-ns#XMLLiteral

To sum up, an RDF graph is a collection (conjunction) of triples. Each triple consists of three terms, a URI or BNode, a URI, and a URI, BNode, or literal term. Literals may be typed or untyped. In SPARQL lingo, an RDF graph that is available for query is part of a *dataset*. A dataset may contain one or more RDF graphs where all but one of the graphs in a dataset have a URI as a label. The unlabeled graph is called the *default* graph. In this paper, we shall only deal with a single default graph in the queried dataset.

Throughout, we use the Turtle concrete syntax for RDF, as it is the syntax employed by SPARQL. Here is a brief introduction to Turtle, but the reader is strongly encouraged to consult the Turtle specification.

The core of Turtle is a direct, minimal representation of a set of triples. Each triple is delimited with a full stop; URIs are delimited by angle brackets; BNodes are indicated by a leading "_:"; and literals (both plain and typed) by straight double quotes. The following four triples exhibit all these forms, including a BNode coreference:

Example 2. **Basic Turtle:**
```
<http://ex.org/sara> <http://ex.org/loves>
                         <http://ex.org/mary>.
<http://ex.org/sara> <http://ex.org/hasFirstName> "Sara".
<http://ex.org/sara> <http://ex.org/knows> _:aBNode.
_:aBNode <http://ex.org/age>
       "8"^^<http://www.w3.org/2001/XMLSchema#integer>.
```

Turtle has a number of abbreviation forms which make it considerably less tedious to read and write. In particular, URIs can be abbreviated with (psuedo) QNames, given an appropriate prefix declaration, as follows:

Example 3. **Moderately Abbreviated Turtle:**
```
@prefix  : <http://ex.org/>.
@prefix xsd: <http://www.w3.org/2001/XMLSchema#>.
:sara :loves :mary.
:sara :hasFirstName "Sara".
:sara :knows _:aBNode.
_:aBNode :age "8"^^xsd:integer.
```

Notice that one can declare a "default" prefix, as we did in this example. Turtle has additional abbreviation forms, but we shall not use them in this paper.

2.2 Semantics

RDF's semantics are given by a simple, if somewhat non-standard, model theory. In what follows, we follow closely the presentation in the RDF Semantics document, and we restrict ourselves to the most basic semantics, that of the graphs themselves, without attending to any of the extended semantic conditions imposed on the special RDF and RDFS vocabulary.

Definition 1. *A* ***simple*** ***interpretation***, *I, of an RDF graph, R (where Sig(R) is the set of terms used in R, i.e., the signature) is a tuple of the form* $< IR, IP, IEXT, IS, IL, IT >$ *where*

- *IR (the domain) is a non-empty set;*
- *IP is the set of properties;*
- $IEXT : IP \rightarrow IR \times IR;$
- *for the set of URIs, U such that* $U \subseteq Sig(R)$, $IS : U \rightarrow (IR \cup IP)$;
- *for the set of plain literals,* $PL \subseteq Sig(R)$, $IL : PL \rightarrow IR$;
- *for the set of typed literals,* $TL \subseteq Sig(R)$, $IT : TL \rightarrow IR$;
- *for the set of BNodes, B such that* $B \subseteq Sig(R)$, $A : B \rightarrow IR$ *and for any non-BNode* $T \in Sig(R)$, $A : T \rightarrow I(T)$.
- *For a triple,* $< s, p, o >$, $I(< s, p, o >) = true$ *if*
    - $I(p) \in IP$;
    - $< A'(s), A'(o) > \in IEXT(I(p))$ *for some* A';

    otherwise $I(< s, p, o >) = false$;
- *For an RDF graph, R,* $I(R) = true$ *if, given some* A', *every triple* $Tr \in R$, $I(Tr) = true$, *and* $I(R) = false$ *otherwise.*

The main thing to attend to is that properties are not interpreted directly as sets of pairs of elements of the domain, as one might expect, but via an additional mapping fucntion ($IEXT$). This is a hook for higher order syntax in RDFS and OWL Full (though the semantics remains robustly first order, in the style of HiLog[3]).

Entailment between basic RDF graphs (called simple entailment) is defined in the usual way: a graph $R1$ simply entails a graph $R2$ if for all I such that $I(R1) = true$, $I(R2) = true$ as well.

3   Core SPARQL: Basic Graph Patterns

3.1   Syntax

Basic graph patterns (BGPs) are the key interface between the query side of things and the data side. A BGP is the only part of a SPARQL query that is sensitive to the semantics of the queried document, and, in fact, at least conceptually speaking, the only part that "interacts" with the data. It should, therefore, be no surprise that a BGP is a slight, but significant, generalization of an RDF graph. The extra bit is in the form of a new sort of term, the query variable. Query variables are similar to BNodes in being, in a sense, existential variables and are globally scoped to the BGP in which they occur. Query variables have a bit more freedom syntactically as they can appear in the predicate, as well as subject or object, of a triple. The set of triples that include triples with query variables are called *triple patterns*. A BGP is a set of triple patterns.

In addition to syntactic freedom, query variables are called out specially from BNodes for two reasons:

- Since BNodes in BGPs are lexically identical to BNodes in a graph serialized to Turtle syntax, it's useful to distinguish between "intentional" query variables and variables that are possibly just part of some example data.
- Query variables and BNodes correspond to *distinguished* and *undistinguished* variables, respectively. Traditionally, a distinguished variable must be bound to a ground term, and thus can only bind to individuals explicitly mentioned in the document. Undistinguished variables do not require a named binding and do not report their bindings in result sets. They are purely existential i.e., they do not require a witness entity present in the graph.

As we shall discuss in the next section, things are not quite so neat in the case of simple entailment since many SPARQL users wanted the ability to query *for* BNodes, primarily to deal with coreference between results (or queries!). Thus, query variables can be bound to BNodes — a rather unusual situation.

The concrete syntax of BGPs is Turtle plus terms with either a leading "?" or leading "$" to indicate a query variable (we shall use "?" exclusively).[11] BGPs are delimited by curly braces.

Example 4. **A BGP (without prefix declarations):**
{ex:sara ex:loves ?who.}

3.2   SPARQL Semantics

The semantics for SPARQL, even restricting attention to simple entailment, is surprisingly complex. BNodes, both in the data and especially in the result set, complicate the picture enormously. Furthermore, in spite of the clear semantics of RDF (which mandates that BNodes are existential variables), many users (and SPARQL implementors and specifiers!) tend to treat BNodes as "graph local" names, e.g., as Skolem constants. For editing applications, this is not an unreasonable attitude, but for the definition of query answers, it is rather odd. Given the lack of systems that correctly and sensibly implement simple entailment (and given the rather high computational complexity of simple entailment), we should not be so surprised that the data structural view of RDF graphs is so prevalent. It is possible that future working groups will chose to retract the existential interpretation of BNodes, given these prevailing attitudes.

A second difficulty is the desire to have SPARQL be *the* query language for the Semantic Web, or at least for all extant Semantic Web languages. Even restricting one's attention to the RDF Semantics document, one finds several sorts of entailment *specified* (simple entailment, RDF entailment, various extensions including RDFS). OWL is a completely different beast. While all these languages have an RDF syntax, not all variants are happy with the RDF semantics. For example, OWL Lite and OWL DL are based on description logics and thus are biased toward a more traditional first order model theory (i.e., where relations are directly identified with sets of tuples). So, some of the syntactic freedom

---

[11] There are other relaxations, including permitting literals in the subject position.

of RDF and SPARQL can cause problems for standard approaches to OWL conjunctive query.

The current SPARQL specification tries to be flexible and to provide useful hooks for dealing, semantically, with all these variations. Unfortunately, the current does not provide any syntax (or protocol features) for determining what semantics one is querying with. Also, there are several unspecified aspects of the semantics (for example, the algebra — see the notion of distinctness). It is hoped that as implementation and use experience is gathered, these problems can be straightfowardly resolved.

Parameterizing the Semantics. For specification purposes, we can divide SPARQL queries into two parts: basic graph patterns and algebraic operations.[12] BGPs are evaluated against a graph and that evaluation produces a *query result* (also known as a *result set*), that is, a set of *bindings* for the query variables in the BGP. A query result is very much like a table in a relational database system (the key difference being the presence of BNodes in the results). Query results are then manipulated by the various algebraic operations of SPARQL. This conception of SPARQL allows for SPARQL queries to be parameterized to the semantics of the graph, while leaving the rest of the language fixed. (From an implementation perspective, such a separation is unlikely to be practical.)

The relationship between a graph, a BGP, and the result set is characterized by an "Entailment regime". An entailment regime is an arbitrary relation between RDF graphs, thus, clearly, RDF entailment and all the various forms of OWL entailment are entailment regimes. This vagueness in specification allows for all sorts of processing of RDF graphs to affect the valid answers to a SPARQL query, including procedural and other *ad hoc* notions.

As we will see below, a result is a substitution of RDF terms for the query variables of a BGP such that the resulting graph is entailed by the queried graph under some entailment regime. Now we need to take into account what may be substituted to form a correct result.

BNode Coreference. It is tempting to take query variables as simple existential variables, and thus BGPs as a mere syntactic variant of RDF graphs. On this view, if a graph simply entails a BGP, then the result set is, in principle, non empty — there is at least one hit on the graph. By testing different groundings of the BGP (i.e., wherein we replace all the query variables with ground terms) we could (impractically) determine the particular bindings that make up the results set.

There are several wrinkles in this picture. The easiest to resolve is the existence of query variables in predicate positions. Essentially, we must ground those variables with properties in the signature of the graph in question before testing for entailment, which is how we (in principle) extract predicate variable bindings anyway.

---

[12] This approach was forcefully articulated by Enrico Franconi and Sergio Tessaris during the development of SPARQL.

Trickier is the fact that BNodes can be returned in query results as values of bindings. There are a number of reasons for this, but the most prominent one is for exhibiting coreference in results sets. For example, take the following graph and BGP (assume an appropriate prefix):

Example 5. **Significant BNode Coreference**
Graph:
    _:x :loves :mary.
    _:x :loves :sheeva.
    _:y :loves :katayun.

BGP:
    ?who :loves ?whom.

Now, if ?who were properly distinguished, then this query would have an empty results set, which is both counterintuitive and unfortunate. If it were properly non-distinguished, then while we would know that all of :mary, :sheeva, and :katayun are loved, we could not tell from the result set that someone loves both :mary and :sheeva (without a subsequent query). The most desirable result set for this query against this graph is:

Table 1. Result set for example 5

?who	?whom
_:a	:mary
_:a	:sheeva
_:b	:katayun

(Note, of course, that the semantics of RDF do not rule out that there is someone who loves all three.)

This result set is very informative. We know that someone loves each of these women, and we know that at least one person loves both *:mary* and *:sheeva*. We definitely want this sort of coreference in result sets. We could achieve the same effect, in some sense, with additional queries. Once we have retrieved all the loved people, we could subsequently test whether each element of the power set of the set of loved people share a lover. It is an understatement to say that this is not at all practical. Interestingly, such coreference between answers in a result set is useful under a wide range of entailment regimes, including those of OWL, though existentials returned in bindings has not, to our knowledge, been considered before.[13]

---

[13] Obviously, one might also want to have coreference *between* result sets of different queries (and thus between result sets and queries). To achieve such "stable BNode" references requires the identification of a larger scope to put the quantifiers outside, perhaps a notion of a "session". One would expect this to be handled on the protocol side of things.

Result Redundancy. A naive application of simple entailment will result in an arbitrary number of results, if there are any. Simple entailment allows for existential generalization. So if there are any hits at all, we can substitute fresh BNodes in for query variables to get a new, but redundant, result. This is highly undesirable, as it arbitrarily bloats the result set. Of course, the graph itself may already contain such redundancy, such as in:

Example 6. **Redundant graph:**
```
:june :loves :sheeva.
_:x :loves :sheeva.
```

The second triple does not add any information, since if we know that if :june :loves :sheeva, we know that *someone* does. Similarly, consider the following result set):

Table 2. Result set with redundancy

?x	?y
:june	:sheeva
_:x	:sheeva

Semantically speaking, the second result does not give us any new information. This result set could be derived from a query on example 6, or from a series of operations (e.g., a projection of another result set). Now, fully *minimizing* the result set might be computationally prohibitive (in particular, just requiring minimality in the result set of a BGP bumps up the complexity of query answering). Many query systems allow for redundancy in the result sets (though SPARQL, like SQL, has a keyword DISTINCT that enforces (some sense of) minimality in the results), but we must ensure that there is a sensible bound on redundant answers. Furthermore, there are some applications (e.g., editing) where sensitivity to the explicit redundancy in the queried graph could be pragmatically interesting, though this is pushing back toward a datastructural view of RDF.

Whichever scenario, we must be careful to give only the *right* amount of redundancy, and that the redundancy be predictable.

The Semantics [14]
To handle all this, plus semantic extensibility, requires a fair bit of machinery. Recall the desiderata:

1. Parameterizable semantics
2. BNodes in results
3. Appropriately minimal redundancy

---

[14] Many thanks to Sergio Tessaris and especially Enrico Franconi for their helpful discussions about SPARQL semantics. Without that assistence, this section would surely be entirely broken.

Different entailment regimes put different constraints on the values of bindings, so "more" expressive entailment relations may miss answers that "less"
expressive entailment relations give (as well as the more obvious vice versa;
in a sense, some less expressive entailment relations allow for more expressive
result sets). For example, in most query focused variants of OWL DL entailment, BNodes cannot appear as bindings of variables (they can only match
non-distinguished variables). Similarly, OWL DL entailment generally does not
allow for the built-in vocabulary to appear as bindings. In order to capture these
distinctions, the scoping set contains the set of admissible bindings for a query
against a graph under an entailment regime.

Definition 2. *Basic Graph Pattern E-matching*[15]
   *Let G be an RDF graph, BGP be a basic graph pattern, B a set of RDF
terms, S a mapping from the query variables in BGP to elements of B, and E
an entailment regime. BGP E-matches with pattern solution S on graph G with
respect to scoping set B if:*

   − *BGP′ is a basic graph pattern that is exactly the same as BGP except that
     all the BNodes in Sig(BGP) are mapped 1-1 to the BNodes in Sig(BGP′)*
   − *B and BGP′ do not share any BNodes.*
   − *G E-entails (G ∪ S(BGP′))*

While the entailment regime is necessary for parameterizing the semantics, it
is not sufficient. We also need B, the "scoping set", to specify the terms which
are legitimate values of bindings. For example, if one wished to use SPARQL to
express traditional conjunctive queries against OWL DL knowledge bases (where
there are no existentials in the result set), one merely needs to specify that the
scoping set can never contain BNodes. Similarly, one can exclude the built-in
vocabulary, or the set of class names. However, typically, B must contain all or
nearly all the non-BNode terms in G. If it excludes terms that are legitimate
bindings, we run the risk of excluding valid answers. It also must contain *enough*
BNodes to handle all the distinctions needed in the result set. Furthermore,
the entailment regime must specify what instantiated BGPs are "syntactically
legal."[16]
   The main oddity in this definition is the third condition: instead of directly entailing $S(BGP)$, G must entail $(G ∪ S(BGP′))$. Let us consider the case where
the entailment regime is simple entailment, and the scoping set, B, is equal

---

[15] This definition is somewhat different from that appearing in the SPARQL specification. in particular, it dispenses with the notion of a *scoping graph* and just reuses
   the original graph. We believe that these definitions are effectively equivalent, but
   since the role of the scoping graph is not explicitly described, it is hard to be entirely
   sure.
[16] In our definition, this is defined by ruling that non-well-formed BGPs for an entailment regime are not entailed by any graph. In the SPARQL document, this is
   specified by an extra condition on entailment, that is, that $S(BGP′)$ must be "in
   the range" of the entailment relation.

to $Sig(G)$. (This is, in fact, the specific semantics currently sanctioned by the SPARQL specification.) We now must consider if the definition of E-matching, instantiated in this way, meets desiderata 2 and 3.

B contains exactly the BNodes in G. When we substitute one into BGP', since this subsitution *preserves* BNode identity, we have stable coreference across different substitutions. Thus we at least enable coreference. Since we combine by simple set union the original graph with $S(BGP')$, BNode identity is preserved between triples in G and in $S(BGP')$. Thus, if there is a match, $G \cup S(BGP')$ will just be G again. If we substitute the "wrong" BNode in for a query variable, we will *not* get an "extra" match (unlike if we use a fresh BNode), since there will be an extra coreference that prevents G from entailing $G \cup S(BGP')$. So, we get exactly the redundancy that is in G and no more.[17] Consider the following example:

Example 7. **Correct redundancy:**
Graph:
```
_:x :loves :sheeva.
_:y :loves :sheeva.
_:z :loves :zarrin.
```

BGP:
```
?who :loves :sheeva
```

Recall that the scoping set is equal to the signature of the original graph, thus, $\{\_:x, \_:y, \_:z, :loves, :sheeva, :zarrin\}$. These are the only candidates for bindings of ?who. Clearly, the only possibly successful candidates are the BNodes, so let us examine each of those substituions when combined with the original graph:

Example 8. $G \cup S(BGP')$:
Where $?who = \_:x$:
```
_:x :loves :sheeva. # The S(BGP') merges with this triple.
_:y :loves :sheeva.
_:z :loves :zarrin.
```

Where $?who = \_:y$:
```
_:x :loves :sheeva.
_:y :loves :sheeva.# The S(BGP') merges with this triple.
_:z :loves :zarrin.
```

Where $?who = \_:z$:
```
_:x :loves :sheeva.
_:y :loves :sheeva.
```

---

[17] The only reason to replace BGP with BGP' is to ensure that there are no shared BNodes between the original graph and the query *except* those introduced by a substitution.

```
_:z :loves :zarrin.
_:z :loves :sheeva.# S(BGP') appears with a spurious co-reference).
```

Clearly, the first two substitutions are entailed by G, whereas the third is not. Consider what happens if we add a fresh BNode to the scoping set not included in $Sig(G)$:

Example 9. $G \cup S(BGP')$:
Where $?who = \_:\text{somethingFresh}$:
```
_:x :loves :sheeva.
_:y :loves :sheeva.
_:z :loves :zarrin.
_:somethingFresh :loves :sheeva.
```

But this *is* simply entailed by G as the last triple is entailed by either the first or second triple alone. Thus, we can recover the exact behavior of unrestricted simple entailment by adding an infinite supply of fresh BNodes to the scoping set. Full minimality is harder to ensure and involves an increase in complexity (as one must "leanify" the results), but also is not required by the current SPARQL specification. In effect, we have a compromise between a full knowledge based approach and a pure datastructural approach.

4   Algebraic Manipulation of Results

Now that we can extract a table from a graph via a BGP, we can manipluate that table in a variety of more or less standard relational ways. The table and algebra orientation of SPARQL is perhaps most obviously distinguishes it from path oriented query languages, where the intermediate objects tend to be *nodes* rather than tables of bindings.[18]

4.1   A Bit of Syntax

A concrete, complete "core" SPARQL query consists of zero or more prefix declarations, a query result form (we shall only consider the **SELECT** form), and a where clause consisting of a number of BGPs with operations between them. Consider this example (without operations):

Example 10. **Core SPARQL query:**
```
PREFIX ex: <http://ex.org/>
SELECT *
  {?who ex:loves ?whom}
```

BGPs are delimited by curly braces, which are required in order to distinguish distinct BGP arguments to various operators.

---

[18] One can typically simulate each approach in the other, at the cost of perspicuity and concision, for example, see [4].

4.2   Familiar Operations

There are three fundamental operations which can be performed on a result set within a SPARQL query: projection, filtering, and conjunction. The project function removes columns from a result set, in the standard way. Projections are specified in the *SELECT* clause by listing the variables[19] whose columns are to be preserved, where * is the identity projection. For example, we can modify the prior example to only give one column (e.g., the lovers, not the loved):

Example 11. **Simple Projection:**
Graph:
```
_:x :loves :mary.
_:x :loves :sheeva.
_:y :loves :katayun.
```
Query:
```
PREFIX ex: <http://ex.org/>
SELECT ?who
  {?who ex:loves ?whom}
```

Evaluating this query against the graph will result in one column of answers. The number of answers will vary with the semantics of the entailment relation (and, if the DISTINCT solution modifier is added, on the particular semantics of DISTINCT), but in any case we will have only two distinguishable answers. In contrast, if we evaluate the same BGP with SELECT * we will get three clearly distinct answers in the results set.

In addition to filtering out columns, we can filter out rows in a result set by testing the value of a binding against a range of functions.[20] Row filters syntactically appear inside a BGP but are understood as operations on a result set, not as part of the core semantics of the query, though, if the base logic has the correct expressiveness, this distinction can be moot. Certainly, in practical query engines, one will push the filters as far down into the query plan as possible to avoid generating inordinately large intermediate tables, or bringing in excess data from disk.

Finally, we can combine result sets using the OPTIONAL or UNION operators. These allow for a weak kind of disjunction in queries, restricted to result sets.

5   Conclusion

There is much missing in SPARQL, and much in SPARQL that we did not touch on in this essay. SPARQL has a rich set of test functions, some aggregation and

---

[19] Note that unlike many query languages, the *SELECT* clause does not determine which variables are distinguished, or even pseudo-distinguished (i.e., taking BNodes as values). BNodes in the BGP are non-distinguished whereas query variables are all distinguished (or pseudo-distinguished if the scoping set contains BNodes).

[20] See the SPARQL specification: http://www.w3.org/TR/rdf-sparql-query/#tests

ordering operators, several interesting query forms (with the most notable being the CONSTRUCT form, which produces an RDF graph from a template and a query result), and the ability to query over multiple identified graphs, or to select graphs based on a query about them. Additionally, there is a minimal protocol for querying a dataset over raw HTTP or as a SOAP based Web Service. Additionally, though not formally specified, the SPARQL query syntax has become the *de facto* standard for conjunctive data query over OWL DL knowledge bases.

SPARQL has many features well suited for the manipulation of semi-structured data beyond merely its graph and RDF orientation. For example, bindings to BNodes or, in the case of certain constructs, optionally bound variables make uniform querying of heterogeneously structured data — in particular, data that is only partially congruous — succinct and effective. Not discussed in this paper, but significant, is the introspective capabilities afforded by graph variables. A single query can set up a series of subqueries that are applied based on some inspection of the metadata of various graphs. Similarly, the controversial DESCRIBE query form which returns an arbitrary, server defined RDF graph that in some way "describes" the query answers makes it easier to *explore* graphs on the fly. This close, in principle, alignment (some would say confusion) between a browsing approach and a more structured query approach is at the heart of the functioning of the web.

References

1. Franz Baader. Logic-based knowledge representation. In M. J. Wooldridge and M. Veloso, editors, *Artificial Intelligence Today, Recent Trends and Developments*, number 1600, pages 13–41. Springer Verlag, 1999.
2. Charles W. Bachman. The programmer as navigator. *Commun. ACM*, 16(11):653–658, 1973.
3. Weidong Chen, Michael Kifer, and David Scott Warren. HILOG: A foundation for higher-order logic programming. *Journal of Logic Programming*, 15(3):187–230, 1993.
4. F. Frasincar, G. Houben, R. Vdovjak, and P. Bar. RAL: An algebra for querying RDF. In *The 3rd International Conference On Web Information Systems Engineering (WISE 2002)*, 2002.
5. R. Goldman, J. McHugh, and J. Widom. From semistructured data to XML: Migrating the Lore data model and query language. In *Workshop on the Web and Databases (WebDB '99)*, pages 25–30, 1999.

Composition of Rule Sets and Ontologies

Uwe Aßmann, Jendrik Johannes, Jakob Henriksson, and Ilie Savga

Institut für Software- und Multimediatechologie
Technische Universität Dresden
uwe.assmann, jendrik.johannes, jakob.henriksson, ilie.savga@tu-dresden.de

In order for ontologies to have the maximum impact, they need to be widely shared. In order to minimize the intellectual effort involved in developing an ontology, they need to be re-used. In the best of all possible worlds, ontologies need to be composed. [45]

Abstract. To master large rule sets in ontologies and other logic-based specifications, the ability to divide them into components plays an important role. While a naive approach treats the rule sets as black-box components and composes them via combinators, their relationships are usually so complicated that this approach fails to be useful in many scenarios. Instead, the components should be "opened" before composition. The paper presents several such "gray-box composition" techniques, namely fragment-based genericity and extension, inline template expansions, semantic macros, and mixin layers. All approaches help to structure large ontologies and rule-based specifications into fine-grained components, from which they can be built up flexibly.

Models or specifications describing domains or systems can easily and quickly grow in size. Big ontologies, such as the Gene Ontology[1], contain thousands of concepts and relationships. Indeed, because it is difficult in general to construct large models, some existing attempts have been criticized for their structure (see e.g. [5]). The same is also valid for large rule-based specifications and ontologies. Important questions to answer are: How to structure a large specification in a good way? How to simplify the specification task for ontology engineers? How to share parts of a model with other models so that the cost of construction is reduced? While several authors have suggested that a division of a large ontology into components can be a decisive help to master the complexity of ontology engineering [34,39], several important questions remain open: How does an adequate component model for ontologies look? Which grain size should it have? Can we reuse small building blocks of ontologies in several contexts? Does component-based ontology engineering scale?

One obvious idea for a solution, the employment of the object-oriented paradigm, is not enough. Inheritance is a concept that is often misinterpreted, either because it can be given several slightly different semantics, depending on

---

[1] http://www.geneontology.org/

P. Barahona et al. (Eds.): Reasoning Web 2006, LNCS 4126, pp. 68–92, 2006.

the context in which it is used [10], or because application engineers have difficulties to distinguish it from part-of relationships [5]. On the other hand, while inheritance provides reuse for types, it does not so for rules: what does it means to inherit from a rule set?

Unfortunately, also other well-known component models from software engineering, such as CORBA [42], or EJB [28], suffer from several problems that prevent their employment in ontological engineering. First of all, these models are *black-box*, in the sense that the components remain unchanged during composition. Often, changes to the interiors of a component are required to make it more apt to its use context, but due to the black-box principle, the only way components can be adapted is by wrapping. Secondly, these classical component models are defined for binary languages. Of course, this is not the level of abstraction on which model components should be reused, which should be suited for modeling tasks in analysis and design. Thirdly, the components are connected by linkers that link function definitions to function calls. However, for rule-based languages, linking predicate definitions to predicate uses would be more important, but this is not supported. Finally, model components should be connected according to other static relationships than the *call* relation, for instance, according to aggregation or inheritance. However, such connections are not possible with current component models.

A typical model composition technique that can be applied to other relations between language constructs than the call relation is *genericity*. It is already employed in most modern object-oriented languages for classes (C++, Java 1.5, Haskell, or Ada95 [25]), but so far, only in a restricted manner in rule-based and ontology languages, with the notable exception of HiLog [11]. Genericity is used to produce specific instances of language constructs (*fragments*) from other *generic fragments*. For instance, specific types can be produced from generic classes. Most often, this is used for type-safe collections: container classes are programmed as generic skeletons and instantiated to type-specific containers better apt for typing. One object-oriented language, BETA, drives the genericity principle to the extreme [33]. In BETA, every fragment that can be produced by the language is considered as a component that can be constructed, instantiated, compiled, and linked in isolation. Furthermore, fragments can contain parametric *slots*, generic parameters that can be filled by other fragments. Hence, BETA components, fragments, are perfectly apt for reuse on all levels of abstraction the language offers. However, this principle of *universal genericity* is not well known and has not been applied to other languages.

This principle, universal genericity, and its cousin, *universal extensibility*, can easily be applied to modeling languages, in particular, rule-based ontology languages, delivering important techniques for component-based ontology engineering, such as type-safe templates, type-safe macros (semantic macros), view-based and aspect-based development. Thus, when ontologies are engineered from fragment components, these principles can be applied to all concepts of an ontology language, so that *ontology lines (ontology families)* can be built from ontology components. Thus, the motivation behind this paper is the following: to show how the elements of an ontology can be composed from fragments.

This paper starts out with an overview on several programming languages that use fragment-based component models. Then, it transfers these concepts to the elements of ontology languages. Basically, ontologies contain concepts, classes, defined by a data definition language (DDL), and expressions, rules or constraints, defined by a data manipulation language (DML). Sections 2–4 transfer fragment-based component models and the related technology of invasive composition to them. We start with invasive composition of queries, using a query language for XML and RDF, Xcerpt, as an example. Then, we look at invasive rule composition for Prolog. Finally, we show how the elements of rule-based ontology languages, can be composed invasively. We demonstrate how F-logic classes can be composed from partial classes, and, in the large, how ontologies can be composed from partial class layers (mixin layers, Section 5). Finally, a comparison to related work (Section 6) completes the paper.

1   Component-Based Engineering with Fragments

Future ontologies will be based on *ontology components*. We argue that the right size of an *ontology component* for component-based ontology management is a *fragment* of the underlying ontology language. Fragment components have been invented in the research on object-oriented systems, and are used there for type-safe adaptation of frameworks and unforeseen evolution, as can be seen from languages, such as BETA. Fragment composition relies on three techniques: universal genericity, universal extension, and an appropriate composition language. These principles allow for a maximal reuse of code and specification pieces, to increase variability, and to improve extension and evolution.

1.1   The BETA Fragment Metaprogramming Environment

The first language which introduced universal genericity is BETA [33]. This language and its development environment was developed as part of the Mjolner project - a project for object-oriented software development environments, conducted by a number of Scandinavian institutes [26].[2] The BETA language is a strongly typed object-oriented language with two main constructs, *pattern* and *object*. Patterns describe classes, procedures, functions and other static concepts, while objects and activation records represents their run-time instances.

What is interesting in the BETA programming language in relation to the context of component-based development, is its solution for modularization, which relies on the notion of fragments, fragment forms, and slots.

Definition 1. *In BETA, a* fragment *is a sentential form, a partial sentence derived by a nonterminal.*

---

[2] Remarkably, the inventors of BETA and its principle of universal genericity stem from the same schools in Scandinavia who invented the principle of object orientation.

Fragments can be plain or generic. A plain, non-generic fragment is a partial sentence of BETA, derived from a non-terminal, containing only terminals. A generic fragment (a *fragment form* or *template*) is a fragment that still contains nonterminals. Hence, a *fragment form* is a set of non-terminal and terminal symbols derived from a non-terminal; it is the basic element to define a module in the BETA system.

Using a specific notation, it is possible to write non-terminals inside forms that can be replaced by other forms (*slots*[3]). Slots have a name and are typed by a syntactic category, i.e., an element of BETA's grammar (which corresponds to a metaclass in a metamodel of BETA). A BETA slot is syntactically structured by the following grammar rule:

```
Slot ::= '<<SLOT' Name ':' Metaclass '>>'          1
       | '<<' Name ':' Metaclass '>>'
```

where '<<', the placeholder token, does not occur in BETA elsewhere and `Metaclass` is an arbitrary nonterminal of the BETA grammar. Finally, when a set of fragments is associated with a name, it is called a *fragment group*.

Example 1. The following example demonstrates a fragment form named `PersonTemplate` of the syntactic category `PatternDecl` with a slot `EmployerSlot` typed by the metaclass `Attribute`. The form is contained in the file `PersonTemplate`.[4]

Listing 1.1. Fragment component in BETA.

```
PersonTemplate = {
    name '/home/assmann/PersonTemplate'
    Person: PatternDecl      // typed by the syntactic category    2
    Person: begin
        PersonMembers: begin name: @ String <<EmployerSlot:Attribute>>    4
            end
    end                                                                    6
}
```

The slot of this form can be bound with the content of some other form. For example, the code in the Listing 1.2 defines a fragment `PersonFiller` that has as its *origin* `PersonTemplate`. The origin construct specifies that the fragment `EmployerSlot` should be substituted for the corresponding slot in the component `PersonTemplate`. Hence, the substitution is *implicit*, in the sense that a definition of a slot is implicitly bound to its use. Since the substitution is typed by a metaclass, it is type-safe.

Listing 1.2. Fragment component in BETA.

```
define fragment component PersonFiller = {                               1
    name ''/home/assmann/PersonFiller''
    origin ''/home/assmann/PersonTemplate''                             3
    EmployerSlot: Attribute     // typed by the syntactic category
    EmployerSlot: employer: @ Employer; salary: Integer                 5
}
```

---

[3] The word slot has here a slightly different meaning than a slot of a frame in frame logic. However, it also indicates a "hole in a template".

[4] For readability, the original BETA brackets (# and #) have been replaced by **begin** and **end**, respectively.

The result of the parameterization or substitution—the *extent* of the fragment—is the composition of the two initial forms and is represented Listing 1.3.

Listing 1.3. Result component in BETA.

```
Person: begin
  name: @ String;                                              2
  employer: @ Employer;
  salary: Integer;                                             4
end
```

Hence, the BETA compiler treats fragments as components; it can even compile fragment forms separately and link them in binary form. As a composition operation, the compiler applies type-safe parameterization, filling a fragment into a slot. Hence, the interface of a BETA component consists of named slots typed by the BETA metamodel. Through this *composition interface*, language constructs flow from fragments to fragment forms: definitions, types, expressions, statements.

Because BETA allows for genericity on all language constructs, we define the following:

Definition 2. *A language is called* universally generic, *if it provides genericity for every language construct.*

1.2   Hyperspace Programming

Hyperspace programming proposes *universal extension*. This principle means that every collection-like language construct can be extended from a use context.

Hyperspace programming also builds on the concepts of fragments and fragment groups (although forms are neglected), and adds the concepts of concerns and hyperslices. Concerns are sets of semantically related fragment groups, which describe one aspect of the software. Concerns can be grouped to hyperslices, declaratively complete concerns, that define all items they use, so that they can be compiled and executed. Finally, hyperslices are composed to an executable system. Several composition operators are available for hyperspace programming. The most interesting one is the *merge* operator, which merges collection-like fragments that have the same name. For instance, when two classes in different hyperslices have been defined under the same name (denoting two different views of a class), the merge operator can merge the classes together, while eliminating replicates and signaling conflicts. The merge operator also merges entire hyperslices, point-wisely applying merges on the contained collection-like constructs.

Hyperspace programming has been realized for Java in the tool Hyper/J [48]. Hyper/J can deal with class and method fragments (signature definitions and method bodies). It can extract semantically related method fragments from Java packages, and group them to concerns. From such concerns, Java hyperslices can be composed. Those are then complete Java packages, which contain several concerns, and can be compiled and executed. Hence, hyperslices correspond to *views* for Java classes that can be composed, merging all contained classes with identical names together, and resulting in complete Java systems.

Example 2. As an example, consider the following two concerns that define views for the classes `Person`.

```
define concern PersonalConcern = {                           1
    class Person {
        String name;                                         3
        int age;
    }                                                        5
}
define concern EmploymentConcern = {                         7
    class Person {
        Employer employer;                                   9
        int salary;
    }                                                        11
    class Employer { }
}                                                            13
define concern PoliticalConcern = {
    class Person {                                           15
        String politicalParty;
        int contribution;                                    17
    }
}                                                            19
define hyperslice Employment =
    PersonalConcern.merge(EmploymentConcern);
define hyperslice PartyMember =                              21
    PersonalConcern.merge(PoliticalConcern);
define hyperslice PersonInfo = Employment.merge(PartyMember);
```

In this example, all concerns define information about persons from different perspectives. Hyperslices can be composed from two basic concerns, merging all their class fragments together with a point-wise merge. Finally, a hyperslice `PersonInfo` assembles a complete Java package that can be reused[5].

That a class in a hyperslice can be merged with another class, can also be interpreted as an extension of one class with another. As a necessary condition, an extensible construct in a hyperslice must have the form of a collection (e.g., classes or method bodies). In general, a merge of two hyperslices can be interpreted as a point-wise extension of all contained constructs. To this end, we can introduce, similarly to slots, *extension points (hooks)* in the constructs that can indicate where a construct can be extended. Hooks obey the following syntax:

```
Hook ::= '<<HOOK' Name ':' Metaclass '>>'
       | '<+' Name ':' Metaclass '+>'                        2
```

With hooks, the above example can be rephrased as extension of hooks [4]:

```
define concern PersonalConcern = {
    class Person {                                           2
        String name;
        <+ personHook: Attribute+>                           4
        int age;
    }                                                        6
}
define concern EmploymentConcern = {                         8
    class Person {
        Employer employer;                                   10
        int salary;
    }                                                        12
    class Employer {
```

---

[5] For composition expressions, we use an object-oriented style, i.e., group composition operations to fragments. Also functional style can be employed.

```
      <+ employerHook:  Attribute+>                                    14
   }
}                                                                      16
define  concern  PoliticalConcern  =  {
   class  Person  {                                                    18
      String  politicalParty ;
      int  contribution ;                                              20
   }
}                                                                      22
define  hyperslice  Employment  =
   PersonalConcern . personHook . extend ( EmploymentConcern ) ;       24
define  hyperslice  Full  =
   Employment . personHook . extend ( PoliticalConcern ) ;
```

resulting in

```
hyperslice  Full  =  {                                                 1
   class  Person  {
      String  name ;                                                   3
      Employer  employer ;
      int  salary ;                                                    5
      String  politicalParty ;
      int  contribution ;                                              7
      int  age ;
   }                                                                   9
   class  Employer  {
   }                                                                   11
}
```

Extension operations have several advantages over merge operations. While merge operations usually provide a shorter notation, extension operations use extension points to steer the composition in a more fine-grained way. Because extension points are explicitly specified, they offer a *extension interface* for fragment components, i.e., inform a composition system where they can be extended. In this way, parts of components can be hidden, i.e., protected against changes, while, when merge operations have to be applied, the component is opened up as a white-box. We conjecture, that such an extension interface is better for component-based engineering, because it provides information hiding [37]. In the following, we will use both operations, supposing that merges and extensions are related, and merges can always be reduced to extensions, given appropriate extension points.

While Hyper/J employs the extension principle only to classes and method bodies, we can generalize it to all collection-like language constructs of a programming or modeling language:

Definition 3. *A language is called* universally extensible, *if it provides extensibility for every collection-like language construct.*

1.3   Distinguishing Modeling-In-The-Large

A further issue is that the comprehension of large systems and models can be improved by the distinction of an *architectural description*. [15] were the first to argue that programs in-the-small are essentially different from programs in-the-large. They suggest that in a system, two layers, architecture and application-specific components, should be distinguished. Then, the architecture gives an overview of the system and abstracts from application-specific details, hiding them in the components, so that the system can be comprehended much more easily. Clearly, this abstraction feature would be useful also to comprehend large ontologies. But what is the *architecture* of an ontology?

With an explicit architecture, appropriate languages can be employed for programming in-the-large and for programming in-the-small that are tailored to their purpose. Depending on the kind of system, researchers have suggested different Architecture Description Languages (ADL). Standard ADL are based on structured, reducible process graphs [21] that are connected by *connectors*, special components responsible for communication. Other architectural languages are expression-based, i.e., rely on side-effect free functions [47]. [14,12] have suggested to use higher-order functions (*skeletons*) to describe architectures. Nothing seems to prevent logic-based architectural languages, but this idea is not yet explored; instead, logic is only used as a specification language for architectural constraints [20]. So, how does the architectural language of an ontology look?

Also, the separation of an architectural aspect introduces two dimensions of reuse: components can be reused for different architectures, and architectures can be reused for components. Beyond simple component-based engineering, this principle strengthens the reuse factor because reuse combinations are quadratic and no longer linear. So, how to reuse the architecture and the components of an ontology?

Unfortunately, architectural description languages cannot easily be transfered to ontologies, because they define component models for *communication architectures*. In an architectural language, the component interface describes data flow in and out of a component, or, which services are provided in the form of procedure calls and returns. Since logic languages are declarative, other types of components interfaces and composition operations have to be developed; classical component models are out of question. We have seen that fragments can be used as components.[6] But how do *fragment composition languages* look?

1.4   Invasive Software Composition

Invasive software composition (ISC) combines the previously presented ideas, combining universal genericity, universal extension, and a language for composition-in-the-large [4]. Firstly, principles of universal genericity and extensibility are supported with a primitive set of explicit composition operators that combine fragments: *bind (parameterization, substitution), extend, copy*, and *rename*. The bind operation fills slots with fragments, the extend operation appends new fragments to the hooks, and the copy and rename operations do what their names indicate. More complex composition operations, such as merge, connectors, or aspect weavers can be reduced to universal genericity and extensibility. Thus, with ISC, several complex composition paradigms, such as generic programming [33], connector-based programming [21], view-based programming [47], or aspect-oriented programming [29] can easily be modeled. Basically, invasive composition reduces all paradigms to the basic techniques of genericity and extensibility.

---

[6] It should be remarked that binary components also consist of fragments, but fragments of a binary language.

Secondly, ISC describes the structure of a system in-the-large with a *composition language*, which glues the basic operations on components together. This language is used not only to specify architectures, but also to build expressions and programs, that describe compositions of fragments in-the-large. That is, composition programs describe how components are plugged together to systems.Essentially, invasive composition consists of a composition algebra in the spirit of [7], but is based on parameterization *and* extension. Finally, while the basic operations are ubiquitous, ISC does not rely on a specific composition language; imperative, functional, and rule-based languages can be employed.

Example 3. Generic programming in the way of BETA can easily be simulated by ISC. The *bind* operation binds slots to fragments, i.e., instead of implicitly binding a slot to a fragment as in BETA, the binding must be done explicit. Examples in Listings 1.1–1.2 would be written in ISC as an explicit parameterization:

Listing 1.4. Explicit binding of forms.

```
PersonTemplate . EmployerSlot . bind ( PersonFiller ) ;
```

which results in the same component as in Listing 1.3. The second mechanism, extensibility, is realized by the ubiquitous operator *extend*. It can be applied to all collection-like constructs in a language. For instance, extending the component **PersonalConcern** from above works in ISC similarly to hyperspaces:

Listing 1.5. Extending forms.

```
define  fragment  component  Employment  =                                      1
       PersonalConcern . personHook . extend ( EmploymentConcern ) ;
```

An important observation is that in general, the principles of invasive composition can be superimposed on all languages. The requirements—bindings rely on slots, i.e., unexpanded nonterminals, extends rely on collection-like language constructs—are general enough that every language, also a rule-based ontology language, can meet them. However, since every language has a data definition (DDL) and a data manipulation sub-language (DML), the task of invasive composition falls into two categories:

Concept Composition. This task composes fragments of the DDL, i.e., classes, types, or views on them are composed. Basically, a set of types is computed from a set of fragments.

Expression Composition. This task is about composing fragments of expressions (DML composition). Basically, expressions, statements, queries, rule sets, or methods are composed from a set of fragment components.

At this point, it should be clear that a fragment-based component model for rule-based ontologies has many advantages, so that a future composition environment for rule-based ontologies should support it. Such a system could, building on the principles of universal genericity, universal extension, and a composition language, offer view-based, connector-based, and aspect-based development techniques, by which large ontologies can more easily be constructed. The rest of the paper applies these principles of invasive software composition to rule-based and ontology languages, transferring several programming paradigms to DDL and DML ontology compositions. We start in the next section with invasive composition of queries.

2   Invasive Query Composition

In this section, we demonstrate the principles of invasive composition on the XML query and transformation language Xcerpt [9]. As in BETA, our approach is metamodel-supported to enable type-safe compositions. For the case of Xcerpt, we assume a metamodel describing all the constructs of the language and their relationships. In addition, to enable universal genericity and extensibility, this metamodel is augmented with *slot* and *hook* constructs, each derived from constructs in the core language metamodel. These additional constructs allow us to explicitly define the variation points (i.e. the interface) of the components.

A difference between Xcerpt, often stressed in its favor, and other XML query and transformation languages [6,17], is the separation in its rules of the way documents are queried and the way the result is constructed.

Listing 1.6. An Xcerpt rule constructing a list of all clerks for each manager from a database document.

```
define  fragment  component  allClerksForManagerConstruct = {
  CONSTRUCT                                                           2
    result {
      all  result {                                                   4
        var  Manager,
        all  var  Clerk                                               6
      }
    }                                                                 8
  FROM
    in {                                                              10
      resource {  ''http://employee.example.com''  }  ,
      management {{                                                   12
        staff {{
          var  Manager -> manager  ,                                  14
          clerks {{
            var  Clerk -> clerk                                       16
          }}
        }}                                                            18
      }}
    }                                                                 20
  END
}                                                                     22
```

In Listing 1.6, we find an Xcerpt rule which extracts information about managers and clerks from a document and constructs the result by listing all clerks for each manager. Thanks to this clear separation of concerns found in Xcerpt, we are able to produce components which can be reused in several rules. In this example, we have made a component out of the query part of the rule in Listing 1.6, to be found in Listing 1.7. This query component can then be re-used in several rules which might construct the result in a different manner.

Listing 1.7. Xcerpt component describing an Xcerpt fragment, a query fetching all managers and clerks from a database document.

```
define fragment component employeeQuery = {
  in {                                                          2
    resource { ''http://employee.example.com'' } ,
    management {{                                               4
      staff {{
        var Manager -> manager ,                               6
        clerks {{
          var Clerk -> clerk                                   8
        }}
      }}                                                       10
    }}
  }                                                            12
}
```

The remaining part of the original rule, found in Listing 1.8, now contains a slot where the query used to be (Line 10). Note that this slot is a valid construct of the extended language description.

Listing 1.8. Xcerpt component describing how to construct an answer, listing all clerks for each manager.

```
define fragment component allClerksForManagerConstruct = {    1
  CONSTRUCT
    result {                                                   3
      all result {
        var Manager ,                                          5
        all var Clerk
      }                                                        7
    }
  FROM                                                         9
    <<employeeQuery : Query>>
  END                                                          11
}
```

Using a composition script (Listing 1.9), we can assemble the two components in Listing 1.8 and 1.7 and produce the complete Xcerpt as expected (Listing 1.6).

Listing 1.9. Composition script producing Listing 1.6

```
allClerksForManagerConstruct.employeeQuery.bind(employeeQuery);
```

In-line template expansions for comprehensibility For ease of specification of the compositions, also *in-line* specifications are possible. They improve comprehensibility, because parameterizations and extensions are seen in the context of their embedding. The composition script would then be included in one component and the overall composition would be specified from there. The component `allClerksForManagerConstruct`, from the previous example, would look a little bit different (Listing 1.10). Instead of specifying a slot on Line 10 in Listing 1.10, a bind operation is performed in-line during composition. Binding the component `employeeQuery` (Listing 1.7) in that position would again produce the expected Xcerpt program (Listing 1.6).

Listing 1.10. Example of in-line template expansion

```
define fragment component allClerksForManagerConstruct = {    1
  CONSTRUCT
    result {                                                   3
      all result {
```

```
        var  Manager,                                                        5
        all  var  Clerk
      }                                                                      7
    }
FROM                                                                         9
    bind(employeeQuery)
END                                                                          11
}
```

Using in-line template expansions in this fashion speeds up the writing of composition-based applications, because components and compositions are specified together.

Semantic macros for context parameterization Semantic macros provide *parameterized in-line compositions,* another form of in-line compositions that go one step beyond type-safe template expansion, because they incorporate context information into the compositions [31]. Instead of parameterizing a slot with a fixed fragment, they take fragments from their application context as parameters, bind them to the slots of a body template, and embed the expanded template in-place, i.e. where the composition was specified:

Listing 1.11. A semantic macro and how to use it.

```
define  semmacro  constructResult(q:Query) = {
    CONSTRUCT                                                                2
      result {
        all  result {                                                       4
          var  Manager,
          all  var  Clerk                                                   6
        }
    }                                                                        8
    FROM
      <<q:Query>>                                                           10
    END
}                                                                           12

fragment  component  result = constructResult(employeeQuery);               14
```

The composed component `result` in Listing 1.11 is constructed on Line 14 by parameterizing the semantic macro `constructResult` with the fragment component `employeeQuery`.

An application of a semantic macro reduces to parameterizations of copies of its fragment form. Every actual parameter that is passed to a semantic macro is equivalent to a parameterization statement that fills a slot of the body template of the semantic macro. For instance, the above application is equivalent to:

```
// copy  template
fragment  component  result = new  constructResult.Body;                    2
// parameterization
result.q.bind(employeeQuery);                                               4
```

In summary, a semantic macro contains a fragment component, which is instantiated with slot parameters and expanded in-place. All bindings are type-safe, i.e., they are controlled by the type specifications of the macro parameters.

Aspect-oriented queries Beyond template expansion, semantic macros offer a limited form of aspect orientation [29]. For instance, one can weave a name component into many slots of a core construction component (aka *joinpoints*):

```
define semmacro constructResult (manager:Name, clerk:Name) = {        2
  CONSTRUCT
    result {
      all result {                                                      4
        var <<manager:Name>>,
        all var <<clerk:Name>>                                          6
      }
    }                                                                   8
  FROM in {
    resource { ''http://employee.example.com'' } ,                     10
    management {{
      staff {{                                                         12
        var <<manager:Name>> -> manager
        clerks {{                                                       14
          var <<clerk:Name>> -> clerk
        }}                                                              16
      }}
    }}                                                                  18
  }
  END                                                                  20
}
define fragment component ManagerComp = { Man }                        22
define fragment component ClerkComp = { Cle }
                                                                       24
fragment component query = constructResult (ManagerComp, ClerkComp);
```

Here, variable names for managers and clerks can be tailored to different names, by weaving some name components over several points in the core query.

Thus, semantic macros offer a simple form of aspect-oriented query language. Furthermore, since semantic macros have parameters that can be filled with information from the application context, they can even tailor the aspect with regard to the context into which it is woven.

3   Invasive Rule Composition

In Section 2, we looked at how to invasively compose fragments of a rule-based language, the XML query and transformation language Xcerpt. In this section, we will look at a more standard form of rule language, Prolog. This section will take us one step closer to demonstrating how it is possible to compose fragment components of rule-based ontology languages. Rules will play a big role in future ontology languages, see Section 4 for further discussion.

In a rule-based language with universal extensibility, all language constructs are extensible that can be embedded into collections [3]. This means that rules can be extended by additional preconditions or conclusions (open rules), predicates can be extended by new members (open predicates), precondition clauses can be extended (open clauses), and rule sets can be extended by new rules (open queries). Such open constructs can be extended by composition programs to add more preconditions, conclusions, clauses, or rules to a query. Below we will look at an example that applies this to Prolog rules.

Listing 1.12 defines a generic depth-first search algorithm in Prolog.

Listing 1.12. Depth-first search algorithm.

```
define fragment component search = {                                   1
  <<SearchCommand:PName>>(X,Y) :-
    <<SearchCommand:PName>>(X,Y,Solution).
```

```
<<SearchCommand:PName>>(X,Y,Solution) :-              3
  <<Edge:PName>>(X,_), <<Edge:PName>>(_,Y),
    depthfirstsearch(X,Y,Solution).                   5
depthfirstsearch(Start,Destination,Solution) :-
    depthfirstsearch(Start,[Start],Destination,Solution).  7
depthfirstsearch(Destination,Path,Destination,Solution) :-
    Solution = Path,<+ActionAtDestination:Predicate+>,!.   9
depthfirstsearch(NodeA,Path,Destination,Solution):-
  <<Edge:PName>>(NodeA,NodeN),                        11
  not(member(NodeN,Path)),
    depthfirstsearch(NodeN,[NodeN|Path],Destination,Solution).  13
}
```

In Listing 1.13, we have a set of facts, but with an unnamed fact-relation. The relations are slots to be filled with a predicate name through a composition program, before the final rule is produced. In this fact-base, all relations will be bound to the same predicate name.

Listing 1.13. Facts for the generic search algorithm.

```
define fragment component whoKnowsWho = {
  <<KnowsAboutRelation:PName>>(amy, lilly).           2
  <<KnowsAboutRelation:PName>>(amy,james).
  <<KnowsAboutRelation:PName>>(lilly ,james).         4
  <<KnowsAboutRelation:PName>>(amy, profSmith).
  <<KnowsAboutRelation:PName>>(james , profSmith).    6
  <<KnowsAboutRelation:PName>>(amy, billGates).
  <<KnowsAboutRelation:PName>>(james , billGates).    8
  <<KnowsAboutRelation:PName>>(profSmith , billGates).
}                                                      10
```

The components in Listing 1.14 define names for parameterizations and a semantic macro.

Listing 1.14. Name components and a semantic macro.

```
define fragment component knows = { knows }
define fragment component connection = { connection }
define semmacro output(v:Variable) = {              2
  write(''found a friend''), write(v)                4
}
```

Listing 1.15 shows the composition program which defines how the fragment components will be put together to produce the complete Prolog program shown in Listing 1.16.

Listing 1.15. Composition program

```
whoKnowsWho. KnowsAboutRelation. bind(knows).        1
search . Edge. bind(knows).
search . SearchCommand. bind(connection).            3
search . ActionAtDestination. extend(output(Destination)).
```

Listing 1.16. Composed Prolog program

```
knows(amy, lilly).
knows(amy,james).                                    2
knows(lilly ,james).
knows(amy, profSmith).                               4
knows(james , profSmith).
knows(amy, billGates).                               6
knows(james , billGates).
                                                     8
connection(X,Y) :- connection(X,Y,Solution).
```

```
connection(X,Y,Solution) :-                                          10
    knows(X,_), knows(_,Y),
    depthfirstsearch(X,Y,Solution).                                  12
depthfirstsearch(Start,Destination,Solution) :-
    depthfirstsearch(Start,[Start],Destination,Solution).            14
depthfirstsearch(Destination,Path,Destination,Solution) :-
    Solution = Path,                                                 16
    write(''found a friend''), write(Destination), !.
depthfirstsearch(NodeA,Path,Destination,Solution):-                  18
    knows(NodeA,NodeN),
    not(member(NodeN,Path)),                                         20
    depthfirstsearch(NodeN,[NodeN|Path],Destination,Solution).
```

Hence, the principles of universal genericity and universal extension, including in-line template parameterization and semantic macros, can be transfered to rule-based logic languages, too. This paves the way for rule components, also in ontology languages, as the next section shows.

4   Invasive Rule-Based Ontology Composition

In Section 3, we looked at how to invasively compose fragments of a rule language, Prolog. While some of the well-known ontology languages, based on Description Logic [38,13], do not include rule constructs, rules have come to play a larger role for ontologies. Recently, much effort has been put into how to solve a long standing issue for the Semantic Web, how to integrate rules with ontology languages [24,23,18,2,36,40].

There exists several approaches to integrating rules and ontologies. For a survey of such approaches, please refer to [27]. Examples of such integrations include, for example, the rule extension of the standardized Web Ontology Language OWL [38], whose XML encoding is known as the Semantic Web Rule Language (SWRL) [24]. Description Logic Programs (DLP) [23] form an intersection between Description Logics and monotonic rules. Such an intersection creates a minimal rule-based ontology language; the entire ontology is described in rules and can be solved in a rule reasoner. Another attempt tries to deviate from the popular approach of extending OWL with rules, instead the lesser language RDF [22] is extended with rules into Extended RDF [1]. The purpose here is not to give an extensive overview of the different integration approaches and their semantics, but rather to make the reader aware of the current trend to include the concept of rules in ontology languages. Different rules languages have been investigated for this kind of integration. However, the most common rule language is Datalog, or one of its extensions. The syntax of these rules are similar to the logic programming rules that were composed in Section 3. Thus, rules are becoming a key ingredient in ontology languages and play an important role in the Semantic Web and its languages.

In the following, we discuss rule-based ontology compositions, i.e., composing concepts and rules together. It should be clear from the previous sections that universal genericity and extensibility can be provided for all concepts of rule-based ontology languages, also classes and rules. As a first example, we consider the extension of base classes in concept inheritance hierarchies, for instance, from legacy ontologies. This is important in ontology integration and alignment. As a second example, we look at the composition of classes with mixin-based inheritance, a systematic structuring of classes, which is useful in particular if the class descriptions grow large. In the following, we use F-logic as a rule-based ontology language [30]. However, since the ideas of universal genericity and universal extensibility applies to every languages, ontology and rule-based ontology languages such as OWL and SWRL can also be treated.

In Section 5, we provide an outlook on what needs to be accomplished to structure ontologies in-the-large. The key idea is to extend mixin-based class composition such that the model can be structured in layers (*mixin layers*), forming a structural outline of the model. Then, every final class is composed from class components, the mixins, each for every layer.

4.1 Base Class Extension

Often, in evolution of ontologies, it is necessary to extend a *base class* of a concept hierarchy. Because inheritance is hard-wired in class specifications, this is usually impossible to do directly. Base class extension can be achieved with design patterns such as Decorator [19], but then, extended and extension information reside in two classes (an effect called *object schizophrenia* [46]). Alternatively, base classes can be re-defined, or multiply defined, i.e., the extension does not introduce a new class, but contributes its features as a *view*. From Section 1, it is clear that the merge operator in hyperspace programming can be applied to merge the views; alternatively, the universal extend operator can be employed.

Example 4. As an example, consider the following F-logic fragment, a simple inheritance hierarchy defining customers. As an integrity constraint, person customers are not allowed to have debts, companies do (:: means inheritance, [] are scope brackets for classes, => means type annotation, and **members** is an implicitly defined hook for the end of a class member list).

Listing 1.17. Base class extension in F-logic.

```
person [name=>string];                                          1
company :: organization [money=>integer];
customer :: person [money=>natural];                            3
FORALL X <- customer [money=>X], X >= 0;  // no debts allowed
companyCustomer :: company;                                     5
companyCustomer :: customer;
personCustomer :: customer;                                     7
```

The base class **person** in this inheritance hierarchy can be extended as follows:

Listing 1.18. Base class extension in F-logic.

```
personExtension [age=>natural];                                 1

// Base class extension with the merge operator                 3
person.merge(personExtension);
// or with an implicit extension point members                  5
person.members.extend(personExtension);
```

which introduces a second definition to the class **person**, enriching it with the feature **age**.

Base class extension is very important for the integration of legacy ontologies into applications, because it makes it easy to enrich legacy inheritance hierarchies with new information. OWL (and thus SWRL) offers base class extension in a similar way by allowing classes and relationships to be re-defined at any time, thus providing a "built-in" merge operator for such concepts.

Hence, in the following, whenever we employ the merge and extend operators for F-logic on classes and relationships, the arguments also hold for OWL and SWRL.

4.2   Mixins Composition

Besides the standard notion of inheritance, several object-oriented languages have employed *mixin-based inheritance* [35,8]. Mixins are partial and abstract classes, i.e, cannot be instantiated to objects. However, they contribute to classes by contributing their features to them (that is why they are called mixins). Because the order, in which several mixins are inherited into a base class, must be explicitly specified, mixin-based inheritance seems to be easier to understand than standard multiple inheritance, in which the strategy of feature resolution is often implicit and hidden [35]. The following is an example in F-logic. The feature `money` is defined and replicated in `company` and `customer`. From which should `companyCustomer` inherit it?

Listing 1.19. Multiple inheritance in F-logic.

```
person [name=>string ];
company [money=>integer ];                                                    2
customer :: person [money=>natural ];
FORALL X <- customer [money=>X] , X >= 0;   // no debts allowed               4
companyCustomer :: company ;
companyCustomer :: customer ;                                                 6
personCustomer :: customer ;
```

With mixin-based inheritance, the example looks as follows:

Listing 1.20. Mixin-based inheritance in F-logic.

```
person [name=>string ];                                                       1
mixin company [money=>integer ];
mixin customer [money=>natural ];                                             3
FORALL X <- customer :: person [money=>X] , X >= 0;   // no debts allowed
companyCustomer = customer . members . extend (company );                     5
personCustomer :: customer ;
```

This example is more comprehensible, because the extension order is explicitly specified: `companyCustomer` is composed by extending `company` with `customer`, which implies that features of `customer` override those of `company`, so that the `companyCustomer` is not permitted to make debts.

If a language does not offer hooks, but generic classes, an alternative to the application of the extend operator exists. Batory has shown how to realize mixin-based inheritance in a universally generic language [44]. The trick is to combine inheritance with parameterization, i.e., the extend operator can be simulated by parameterizing a superclass reference. Then, a mixin becomes a class with a parameterized superclass:

Listing 1.21. Mixin-based inheritance in generic F-logic.

```
person [ name=>string ] ;
company::<<super : Class >>[money=>integer ] ;                              2
customer::<<super : Class >>[money=>natural ] ;
FORALL X <- customer [money=>X] , X >= 0;   // no debts allowed            4

companyCustomer = customer . super . bind (company ) ;                      6
personCustomer = customer . super . bind ( person ) ;
```

In this way, company becomes a superclass of companyCustomer, which means that its features are overridden.

5 Applications

Mixins can systematically be arranged in layers, which structures a class model in-the-large [44]. This is further explored in this section.

5.1 Composing Class Variants with Mixins

Mixins can be arranged in layers, so that each layer realizes a concern of the domain. When there exist variants for mixins on each layer, the result is a variant space for class composition.

Example 5. When modeling graphs with a graph ontology, many concerns play a role, for instance, whether or not the nodes should have a type (core concern), whether or not there should be explicit edge objects (explicit edges concern) or whether the graph should be unidirectional or bidirectional (symmetry concern). Every concern leads to one or several variabilities, i.e., modeling decisions about the features of the class with regard to the concerns (=>> means a set of typed objects).

```
concern  core = {                                                          1
    Core           ::  Thing ;
    UntypedNode  ::  Core [name=>string ] ;                                3
    TypedNode    ::  UntypedNode [ type=>string ] ;
}                                                                          5
concern edge = {
    Neighbor  ::  Thing ;                                                   7
    Node  ::  Neighbor ;
    Edge  ::  Neighbor ;                                                    9
    ForwardEdges [ outgoing=>>Neighbor ; fanOut=>int ] ;
    BackwardEdges [ incoming=>>Neighbor ; fanIn=>int ] ;                    11
}
concern symmetry = {                                                       13
    Unidirectional = ForwardEdges ;
    Bidirectional = ForwardEdges . members . extend ( BackwardEdges ) ;     15
}
```

When a graph node it modeled, its features have to be selected according to the variability decisions: for instance, a graph node should be composed from a core concern, talking about names and/or types; an edge concern, talking about neighbor edges or edge objects (outgoing, fan-out); and a symmetry concern, talking about also incoming edges. Hence, composing a graph node means to select one alternative mixin from every concern and extend the core class with them. For instance, a typed node with bidirectional relations is composed as follows:

```
TypedNodeBidirectional  =  TypedNode.members.extend(Bidirectional);
```

resulting in

```
TypedNodeBidirectional  ::  Thing  [                              1
   name=>string;
   type=>string;                                                  3
   outgoing=>>Neighbor;  fanOut=>int;
   incoming=>>Neighbor;  fanIn=>int;                              5
];
```

On the other hand, an untyped node with forward relations is composed as follows:

```
UntypedNodeUnidirectional =
   UntypedNode.members.extend(Unidirectional);
```

resulting in

```
UntypedNodeUnidirectional  ::  Thing  [                           1
   name=>string;
   outgoing=>>Neighbor;  fanOut=>int;                             3
];
```

Similarly, other ingredients of a graph, edges or graph objects can be composed [44,43].

With mixins, classes can systematically be defined in variants. Variants can offer alternative interfaces for concerns, or alternative implementations for an interface. Using variants of mixins for a concern leads to different composition results. All variants for all concerns form a variant space, and the selection of a mixin for a variant means to select a variant configuration.

Usually a mixin characterizes one concern of a class, for instance, a role in a collaboration. Recent research has found out that associations between classes define roles that an object plays in a certain context (the roles taking part in an association form a *collaboration* [16]). Hence, mixins characterize the behavior of a class in a certain collaboration context, and if the behavior of the class should be modeled in variants, mixins can model the behavioral variants. In our example, the concerns describe the behavior of a graph node in the context of other graph nodes, i.e., in a collaboration with other nodes and edges of a graph. Hence, variants of such collaborative behavior can be modeled systematically, grouped to concerns, and composed to classes in the variant space for graphs.

For ontology engineering, mixin composition is useful in several respects. First, it should be employed, if an ontology must be modeled in a variant space, i.e., if several basic variability decisions (modeling alternatives) exist, and all combinations of these alternatives form valid domain objects. Such ontology variant spaces are by no means restricted to mathematical domains like the graphs, but relate to all domains, where collaborations of an object or concept can be varied. Then, collaboration variants can be composed by mixin composition. Additionally, commercial reasons may create a need for mixin composition. Most often, business domains, such as business rules or product data domains, require variant spaces, because they form the backbone of a product line, a set of products that differ only marginally, but should be sold separately. With mixin composition, it is easy to model the feature space of a product line systematically.

Next, it is well-known that many classifications are based on *dimensions (facet classifications)* [49]. Whenever objects have several orthogonal partitions, facets can be defined, independent classification dimensions, in which objects can be described, and whose cross-product gives the whole characterization. Because every facet provides a basic variability decision for the model, a concrete classification selects a combination of variants. Hence, facet spaces form *orthogonal variant spaces* for ontologies. Furthermore, facet classifications may underly restriction constraints [49]. Then, the facets are not independent, but several combinations are excluded. For instance, it might be prohibited for a graph to contain both untyped and typed edges. Such illegal combinations can be excluded from the variant space by integrity constraints, but, anyway, faceted domains are subject to concern modeling and mixin composition.

5.2 Composing Class Variant Spaces with Mixin Layers

Mixin compositions form singular objects or concepts. However, for a set of collaborating concepts or objects, layers can group dependent mixin variants of all collaborating objects together. Then, we speak of *mixin layer composition* [44]. Composing mixin layers means to compose all classes of the model together from all collaborating mixin parts. To this end, collaborating mixins are grouped in layers. These mixin layers, like single mixins, can be defined in variants, and every variant forms an aligned, syntonic set of mixins who collaborate consistently. Hence, a concern that crosscuts several objects, can be described by a single layer of collaborating mixins. If several variants of the layer exist, the appropriate realization of the concern can be chosen by selecting a mixin layer variant, containing a set of coherently collaborating mixins. This coherent selection is very important for defining consistent large ontologies: in one go, large collaborations of concepts and objects can be selected and wired together easily.

Example 6. For the graph ontology, apart from graph nodes, also graph edges and graph objects must be modeled. Naturally, since all these concepts interact, they should be modeled consistently. For instance, depending on whether a unidirectional or bidirectional graph is modeled, edges and nodes must fit together; either both have to model only the forward relationship or both have to model also the backward relationship.

```
concern core = {
  layer UntypedCore = {                                              2
    Node   ::  Thing [name=>string];
    Edge   ::  Thing;                                                4
    Graph  ::  Thing[name=>string; nodes=>>Node, edges=>>Edge];
  }                                                                  6
  layer TypedCore = {
    Node   ::  Thing[name=>string;type=>string];                    8
    Edge   ::  Thing[type=>string];
    Graph  ::  Thing[name=>string; nodes=>>Node, edges=>>Edge];     10
  }
}                                                                   12
concern edge = {
  layer ForwardRelation {                                           14
    Node[outgoing=>>Edge; fanOut=>int];
    Edge[Node=>successor];                                          16
```

```
   Graph [sources=>>Node];
   Sink::Node;   FORALL X:  Sink[fanOut=>X], X=0. // no successors    18
}
layer BackwardRelation {                                              20
   Node[incoming=>>Edge; fanIn=>int];
   Edge[Node=>predecessor];                                          22
   Graph[sinks=>>Node];
   Source::Node;   FORALL X:  Source[fanIn=>X], X=0. // no           24
       predecessors
}
}                                                                    26
concern symmetry = {
   layer Unidirectional = ForwardRelation;                          28
   layer Bidirectional  = ForwardRelation.merge(BackwardRelation);
}                                                                    30
```

A mixin layer has to define an extension for every corresponding core object. (Here, in this simple case, the correlation is indicated by the same name, but more complicated schemes can be applied.) This time, the graph ontology is composed from mixin layer variants:

```
UntypedForwardGraph  = UntypedCore.merge(Unidirectional);
TypedSymmetricGraph  = TypedCore.merge(Bidirectional);              2
```

resulting in

```
UntypedForwardGraph = {
   Node::Thing[name=>string; outgoing=>>Edge;fanOut=>int];          2
   Sink::Node;   FORALL X:  Sink[fanOut=>X], X=0. // no successors
   Edge::Thing[Node=>successor];                                    4
   Graph::Thing[name=>string;nodes=>>Node;edges=>>Edge;sources=>>Node];
}                                                                   6
TypedSymmetricGraph = {
   Node  ::Thing[name=>string;type:string;outgoing=>>Edge;          8
                 incoming=>>Edge;fanIn=>int;fanOut=>integer];
   Source::Node;   FORALL X:  Source[fanIn=>X], X=0. // no predecessors  10
   Sink::Node;   FORALL X:  Sink[fanOut=>X], X=0. // no successors
   Edge ::Thing[type=>string;Node=>successor;Node=>predecessor];    12
   Graph::Thing[name=>string;nodes=>>Node,edges=>>Edge,
                 sources=>>Node;sinks=>>Node];                      14
}
```

Essentially, mixin layers are hyperslices that group collaborating mixins together. For ontology engineering, mixin layer composition enables the composition of partial classes, together with their constraints. Integrity constraints and production rules can be composed together with mixins and mixin layers, and they can be parameterized and extended in the same way as seen in the previous sections.

Mixin layers provide an important type of fragment components for component-based ontology engineering. Classes in an ontology, together with their relations, integrity constraints, and production rules, may be composed from consistently defined mixin layers. This composition style is very important for large ontologies that must be designed in variant spaces, and have sets of collaborating concepts. Whenever interaction between concepts of an ontology is required, mixin layer composition is a good means to specify all classes, relationships, and constraints together. Due to the layering, this improves comprehensibility of the ontology, because larger ontologies are constructed from smaller building blocks in a structured way.

6   Related Work

In contrast to component-based ontology composition, which attempts to construct an ontology from scratch, ontology alignment attempts to integrate legacy ontology components [45]. Of course, this is a related approach, which is important as such, because the world of ontologies will be heterogeneous, evolving, and legacy-aware. However, universal genericity and universal extension are two basic principles that will also improve ontology alignment work, as can be seen from the section on base class extension and mixin composition.

[34] presents an ontology composition algebra ONION that is mainly tailored to the integration of existing ontologies. It is a set-based algebra, with union, intersection, difference and selection as basic operations. Hence, merges and extensions are realized by set union. However, the ONION algebra lacks parameterization and extension of hooks. Since it offers merges mainly on concepts, it is similar to hyperspace programming. On the other hand, ONION offers articulation rules, which create relationships between concepts in different ontologies (homonymic mappings).

A second-order logic programming language directly provides the parameterizations and extensions of invasive component models, in the form of higher order functions and clauses. However, full second-order logic programming is undecidable. Hence, one could say that the decisive difference of a fragment-based composition system to a second-order language is that the invasive composition operations are executed in a stage before the actual system *(staged metaprogramming)* [41]. Hence, a fragment component model relies on staged metaprogramming principles.

Lämmel's work on language composition has applied static metaprogramming to attribute grammars [32]. He uses the λ-calculus as a composition language (with the bind operation), realizes extend operations by function composition, and is able to compose attribute grammar components. Fragment-based composition works in this spirit, but can be universally applied to all languages.

7   Conclusions

This paper has explained several techniques that will help the ontology engineer to define architectures of ontologies, i.e., structures of ontologies in-the-large. Templates, semantic macros, views, mixin layers allow for structuring concepts, relationships, and entire ontologies into components, which can be constructed and comprehended in isolation, but reused in many ontologies. These techniques, successfully applied in software engineering for programs and system models, will certainly contribute to the future field of component-based ontology engineering.

Acknowledgment

This research has been co-funded by the European Commission and by the Swiss Federal Office for Education and Science within the 6th Framework Programme project REWERSE number 506779 (cf. http://rewerse.net).

References

1. A. Analyti, G. Antoniou, C. V. Damásio, and G. Wagner. Stable model theory for extended rdf ontologies. In *Int. Semantic Web Conference*, pages 21–36, 2005.
2. G. Antoniou. Nonmonotonic rule systems using ontologies. In *Proc. Intl. Workshop on Rule Markup Languages for Business Rules on the Semantic Web*, 2002.
3. U. Aßmann. Beyond generic component parameters. In *CD '02: Proceedings of the IFIP/ACM Working Conference on Component Deployment*, pages 141–154, London, UK, 2002. Springer-Verlag.
4. U. Aßmann. *Invasive Software Composition*. Springer-Verlag, Feb. 2003.
5. S. Barry, J. Williams, and S. Schulze-Kremer. The ontology of the Gene Ontology. In *AMIA 2003 – Annual Symposium of the American Medical Informatics Association*, 2003.
6. S. Boag and D. C. et. al. (editors). XQuery 1.0: An XML Query Language. W3C Candidate Recommendation 3 November 2005, 3 November 2005. Available at `http://www.w3.org/TR/xquery/`.
7. G. Bracha. *The Programming Language Jigsaw: Mixins, Modularity and Multiple Inheritance*. Ph.D. thesis, Dept. of Computer Science, University of Utah, Mar. 1992.
8. G. Bracha and W. Cook. Mixin-based inheritance. In N. Meyrowitz, editor, *Proceedings of OOPSLA ECOOP '90*, number 25(10) in ACM SIGPLAN Notices, pages 303–311. ACM Press, New York, Oct. 1990.
9. F. Bry and S. Schaffert. The XML query language Xcerpt: Design principles, examples, and semantics. In *Web and Databases, Proc of the 2nd Int. Workshop*, LNCS2593. Springer Verlag, 2002.
10. G. Castagna. Covariance and contravariance: Conflict without a cause. *ACM Transactions on Programming Languages and Systems*, 17(3):431–447, May 1995.
11. W. Chen, M. Kifer, and D. S. Warren. HiLog: A Foundation for Higher-Order Logic Programming. *Journal of Logic Programming*, 15(3):187–230, Feb. 1993.
12. M. Cole. *Algorithmic Skeletons: Structured Management of Parallel Computation*. Monograms. MIT Press, Cambridge, MA, 1989.
13. Dan Brickley and R.V. Guha. RDF Vocabulary Description Language 1.0: RDF Schema. W3C Recommendation, 10 February 2004. Available at `http://www.w3.org/TR/rdf-schema/`.
14. J. Darlington, Y.-K. Guo, H. W. To, and J. Yang. Functional skeletons for parallel coordination. *Lecture Notes in Computer Science*, 966:55, 1995.
15. F. DeRemer and H. Kron. Programming in the Large vs. Programming in the Small. *IEEE Transactions on Software Engineering*, 2(2):80–86, June 1976.
16. D. F. D'Souza and A. C. Wills. *Objects, Components and Frameworks with UML: The Catalysis Approach*, chapter 6, page 816. Object Technology Series. Addison-Wesley, 1st edition, 1998.
17. J. C. (editor). XSL Transformations (XSLT) Version 1.0. W3C Recommendation 16 November 1999, 16 November 1999. Available at `http://www.w3.org/TR/xslt`.
18. T. Eiter, T. Lukasiewicz, R. Schindlauer, and H. Tompits. Combining answer set programming with description logics for the semantic web. In *Proc. of the Int. Conference of Knowledge Representation and Reasoning (KR'04)*, 2004.
19. E. Gamma, R. Helm, R. Johnson, and J. Vlissides. *Design Patterns: Elements of Reusable Object-Oriented Software*. Addison Wesley, Reading, MA, 1994.

20. D. Garlan. Formal modeling and analysis of software architecture: Components, connectors, and events. In M. Bernardo and P. Inverardi, editors, *Formal Methods for Software Architectures, Third Int. School on Formal Methods for the Design of Computer, Communication and Software Systems: Software Architectures (SFM 2003), Advanced Lectures*, volume 2804 of *Lecture Notes in Computer Science*, pages 1–24. Springer, Sept. 2003.

21. D. Garlan and Z. Wang. Acme-based Software Architecture Interchange. In P. Ciancarini and A. Wolf, editors, *Proc. 3rd Int. Conf. on Coordination Models and Languages*, volume 1594 of *Lecture Notes in Computer Science*, pages 340–354. Springer, Heidelberg, Apr. 1999.

22. Graham Klyne and Jeremy J. Carroll. Resource Description Framework (RDF): Concepts and Abstract Syntax. W3C Recommendation, 10 February 2004. Available at `http://www.w3.org/TR/rdf-concepts/`.

23. B. Grosof, I. Horrocks, R. Volz, and S. Decker. Description logic programs: Combining logic programs with description logic. In *Proceedings of 12th Int. Conference on the World Wide Web*, 2003.

24. I. Horrocks and P. F. Patel-Schneider. A proposal for an OWL rules language. In *Proc. of the Thirteenth Int. World Wide Web Conference (WWW 2004)*, pages 723–731. ACM, 2004.

25. Int. Organization for Standardization. *Ada 95 Reference Manual. The Language. The Standard Libraries*, Jan. 1995. ANSI/ISO/IEC-8652:1995.

26. L. K. J., M. Löfgren, O. Lehrmann Madsen, and B. Magnusson, editors. *Object-Oriented Environments—The Mjoelner Approach*. Prentice Hall, New York, 1994.

27. Jan Maluszynski et. al. Combining Rules and Ontologies. A survey. . Technical report, REWERSE Deliverable, March 2005. `http://rewerse.net/deliverables/m12/i3-d3.pdf`.

28. JavaSoft. *Enterprise Java Beans (TM)*, Apr. 2000. Version 2.0.

29. G. Kiczales, J. Lamping, A. Mendhekar, C. Maeda, C. Lopes, J.-M. Loingtier, and J. Irwin. Aspect-oriented programming. In *Proceedings of the European Conference on Object-Oriented Programming (ECOOP 97)*, volume 1241 of *Lecture Notes in Computer Science*, pages 220–242. Springer, Heidelberg, 1997.

30. M. Kifer. Rules and ontologies in F-logic. In N. Eisinger and J. Maluszynski, editors, *Reasoning Web, First Int. Summer School 2005, Msida, Malta, July 25-29, 2005, Tutorial Lectures*, volume 3564 of *Lecture Notes in Computer Science*, pages 22–34. Springer, 2005.

31. S. Krishnamurthi, M. Felleisen, and B. F. Duba. From Macros to Reusable Generative Programming. In U. W. Eisenecker and K. Czarnecki, editors, *Generative Component-based Software Engineering (GCSE)*, number 1799 in Lecture Notes in Computer Science. Springer, Heidelberg, Oct. 1999.

32. R. Lämmel. *Functional Meta-Programs – Towards Reusability in the Declarative Paradigm*. PhD thesis, Universität Rostock, 1999.

33. O. Lehrmann Madsen, B. Möller-Pedersen, and K. Nygaard. *Object-Oriented Programming in the BETA Programming Language*. Addison Wesley, Reading, MA, 1993.

34. P. Mitra and G. Wiederhold. An ontology-composition algebra. In S. Staab and R. Studer, editors, *Handbook on Ontologies*, Int. Handbooks on Information Systems, pages 93–116. Springer, 2004.

35. D. A. Moon. Object-oriented programming with flavours. In *Proceedings of OOPSLA'86*, number 21(11) in ACM SIGPLAN Notices, pages 1–8. ACM Press, New York, Oct. 1986.

36. B. Motik, U. Sattler, and R. Studer. Query Answering for OWL-DL with Rules. *J. of Web Semantics*, 3:41–60, 2005.

37. D. L. Parnas. On the criteria to be used in decomposing systems into modules. *Communications of the ACM*, 15(12):1053–1058, Dec. 1972.

38. P. F. Patel-Schneider, P. Hayes, and I. Horrocks. OWL web ontology language semantics and abstract syntax. W3C Recommendation, 10 February 2004. Available at http://www.w3.org/TR/owl-semantics/.

39. A. L. Rector, C. Wroe, J. Rogers, and A. Roberts. Untangling taxonomies and relationships: personal and practical problems in loosely coupled development of large ontologies. In *K-CAP*, pages 139–146. ACM, 2001.

40. R. Rosati. Semantic and computational advantages of the safe integration of ontologies and rules. In F. Fages and S. Soliman, editors, *Principles and Practice of Semantic Web Reasoning*, LNCS3703, pages 50–64. Springer Verlag, 2005.

41. T. Sheard. Using MetaML: A staged programming language. Number 1608 in Lecture Notes in Computer Science, pages 207–239. Springer, Heidelberg, 1999.

42. J. Siegel. OMG overview: CORBA and the OMA in enterprise computing. *Communications of the ACM*, 41(10):37–43, Oct. 1998.

43. Y. Smaragdakis and D. Batory. Implementing layered designs with mixin layers. volume 1445, page 550. Springer, Heidelberg, 1998.

44. Y. Smaragdakis and D. Batory. Mixin layers: an object-oriented implementation technique for refinements and collaboration-based designs. *ACM Transactions on Software Engineering and Methodology*, 11(2):215–255, 2002.

45. M. K. Smith, C. Welty, and D. L. McGuinness. OWL web ontology language guide. Technical report, W3C Recommendation, Feb. 2004. http://www.w3.org/TR/owl-guide.

46. C. Szyperski. *Component Software: Beyond Object-Oriented Programming*. Addison-Wesley, New York, 1998.

47. P. Tarr, H. Ossher, W. Harrison, and S. Sutton. N degrees of separation: Multidimensional separation of concerns. In *Proceedings of ICSE'99*, pages 107–119, Los Angeles CA, USA, 1999.

48. P. L. Tarr and H. Ossher. Hyper/J^{TM}: Multi-dimensional separation of concerns for java^{TM}. In *ICSE*, pages 729–730. IEEE Computer Society, 2001.

49. Y. Tzitzikas, N. Spyratos, P. Constantopoulos, and A. Analyti. Extended faceted ontologies. *Lecture Notes in Computer Science*, 2348:778, 2002.

Reasoning with Rules and Ontologies*

Thomas Eiter[1], Giovambattista Ianni[1], Axel Polleres[2],
Roman Schindlauer[1], and Hans Tompits[1]

[1] Institut für Informationssysteme, Technische Universität Wien
Favoritenstraße 9-11, A-1040 Vienna, Austria
{eiter, ianni, roman, tompits}@kr.tuwien.ac.at
[2] Universidad Rey Juan Carlos, 28933 Móstoles, Spain
axel@polleres.net

Abstract. For realizing the Semantic Web vision, extensive work is underway
for getting the layers of its conceived architecture ready. Given that the Ontology Layer has reached a certain level of maturity with W3C recommendations
such as RDF and the OWL Web Ontology Language, current interest focuses on
the Rules Layer and its integration with the Ontology Layer. Several proposals
have been made for solving this problem, which does not have a straightforward
solution due to various obstacles. One of them is the fact that evaluation principles like the closed-world assumption, which is common in rule languages,
are usually not adopted in ontologies. Furthermore, naively adding rules to ontologies raises undecidability issues. In this paper, after giving a brief overview
about the current state of the Semantic-Web stack and its components, we will
discuss nonmonotonic logic programs under the answer-set semantics as a possible formalism of choice for realizing the Rules Layer. We will briefly discuss
open issues in combining rules and ontologies, and survey some existing proposals to facilitate reasoning with rules and ontologies. We will then focus on
description-logic programs (or *dl-programs*, for short), which realize a transparent integration of rules and ontologies supported by existing reasoning engines,
based on the answer-set semantics. We will further discuss a generalization of dl-
programs, viz. HEX-*programs*, which offer access to different ontologies as well
as higher-order language constructs.

1 Introduction

For the realization of the Semantic Web, the integration of different layers of its conceived architecture is a fundamental issue. In particular, the integration of *rules* and
ontologies is currently under investigation, and many proposals in this direction have
been made. They range from homogeneous approaches, in which rules and ontologies
are combined in the same logical language (e.g., in SWRL and DLP [31,24]), to hybrid
approaches in which the predicates of the rules and the ontology are distinguished and
suitable interfacing between them is facilitated, like, e.g., [18,14,59,30] (see [4] for a

* This research has been partially supported by the European Commission within the FP6 project
REWERSE (IST 506779, http://rewerse.net), by the Austrian Science Fund (FWF)
project P17212-N04, and by the CICyT of Spain project TIC-2003-9001-C02.

P. Barahona et al. (Eds.): Reasoning Web 2006, LNCS 4126, pp. 93–127, 2006.

survey about such approaches). While the former approaches provide a seamless semantic integration of rules and ontologies, they suffer from problems concerning either limited expressiveness or undecidability, because of the interaction between rules and ontologies. Furthermore, they are not (or only to a limited extent) capable of dealing with ontologies having different formats and semantics (like, e.g., RDF Schema and OWL DL, which have some semantic incompatibilities) at the same time. This can be handled, in a fully transparent way, by approaches which keep rules and ontologies separate. Here, ontologies are treated as external sources of information, which are accessed by rules that also may provide input to the ontologies. In view of well-defined interfaces, the precise semantic definition of ontologies and their actual structure does not need to be known. This in particular facilitates ontology access as a Web service, where also privacy issues might be involved (e.g., a customer taxonomy in a financial domain).

In this paper, we shall consider reasoning with rules and ontologies from the *answer-set programming* (ASP) [6] perspective. The latter is nowadays a general term for a powerful knowledge representation (KR) and declarative programming paradigm which includes many language features from nonmonotonic logics, as well as support for reasoning with constraints and preferences. ASP has recently been used as a reliable specification tool in a number of promising applications. For instance, several tasks in information integration, knowledge management, security management, and configuration, which require complex reasoning capabilities, have been successfully tackled using ASP. In particular, these applications have been explored in several recent projects funded by the European Commission (e.g., the projects WASP [61], INFOMIX [35], and ICONS [33]).

Some attractive benefits of ASP are summarized as follows:

- *Full declarativity:* ASP is fully declarative. The order of rules and atoms in a logic program is not important, and, in general, no knowledge of the operational semantics a specific solver adopts is required.
- *Decidability:* ASP programs are, in their basic flavor, decidable. No special restrictions are needed in order to keep this important property.
- *Support of nonmonotonicity:* ASP supports strong negation as well as negation as failure. The latter facilitates default reasoning and nonmonotonic inheritance.
- *Nondeterminism:* Concepts may be defined which "range" over a space of choices without any particular restriction. Combined with extensions for preferences and different kinds of constraints, this enables a compact specification of search and optimization problems.
- *Scalability:* Despite the computational expressiveness of ASP, current state-of-the-art solvers, such as DLV [36], GnT [34], or Cmodels-3 [38], have reached a level of maturity which allows them to deal even with large datasets.

We refer to [60] for a repository of ASP solvers, and to [63] for a comprehensive report on recent ASP applications; a showcase collection is available online at

`http://www.kr.tuwien.ac.at/projects/WASP/showcase.html.`

In the Semantic Web perspective, significant efforts have been made to highlight the benefits of ASP for the Rules Layer of the Semantic Web architecture and its

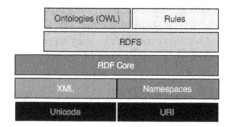

Fig. 1. Ontology and rule languages in the Semantic-Web layer cake

interactions with the Ontology Layer. A variety of upcoming applications supports adopting ASP as a formalism for realizing the Rules Layer. The inherent nondeterminism and the possibility to enrich the semantics with weak (i.e., soft) constraints make ASP a well-suited candidate for applications like Web-service matchmaking and ontology alignment [58]. It is worth mentioning that an ASP application for Web-service composition [49] earned first prize in the EEE Web-Service Composition Contest [13].

The remainder of this paper is organized as follows. The next section contains preliminaries on the relevant parts of the Semantic Web architecture, and Section 3 introduces ASP. In Section 4, we point out issues in combining rules and ontologies, and briefly survey approaches in this direction. After that, Section 5 presents nonmonotonic *description-logic programs* (or *dl-programs*, for short) as an example of an approach for combining rules and ontologies. The subsequent Section 6 presents an extension of this approach towards an integration of rules and general external software, in which the usage of higher-order predicates is facilitated. Finally, Section 7 provides a short discussion and concludes the paper.

In order to have a cohesive flow and to illustrate the different ASP extensions, we introduce an example in a storyboard-like fashion, which will serve as a running example throughout the paper.

2   Ontology Formalisms

Rules and ontologies represent two main components in the Semantic-Web vision which are expected to tightly interplay for making this vision a reality. In order to illustrate a plausible scenario where rules and ontologies interact, we will incrementally build a simple, yet conceivable, example.

Example 1 (Motivating Example, Part I). The Reasoning-Web Summer School is planning the organization of its social dinner. In order to make the attendees happy with this event and to make them familiar with ontologies, they decide to ask them to declare their preferences about wines, in terms of a class description reusing the (in)famous Wine Ontology [62]. The organizers realize that only one kind of wine would not achieve the goal of fulfilling all the attendees' preferences. Thus, they aim at automatically finding the cheapest selection of bottles such that any attendee can have his or her preferred wine at the dinner.

The organizers quickly realize that several building blocks are needed to accomplish this task. First of all, a good formalism to express the domain of interest (involving wines, their properties, and bottles) is needed. So they search among the currently available technologies and return with a strange brew of acronyms such as RDF, RDFS, and OWL.   □

The realization of reasoning with rules and ontologies affects basically four components of the so-called "Semantic-Web layer cake" [7]: *RDF*, *RDFS*, the *Ontology Layer*, and the *Rules Layer*. A slightly simplified version of this relevant part of the architecture proposal for the Semantic Web is shown in Fig. 1.

Layered on top of standards which mainly serve to provide common syntax for information exchange on the Web, the *Resource Description Framework* (RDF) [57,27] provides a common flexible data model for the Semantic Web. Based on arbitrary labeled graphs, RDF does not enforce a particular data schema upfront. Next, *RDF Schema* (RDFS) provides facilities to define simple taxonomies among concepts and relations.

While RDFS as such could already be viewed as a simple ontology language, in order to provide more expressiveness for describing formal conceptualizations, the *Ontology Layer* was introduced and is realized by means of the OWL Web Ontology Language [11], which can be seen as a syntactic variant of an expressive description logic.

As we already see in Fig. 1, the "Semantic-Web layer cake" is in fact not strictly layered, since rules and ontologies appear side by side. Whereas RDF, RDFS, and OWL have already achieved an acceptable level of maturity as W3C recommendations, it is not yet completely clear where and how to fit in rules, possibly involving nonmonotonicity, preferences, or other expressive features. Defining a proper standard for integrating the plethora of rules languages around is yet to be investigated by W3C's recently established *Rule Interchange Format* (RIF) working group.[3]

A natural choice of rule languages relevant for the integration of rules and ontologies are those originating from logic programming and nonmonotonic reasoning, in particular languages which are based on the *answer-set programming paradigm* (cf., e.g., [6]), on which we focus here. The latter paradigm is a purely declarative problem-solving formalism which gained increasing momentum in the knowledge-representation community over the last decade.

Before introducing this paradigm in more detail though, we briefly recapitulate the established building blocks RDF(S) and OWL, and discuss their formal underpinnings.

2.1   RDF(S)

The *Resource Description Framework* (RDF) defines the data model for the Semantic Web. Driven by the goal of a least possible commitment to a particular data schema, the simplest possible structure for representing information was chosen in RDF, a labeled graph. An RDF graph can be viewed as a set of its directed edges, commonly represented by triples of form ⟨*Subject Predicate Object*⟩, also called *statements*.

---

[3] cf. http://www.w3.org/2005/rules/wg/charter.

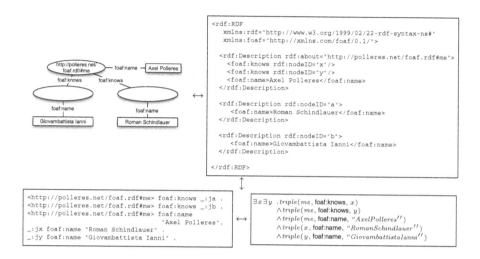

Fig. 2. Different representations of RDF

Predicates, also referred to as *properties* in RDF terminology, denote the labels, and link a *resource*, identified by a URI, with another resource, datatype literal, or XML literal.

Moreover, RDF graphs may contain anonymous ("blank") nodes, in order to express incomplete information or queries. Fig. 2 shows an example demonstrating three common notions for RDF graphs: RDF/XML syntax, N-Triples, and representing an RDF graph as a closed first-order formula where blank nodes are conceived as existentially quantified variables. We use the ternary predicate *triple* to represent RDF statements: Alternative representations, like representing triples $\langle S\ P\ O\rangle$ by $P(S, O)$, have some disadvantage for RDF, as we will see below.

This graphs contains the following information: The resource

"http://polleres.net/foaf.rdf#me"

with the name "Axel Polleres" knows someone named "Giovambattista Ianni" and someone named "Roman Schindlauer". Terms like foaf:knows are shortcuts for full URIs like http://xmlns.com/foaf/0.1/knows,[4] i.e., using so-called *namespace prefixes* from XML, for ease of legibility.

Moreover, basic RDF defines a special property rdf:type, which allows the specification of "is-a" relations, such as, for instance,

$\langle$http://polleres.net/foaf.rdf#me rdf:type foaf:Person$\rangle$.

RDF supports two basic types, viz. rdf:Property and rdf:XMLLiteral, and a basic set of XML schema datatypes.

---

[4] This represents typical information which you might find in a so-called *FOAF description*, an RDF vocabulary for expressing personal information with growing popularity, see http://www.foaf-project.org/.

Table 1. Semantics of RDFS

$\forall S, P, O.(triple(S, P, O) \supset triple(P, \mathsf{rdf:type}, \mathsf{rdf:Property}))$,

$\forall S, P, O.(triple(S, P, O) \supset triple(S, \mathsf{rdf:type}, \mathsf{rdfs:Resource}))$,

$\forall S, P, O.(triple(S, P, O) \supset triple(O, \mathsf{rdf:type}, \mathsf{rdfs:Resource}))$,

$\forall S, P, O.(triple(S, P, O), triple(P, \mathsf{rdfs:domain}, C)) \supset triple(S, \mathsf{rdf:type}, C))$,

$\forall S, P, O, C.(triple(S, P, O) \wedge triple(P, \mathsf{rdfs:range}, C) \supset triple(O, \mathsf{rdf:type}, C))$,

$\forall C.(triple(C, \mathsf{rdf:type}, \mathsf{rdfs:Class}) \supset triple(C, \mathsf{rdfs:subClassOf}, \mathsf{rdfs:Resource})$,

$\forall C_1, C_2, C_3.((triple(C_1, \mathsf{rdfs:subClassOf}, C_2) \wedge$
$\qquad triple(C_2, \mathsf{rdfs:subClassOf}, C_3)) \supset triple(C_1, \mathsf{rdfs:subClassOf}, C_3)$,

$\forall S, C_1, C_2.((triple(S, \mathsf{rdf:type}, C_1) \wedge$
$\qquad triple(C_1, \mathsf{rdfs:subClassOf}, C_2)) \supset triple(S, \mathsf{rdf:type}, C_2))$,

$\forall S, C.(triple(S, \mathsf{rdf:type}, C) \supset triple(C, \mathsf{rdf:type}, \mathsf{rdfs:Class})$,

$\forall C.(triple(C, \mathsf{rdf:type}, \mathsf{rdfs:Class}) \supset triple(C, \mathsf{rdfs:subClassOf}, C)$,

$\forall P_1, P_2, P_3.((triple(P_1, \mathsf{rdfs:subPropertyOf}, P_2) \wedge$
$\qquad triple(P_2, \mathsf{rdfs:subPropertyOf}, P_3)) \supset triple(P_1, \mathsf{rdfs:subPropertyOf}, P_3))$,

$\forall S, P_1, P_2, O.(triple(S, P_1, O) \wedge triple(P_1, \mathsf{rdfs:subPropertyOf}, P_2) \supset triple(S, P_2, O))$,

$\forall P.(triple(P, \mathsf{rdf:type}, \mathsf{rdf:Property}) \supset triple(P, \mathsf{rdfs:subPropertyOf}, P))$

The semantics of RDF can be essentially viewed as corresponding to the first-order representation chosen in Fig. 2 plus entailment of several axiomatic triples, such as that the triple ⟨ X rdf:type rdf:Property ⟩ is an axiom for all X which occur in the predicate position of any other triple. In particular, this also makes, for instance, ⟨ rdf:type rdf:type rdf:Property ⟩ an axiom.

The semantics of RDF involves some more peculiarities in the handling of XML literals, RDF containers, and lists. Most remarkably, it should be noted that the RDF vocabulary contains an infinite number of predefined properties rdf:_1, rdf:_2, ... for container membership, and thus gives rise to an infinite number of axiomatic triples ⟨rdf:_1 rdf:type rdf:Property⟩, ... We refer the interested reader to [27] for details.

RDF Schema (RDFS) is a semantic extension of basic RDF essentially by giving special meaning to the properties rdfs:subClassOf and rdfs:subPropertyOf, as well as to several types (like rdfs:Class, rdfs:Resource, rdfs:Literal, rdfs:Datatype etc.), in order to express simple taxonomies and hierarchies among properties and resources.

The semantics of RDFS can to a large extent be approximated by a set of sentences of first-order logic (FOL), reusing the notion from above (see Table 1)[5] plus the axiomatic triples from [27, Sections 3.1 and 4.1]. Note that our choice of using a ternary predicate *triple* in favor of a binary representation helped us to avoid higher-order-like rules such as $\forall S, P, O.\ P(S, O) \supset$ rdf:type $(P, \mathsf{rdf:Property})$ in this axiomatization. Again, we do

---

[5] We use '⊃' for material implication to avoid confusion with '←' as commonly used in logic programming.

Table 2. Expressing OWL DL Property axioms to DL and FOL

OWL property axioms as RDF Triples	DL syntax	FOL short representation
$\langle P$ rdfs:domain $C\rangle$	$\top \sqsubseteq \forall P^-.C$	$\forall x, y : P(x,y) \supset C(x)$
$\langle P$ rdfs:range $C\rangle$	$\top \sqsubseteq \forall P.C$	$\forall x, y : P(x,y) \supset C(y)$
$\langle P$ owl:inverseOf $P_0\rangle$	$P \equiv P_0^-$	$\forall x, y : P(x,y) \equiv P_0(y,x)$
$\langle P$ rdf:type owl:SymmetricProperty $\rangle$	$P \equiv P^-$	$\forall x, y : P(x,y) \equiv P(y,x)$
$\langle P$ rdf:type owl:FunctionalProperty $\rangle$	$\top \sqsubseteq\; \leqslant 1P$	$\forall x, y_1, y_2 : P(x,y_1) \wedge P(x,y_2) \supset y_1 = y_2$
$\langle P$ rdf:type owl:InverseFunctionalProperty $\rangle$	$\top \sqsubseteq\; \leqslant 1P^-$	$\forall x_1, x_2, y : P(x_1,y) \wedge P(x_2,y) \supset x_1 = x_2$
$\langle P$ rdf:type owl:TransitiveProperty $\rangle$	$P^+ \sqsubseteq P$	$\forall x, y, z : P(x,y) \wedge P(y,z) \supset P(x,z)$

not elaborate upon peculiarities and additional rules or axioms in the context of RDF containers and XML literals here.

2.2 Description Logics and the OWL Web Ontology Language

The next layer in the Semantic-Web stack serves to formally define shared conceptualizations, i.e., ontologies [25], on top of the RDF/RDFS data model. In order to formally specify such domain models, the W3C has chosen a language which is close to a syntactic variant of an expressive but still decidable description logic (DL), namely $\mathcal{SHOIN}(D)$. More precisely, the OWL DL variant coincides with this description logic, at the cost of imposing several restrictions on the usage of RDF(S). These restrictions (e.g., disallowing that a resource is used both as a class and an instance) are lifted in OWL Full which combines the description logic flavor of OWL DL and the syntactic freedom of RDF(S). For an in-depth discussion of the peculiarities of OWL Full, we refer the interested reader to the language specification [11] and restrict our observations to OWL DL here.

While RDFS itself may already be viewed as a simple ontology language, OWL adds several features beyond the simple definition of hierarchies (rdfs:subPropertyOf, rdfs:subClassOf) to define relations between properties and classes.

As for properties, OWL allows to specify transitive, symmetric, functional, inverse functional, and inverse properties. The correspondences of respective OWL properties and classes with description logics and first-order logic axioms expressible in OWL can be found in Table 2. Note that we switch to the binary representation $P(S, O)$ of triples here, since in description logics (and thus in OWL DL), predicate names and resources are assumed to be disjoint.

Moreover, OWL allows the specifications of complex class descriptions to be used in rdfs:subClassOf statements. Complex descriptions may involve class definitions in terms of union or intersection of other classes, as well as restrictions on properties. Table 3 gives an overview of the expressive possibilities of OWL for class descriptions and its semantic correspondences with description logics and first-order logics.[6] Such class descriptions can be related to each other using rdfs:subClassOf, owl:equivalentClass, or owl:disjointWith keywords, which allow us to express description-logic axioms of the form $C_1 \sqsubseteq C_2$, $C_1 \equiv C_2$, or $C_1 \sqcap C_2 \sqsubseteq \bot$, respectively, in OWL.

---

[6] We use a simplified notion for the first-order logic translation here—actually, the translation needs to be applied recursively for any complex description-logic term. For a formal specification of the correspondence between description-logic expressions and first-order logic, cf. [5].

Table 3. Mapping of OWL DL Complex Class Descriptions to DL and FOL

OWL complex class descriptions[*]	DL syntax	FOL short representation
owl:Thing	$\top$	$x = x$
owl:Nothing	$\bot$	$\neg x = x$
owl:intersectionOf $(C_1 \ldots C_n)$	$C_1 \sqcap \ldots \sqcap C_n$	$\bigwedge C_i(x)$
owl:unionOf $(C_1 \ldots C_n)$	$C_1 \sqcup \ldots \sqcup C_n$	$\bigvee C_i(x)$
owl:complementOf (C)	$\neg C$	$\neg C(x)$
owl:oneOf $(o_1 \ldots o_n)$	$\{o_1 \ldots o_n\}$	$\bigvee x = o_i$
owl:restriction $(P$ owl:someValuesFrom $(C))$	$\exists P.C$	$\exists y. P(x,y) \wedge C(y)$
owl:restriction $(P$ owl:allValuesFrom $(C))$	$\forall P.C$	$\forall y. P(x,y) \supset C(y)$
owl:restriction $(P$ owl:value $(o))$	$\exists P.\{o\}$	$P(x,o)$
owl:restriction $(P$ owl:minCardinality $(n))$	$\geqslant nP$	$\exists_{i=1}^{n} y_i . \bigwedge_{j=1}^{n} P(x, y_j) \wedge \bigwedge_{i \neq j} y_i \neq y_j$
owl:restriction $(P$ owl:maxCardinality $(n))$	$\leqslant nP$	$\forall_{i=1}^{n+1} y_i . (\bigwedge_{j=1}^{n} P(x, y_i) \supset \bigvee_{i \neq j} y_i = y_j)$

[*]For reasons of legibility, we use a variant of the OWL abstract syntax [47] in this table.

Finally, OWL allows to express explicit equality or inequality relations between individuals by means of the owl:sameAs and owl:differentFrom properties, e.g., the triples

⟨http://www.polleres.net/foaf.rdf#me owl:sameAs
http://polleres.net/foaf.rdf#me⟩ and

⟨http://polleres.net/foaf.rdf#me owl:differentFrom
http://www.gibbi.com/foaf.rdf#me⟩

boil down to

http://www.polleres.net/foaf.rdf#me=http://polleres.net/
foaf.rdf#me ∧ http://polleres.net/foaf.rdf#me ≠
http://www.gibbi.com/foaf.rdf#me.

For details on the description logics notion used in the Tables 2 and 3, we refer the interested reader to, e.g., [5]. For our purposes, basic understanding of the corresponding definitions in term of first-order logic will be sufficient. What makes description logics the formalism of choice is the fact that it defines a *decidable fragment* of first-order logic, i.e., queries for entailment of subclass relationships or class membership of a particular individual are effectively computable.

Example 2 (Ontologies in Description Logics). Taking the wine ontology from [62], let us illustrate some of the conceptualizations therein in their corresponding description-logics syntax:

$$Wine \sqsubseteq PotableLiquid \sqcap\, = 1 hasMaker \sqcap \forall hasMaker.Winery;$$
$$Wine \sqsubseteq\, \geq 1 madeFromGrape \sqcap\, = 1 hasFlavor;$$
$$\forall hasColor^{-}.\top \sqsubseteq \{\text{``White''}, \text{``Rose''}, \text{``Red''}\};$$
$$WhiteWine \equiv Wine \sqcap \forall hasColor.\{\text{``White''}\}.$$

This knowledge base expresses the following information: A wine is a potable liquid, having exactly one maker, who is a member of the class *Winery*. Moreover, wines are made from at least one sort of grapes and have exactly one of the flavors, and one of the colors "*White*", "*Rose*", and "*Red*". A *WhiteWine* is a wine with color "*White*". Finally, *Welschriesling* is an instance of *WhiteWine*.   □

3   Answer-Set Programming

After having introduced some foundations of the Semantic Web in terms of a data model (RDF) and ontology languages (RDFS and OWL), let us now turn to logic programs as a way to realize the Semantic-Web Rules Layer. For illustration purposes, consider the following continuation of our running example:

Example 3 (Motivating Example, Part II). As soon as the wine domain is described, the social-dinner organizers now have to face the problem of quickly modeling rules that describe a set of bottles that are suitable for all the participants, and to express the choice criteria among these candidate sets. They realize soon that domain-description languages accomplished their job well, but now they need some different tool: First, how to express possible choices of bottles? How to determine the set of attendees (say, the class *nonSatisfied*) that are *not* assigned a compliant bottle? Unfortunately, under an open-world assumption, no attendee can be entailed as belonging to this class. Moreover, is it possible to exclude the situations where *nonSatisfied* is non-empty, and where the price of this selection of bottles is possibly minimal?

They conclude that a rule-based formalism with disjunction and nonmonotonic features would be the most appropriate formalism, and, among others, choose to investigate on the characteristics of ASP (answer-set programming).   □

Answer-set programming has its roots in the seminal work by Gelfond and Lifschitz [22], who presented a semantics for logic programs with negation as failure and strong negation, where multiple *answer sets* (or *stable models*) may be ascribed to a program. This inherent nondeterminism can be exploited to represent different solutions to a problem in the answer sets of a logic program, as fostered, e.g., in [39,42,44].

3.1   Syntax

Let Φ be a first-order vocabulary with nonempty finite sets of constant and predicate symbols, but no function symbols.[7] Let $\mathcal{X}$ be a set of variables. A *term* is either a variable from $\mathcal{X}$ or a constant symbol from Φ. An *atom* is an expression of the form $p(t_1, \ldots, t_n)$, where p is a predicate symbol of arity $n \geq 0$ from Φ, and $t_1, \ldots, t_n$ are terms. A *literal* l is either an atom or an expression of form $-p$, where "$-$" denotes *strong negation* and p is an atom. The *complementary literal* $-l$ of l is $-p$ if $l = p$ and p if $l = -p$. A *negation-as-failure literal* (or *NAF-literal*) is either a literal or an expression of form *not* l, where "*not*" denotes *negation as failure*, or *default negation*, and l is a literal. A *disjunctive rule* (or simply a *rule*) r is an expression of the form

$$a_1 \vee \cdots \vee a_l \leftarrow b_1, \ldots, b_k, \text{not } b_{k+1}, \ldots, \text{not } b_m, \qquad (1)$$

where $l \geq 0$, $m \geq k \geq 0$, and all a_i and b_j are literals. The disjunction $a_1 \vee \cdots \vee a_l$ is the *head* of r, while the conjunction $b_1, \ldots, b_k, \text{not } b_{k+1}, \ldots, \text{not } b_m$ is the *body* of r, where $b_1, \ldots, b_k$ (resp., *not* $b_{k+1}, \ldots, \text{not } b_m$) is the *positive* (resp., *negative*) *body*

---

[7] Gelfond and Lifschitz allowed function symbols and inconsistent answer sets in their seminal paper [22]. Current ASP solvers have limited support of function symbols, while inconsistent answer sets are not allowed as valid answers.

of r. We use $H(r)$ to denote the set of all head literals $\{a_1, \ldots, a_l\}$ of r, and $B(r)$ to denote the set of all body literals $B^+(r) \cup B^-(r)$ of r, where $B^+(r) = \{b_1, \ldots, b_k\}$ and $B^-(r) = \{b_{k+1}, \ldots, b_m\}$.

A *disjunctive program* (or simply *program*) P is a finite set of (disjunctive) rules.

If the body of a rule r is empty (i.e., if $B(r) = \emptyset$), then r is a *fact*, and we often omit "$\leftarrow$" in such a case. A rule is *positive* if $B^-(r) = \emptyset$, and *normal* if the head of r is a literal. Similarly, a program is *positive* resp. *normal*, if each rule in it is positive resp. normal. A rule without head literals is an *(integrity) constraint*.

Example 4 (Simple Wine Program). The following program is a simplistic representation of a part of the wine scenario described previously, in which a plain ontology is natively represented within the logic program.

% *A suite of wine bottles and their kinds*
wineBottle("SelaksIceWine");   isA("SelaksIceWine", "whiteWine");
                                isA("SelaksIceWine", "sweetWine");
wineBottle("CheninBlanc");   isA("CheninBlanc", "whiteWine");
                                isA("CheninBlanc", "dryWine");
wineBottle("Chardonnay");   isA("Chardonnay", "whiteWine");
                                isA("Chardonnay", "dryWine");
wineBottle("ChiantiClassico"); isA("ChiantiClassico", "redWine");
                                isA("ChiantiClassico", "dryWine");
wineBottle("TaylorPort");   isA("TaylorPort", "redWine");
                                isA("TaylorPort", "sweetWine").

% *Persons and their preferences*
person("axel");   preferredWine("axel", "whiteWine");
person("gibbi");   preferredWine("gibbi", "redWine");
person("roman");   preferredWine("roman", "dryWine").

% *Available bottles a person likes*
compliantBottle$(X, Z) \leftarrow$ preferredWine(X, Y), isA(Z, Y).

The last rule describes bottles which are compliant with a person's preference.   □

Let us now consider a more elaborate version of this program.

Example 5 (Wine Program II). Compared to Example 4, we add the following rules:

doesNotLike$(X, Z) \leftarrow$ person(X), wineBottle(Z), not compliantBottle(X, Z).

% *This rule generates multiple answer sets*
bottleChosen$(X) \vee -$bottleChosen$(X) \leftarrow$ compliantBottle(Y, X).

% *Ensure that each person gets a bottle*
hasBottleChosen$(X) \leftarrow$ bottleChosen(Z), compliantBottle(X, Z);
$\leftarrow$ person(X), not hasBottleChosen(X).

The first rule concludes that somebody does not like wine bottles which do no comply with the personal desires. The second rule generates different worlds: ones in which a given bottle is chosen and others in which it is not. The third rule, together with the constraint, prunes all worlds (under closed-world assumption, CWA) in which some person has no bottle chosen.

Moreover, note that the second rule (the "choice" rule) may be equivalently replaced with

$$-bottleChosen(X) \leftarrow not\ bottleChosen(X),\ compliantBottle(Y,X);$$
$$bottleChosen(X) \leftarrow not\ -bottleChosen(X),\ compliantBottle(Y,X).$$

Under the answer-set semantics (introduced next), this pair of rules enforces that either $bottleChosen(X)$ or $-bottleChosen(X)$ is included in an answer set (but not both), providing it contains $compliantBottle(Y,X)$. ◻

3.2 Semantics

The *Herbrand universe* of a program P, denoted HU_P, is the set of all constant symbols appearing in P. If there is no such constant symbol, then $HU_P = \{c\}$, where c is an arbitrary constant symbol from Φ. As usual, terms, atoms, literals, rules, programs, etc. are *ground* iff they do not contain any variables. The *Herbrand base* of a program P, denoted HB_P, is the set of all ground (classical) literals that can be constructed from the predicate symbols appearing in P and the constant symbols in HU_P. A *ground instance* of a rule $r \in P$ is obtained from r by replacing every variable that occurs in r by a constant symbol from HU_P. We use $ground(P)$ to denote the set of all ground instances of rules in P.

A set of literals $X \subseteq HB_P$ is *consistent* iff $\{p, -p\} \nsubseteq X$ for every atom $p \in HB_P$. An *interpretation* I relative to a program P is a consistent subset of HB_P. A *model* of a positive program P is an interpretation $I \subseteq HB_P$ such that $B(r) \subseteq I$ implies $H(r) \cap I \neq \emptyset$, for every $r \in ground(P)$. An *answer set* of a positive program P is a minimal model of P with respect to set inclusion. In particular, if P is positive and does not involve disjunction, then there exists a single answer set (if one exists).

Example 6 (Simple Wine Program, continued). Our simple wine program does not contain disjunction. Its Herbrand universe is

$$HU_P = \{\text{"SelaksIceWine"}, \text{"CheninBlanc"}, \text{"Chardonnay"}, \text{"ChiantiClassico"},$$
$$\text{"TaylorPort"}, \text{"whiteWine"}, \text{"redWine"}, \text{"sweetWine"}, \text{"dryWine"},$$
$$\text{"axel"}, \text{"gibbi"}, \text{"roman"}\}$$

and its single answer set consists of all the facts of the program, together with the following items:

$compliantBottle(\text{"axel"}, \text{"SelaksIceWine"});$
$compliantBottle(\text{"axel"}, \text{"CheninBlanc"});$
$compliantBottle(\text{"axel"}, \text{"Chardonnay"});$
$compliantBottle(\text{"gibbi"}, \text{"ChiantiClassico"});$
$compliantBottle(\text{"gibbi"}, \text{"TaylorPort"});$
$compliantBottle(\text{"roman"}, \text{"CheninBlanc"});$
$compliantBottle(\text{"roman"}, \text{"Chardonnay"});$
$compliantBottle(\text{"roman"}, \text{"ChiantiClassico"}).$

◻

The *Gelfond-Lifschitz reduct* [22] of a program P relative to an interpretation $I \subseteq HB_P$, denoted P^I, is the ground positive program that is obtained from $ground(P)$ by

(i) deleting every rule r such that $B^-(r) \cap I \neq \emptyset$, and
(ii) deleting the negative body from every remaining rule.

An *answer set* of a program P is an interpretation $I \subseteq HB_P$ such that I is an answer set of P^I.

Note that, for positive P, $P^I = ground(P)$, and thus the answer sets of P are its minimal models, as we recall from above. This applies to the program in Example 4.

Example 7 (Wine Program II, continued). Let us extend the answer set of the program in Example 4 by the atoms

> *doesNotLike*("*axel*", "*ChiantiClassico*"), *doesNotLike*("*axel*", "*TaylorPort*"),
> *doesNotLike*("*gibbi*", "*SelaksIceWine*"), *doesNotLike*("*gibbi*", "*CheninBlanc*"),
> *doesNotLike*("*gibbi*", "*Chardonnay*"), *doesNotLike*("*roman*", "*SelaksIceWine*"),
> *doesNotLike*("*roman*", "*TaylorPort*"), $-$*bottleChosen*("*SelaksIceWine*"),
> $-$*bottleChosen*("*CheninBlanc*"), *bottleChosen*("*Chardonnay*"),
> *bottleChosen*("*ChiantiClassico*"), $-$*bottleChosen*("*TaylorPort*"),
> *hasBottleChosen*("*axel*"), *hasBottleChosen*("*roman*"),
> *hasBottleChosen*("*gibbi*"),

and let I be the resulting interpretation. Then, the program P^I contains all ground instances of positive rules on HU_P, plus the rules (originally containing negation in P)

$$doesNotLike(c, c') \leftarrow person(c), wineBottle(c'),$$

where (c, c') is from the set

> {("*axel*", "*ChiantiClassico*"), ("*axel*", "*TaylorPort*"), ("*gibbi*", "*SelaksIceWine*"),
> ("*gibbi*", "*CheninBlanc*"), ("*gibbi*", "*Chardonnay*"), ("*roman*", "*TaylorPort*"),
> ("*roman*", "*SelaksIceWine*")}.

As easily checked, I satisfies all rules in P^I, and moreover is a minimal model of P^I. Therefore, I is an answer set of P. However, other answer sets do exist.   □

3.3   Reasoning Tasks

The main reasoning tasks associated with programs under the answer-set semantics are the following:

- decide whether a given program P has an answer set;
- given a program P and ground literals $l_1, \ldots, l_n$, decide whether $l_1, \ldots, l_n$ simultaneously hold in every (resp., some) answer set of P (this is known as *cautious* resp. *brave reasoning*);
- given a program P and nonground literals $l_1, \ldots, l_n$ over variables $X_1, \ldots, X_k$, list all assignments ν of values to $X_1, \ldots, X_k$ such that $l_1\nu, \ldots, l_n\nu$ is cautiously (resp., bravely) true (*query answering*); and
- compute the set of all answer sets of a given program P.

Example 8 (Simple Wine Program, continued). In our simple wine program, we have a single answer set, and thus cautious and brave reasoning coincides. For instance, *compliantBottle("axel", "SelaksIceWine")* is both a cautious as well as a brave consequence of the program. For the query *person(X)*, we obtain the answers *"axel"*, *"gibbi"*, and *"roman"*.   □

Example 9 (Wine Program II, continued). The more elaborated wine program has 20 answer sets, corresponding to the possibilities whether a bottle is being chosen or not. The cautious query *bottleChosen("SelaksIceWine")* fails, while the brave query *bottleChosen("SelaksIceWine")* succeeds. For the query *bottleChosen(X)*, we obtain no answer under cautious reasoning.   □

The basic ASP language, as introduced above, has been extended in the literature with many features like *weak constraints* [8], *aggregates* [20] (as familiar from database query languages), or *cardinality* and *weight constraints* [45]. The fruitful combination of these features allowed ASP to become an important knowledge-representation formalism for declaratively solving AI problems.

Example 10 (Wine Program III). Suppose we want to single out situations in which a smallest number of bottles is chosen. This is effected in DLV [36] by the weak constraint

$$:\sim bottleChosen(X) \, [1].$$

Intuitively, each fact *bottleChosen(c)* in an answer set is assigned a penalty of 1, and total penalties are minimized. In our example, the optimum are two bottles (e.g., *bottleChosen("Chardonnay")* and *bottleChosen("ChiantiClassico")*). For a formal definition of the syntax and semantics of weak constraints, and a refinement using priority levels, we refer to [36].   □

4 Combining Rules with Ontologies

Motivated by our wine selection example, we have illustrated that answer-set programming might be a good candidate for filling the gap extending the Semantic-Web layers with a suitable rules component. However, there are several obstacles in finding the right combination of rich ontology languages such as OWL, which are based on classical logic, with logic-programming based languages such as answer-set programming (see also [53] for a discussion).

4.1 Logic Programming vs. Classical Logic

As well-known, the core of logic programming, i.e., definite positive programs, has a direct correspondence with the Horn subset of classical first-order logic. To wit, a rule of form (1) which is definite (i.e., when $l = 1$) and *not*-free (i.e., when $m = k$) can be read as a first-order sentence

$$(\forall) \, b_1 \wedge \ldots \wedge b_k \supset a \tag{2}$$

where ($\forall$) denotes the universal closure operator. This subset of first-order logic allows for a sound and complete decision procedure for entailment of ground atomic formulae, which is in the function-free (datalog) case computable in finite polynomial time.

However, there are some slight but important differences between the logic-programming view and the first-order view already for definite programs.

Non-ground entailment. The first divergence becomes apparent already in case of positive programs. The logic-programming semantics is defined in terms of minimal Herbrand models, i.e., sets of ground facts. Take for example the logic program

$potableLiquid(X) \leftarrow wine(X);$
$wine(X) \leftarrow whiteWine(X);$
$whiteWine(\text{``}Welschriesling\text{''}).$

Both the logic-program reading and the Horn-clause reading of this program yields the entailment of facts $whiteWine(\text{``}WelschRiesling\text{''})$, $wine(\text{``}WelschRiesling\text{''})$, and $potableLiquid(\text{``}WelschRiesling\text{''})$. The first-order reading of the program would allow further non-factual inferences, such as

$wine(\text{``}WelschRiesling\text{''}) \supset potableLiquid(\text{``}WelschRiesling\text{''})$ and
$\forall X . whiteWine(X) \supset PotableLiquid(X),$

which are not entailed by the logic program. Logic programs, minimal Herbrand models (and answer sets as their extension) are mainly concerned with facts.

Negation as failure vs. classical negation. Divergences become more severe when considering programs with negation. Negation as failure *not* is evaluated with respect to a closed-world assumption (CWA) whereas negation in description logics and thus in OWL (owl:complementOf) is interpreted classically. Let us again demonstrate this with a small example:

$wine(X) \leftarrow whiteWine(X);$
$nonWhite(X) \leftarrow not\ whiteWine(X);$
$wine(myDrink).$

Not given any additional information, under the answer-set semantics this program entails both bravely and cautiously the fact $nonWhite(myDrink)$. However, this conclusion would not be justified in a first-order or description-logics reading of the above program, such as:

$\forall X. (WhiteWine(X) \supset Wine(X)) \wedge$ $WhiteWine \sqsubseteq Wine$
$\forall X. (\neg WhiteWine(X) \supset NonWhite(X)) \wedge$ $\neg WhiteWine \sqsubseteq NonWhite$
$Wine(myDrink).$ $myDrink \in Wine.$

The reason for this is the different purposes classical negation and negation as failure serve: the latter to be understood as modeling (defeasible) default assumptions with nonmonotonic behavior. While some people argue that such a kind of nonmonotonic negation is unsuitable for an open environment like the Web, there are several applications, e.g., in information integration, where negation as failure has proved particularly useful (see Subsection 5.3).

Strong negation vs. classical negation. Note that also strong negation, as used in ASP has a slightly different flavor than its classical counterpart. That is, the following two representations of a logic program and an OWL knowledge base again slightly diverge:

$$Wine(X) \leftarrow Whitewine(X); \qquad Whitewine \sqsubseteq Wine;$$
$$-Wine(myDrink). \qquad\qquad myDrink \in \neg Wine.$$

Whereas the description-logic knowledge base would entail $myDrink \in \neg white Wine$, the corresponding fact $-white Wine(myDrink)$ is not a justified conclusion in a logic-programming setting, i.e., neither the law of the excluded middle nor contraposition does hold upfront in ASP. Nonetheless, one can "emulate" classical behavior of certain predicates in ASP. For instance, adding a rule $white Wine(X) \vee -white Wine(X)$ in the above example would achieve this.

Logic Programming and equality. Answer-set programming engines typically deploy a unique-names assumption (UNA) and do not support real equality reasoning, i.e., equality in the head of rules. This does not comply necessarily with the view in classical logic, and thus with RDF and OWL, where no such assumption is made. While equality "=" and inequality "≠" predicates are allowed in rule bodies, they represent syntactic equality and (default) negation thereof only. This shall not be confused with OWL's owl:sameAs and owl:differentFrom directives. Following up the example from Section 2.2, consider the following rule base:

$knowsOtherPeople(X) \leftarrow knows(X,Y), X \neq Y;$
$knows(\text{"http://polleres.net/foaf.rdf\#me"},$
          $\text{"http://www.polleres.net/foaf.rdf\#me"}).$

Under standard ASP semantics where UNA is deployed, "≠" amounts to "$not =$". Thus,

$knowsOtherPeople(\text{"http://polleres.net/foaf.rdf\#me"})$

would be entailed.

Enabling reasoning with equality has usually a very high computational cost. Indeed, common description-logic reasoners like FACT++ [55] or RACER [26] also do not support full equality reasoning and nominals.

Decidability. Finally, the probably largest obstacle towards combining the description-logics world of OWL and the logic-programming world of ASP stems from the fact that these two worlds face undecidability issues from two completely different angles.

Indeed, decidability of ASP follows from the fact that it is based on function-free Horn logic where ground entailment can be determined by checking finite subsets of the Herbrand base, i.e., decidability and termination of evaluation strategies is guaranteed by the finiteness of the domain. However, this is not so for description logics. Decidability of reasoning tasks such as satisfiability, class subsumption, or class membership in description logics is often strictly dependent from the combination of constructs which are allowed in the terminological language.

It is often possible to prove decidability by means of the so called *tree-model property.* This property basically says that a description-logic knowledge base has a model iff it has a finite tree shaped model whose depth and branching factor are bounded by the size of the knowledge base [5]. In general, it is possible to attempt to prove decidability by means of a generic finite-model property, although it is worth noting that $\mathcal{SHOIN}$ neither has the tree-model property nor the finite-model property [32].

Unfortunately, it is difficult to combine two decidable fragments coming from the two worlds. As shown in [37], the naive combination of even a very simple description logic with an arbitrary Horn logic is undecidable.

4.2 Strategies for Combining Rules and Ontologies

As one can expect by the above-mentioned problems, combining the two worlds of logic programming and classical logic, underlying description logics, is not straightforward.

However, a naive combination of description logics and Horn rules could be imagined as a possible approach for the Rules Layer of the Semantic Web. Indeed, the *Semantic Web Rule Language* (SWRL) [31] proposal, a recent W3C member submission, straightforwardly extends OWL DL in this spirit. Given an OWL knowledge base, SWRL allows to extend it by Horn rules using unary and binary atoms representing classes (concepts) and roles (properties), respectively. This allows, for instance, combined knowledge bases such as the following:

$$
\begin{aligned}
&shareFood(W1, W2) \leftarrow hasDrink(D, W1), hasDrink(D, W2), \\
&Whitewine \sqsubseteq Wine; \\
&\text{"}Trout\ grilled\text{"} \in Dish; \\
&(\text{"}Trout\ grilled\text{"}, \text{"}WelschRiesling\text{"}) \in hasDrink,
\end{aligned}
\tag{3}
$$

where the definition of the role "*shareFood*" by means of the first rule is not expressible directly in description logic alone. However, as mentioned above, this freedom comes at he cost of undecidability in the general case.

On the other extreme, the overcautious approach of allowing interoperability only on the intersection of description logics and Horn logic seems to be too restricted. Grosof *et al.* [24] have defined this intersection where the logic-programming and description-logic worlds coincides which they call DLP. However, such an approach leaves a rule and ontology language with very restrictive expressivity. Layering several extensions in the direction of logic programming and ASP on top of the DLP fragment have lead to the *Web Rule Language* (WRL) [2] proposal, an alternative W3C member submission.

In the following, we want to take a closer look at approaches which go beyond DLP but still retain decidability in a more cautious integration than SWRL. Especially, when we want to combine full description logics with full answer-set programming (i.e., not only Horn Rules), things become more involved. In principle, the different approaches in the literature can be divided into two major streams, as described below.

Interaction of ontologies and rules with tight semantic integration. Rules are introduced by adapting existing semantics for rule languages directly in the Ontology Layer. The DLP fragment on the one end and the undecidable SWRL approach on the other mark two extremes of this stream. Nonetheless, in between, recently several proposals have been made to extend expressiveness while still retaining decidability, remarkably

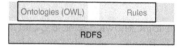 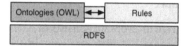

Fig. 3. Integrating Ontologies and Rules by defining "safe interaction" (left) vs. "safe interfaces" (right)

several attempts in the ASP field. Common to these approaches are syntactic restrictions of the combined language in a way that guarantees "safe interaction" of the rules and ontologies parts of the language (see Fig. 3).

The first such approach, $\mathcal{AL}$-Log [12], extends the description logic $\mathcal{AL}$ by Horn rules, but with the additional "safety" restriction that every variable of a rule r must appear in at least one of the rule atoms occurring in the body of r, where rule atoms are those predicates which do not appear in the description-logic knowledge base part, but only in rules. This restriction, which retains decidability, is for instance violated by (3). The decidability result for such so-called *DL-safe rules* is extended to a more expressive description logic $\mathcal{SHIQ}$ in [43] bringing us closer to OWL.

Another approach [29] in this direction shows decidability for query answering in $\mathcal{ALCHOQ}(\sqcup, \sqcap)$ with DL-safe rules by an embedding in extended conceptual logic programming, a decidable extension of the answer-set semantics by open domains.

The most recent work in this direction [51,52,53] loosens the safety restriction further, by allowing non-rule atoms also in rule heads, and also gives a nonmonotonic semantics for non-Horn rules in the spirit of answer-set programming.

Integration of ontologies and rules with strict semantic separation. In this setting, ASP should play a central role in the Rules Layer, while OWL/RDF flavors would keep their purpose of description languages, not aimed at intensive reasoning jobs, in the underlying Ontology Layer. The two layers are kept strictly separate and only communicate via a "safe interface", but do not impose syntactic restrictions on either the rules or the ontology part (see again Fig. 3).

From the Rules Layer point of view, ontologies are dealt with as an external source of information whose semantics is treated separately. Nonmonotonic reasoning and rules are allowed in a decidable setting, as well as arbitrary mixing of closed and open world reasoning. This approach typically involves special predicates in rule bodies which allow queries to a description-logic knowledge base, and exchange factual knowledge, Examples for this type of interaction are [18,14,41] and the call of external description-logic reasoners in the TRIPLE [54] rules engine. In the remainder of this paper, we will focus on nonmonotonic *description-logic programs* [18,14] as a showcase solution among these approaches.

For excellent surveys which classify the numerous proposals for combining rules and ontologies we refer the interested reader to [4,46].

5   Nonmonotonic Description-Logic Programs

In this section, we introduce *description-logic programs* (or simply *dl-programs*), which are a novel combination of normal programs and description-logic knowledge bases.

5.1   Syntax

Informally, a dl-program consists of a description-logic knowledge base L and a generalized program P, which may contain queries to L. Roughly, in such a query, it is asked whether a certain description-logic axiom or its negation logically follows from L or not.

A *dl-query* $Q(\mathbf{t})$ is either

(a) a concept inclusion axiom F or its negation $\neg F$; or
(b) of the form $C(t)$ or $\neg C(t)$, where C is a concept and t is a term; or
(c) of the form $R(t_1, t_2)$ or $\neg R(t_1, t_2)$, where R is a role and t_1, t_2 are terms.

A *dl-atom* is an expression of the form

$$DL[S_1 op_1 p_1, \ldots, S_m op_m p_m; Q](\mathbf{t}), \tag{4}$$

where $m \geq 0$, and such that each S_i is either a concept or a role, $op_i \in \{\uplus, \cup\}$, p_i is a unary resp. binary predicate symbol, and $Q(\mathbf{t})$ is a dl-query. We call $p_1, \ldots, p_m$ the *input predicate symbols* of (4). Intuitively, $op_i = \uplus$ (resp., $op_i = \cup$) increases S_i (resp., $\neg S_i$) by the extension of p_i.

A *dl-rule* r has the form (1),[8] where any literal $b_1, \ldots, b_m \in B(r)$ may be a dl-atom. We denote by $\widetilde{B}^+(r)$ (resp., $\widetilde{B}^-(r)$) the set of all dl-atoms in $B^+(r)$ (resp., $B^-(r)$). A *dl-program* $KB = (L, P)$ consists of a description-logic knowledge base L and a finite set P of dl-rules.

Positive and normal dl-rules are defined like for ordinary programs. A dl-program $KB = (L, P)$ is *positive*, if P is "*not*"-free, and is *normal*, if rule heads are literals (i.e., if $l = 1$ in (1)).

We illustrate dl-programs in terms of our running example.

Example 11 (Wine program, OWL). Suppose now that an ontology is available, formulated in OWL, which describes information about available wine bottles (as instances of a concept *Wine*), and contains (among others) further concepts *SweetWine*, *DryWine*, *RedWine*, and *WhiteWine* for different types of wine. The earlier program is modified by fetching the wines now from the ontology, using the following rule:

> % A suite of wine bottles and their kinds
> $wineBottle(X) \leftarrow DL[\text{``}Wine\text{''}](X).$

The *isA* predicate can then be defined by means of the following rules:

> % A suite of wine bottles and their kinds
> $isA(X, \text{``}sweetWine\text{''}) \leftarrow wineBottle(X), DL[\text{``}SweetWine\text{''}](X);$
> $isA(X, \text{``}dryWine\text{''}) \leftarrow wineBottle(X), DL[\text{``}dryWine\text{''}](X);$
> $isA(X, \text{``}redWine\text{''}) \leftarrow wineBottle(X), DL[\text{``}redWine\text{''}](X);$
> $isA(X, \text{``}whiteWine\text{''}) \leftarrow wineBottle(X), DL[\text{``}WhiteWine\text{''}](X).$

However, the *isA* predicate may be eliminated; instead of

> $compliantBottle(X, Z) \leftarrow preferredWine(X, Y), isA(Z, Y),$

we may write simply use

---

[8] In [18], only rules with $l = 1$ are considered; the extension to arbitrary l is straightforward.

% A suite of wine bottles and their kinds:

$$wineBottle(X) \leftarrow DL[``Wine"](X). \tag{5}$$

% Persons and their preferences:

$$person(``axel"); \quad preferredWine(``axel", ``whiteWine"); \tag{6}$$
$$person(``gibbi"); \quad preferredWine(``gibbi", ``redWine"); \tag{7}$$
$$person(``roman"); \quad preferredWine(``roman", ``dryWine"). \tag{8}$$

% Available bottles a person likes:

$$compliantBottle(X, Z) \leftarrow preferredWine(X, ``SweetWine"), wineBottle(Z), \\ DL[``SweetWine"](Z); \tag{9}$$

$$compliantBottle(X, Z) \leftarrow preferredWine(X, ``DryWine"), wineBottle(Z), \\ DL[``DryWine"](Z); \tag{10}$$

$$compliantBottle(X, Z) \leftarrow preferredWine(X, ``RedWine"), wineBottle(Z), \\ DL[``RedWine"](Z); \tag{11}$$

$$compliantBottle(X, Z) \leftarrow preferredWine(X, ``WhiteWine"), wineBottle(Z), \\ DL[``WhiteWine"](Z). \tag{12}$$

% Available bottles a person dislikes:

$$doesNotLike(X, Z) \leftarrow person(X), wineBottle(Z), not\ compliantBottle(X, Z). \tag{13}$$

% Generation of multiple answer sets:

$$bottleChosen(X) \vee -bottleChosen(X) \leftarrow compliantBottle(Y, X). \tag{14}$$

% Ensuring that each person gets a bottle:

$$hasBottleChosen(X) \leftarrow bottleChosen(X), compliantBottle(X, Z); \tag{15}$$
$$\leftarrow person(X), not\ hasBottleChosen(X). \tag{16}$$

Fig. 4. dl-program for wine selection

$$compliantBottle(X, Z) \leftarrow preferredWine(X, c), wineBottle(Z), DL[c](Z),$$

for each $c \in \{``SweetWine", ``DryWine", ``RedWine", ``WhiteWine"\}$. The resulting program is depicted in Fig. 4. Notice that Rules (5)–(12) form a positive normal dl-program. □

Example 12 (Wine program, OWL II). Suppose now that we learn that there is a bottle, *"SelaksIceWine"*, which is a white wine and not dry. We may add this information to the logic program using the facts

$$white(``SelaksIceWine") \text{ and } not\_dry(``SelaksIceWine").$$

In our program, we may pass this information to the ontology by adding in the dl-atoms the operations

"*WhiteWine*" ⊎ *white* and "*DryWine*"⊎*not_dry*.

For instance, $DL[\text{``}Wine\text{''}](X)$ is changed to $DL[\text{``}WhiteWine\text{''}\uplus white, \text{``}DryWine\text{''}\uplus not\_dry; \text{``}Wine\text{''}](X)$. □

5.2 Semantics

We first define Herbrand interpretations and the truth of dl-programs in Herbrand interpretations. In the sequel, let $KB = (L, P)$ be a dl-program.

The *Herbrand base* of P, denoted HB_P, is the set of all ground literals with a standard predicate symbol that occurs in P and constant symbols in Φ. We denote by DL_P be the set of all ground instances of dl-atoms with constant symbols in Φ.

An *interpretation* I *relative to* P is a consistent subset of HB_P. We say that I is a *model* of $\ell \in HB_P$ under L, denoted $I \models_L \ell$, iff $\ell \in I$, and of a ground dl-atom a of form (4) under L, denoted $I \models_L a$, iff $L \cup \bigcup_{i=1}^{m} A_i(I) \models Q(\mathbf{t})$, where

- for $op_i = \uplus$, $A_i(I) = \{S_i(\mathbf{e}) \mid p_i(\mathbf{e}) \in I\}$, and
- for $op_i = \ominus$, $A_i(I) = \{\neg S_i(\mathbf{e}) \mid p_i(\mathbf{e}) \in I\}$.

We say that I is a *model* of a ground dl-rule r under L, denoted $I \models_L r$, iff $I \models_L H(r)$ whenever $I \models_L l$ for all $l \in B^+(r)$ and $I \not\models_L l$ for all $l \in B^-(r)$. Furthermore, I is a model of a dl-program $KB = (L, P)$, denoted $I \models KB$, iff $I \models_L r$ for all $r \in ground(P)$. We say that KB is *satisfiable* (resp., *unsatisfiable*) iff it has some (resp., no) model.

Note that the herein introduced dl-atoms are *monotonic*: A ground dl-atom a is said to be monotonic whenever given two interpretations $I' \subseteq I''$ it holds that if $I' \models_L a$ then $I'' \models_L a$ as well.

Example 13 (Wine program, OWL, continued). Consider the interpretation

$$I = \{wineBottle(\text{``}TaylorPort\text{''}), preferredWine(\text{``}gibbi\text{''}, \text{``}redWine\text{''}),$$
$$isA(\text{``}TaylorPort\text{''}, \text{``}redWine\text{''})\},$$

and the rule r, given by:

$$isA(\text{``}TaylorPort\text{''}, \text{``}redWine\text{''}) \leftarrow wineBottle(\text{``}TaylorPort\text{''}),$$
$$DL[\text{``}RedWine\text{''}](\text{``}TaylorPort\text{''}).$$

Suppose "*RedWine*"("*TaylorPort*") is true in the ontology. Then, we have that $I \models_L DL[\text{``}RedWine\text{''}](\text{``}TaylorPort\text{''})$, and hence $I \models_L r$. On the other hand, $I \not\models_L s$, where s is given by

$$compliantBottle(\text{``}gibbi\text{''}, \text{``}TaylorPort\text{''}) \leftarrow preferredWine(\text{``}gibbi\text{''}, \text{``}redWine\text{''}),$$
$$wineBottle(\text{``}TaylorPort\text{''}),$$
$$DL[\text{``}RedWine\text{''}](\text{``}TaylorPort\text{''}),$$

since I contains all atoms in the body of s but not $H(s) = compliantBottle(\text{``}gibbi\text{''}, \text{``}TaylorPort\text{''})$. □

Minimal-model semantics of positive dl-programs. We first consider positive dl-programs. Like for ordinary positive programs, every nondisjunctive positive dl-program which is satisfiable has a single minimal model, which naturally characterizes its semantics. Observe that, as pointed out above, dl-atoms considered here are monotonic.

For ordinary normal positive programs P, it is well-known that the intersection of two models of P is also a model of P. A similar result holds for dl-programs.

Theorem 1. *Let $KB = (L, P)$ be a normal positive dl-program. If the interpretations $I_1, I_2 \subseteq HB_P$ are models of KB, then $I_1 \cap I_2$ is also a model of KB.*

As an immediate corollary of this result, every satisfiable positive dl-program KB has a unique least model, denoted M_{KB}, which is contained in every model of KB.

Corollary 1. *Let $KB = (L, P)$ be a normal positive dl-program. If KB is satisfiable, then there is a unique model $I \subseteq HB_P$ of KB such that $I \subseteq J$ for all models $J \subseteq HB_P$ of KB.*

Example 14. Consider Rules (5)–(12) in Fig. 4. Combined with the classical wine ontology, which is consistent, they have a single minimal model.   □

On the other hand, if a dl-program contains disjunction, then multiple minimal models of KB may exist.

Example 15. Consider again the program in Fig. 4, and disregard the rules containing default negation "*not*". In the wine ontology, each class *RedWine*, *WhiteWine*, and *DryWine* has several instances (and some of them have common instances, e.g., "*TaylorPort*"). Therefore, for each of *axel*, *gibbi*, and *roman*, multiple possibilities to choose a compliant bottle exist. In combination, they give rise to multiple answer sets of the reduced program.   □

Strong answer-set semantics of dl-programs. We now define the *strong answer-set semantics* of general dl-programs. It reduces to the minimal model semantics for positive dl-programs, using a generalized transformation that removes all NAF-literals.

In the sequel, let $KB = (L, P)$ be a dl-program.

Definition 1. *The* strong dl-reduct *of P relative to L and an interpretation $I \subseteq HB_P$, denoted sP_L^I, is the set of all dl-rules obtained from $ground(P)$ by*

(i) *deleting every dl-rule r such that $I \models_L \ell$ for some $\ell \in B^-(r)$, and*
(ii) *deleting from each remaining dl-rule r all literals in $B^-(r)$.*

Note that (L, sP_L^I) is a positive dl-program. Moreover, by Corollary 1, it has a least model if it is satisfiable and normal.

Definition 2. *Let $KB = (L, P)$ be a dl-program. A* strong answer set *of KB is an interpretation $I \subseteq HB_P$ such that I is a minimal model of (L, sP_L^I).*

Example 16 (Wine program, OWL continued). Suppose that the concept *RedWine* possesses the instances "*TaylorPort*" and "*ChiantiClassico*", *WhiteWine* the instance

"*SelaksIceWine*", and *DryWine* the instance "*ChateauMargaux*", and assume that *SweetWine* is empty. Note that these concepts are all subconcepts of *Wine*.

Consider the interpretation I which includes, besides the facts in the program, the following items:

> $compliantBottle$ ("*axel*", "*SelaksIceWine*");
> $compliantBottle$ ("*gibbi*", "*TaylorPort*");
> $compliantBottle$ ("*gibbi*", "*ChiantiClassico*");
> $compliantBottle$ ("*roman*", "*ChateauMargaux*");

> $bottleChosen$ ("*axel*"); $bottleChosen$ ("*gibbi*"); $bottleChosen$ ("*roman*");
> $hasBottleChosen$ ("*axel*"); $hasBottleChosen$ ("*gibbi*");
> $hasBottleChosen$ ("*roman*");

> $doesNotLike$ ("*axel*", "*TaylorPort*");
> $doesNotLike$ ("*axel*", "*ChiantiClassico*");
> $doesNotLike$ ("*axel*", "*ChateauMargaux*");
> $doesNotLike$ ("*gibbi*", "*SelaksIceWine*");
> $doesNotLike$ ("*gibbi*", "*ChateauMargaux*");
> $doesNotLike$ ("*roman*", "*SelaksIceWine*");
> $doesNotLike$ ("*roman*", "*TaylorPort*");
> $doesNotLike$ ("*roman*", "*ChiantiClassico*").

It can be checked that I is a strong answer set of KB. Indeed, I satisfies all positive rules in P, as well as all rules of form

$$doesNotLike(p, w) \leftarrow person(p), wineBottle(w),$$

stemming from Rule (13) in Fig. 4, for each pair p, w such that $compliantBottle(p, w)$ is not contained in I. Furthermore, Rule (16) vanishes in the reduction. Thus, I is a model of (L, sP_L^I). Moreover, I is minimal as no facts can be removed from it without losing modelhood. Therefore, I is an strong answer set of KB. $\square$

The following result shows that the strong answer-set semantics of a dl-program $KB = (L, P)$ conservatively extends the ordinary answer-set semantics of P.

Theorem 2. *Let $KB = (L, P)$ be a dl-program without dl-atoms. Then, $I \subseteq HB_P$ is a strong answer set of KB iff it is an answer set of the ordinary program P.*

As desired, strong answer sets of a dl-program KB are also models, and, moreover, minimal.

Theorem 3. *Let $KB = (L, P)$ be a dl-program and let M be a strong answer set of KB. Then, (a) M is a model of KB, and (b) M is a minimal model of KB.*

Proof. (a) Let I be a strong answer set of KB. To show that I is also a model of KB, we have to show that $I \models_L r$ for all $r \in ground(P)$. Consider any $r \in ground(P)$. Suppose that $I \models_L \ell$ for all $\ell \in B^+(r)$ and $I \not\models_L \ell$ for all $\ell \in B^-(r)$. Then, the dl-rule r' that is obtained from r by removing all the literals in $B^-(r)$ is contained in sP_L^I. Since I is a minimal model of (L, sP_L^I) and thus in particular a model of (L, sP_L^I), it follows that I is a model of r'. Since $I \models_L \ell$ for all $\ell \in B^+(r')$ and $I \not\models_L \ell$ for all $\ell \in B^-(r') = \emptyset$,

it follows that $I \models_L \ell'$ for some $\ell' \in H(r)$. This shows that $I \models_L r$. Also, each rule $r \in ground(P)$ having no counterpart in sP_L^I is trivially modeled by I since $I \not\models B(r)$.
Hence, I is a model of KB.

(b) By Part (a), every strong answer set I of KB is a model of KB. We show that I is a minimal model of KB. Towards a contradiction, suppose that there exists a model J of KB such that $J \subset I$. Since J is a model of KB, it follows that J is also a model of (L, sP_L^I). As every dl-atom in DL_P is monotonic relative to KB, it then follows that $sP_L^I \subseteq sP_L^J$. Hence, J is also a model of (L, sP_L^I). But this contradicts that I is a minimal model of (L, sP_L^I). Hence, I is a minimal model of KB. $\qquad\square$

Note that every normal positive dl-program KB has at most one strong answer set, which coincides with the single minimal model of KB.

5.3 Further Examples

Closed-world reasoning. As stressed in Section 4, it is acknowledged that many Semantic-Web application scenarios require some form of closed-world reasoning [1,28].

Using dl-programs, the CWA may be easily expressed on top of an external knowledge base which can be queried through suitable dl-atoms. We show this here for a description-logic knowledge base L.

Intuitively given a concept C, its negated version $\bar{C}$ (under CWA) is defined by adding to a given dl-program the rule

$$\bar{C}(X) \leftarrow not\ DL[C](X)$$

For example, given that $L = \{\ WhiteWine \sqsubseteq Wine,\ Wine(``ChiantiClassico")\}$, for concepts $WhiteWine$ and $Wine$, the CWA infers $\neg WhiteWine(``ChiantiClassico")$.

As well known, the CWA can lead to inconsistent conclusions. If, in the above example, L contains further axioms

$$Wine = WhiteWine \sqcup \neg RedWine \text{ and}$$
$$\bot = WhiteWine \sqcap \neg RedWine,$$

then the CWA infers

$$\overline{WhiteWine}(``ChiantiClassico") \text{ and } \overline{RedWine}(``ChiantiClassico"),$$

which is inconsistent with L.

We can check inconsistency of the CWA with the further rule

$$fail \leftarrow DL[\ WhiteWine \uplus \overline{WhiteWine},\ RedWine \uplus \overline{RedWine};\ \bot](b),\ not\ fail,$$

where $\bot$ is the empty concept (entailment of $\bot(b)$, for any constant b, is tantamount to inconsistency).

Workarounds to these semantic difficulties are well known in the literature: minimal-model reasoning, or the extended closed-world assumption (ECWA), for instance, avoid the problem of CWA inconsistency [9,23]. These extensions can be easily implemented in the framework of dl-programs, by means of a suitable encoding that computes minimal models of a knowledge base L. Intuitively, building minimal models of L corresponds to concluding as much negative facts as possible while keeping consistency.

Default reasoning. By *maximizing* rather than *minimizing* extensions, default reasoning, as in the approach by Poole [48], on top of a description-logic knowledge base may be supported. The rationale is to associate to individuals default values for concept and roles. Default information is maximized, in the sense that it is propagated as much as possible unless inconsistency arises.

Although acknowledged as being essential for modeling reasoning in the Semantic-Web context (see, e.g., [3]), description-logic knowledge bases do not allow nonmonotonic inheritance. This often causes many ontology design problems, especially in those cases where overriding some default-concept property value is the most natural way of defining a subclass. Defaults are especially tailored at implementing nonmonotonic inheritance. For example, the rules

$$shouldbewhite(W) \leftarrow DL[sparklingWine](W), not\ nonwhite(W),$$
$$nonwhite(W) \leftarrow DL[WhiteWine \uplus shouldbewhite; \neg WhiteWine](W)$$

on top of a part, L, of the wine ontology express that sparkling wines are white by default. Given

$$L = \{\ sparklingWine(``VeuveCliquot"),$$
$$(sparklingWine \sqcap \neg whiteWine)(``Lambrusco")\},$$

we then can conclude $white(``VeuveCliquot")$ and $nonwhite(``Lambrusco")$.

5.4   Additional Features of dl-programs

An interesting fragment of dl-programs are *stratified dl-programs*, which are, intuitively, composed of hierarchic layers of positive dl-programs linked via default negation. This generalization of the classic notion of stratification embodies a fragment of the language having single answer sets. Semantics for programs (or sub-programs) belonging to this fragment can be evaluated at a less expensive computational cost [15].

Furthermore, it is possible to evaluate dl-programs either under *weak answer-set semantics* [18] and a *well-founded semantics* [19]. The former does not make any assumption on the nature of a dl-atom (whereas *monotonic* dl-atoms are treated explicitly in the semantics discussed here), while the latter is a generalization of the traditional well-founded semantics [56] for dl-programs.

5.5   Prototype Implementation

A fully operational prototype, named *NLP-DL*, ready for experiments, is available via a Web interface at

```
http://www.kr.tuwien.ac.at/staff/roman/semweblp/
```

The system accepts nondisjunctive dl-programs as input,[9] given by an ontology formulated in OWL DL (as processed by RACER [26]) and a set of dl-rules in the language above, where $\leftarrow$, $\uplus$, and $\cup$, are written as ":-", "+=", and "-=", respectively. The following reasoning tasks are featured:

---

[9] An implementation of disjunctive dl-programs is available through dlvhex, an implementation of HEX-programs (see next section for details about HEX-programs and dlvhex).

(i) *Computing models (answer sets or the well-founded model) of a given dl-program:* For computing the answer sets, a preliminary computation of the well-founded model may be issued, which semantically approximates the answer sets—this is exploited for optimization.

(ii) *Evaluating a given query on a given dl-program:* Under the answer-set semantics, both *brave reasoning* and *cautious reasoning* are available.

The system architecture integrates the external DLV [36] and RACER engines, the latter being embedded into a caching module, a well-founded semantics module, an answer-set semantics module, a pre-processing module, and a post-processing module.

Each internal module has been implemented using the PHP scripting language; the overhead is insignificant, provided that most of the computing power is devoted to the execution of the two external reasoners. In particular, efficient usage of RACER is critical for the system performance. Respective techniques, mainly based on caching query results and exploiting monotonicity of description-logic reasoning, are described in [15].

6 Extensions

Example 17 (Motivating Example, Part III). Now that a machinery, automatically generating a selection of wine bottles for the social dinner, is ready, the organizers wonder whether it is possible to accomplish this task in a better way. After all, the Semantic Web envisions a world where machine-to-machine protocols express their full potential, and people are freed from most annoying jobs. In this context, multiple domain descriptions (i.e., multiple ontologies), possibly with differing semantics, may interact closely and have to be ready for information exchange.

For instance, most of the attendees may have his or her own FOAF [21] description on-line. These description might potentially publish all the public data about an attendee, including his or her preferred wine. However, now the organizers notice that they need some formalism powerful enough to interface several formalisms and multiple ontologies at once.   □

6.1 HEX-programs

HEX-programs generalize dl-programs with regard to the following features:

– The notion of a dl-atom is generalized to that of an *external atom*. The latter kind of atom may bind knowledge coming from different external formalisms, with possibly differing semantics. Also, an external atom can delegate special tasks to traditional programs (such as string processing), for which logic programming is not tailored at. For instance, it is possible to merge RDF ontologies with OWL ontologies, as in the following small program:

$$triple(X, Y, Z) \leftarrow url(U), \&rdf[U](X, Y, Z);$$
$$\leftarrow \&DLinconsistent[triple].$$

Also, possible external sources of knowledge can be merged with arbitrary strategies, and can bring in new symbols not appearing elsewhere in a given program ("value invention").

- It is made possible to quantify over sets of concepts just as it is done with individuals, and to freely exchange the former objects with the latter ones. These meta-reasoning features are enabled by means of *higher-order atoms*, such as in the rule

$$\text{“wine:Wine”}(X) \leftarrow triple(X, \text{“rdf:type”}, \text{“wine:Wine”}).$$

- Logic programs are made compatible with naming conventions employed in the Semantic-Web world. Thus, a directive such as

$$\#namespace(wine, \texttt{“http://www.w3.org/TR/2003/}$$
$$\texttt{PR-owl-guide-20031209/wine\#”})$$

allows to interpret the constant symbol "wine:Wine" as a shortcut for the symbol

```
"http://www.w3.org/TR/2003/PR-owl-guide-20031209/
wine#Wine".
```

In this section, we briefly discuss HEX-programs; for further details, see [14].

6.2   Syntax and Semantics

HEX-programs are built on mutually disjoint sets $\mathcal{C}$, $\mathcal{X}$, and $\mathcal{G}$ of *constant names, variable names*, and *external predicate names*, respectively. Unless stated otherwise, elements from $\mathcal{X}$ (resp., $\mathcal{C}$) are denoted with first letter in upper case (resp., lower case); elements from $\mathcal{G}$ are prefixed with " & ".[10] Constant names serve both as individual and predicate names. Importantly, $\mathcal{C}$ may be infinite.

Elements from $\mathcal{C} \cup \mathcal{X}$ are called *terms*. A *higher-order atom* (or *atom*) is a tuple $(Y_0, Y_1, \ldots, Y_n)$, where $Y_0, \ldots, Y_n$ are terms; $n \geq 0$ is its *arity*. Intuitively, Y_0 is the predicate name; we thus also use the familiar notation $Y_0(Y_1, \ldots, Y_n)$. The atom is *ordinary*, if Y_0 is a constant. For example, $(x, rdf{:}type, c)$ and $node(X)$ are ordinary atoms, while $D(a, b)$ is a higher-order atom. An *external atom* is of the form

$$\&g[Y_1, \ldots, Y_n](X_1, \ldots, X_m),$$

where $Y_1, \ldots, Y_n$ and $X_1, \ldots, X_m$ are two lists of terms (called *input list* and *output list*, respectively), and $\&g \in \mathcal{G}$ is an external predicate name. We assume that $\&g$ has fixed lengths $in(\&g) = n$ and $out(\&g) = m$, respectively. Intuitively, an external atom provides a way for deciding the truth value of an output tuple depending on the extension of a set of input predicates.

Example 18. The external atom $\&reach[edge, a](X)$ may compute the nodes reachable in the graph *edge* from the node a. Here, $in(\&reach) = 2$ and $out(\&reach) = 1$.   □

A HEX-*program*, P, is a finite set of rules of form (1), where literals in the heads of rules are (higher-order) atoms, and literals in the bodies of rules contain either (higher-order) atoms or external atoms.

---

[10] In [14], " # " is used instead of " & "; the change is motivated to be in accord with the syntax of the prototype system.

The semantics of HEX-programs generalizes the answer-set semantics [22], and is defined using the *FLP-reduct* [20], which is more elegant than the traditional reduct and ensures minimality of answer sets.

The *Herbrand base* of a HEX-program P, denoted HB_P, is the set of all possible ground versions of atoms and external atoms occurring in P obtained by replacing variables with constants from $\mathcal{C}$. The grounding of a rule r, $ground(r)$, is defined accordingly, and the grounding of program P is $ground(P) = \bigcup_{r \in P} ground(r)$.

Example 19. For $\mathcal{C} = \{edge, arc, a, b\}$, ground instances of $E(X, b)$ are, for instance, $edge(a, b)$, $arc(a, b)$, and $arc(arc, b)$; ground instances of $\&reach[edge, N](X)$ are $\&reach[edge, edge](a)$, $\&reach[edge, arc](b)$, and $\&reach[edge, edge](edge)$, etc. □

An *interpretation relative to* P is any subset $I \subseteq HB_P$ containing only atoms. We say that I is a *model* of atom $a \in HB_P$, denoted $I \models a$, if $a \in I$. With every external predicate name $\&g \in \mathcal{G}$ we associate an $(n+m+1)$-ary Boolean function $f_{\&g}$ (called *oracle function*) assigning each tuple $(I, y_1 \ldots, y_n, x_1, \ldots, x_m)$ either 0 or 1, where $n = in(\&g)$, $m = out(\&g)$, $I \subseteq HB_P$, and $x_i, y_j \in \mathcal{C}$. We say that $I \subseteq HB_P$ is a *model* of a ground external atom $a = \&g[y_1, \ldots, y_n](x_1, \ldots, x_m)$, denoted $I \models a$, iff $f_{\&g}(I, y_1 \ldots, y_n, x_1, \ldots, x_m) = 1$.

Example 20. Associate with the external predicate name $\&reach$ a function $f_{\&reach}$ such that $f_{\&reach}(I, E, A, B) = 1$ iff B is reachable in the graph E from A. Let $I = \{e(b, c), e(c, d)\}$. Then, I is a model of the external atom $\&reach[e, b](d)$ since $f_{\&reach}(I, e, b, d) = 1$. □

Let r be a ground rule. We define (i) $I \models H(r)$ iff there is some $a \in H(r)$ such that $I \models a$, (ii) $I \models B(r)$ iff $I \models a$ for all $a \in B^+(r)$ and $I \not\models a$ for all $a \in B^-(r)$, and (iii) $I \models r$ iff $I \models H(r)$ whenever $I \models B(r)$. We say that I is a *model* of a HEX-program P, denoted $I \models P$, iff $I \models r$ for all $r \in ground(P)$.

The *FLP-reduct* [20] of P with respect to $I \subseteq HB_P$, denoted fP^I, is the set of all $r \in ground(P)$ such that $I \models B(r)$. $I \subseteq HB_P$ is an *answer set of* P iff I is a minimal model of fP^I.

Differences between the FLP-reduct and the strong dl-reduct. The two above semantics are not equivalent in the presence of nonmonotonic external atoms, where the notion of monotonicity for an external atom generalizes that for dl-atoms. Let us assume to have an external predicate $\&neg$, defined in such a way that the ground atom $\&neg[p](a)$ satisfies $I \not\models \&neg[p](a)$ whenever an interpretation I is such that $I \models p(a)$ (i.e., $\&neg$ reproduces the behavior of the usual negation as failure). The program P, consisting of the single rule

$$p(a) \leftarrow not \ \&neg[p](a),$$

has $S_1 = \{p(a)\}$ as a strong answer set. However, also $S_2 = \emptyset$ is a strong answer set of P, thus S_1 is not minimal. It is often desirable that answer sets are incomparable as in the above case: intuitively, self-supportedness of an atom such as in the rule $p(a) \leftarrow p(a)$ should not give evidence of the truth of $p(a)$.

The FLP-reduct overcomes these drawbacks. Indeed, it can be proven that this reduct produces only incomparable answer sets: under FLP semantics, S_1 is not an answer set.

6.3 Further Examples

With HEX-programs, it is possible to extract information from different sources in the same program.

Assume we want to invite all friends of Axel Polleres for dinner, and that their wine preferences are given by means of their FOAF descriptions. To this end, we introduce the *&rdf* atom for dealing with RDF sources, and the *&dlC* atom that mimics partially the semantics of a dl-atom. An atom $\&rdf[u](s, p, o)$ is true if $\langle s\ p\ o\rangle$ is an RDF triple asserted at URI u. Also, $\&dlC[u, c](x)$ is true if x is an individual which can be proved to belong to class c in the knowledge base located at URI u (under OWL semantics).

First, namespace directives allow us to deal with individuals and concepts (constant symbols) coming from different Web sources:

$\#namespace(wine,$ "http://www.w3.org/TR/2003/
              PR-owl-guide-20031209/wine#");

$\#namespace(foaf,$ "http://xmlns.com/foaf/0.1/");

$\#namespace(rdf,$ "http://www.w3.org/1999/02/
              22-rdf-syntax-ns#");

$\#namespace(foafplus,$ "http://www.example.org/foafplus");

$\#namespace(rdfs,$ "http://www.w3.org/2000/01/rdf-schema#").

```
<foaf:PersonalProfileDocument rdf:about="">
  <foaf:maker rdf:resource="#me"/>
  <foaf:primaryTopic rdf:resource="#me"/>
  ...
</foaf:PersonalProfileDocument>

  <foaf:Person rdf:ID="me">
    <foaf:name>Axel Polleres</foaf:name>
    ...
    <foaf:knows>
      <foaf:Person>

        <foaf:name>Giovambattista Ianni</foaf:name>
        <foaf:mbox>ianni@mat.unical.it</foaf:mbox>
        <rdfs:seeAlso rdf:resource=
         "http://www.gibbi.com/test_foaf.gibbi.rdf"/>
      </foaf:Person>
    </foaf:knows>
      ...
    <foafplus:winePreference rdf:resource="&vin;SweetWine"/>
  </foaf:Person>
```

Fig. 5. An example FOAF description, extended with the foafplus:winePreference property

Suppose now that a FOAF description is given, like in Fig. 5. This FOAF description is enriched with the property `foafplus:winePreference` which expresses a wine preference for a given person. This small description can be interfaced with a HEX-program in the following way:

$$Y(X, Z, triple) \leftarrow \& rdf[U](X, Y, Z), foafurl(U);$$
$$T(X, triple) \leftarrow \text{"rdf:type"}(X, T, triple).$$

The above rules materialize the RDF triples contained in Axel's FOAF description.

Then, the predicate *preferredWine* is now computed by extracting data from external descriptions of Axel's friends (note that further external ontologies are consulted whose locations depend on the first consulted ontology):

$$mainEntity(M, triple) \leftarrow \text{"foaf:primaryTopic"}(X, M, triple),$$
$$\text{"foaf:PersonalProfileDocument"}(X, triple);$$
$$community(A, Y) \leftarrow \text{"foaf:knows"}(X, A, triple),$$
$$\text{"rdfs:seeAlso"}(A, Y, triple);$$
$$preferredWine(M, Y) \leftarrow \text{"foafplus:winePreference"}(M, Y, triple),$$
$$mainEntity(M, triple);$$
$$preferredWine(X, Y) \leftarrow community(X, U),$$
$$\& rdf[U](\text{"foafplus:winePreference"}, Y).$$

The next rule facilitates the quantification over concept names given to the predicate `&dlC`:

$$compliantBottle(X, Z) \leftarrow wineurl(U), preferredWine(X, Y),$$
$$\& dlC[U, Y](Z).$$

Note that this rule allows to generalize, for instance, Rules (9)–(12) of the program given in Fig. 4. The rest of the program is very similar to the latter one:

$$bottleChosen(X) \vee -bottleChosen(X) \leftarrow compliantBottle(Y, X);$$
$$hasBottleChosen(X) \leftarrow bottleChosen(Z), compliantBottle(X, Z);$$

$$\leftarrow preferredWine(X, Y), not\ hasBottleChosen(X);$$
$$:\sim bottleChosen(X)\ [1].$$

6.4 Prototype Implementation

An experimental prototype for evaluating HEX-programs, called dlvhex, is available and executable on the Web at

http://www.kr.tuwien.ac.at/research/dlvhex/

Apart from implementing the semantics of HEX-programs, dlvhex supports a number of built-in functions as well as integrity and weak constraints. Its further development is work in progress.

The principle behind dlvhex is to represent a framework that integrates a native answer-set solver—here, DLV [36]—and the external reasoners underlying the external atoms. Optionally, dlvhex can integrate DLT [10] as a pre-parser to allow for templates and frame syntax within HEX-programs. Due to the bidirectional nature of external atoms, they cannot be evaluated prior to calling the answer-set solver. Instead, dlvhex builds the dependency graph of the HEX-program, identifying minimal sets of nodes that involve external atoms, which have to be solved by specifically tailored algorithms. This strategy, which is described in more detail in [16] and [17], relies basically on a modified version of the well-known splitting-set theorem for ordinary logic programs [40].

The evaluation functions of the external atoms are defined completely independent from dlvhex by so called *plug-ins*, which can contain the implementations of several atoms. The currently available external atoms are the *RDF Plug-in*, the *Description-Logics Plug-in* and the *String Plug-in*, described below.

The RDF Plug-in. The RDF plug-in currently provides a single external atom, the &*rdf* atom, which enables the user to import RDF triples from any RDF knowledge base. It takes a single constant as input, which denotes the RDF source (a file path or a Web address). The &*rdf* atom interfaces with the RAPTOR RDF library.

The Description-Logics Plug-in. In order to model dl-programs [18] in terms of HEX-programs, the Description-Logics Plug-in has been developed. This plug-in includes three external atoms (these atoms, in accord to the semantics of dl-programs, also allow for extending a description-logic knowledge base, before submitting a query, by means of the atoms' input parameters):

- the &*dlC* atom, which queries a concept (specified by an input parameter of the atom) and retrieves its individuals;
- the &*dlR* atom, which queries an object property and retrieves its individual pairs;
- the &*dlDR* atom, which queries a datatype property and retrieves its pairs; and
- the &*dlConsistent* atom, which tests the (possibly extended) description-logic knowledge base for consistency.

The Description-Logics Plug-in can access OWL ontologies, i.e., description-logic knowledge bases in the language $\mathcal{SHOIN}(\mathbf{D})$, utilizing the RACER [26] reasoning engine.

The String Plug-in. The task of the String Plug-in is to realize simple string manipulations.

Currently, dlvhex, together with the presented plug-ins, are available as source packages. Moreover, a toolkit for developing custom plug-in is supplied as well, embedded in the GNU auto-tools environment, which takes care for the low-level, system-specific build process and which allows the plug-in author to concentrate his or her efforts on the implementation of the plug-in's actual core functionality.

7   Discussion and Conclusion

We have considered reasoning with rules and ontologies, taking an answer-set programming perspective. A number of approaches for combining rules and ontologies have been presented so far, and the quest for the Holy Grail of an ideally suited formalism (which might not exist) is still ongoing. As we have briefly discussed, a number of issues come up when combining rules as in logic programming and ontologies formalized in classical logic. Bridging the quite different worlds of logic programs and ontologies has been attempted in different approaches, which may be grouped in "tightly" coupled and "loosely" coupled approaches.

The approach which is closest in spirit to dl-programs is Rosati's $\mathcal{DL}+log$ formalism [52,53], which extends his previous work [50,51]. In this approach, predicates are split into *ontology predicates* and into *logic-program (datalog) predicates*. A notion of model of a combined rule and ontology knowledge base is defined using a two-step reduct in which, in the first step, the ontology predicates are eliminated under the open-world assumption (OWA) and, in the second step, the negated logic-programming predicates under the closed-world assumption (CWA). As shown by Rosati, the emerging formalism (which focuses on first-order models under the standard-names assumption), is decidable provided that conjunctive-query answering over the underlying ontology is decidable. The main differences between $\mathcal{DL}+log$ and dl-programs are as follows:

- $\mathcal{DL}+log$ is a tight coupling, while dl-programs provide a loose coupling of rules and ontologies.
- While extensions of dl-programs to integrate ontologies even in different formats are straightforward, there is no corresponding counterpart in $\mathcal{DL}+log$.
- The approach of dl-atoms is more flexible for mixing different reasoning modalities, such as consistency checking and logical consequence. In the realm of HEX-programs, almost arbitrary combinations can be conceived.
- The coupling as realized in dl-programs aims at facilitating interoperability of existing reasoning systems and software (such as DLV and RACER). On the other hand, the loose coupling requires a bridging between the two worlds of ontologies and rules, which has to be provided by the user. In particular, this applies to the individuals at the instance level.

The development and theoretical study of HEX-programs is ongoing. Algorithms and techniques for efficient implementation are in an advanced stage of progression. In a sense, rules are per se a form or knowledge that needs to be exchanged and evaluated under different semantics. To this end, we are developing an exchange format aimed at fitting answer-set programming in the RuleML standard. In conclusion, although quite some efforts have been spent on combining rules and ontologies, there is still a lot of work to be done.

References

1. A. Analyti, G. Antoniou, C. V. Damásio, and G. Wagner. Stable Model Theory for Extended RDF Ontologies. In *Proc. Fourth International Semantic Web Conference (ISWC 2005)*, pp. 21–36, 2005.
2. J. Angele, H. Boley, J. de Bruijn, D. Fensel, P. Hitzler, M. Kifer, R. Krummenacher, H. Lausen, A. Polleres, and R. Studer. Web Rule Language (WRL), Sept. 2005. W3C Member Submission, http://www.w3.org/Submission/WRL/.

3. G. Antoniou. Nonmonotonic Rule Systems on Top of Ontology Layers. In *Proc. First International Semantic Web Conference (2002)*, volume 2342 of *Lecture Notes in Computer Science (LNCS)*, pp. 394–398, 2002.

4. G. Antoniou, C. V. Damásio, B. Grosof, I. Horrocks, M. Kifer, J. Maluszynski, and P. F. Patel-Schneider. Combining Rules and Ontologies: A survey. Technical Report IST506779/Linköping/I3-D3/D/PU/a1, Linköping University, February 2005. IST-2004-506779 REWERSE Deliverable I3-D3. http://rewerse.net/publications/.

5. F. Baader, D. Calvanese, D. L. McGuinness, D. Nardi, and P. F. Patel-Schneider, editors. *The Description Logic Handbook: Theory, Implementation, and Applications*. Cambridge University Press, 2003.

6. C. Baral. *Knowledge Representation, Reasoning, and Declarative Problem Solving*. Cambridge University Press, Cambridge, UK, 2003.

7. T. Berners-Lee. Web for Real People, April 2005. Keynote Speech at the 14th World Wide Web Conference (WWW2005). Slides available at http://www.w3.org/2005/Talks/0511-keynote-tbl/.

8. F. Buccafurri, N. Leone, and P. Rullo. Enhancing Disjunctive Datalog by Constraints. *IEEE Transactions on Knowledge and Data Engineering*, 12(5):845–860, 2000.

9. M. Cadoli and M. Lenzerini. The Complexity of Propositional Closed World Reasoning and Circumscription. *Journal of Computer and System Sciences*, 43:165–211, April 1994.

10. F. Calimeri, G. Ianni, G. Ielpa, A. Pietramala, and M. C. Santoro. A System with Template Answer Set Programs. In *Proc. Ninth European Conference on Artificial Intelligence (JELIA 2004)*, volume 3229 of *Lecture Notes in AI (LNAI)*, pp. 693–697. Springer Verlag, 2004.

11. M. Dean, G. Schreiber, S. Bechhofer, F. van Harmelen, J. Hendler, I. Horrocks, D. L. McGuinness, P. F. Patel-Schneider, and L. A. Stein. OWL Web Ontology Language Reference, Feb. 2004. W3C Recommendation.

12. F. M. Donini, M. Lenzerini, D. Nardi, and A. Schaerf. $\mathcal{AL}$-log: Integrating Datalog and Description Logics. *Journal of Intelligent Information Systems (JIIS)*, 10(3):227–252, 1998.

13. The 2005 IEEE International Conference on e-Technology, e-Commerce and e-Service (EEE-05) contest. http://www.comp.hkbu.edu.hk/~eee05/contest/.

14. T. Eiter, G. Ianni, R. Schindlauer, and H. Tompits. A Uniform Integration of Higher-Order Reasoning and External Evaluations in Answer Set Programming. In *Proc. 19th International Joint Conference on Artificial Intelligence (IJCAI 2005)*. Morgan Kaufmann, 2005.

15. T. Eiter, G. Ianni, R. Schindlauer, and H. Tompits. Nonmonotonic Description Logic Programs: Implementation and Experiments. In F. Baader and A. Voronkov, editors, *Proc. Eleventh International Conference on Logic for Programming, Artificial Intelligence, and Reasoning (LPAR 2004)*, number 3452 in LNCS, pp. 511–527. Springer, 2005.

16. T. Eiter, G. Ianni, R. Schindlauer, and H. Tompits. Effective Integration of Declarative Rules with External Evaluations for Semantic Web Reasoning. In Y. Sure and J. Domingue, editors, *Proc. Third European Semantic Web Conference (ESWC 2006)*, number 4011 in LNCS, pp. 273–287. Springer, 2006.

17. T. Eiter, G. Ianni, R. Schindlauer, and H. Tompits. Towards Efficient Evaluation of HEX Programs. In J. Dix and A. Hunter, editors, *Proc. Eleventh International Workshop on Nonmonotonic Reasoning (NMR 2006), Answer Set Programming Track*, pp. 40–46, 2006.

18. T. Eiter, T. Lukasiewicz, R. Schindlauer, and H. Tompits. Combining Answer Set Programming with Description Logics for the Semantic Web. In *Proc. Ninth International Conference on Principles of Knowledge Representation and Reasoning (KR2004)*, pp. 141–151, 2004.

19. T. Eiter, T. Lukasiewicz, R. Schindlauer, and H. Tompits. Well-Founded Semantics for Description Logic Programs in the Semantic Web. In *Proc. ISWC 2004 Workshop on Rules and Rule Markup Languages for the Semantic Web (RuleML 2004)*, volume 3323 of *Lecture Notes in Computer Science (LNCS)*, pp. 81–97. Springer Verlag, 2004.

20. W. Faber, N. Leone, and G. Pfeifer. Recursive Aggregates in Disjunctive Logic Programs: Semantics and Complexity. In *Proc. Ninth European Conference on Artificial Intelligence (JELIA 2004)*, number 3229 in Lecture Notes in AI (LNAI), pp. 200–212. Springer Verlag, 2004.
21. The Friend of a Friend (FOAF) Project. http://www.foaf-project.org/.
22. M. Gelfond and V. Lifschitz. Classical Negation in Logic Programs and Disjunctive Databases. *New Generation Computing*, 9:365–385, 1991.
23. M. Gelfond, H. Przymusinska, and T. C. Przymusinski. The Extended Closed World Assumption and its Relationship to Parallel Circumscription. In *Proc. Fifth ACM SIGACT-SIGMOD Symposium on Principles of Database Systems (PODS '86)*, pp. 133–139, 1986.
24. B. N. Grosof, I. Horrocks, R. Volz, and S. Decker. Description Logic Programs: Combining Logic Programs with Description Logics. In *Proc. Twelfth International World Wide Web Conference (WWW 2003)*, pp. 48–57, 2003.
25. T. R. Gruber. A Translation Approach to Portable Ontology Specifications. *Knowledge Acquisition*, 5:199–220, 1993.
26. V. Haarslev and R. Möller. RACER System Description. In *Proc. First International Joint Conference on Automated Reasoning (IJCAR 2001)*, volume 2083 of *Lecture Notes in Computer Science (LNCS)*, pp. 701–705. Springer Verlag, 2001.
27. P. Hayes. RDF semantics. http://www.w3.org/TR/rdf-mt/.
28. J. Heflin and H. Munoz-Avila. LCW-Based Agent Planning for the Semantic Web. In *Proc. AAAI Workshop on Ontologies and the Semantic Web*, pp. 63–70, 1998.
29. S. Heymans, D. V. Nieuwenborgh, and D. Vermeir. Nonmonotonic Ontological and Rule-Based Reasoning with Extended Conceptual Logic Programs. In *Proc. Second European Semantic Web Conference (ESWC 2005)*, volume 3532 of *Lecture Notes in Computer Science (LNCS)*, pp. 392–407. Springer Verlag, 2005.
30. S. Heymans, D. V. Nieuwenborgh, and D. Vermeir. Preferential Reasoning on a Web of Trust. In *Proc. Fourth International Semantic Web Conference (ISWC 2005)*, volume 3729 of *Lecture Notes in Computer Science (LNCS)*, pp. 368–382. Springer Verlag, 2005.
31. I. Horrocks, P. F. Patel-Schneider, H. Boley, S. Tabet, B. Grosof, and M. Dean. SWRL: A Semantic Web Rule Language Combining OWL and RuleML, May 2004. W3C Member Submission. http://www.w3.org/Submission/SWRL/.
32. I. Horrocks, U. Sattler, and S. Tobies. Practical Reasoning for Very Expressive Description Logics. *Logic Journal of the IGPL*, 8(3):239–264, 2000.
33. ICONS homepage, since 2001. http://www.icons.rodan.pl/.
34. T. Janhunen, I. Niemelä, D. Seipel, P. Simons, and J.-H. You. Unfolding Partiality and Disjunctions in Stable Model Semantics. *ACM Transactions on Computational Logic*, 7(1):1–37, 2006.
35. N. Leone, G. Gottlob, R. Rosati, T. Eiter, W. Faber, M. Fink, G. Greco, G. Ianni, E. Kałka, D. Lembo, M. Lenzerini, V. Lio, B. Nowicki, M. Ruzzi, W. Staniszkis, and G. Terracina. The INFOMIX System for Advanced Integration of Incomplete and Inconsistent Data. In *Proc. 24th ACM SIGMOD International Conference on Management of Data (SIGMOD 2005)*, pp. 915–917. ACM Press, 2005.
36. N. Leone, G. Pfeifer, W. Faber, T. Eiter, G. Gottlob, S. Perri, and F. Scarcello. The DLV System for Knowledge Representation and Reasoning. *ACM Transactions on Computational Logic*, 2005. To appear. Available at http://www.arxiv.org/ps/cs.AI/0211004.
37. A. Y. Levy and M.-C. Rousset. Combining Horn Rules and Description Logics in CARIN. *Artificial Intelligence*, 104(1-2):165–209, 1998.
38. Y. Lierler. Disjunctive Answer Set Programming via Satisfiability. In *Proc. Eighth International Conference on Logic Programming and Nonmonotonic Reasoning (LPNMR 2005)*, volume 3662 of *Lecture Notes in Computer Science (LNCS)*, pp. 447–451. Springer Verlag, 2005.

39. V. Lifschitz. Answer Set Planning. In *Proc. 16th International Conference on Logic Programming (ICLP '99)*, pp. 23–37. MIT Press, 1999.
40. V. Lifschitz and H. Turner. Splitting a Logic Program. In *Proc. Eleventh International Conference on Logic Programming (ICLP '94)*, pp. 23–38. MIT Press, 1994.
41. T. Lukasiewicz. Stratified Probabilistic Description Logic Programs. In *Proc. ISWC 2005 Workshop on Uncertainty Reasoning for the Semantic Web*, pp. 87–97, 2005.
42. W. Marek and M. Truszczyński. Stable Logic Programming - An Alternative Logic Programming Paradigm. In K. Apt, W. Marek, and M. Truszczyński, editors, *The Logic Programming Paradigm*, pp. 375–398. Springer Verlag, 1999.
43. B. Motik, U. Sattler, and R. Studer. Query Answering for OWL-DL with Rules. *Journal of Web Semantics: Science, Services and Agents on the World Wide Web*, 3(1):41–60, 2005.
44. I. Niemelä. Logic Programs with Stable Model Semantics as a Constraint Programming Paradigm. *Annals of Mathematics and Artificial Intelligence*, 25(3-4):241–273, 1999.
45. I. Niemelä, P. Simons, and T. Soininen. Stable Model Semantics of Weight Constraint Rules. In *Proc. Fifth International Conference on Logic Programming and Nonmonotonic Reasoning (LPNMR '99)*, volume 1730 of *Lecture Notes in AI (LNAI)*, pp. 107–116. Springer Verlag, 1999.
46. J. Z. Pan, E. Franconi, S. Tessaris, G. Stamou, V. Tzouvaras, L. Serafini, I. R. Horrocks, and B. Glimm. Specification of Coordination of Rule and Ontology Languages. Project Deliverable D2.5.1, KnowledgeWeb NoE, June 2004.
47. P. F. Patel-Schneider, P. Hayes, and I. Horrocks. OWL Web Ontology Language Semantics and Abstract Syntax, Feb. 2004. W3C Recommendation.
48. D. Poole. A Logical Framework for Default Reasoning. *Artificial Intelligence*, 36:27–47, 1988.
49. A. Rainer. Web Service Composition under Answer Set Programming. In *Proc. KI 2005 Workshop "Planen, Scheduling und Konfigurieren, Entwerfen" (PuK 2005)*, 2005.
50. R. Rosati. Towards Expressive KR Systems Integrating Datalog and Description Logics: Preliminary Report. In *Proc. 1999 International Workshop on Description Logics (DL '99)*, volume 22 of *CEUR Workshop Proceedings*, pp. 160–164. CEUR-WS.org, 1999.
51. R. Rosati. On the Decidability and Complexity of Integrating Ontologies and Rules. *Journal of Web Semantics*, 3(1):61–73, 2005.
52. R. Rosati. $\mathcal{DL}+log$: Tight Integration of Description Logics and Disjunctive Datalog. In *Proc. Tenth International Conference on Principles of Knowledge Representation and Reasoning (KR 2006)*, pp. 68–78. AAAI Press, 2006.
53. R. Rosati. Reasoning with Rules and Ontologies. In P. Barahona, F. Bry, E. Franconi, U. Sattler, and N. Henze, editors, *Reasoning Web, Second International Summer School 2006, Lissabon, Portugal, September 25-29, 2006, Tutorial Lectures*, Lecture Notes in Computer Science (LNCS). Springer Verlag, 2006. This volume.
54. M. Sintek and S. Decker. TRIPLE - A Query, Inference, and Transformation Language for the Semantic Web. In *Proc. First International Semantic Web Conference (ISWC 2002)*, volume 2342 of *Lecture Notes in Computer Science (LNCS)*, pp. 364–378, 2002.
55. D. Tsarkov and I. Horrocks. Fact++ Description Logic Reasoner: System Description. In *Proc. Third International Joint Conference on Automated Reasoning (IJCAR 2006)*, 2006.
56. A. Van Gelder, K. A. Ross, and J. S. Schlipf. The Well-Founded Semantics for General Logic Programs. *Journal of the ACM*, 38(3):620–650, 1991.
57. W3C. The Resource Description Framework. http://www.w3.org/RDF/.
58. K. Wang, G. Antoniou, R. W. Topor, and A. Sattar. Merging and Aligning Ontologies in dl-Programs. In *Proc. First International Conference on Rules and Rule Markup Languages for the Semantic Web (RuleML 2005)*, pp. 160–171, 2005.

59. K. Wang, D. Billington, J. Blee, and G. Antoniou. Combining Description Logic and Defeasible Logic for the Semantic Web. In *Proc. ISWC 2004 Workshop on Rules and Rule Markup Languages for the Semantic Web (RuleML 2004)*, volume 3323 of *Lecture Notes in Computer Science (LNCS)*, pp. 170–181. Springer Verlag, 2004.

60. ASPLIB: The Answer Set Programming Satisfiability Library. `http://dit.unitn.it/~wasp/Solvers/index.html`.

61. WASP homepage, since 2002. `http://wasp.unime.it/`.

62. The Wine Ontology. `http://www.w3.org/TR/owl-guide/wine.rdf`.

63. S. Woltran. Answer Set Programming: Model Applications and Proofs-of-Concept. Technical Report WP5, Working Group on Answer Set Programming (WASP, IST-FET-2001-37004), July 2005. Available at `http://www.kr.tuwien.ac.at/projects/WASP/report.html`.

Integrating Ontologies and Rules: Semantic and Computational Issues

Riccardo Rosati

Dipartimento di Informatica e Sistemistica
Università di Roma "La Sapienza"
Via Salaria 113, 00198 Roma, Italy
rosati@dis.uniroma1.it

Abstract. We present some recent results on the definition of logic-based systems integrating ontologies and rules. In particular, we take into account ontologies expressed in Description Logics and rules expressed in Datalog (and its nonmonotonic extensions). We first introduce the main issues that arise in the integration of ontologies and rules. In particular, we focus on the following aspects: (i) from the semantic viewpoint, ontologies are based on open-world semantics, while rules are typically interpreted under closed-world semantics. This semantic discrepancy constitutes an important obstacle for the definition of a meaningful combination of ontologies and rules; (ii) from the reasoning viewpoint, the interaction between an ontology and a rule component is very hard to handle, and does not preserve decidability and computational properties: e.g., starting from an ontology in which reasoning is decidable and a rule base in which reasoning is decidable, reasoning in the formal system obtained by integrating the two components may not be a decidable problem. Then, we briefly survey the main approaches for the integration of ontologies and rules, with special emphasis on how they deal with the above mentioned issues, and present in detail one of such approaches, i.e., $\mathcal{DL}+log$. Finally, we illustrate the main open problems in this research area, pointing out what still prevents us from the development of both effective and expressive systems able to integrate ontologies and rules.

1 Introduction

1.1 Ontologies and Description Logics

The integration of ontologies and rules has recently received considerable attention in the research on ontologies and the Semantic Web (see e.g.,[24,2]). Description Logics (DLs) [6] are currently playing a central role in this field. DLs are a family of knowledge representation formalisms based on first-order logic (in fact, almost all DLs coincide with decidable fragments of function-free first-order logic with equality) and exhibiting well-understood computational properties. In the last years, a significant body of the Semantic Web research was devoted to defining a suitable language for ontology modeling [33]. In 2004, this endeavor

P. Barahona et al. (Eds.): Reasoning Web 2006, LNCS 4126, pp. 128–151, 2006.

resulted in the Web Ontology Language (OWL). OWL is based on Description Logics, and has successfully been applied to numerous problems in computer science, such as information integration or metadata management. Prototypes of OWL reasoners, such as RACER, FaCT++, Pellet, or KAON2, have been implemented and applied in research projects; commercial implementations and projects using them are currently emerging.

1.2   Limitations of Current Ontology Formalisms

However, the experience in building practical applications has revealed several shortcomings of OWL and, in general, of Description Logics. In particular, the typical expressiveness of DLs does not allow for addressing the following aspects:

- the possibility of defining predicates of arbitrary arity (not just unary and binary)
- the use of variable quantification beyond the tree-like structure of DL concepts (many DLs actually correspond to subsets of the two-variable fragment of first-order logic)
- the possibility of formulating expressive queries over DL knowledge bases (beyond concept subsumption and instance checking)
- the possibility of formalizing various forms of closed-world reasoning over DL knowledge bases
- more generally, the possibility of expressing forms of nonmonotonic knowledge, like default rules [34]

The issue of how to overcome these limitations of OWL and DLs is currently receiving a lot of attention in the Semantic Web community [1]. In this respect, we observe that several of the representational abilities which are missing in DLs require *nonmonotonicity* of the underlying logical formalism. This is in contrast with the well-known monotonic nature of classical first-order logic, which corresponds to the following property: if a theory T entails a conclusion ϕ, then, for every formula ψ, the theory $T \cup \{\psi\}$ entails ϕ. Such a property dos not hold anymore in the presence of closed-world knowledge and default knowledge [34,7].

This implies that the attempt to extend the expressive abilites of DLs, in order to fully overcome the above limitations, requires to leave the realm of classical first-order logic, and to look at nonmonotonic logic.

1.3   Rule-Based Knowledge Representation

Almost all the kinds of knowledge that cannot be formally addressed in a classical, first-order logic setting have a "rule-like" form, i.e., can be expressed by statements of the form "if the precondition ψ holds then the conclusion ϕ holds", where the precondition and the conclusion are logical properties.

However, such a piece of knowledge cannot simply be formalized through the standard material implication of classical logic: in other words, it is not possible to capture the intended meaning of the above statement by an implication in classical first-order logic of the form $\psi \to \phi$.

In this respect, a very relevant role is played by research in logic programming. In fact, logic program rules are implications with a non-standard semantics. And, in the context of ontologies, nonmonotonic extensions of logic programming are of particular interest [7].

Therefore, rule-based formalisms grounded in logic programming have repeatedly been proposed as a possible solution to overcome the above limitations, so adding a rule layer on top of OWL is nowadays seen as the most important task in the development of the Semantic Web language stack. The Rule Interchange Format (RIF) working group of the World Wide Web Consortium (W3C) is currently working on standardizing such a language.

Most of the proposals in this field focus on logic programs expressed in Datalog (and its nonmonotonic extensions) [14]. With respect to DLs, Datalog allows for using predicates of arbitrary arity, the explicit use of variables, and the ability of expressing more powerful queries. Moreover, its nonmonotonic features (in particular, the negation-as-failure operator *not*) allow for expressing default rules and forms of closed-world reasoning.

1.4   Integrating DLs and Rules: Main Issues

Many semantic and computational problems have emerged in the combination of DLs and rule-based representation formalisms. Among them, we concentrate on the following main issues/goals:

(1) *OWA vs. CWA:* DLs are fragments of first-order logic (FOL), hence their semantics is based on the *Open World Assumption* (OWA) of classical logic, while rules are based on a *Closed World Assumption* (CWA), imposed by the different semantics for logic programming and deductive databases (which formalize various notions of information closure). How to integrate the OWA of DLs and the CWA of rules in a "proper" way? i.e., how to merge monotonic and nonmonotonic logical subsystems from a semantic viewpoint?

(2) *UNA vs. non-UNA:* some DLs, in particular the ones specifically tailored for the Semantic Web, i.e., OWL and OWL-DL, are not based on the *Unique Name Assumption* (UNA) (we recall that the UNA imposes that different terms denote different objects). On the other hand, the standard semantics of Datalog rules is based on the UNA (see e.g. [12] for a discussion on this semantic discrepancy). How to define a non-UNA-based semantics for DLs and rules? and most importantly, is it possible to reason under the non-UNA-based semantics by exploiting standard (i.e., UNA-based) Datalog engines?

(3) *decidability preservation:* as shown by the first studies in this field [28], decidability (and complexity) of reasoning is a crucial issue in systems combining DL knowledge bases and Datalog rules. In fact, in general this combination does not preserve decidability, i.e., starting from a DL knowledge base in which reasoning is decidable and a set of rules in which reasoning is decidable, reasoning in the knowledge base obtained by integrating these two components may not be a decidable problem.

(4) *modularity of reasoning:* can reasoning in DL knowledge bases augmented with rules be performed in a modular way, strongly separating reasoning

about the DL component and reasoning about the rule component? This is a very desirable property, since it allows for defining reasoning techniques (and engines) on top of deductive methods (and implemented systems) developed separately for DLs [6] and for Datalog and its nonmonotonic extensions [16].

1.5   Structure of the Paper

The paper is structured in the following way. We start by briefly introducing Description Logics in Section 2, and Datalog and its nonmonotonic extensions in Section 3. Then, in Section 4 we analyze the main issues that arise when integrating Description Logics and rules. In Section 5 we review the main approaches to the integration of ontologies and Datalog rules. Then, in Section 6 we present $\mathcal{DL}+log$, one of the most powerful formalisms integrating Descrition Logics and Datalog rules: in particular, we show how $\mathcal{DL}+log$ deals with the main issues previously discussed. Finally, in Section 7 we briefly illustate some of the main open problems towards the integration of Description Logics and Datalog rules.

2   Description Logics

We start by introducing Description Logics. For a more detailed introduction to this topic, we refer the reader to [6].

Description Logics (DLs) are logics that represent the domain of interest in terms of *concepts*, denoting sets of objects, and *roles*, denoting binary relations between (instances of) concepts. Complex concept and role expressions are constructed starting from a set of atomic concepts and roles by applying suitable constructs.

Different DLs allow for different constructs. Properties of concepts and roles are specified through inclusion assertions, stating that every instance of a concept (respectively, role) is also an instance of another concept (respectively, role).

As an example of a DL, in the following we formally introduce $\mathcal{ALC}$, which actually constitutes a subset of the DLs of the OWL family defined as ontology languages.

2.1   Syntax

In $\mathcal{ALC}$, concepts and roles are formed according to the following syntax:

$$C ::= \top \mid \bot \mid A \mid C_1 \sqcap C_2 \mid C_1 \sqcup C_2 \mid \neg C \mid \exists P.C \mid \forall P.C$$

where A denotes an atomic concept, P denotes an atomic role, and C_1, C_2 denote general concept expressions.

A DL *knowledge base* (KB) $\mathcal{K} = (\mathcal{T}, \mathcal{A})$ represents the domain of interest in terms of two components, a *TBox* $\mathcal{T}$, specifying the intensional knowledge, and an *ABox* $\mathcal{A}$, specifying extensional knowledge.

A TBox is formed by a set of *inclusion assertions* of the form

$$C_1 \sqsubseteq C_2$$

where C_1 and C_2 are general concepts. As we said before, such an inclusion assertion expresses that all instances of concept C_1 are also instances of concept C_2.

An ABox is formed by a set of *membership assertions* on atomic concepts and on atomic roles, of the form

$$C(a), \qquad P(a,b)$$

stating respectively that the object denoted by the constant a is an instance of the concept C and that the pair of objects denoted by the pair of constants (a,b) is an instance of the role P.

2.2   Semantics

The semantics of a DL is given in terms of standard first-order interpretations. Formally, a *DL-interpretation* $\mathcal{I} = (\Delta^{\mathcal{I}}, \cdot^{\mathcal{I}})$ consists of an interpretation domain $\Delta^{\mathcal{I}}$ and an *interpretation function* $\cdot^{\mathcal{I}}$ defined as follows. First, $\mathcal{I}$ assigns to each atomic concept A a subset $A^{\mathcal{I}}$ of $\Delta^{\mathcal{I}}$, and to each role P a binary relation $P^{\mathcal{I}}$ over $\Delta^{\mathcal{I}}$:

$$\top^{\mathcal{I}} = \Delta^{\mathcal{I}}$$
$$\bot^{\mathcal{I}} = \emptyset$$
$$A^{\mathcal{I}} \subseteq \Delta^{\mathcal{I}}$$
$$P^{\mathcal{I}} \subseteq \Delta^{\mathcal{I}} \times \Delta^{\mathcal{I}}$$

Based on the above interpretation of atomic predicates, $\mathcal{I}$ assigns a subset of $\Delta^{\mathcal{I}}$ to general concept expression. For the constructs of $\mathcal{ALC}$, the interpretation of general concepts is defined inductively as follows:

$$\neg C^{\mathcal{I}} = \Delta^{\mathcal{I}} \setminus C^{\mathcal{I}}$$
$$C_1 \sqcap C_2^{\mathcal{I}} = C_1^{\mathcal{I}} \cap C_2^{\mathcal{I}}$$
$$C_1 \sqcup C_2^{\mathcal{I}} = C_1^{\mathcal{I}} \cup C_2^{\mathcal{I}}$$
$$\exists P.C^{\mathcal{I}} = \{d \in \Delta^{\mathcal{I}} \mid \exists d'.(d,d') \in P^{\mathcal{I}} \text{ and } d' \in C^{\mathcal{I}}\}$$
$$\forall P.C^{\mathcal{I}} = \{d \in \Delta^{\mathcal{I}} \mid \forall d'.(d,d') \in P^{\mathcal{I}} \text{ implies } d' \in C^{\mathcal{I}}\}$$

A concept C is *satisfiable* if there exists an interpretation $\mathcal{I}$ such that $C^{\mathcal{I}} \neq \emptyset$, otherwise C is unsatisfiable. An interpretation $\mathcal{I}$ is a *model* of a concept C if $\mathcal{I}$ satisfies C.

A DL-interpretation $\mathcal{I}$ is a *model* of an inclusion assertion $C_1 \sqsubseteq C_2$, if $C_1^{\mathcal{I}} \subseteq C_2^{\mathcal{I}}$.

To specify the semantics of membership assertions, we extend the interpretation function to constants, by assigning to each constant a an object $a^{\mathcal{I}} \in \Delta^{\mathcal{I}}$.[1] A DL-interpretation $\mathcal{I}$ is a model of a membership assertion $C(a)$, (resp., $P(a,b)$) if $a^{\mathcal{I}} \in C^{\mathcal{I}}$ (resp., $(a^{\mathcal{I}}, b^{\mathcal{I}}) \in P^{\mathcal{I}}$).

Given an (inclusion, or membership) assertion α, and a DL-interpretation $\mathcal{I}$, we denote by $\mathcal{I} \models \alpha$ the fact that $\mathcal{I}$ is a model of α. A *model of a KB* $\mathcal{K} = (\mathcal{T}, \mathcal{A})$ is a DL-interpretation $\mathcal{I}$ that is a model of all assertions in $\mathcal{T}$ and $\mathcal{A}$. A KB is *satisfiable* if it has at least one model. A KB $\mathcal{K}$ *entails* an assertion α, written $\mathcal{K} \models \alpha$, if all models of $\mathcal{K}$ are also models of α. Analogously, a TBox $\mathcal{T}$ entails an assertion α, written $\mathcal{T} \models \alpha$, if all models of $\mathcal{T}$ are also models of α.

Observe that $\mathcal{ALC}$ (and, in practice, every DL) is actually a fragment of function-free first-order logic, with a special syntax which avoids the explicit use of variable symbols. In fact, it is immediate to verify that a DL knowledge base $\mathcal{K}$ is semantically equivalent to a FOL theory $FO(\mathcal{K})$ in which each assertion in the knowledge base is expressed by a first-order sentence (for details on such a translation see [6]). For instance, the TBox inclusion assertion

$$A_1 \sqcap \exists P_1.A_2 \sqsubseteq \forall P_2.A_3 \sqcup \neg A_4$$

is equivalent to the first-order sentence

$$\forall x. A_1(x) \wedge (\exists y. P_1(x, y) \wedge A_2(y)) \rightarrow (\forall z. P_2(x, z) \rightarrow A_3(z)) \vee \neg A_4(x)$$

Finally, we remark that, due to the above FOL semantics, DLs are interpreted over an unbound (possibly infinite) domain. Moreover, unique names are not always assumed[2].

3   Disjunctive Datalog

In this section be briefy recall disjunctive Datalog [14], denoted by $\text{Datalog}^{\neg\vee}$, which is the well-known nonmonotonic extension of Datalog with negation as failure and disjunction.

3.1   Syntax

We start from a predicate alphabet, a constant alphabet, and a variable alphabet. An *atom* is an expression of the form $p(X)$, where p is a predicate of arity n and X is a n-tuple of variables and constants. If no variable symbol occurs in X, then $p(X)$ is called a *ground atom* (or *fact*). A $\text{Datalog}^{\neg\vee}$ rule R is an expression of the form

$$p_1(X_1) \vee \ldots \vee p_n(X_n) \leftarrow r_1(Y_1), \ldots, r_m(Y_m), \textit{not } s_1(W_1), \ldots, \textit{not } s_k(W_k)$$

---

[1] We recall that, if we enforce the unique name assumption on constants, then the interpretation $a^{\mathcal{I}}$ of each constant a must be such that, for each constant b different from a, $b^{\mathcal{I}} \neq a^{\mathcal{I}}$ [6].

[2] Even though some DLs are based on the UNA, the most expressive ones, like the ones in the OWL family, are not.

such that $n \geq 0$, $m \geq 0$, $k \geq 0$, each $p_i(X_i)$, $r_i(Y_i)$, $s_i(W_i)$ is an atom and every variable occurring in R must appear in at least one of the atoms $r_1(Y_1), \ldots, r_m(Y_m)$. This last condition is known as the *Datalog safeness* condition for variables. The variables occurring in the atoms $p_1(X_1), \ldots, p_n(X_n)$ are called the *head variables* of R. If $n = 0$, we call R a *constraint*.

A a *Datalog$^{\neg\vee}$* program is a set of Datalog$^{\neg\vee}$ rules. If, for all $R \in \mathcal{P}$, $n \leq 1$, $\mathcal{P}$ is called a *Datalog$^{\neg}$* program. If, for all $R \in \mathcal{P}$, $k = 0$, $\mathcal{P}$ is called a *positive disjunctive Datalog* program. If, for all $R \in \mathcal{P}$, $n \leq 1$ and $k = 0$, $\mathcal{P}$ is called a *positive Datalog* program. If there are no occurrences of variable symbols in a rule R, then R is called a *ground* rule. A *ground* program is a program containing only ground rules.

3.2 Semantics

The semantics of disjunctive Datalog is given in terms of *stable models* of a program $\mathcal{P}$, which we recall below.

The *ground instantiation of* $\mathcal{P}$, denoted by $G(P)$, is the program obtained from $\mathcal{P}$ by replacing every rule R in $\mathcal{P}$ with the set of ground rules obtained by applying all possible substitutions of variables in R with constants occurring in $\mathcal{P}$ (such a set of constants is called the Herbrand universe of $\mathcal{P}$).

We denote by $HB(\mathcal{P})$ the *Herbrand base* of $\mathcal{P}$, i.e. the set of all ground instantiations of predicates occurring in $\mathcal{P}$ over the Herbrand universe of $\mathcal{P}$.

A *Datalog interpretation* I of $\mathcal{P}$ is a subset of $HB(\mathcal{P})$. I satisfies a positive ground rule

$$p_1 \vee \ldots \vee p_n \leftarrow r_1, \ldots, r_m \tag{1}$$

if the following condition holds: if each atom in $\{r_1, \ldots, r_m\}$ belongs to I, then at least one atom p_i belongs to I.

I is a *model* of $\mathcal{P}$ if I satisfies each rule in $G(\mathcal{P})$. A model of $\mathcal{P}$ is *minimal* if it does not properly contain any other model of $\mathcal{P}$.

Given a Datalog interpretation $I \subseteq HB(\mathcal{P})$, the *GL-reduct* of $\mathcal{P}$ with respect to I (denoted as $GL(\mathcal{P}, I)$) is the program obtained from $G(\mathcal{P})$ by removing all clauses of the form (1) such that there exists $s_j \in I$ for some $j \in \{1, \ldots, k\}$, and by removing all negated predicates of the form $not\ s_i$ from the remaining clauses.

A Datalog interpretation $I \subseteq HB(\mathcal{P})$ is a *stable model* of $\mathcal{P}$ if I is a minimal model of $GL(G(\mathcal{P}), I)$.

We say that a program $\mathcal{P}$ entails a ground query (i.e., a ground literal predicate) $q(\bar{a})$, denoted as $\mathcal{P} \models q(\bar{a})$, if $q(\bar{a})$ belongs to all stable models of $\mathcal{P}$.

We remark that, based on the above semantics, every disjunctive Datalog program is interpreted over a finite domain, which coincides with the set of constants occurring in the program. Moreover, every Datalog interpretation enforces the unique name assumption (different constants are interpreted as different objects).

4 Integrating DLs and Rules: Main Issues

In this section we address the main issues arising when trying to combine DLs and (disjunctive) Datalog in a single formalism.

Syntax. From the syntactic viewpoint, integrating a DL with (disjunctive) Datalog simply means the possibility of writing a "hybrid" knowledge base containing a TBox, an ABox, and a set of Datalog rules.

Semantics. From the semantic viewpoint, the meaning of such an integrated knowledge base can be provided in two ways:

1. the whole knowledge base is considered as a first-order theory, by interpreting Datalog rules as first-order implications. More specifically, let R be the following Datalog$^{\neg\vee}$ rule:

$$p_1(X_1, c_1) \vee \ldots \vee p_n(X_n, c_n) \leftarrow$$
$$r_1(Y_1, d_1), \ldots, r_m(Y_m, d_m),$$
$$s_1(Z_1, e_1), \ldots, s_k(Z_k, e_k),$$
$$not\ u_1(W_1, f_1), \ldots, not\ u_h(W_h, f_h)$$

where each X_i, Y_i, Z_i, W_i is a set of variables and each c_i, d_i, e_i, f_i is a set of constants. Then, we denote by $FO(R)$ the first-order sentence

$$\forall \overline{x}_1, \ldots, \overline{x}_n, \overline{y}_1, \ldots, \overline{y}_m, \overline{z}_1, \ldots, \overline{z}_k, \overline{w}_1, \ldots, \overline{w}_h.$$
$$r_1(\overline{y}_1, d_1) \wedge \ldots \wedge r_m(\overline{y}_m, d_m) \wedge$$
$$s_1(\overline{z}_1, e_1) \wedge \ldots \wedge s_k(\overline{z}_k, e_k) \wedge$$
$$\neg u_1(\overline{w}_1, f_1) \wedge \ldots \wedge \neg u_h(\overline{w}_h, f_h) \rightarrow p_1(\overline{x}_1, c_1) \vee \ldots \vee p_n(\overline{x}_n, c_n)$$

and, given a Datalog$^{\neg\vee}$ program $\mathcal{P}$, we denote by $FO(\mathcal{P})$ the set of first-order sentences $\{FO(R) \mid R \in \mathcal{P}\}$.

Finally, the semantics of a knowledge base $(\mathcal{K}, \mathcal{P})$ composed of a DL-KB $\mathcal{K}$ and a Datalog program $\mathcal{P}$ is given by the first-order theory corresponding to the union of $FO(\mathcal{P})$ and the first-order translation $FO(\mathcal{K})$ of $\mathcal{K}$.

While the above semantic account has the advantage of being clear and easy to define, it has the drawback of not being conservative with respect to the semantics of Datalog rules. In other words, the meaning of a Datalog program $\mathcal{P}$ in the new semantics is different from its meaning according to the standard Datalog semantics (the CWA of Datalog is missing in the new semantics).

2. the semantics is defined in a way such that it is a "conservative extension" of both the DL and Datalog. However, this is not as immediate as the above semantic account, due to the different semantic nature of the two formalisms: in fact, one has to simultaneously deal with two semantic discrepancies: the OWA of DLs and the CWA of Datalog on the one side, and the UNA of Datalog and the absence of the UNA of (some) DLs on the other side. In Section 6 we will define such a semantics.

Reasoning. From the reasoning perspective, an important aspect is the "degree of integration" of the two components (the DL-KB and the Datalog program). Indeed, as we will explain in Section 5, the complexity of reasoning in systems combining DLs and rules is directly related to such a degree of integration. In particular, it is well-known that the "full" interaction between a DL-KB and a Datalog program leads to undecidability of reasoning under the above presented FOL semantics, even for extremely simple DLs [28]. On the other side of the spectrum, rules may not interact at all with the DL-KB, and of course this kind of (uninteresting) integration is not problematic at all with respect to the reasoning task, since the two components can be processed separately by standard (DL and Datalog) reasoners.

Obviously, in order to represent some kind of significant interaction, the DL KB and the rules have to share some predicate symbols. A measure of the degree of interaction between the two components depends on these shared predicates, and on how they can be used within DL statements and rules.

More specifically, the alphabet of predicates is divided into *DL predicates* and *Datalog predicates*, where Datalog predicates are the ones that do not occur in the DL-KB, while DL predicates may occur both in the DL-KB and in rules. Then:

 - the full interaction does not make any assumption on the form of rules based on the above classification of predicates;
 - the loose interaction imposes some limitations on the use of DL predicates in rules.

For instance, as we will illustrate in Section 5, a common approach to the loose integration of DLs and rules is realized through the so-called *DL-safeness* condition for Datalog rules. This is a syntactic condition that can be expressed as follows: *every variable occurring in an atom with a DL predicate must occur in a atom with a Datalog predicate in the body of the rule*. Such a condition is sufficient to allow for a nice computational behaviour of reasoning, but has the drawback of restricting the expressiveness of the combined language thus defined. E.g., DL-safe rules are not able to express arbitrary *conjunctive queries* to the DL-KB. Conjunctive queries correspond to a simple form of non-recursive Datalog rules, are computable in many DLs, and there are known algorithms for conjunctive query algorithms in many DLs [9,32]. Therefore, DL-safeness seems to imply a too severe limitation in the expressiveness of rules.

Finally, another measure of the degree of integration lies in the direction of the *information flow* between DL-KB and rules, which may be either bidirectional (from the DL-KB to the rules and vice versa), or unidirectional (only from the DL-KB to the rules). In the latter case, the presence of rules does not affect the semantics of DL predicates. Often, the restriction to the unidirectional flow is realized through the syntactic restriction that DL predicates may not occur in the head of rules (they can only occur in the body of rules).

We conclude this section with two examples of knowledge bases combining DLs and rules.

Example 1. Let $\mathcal{B} = (\mathcal{K}, \mathcal{P})$ be the knowledge base reported in Figure 1, where the DL-KB $\mathcal{K}$ defines an ontology about persons, and the disjunctive Datalog program $\mathcal{P}$ defines nonmonotonic rules about students. For the sake of readability, we denote DL predicates by uppercase names, and denote Datalog predicates by lowercase names.

It is immediate to verify that $\mathcal{B}$ satisfies the DL-safe condition described above.   ∎

$PERSON \sqsubseteq \exists FATHER^-.MALE$
$MALE \sqsubseteq PERSON$
$FEMALE \sqsubseteq PERSON$
$FEMALE \sqsubseteq \neg MALE$
$MALE(Bob)$
$PERSON(Mary)$
$PERSON(Paul)$

(a) DL-KB $\mathcal{K}$ (ontology about persons)

$boy(X) \leftarrow enrolled(X, c1), PERSON(X), not\ girl(X)\ [R1]$
$girl(X) \leftarrow enrolled(X, c2), PERSON(X)\ [R2]$
$boy(X) \lor girl(X) \leftarrow enrolled(X, c3), PERSON(X)\ [R3]$
$FEMALE(X) \leftarrow girl(X)\ [R4]$
$MALE(X) \leftarrow boy(X)\ [R5]$
$enrolled(Paul, c1)$
$enrolled(Mary, c1)$
$enrolled(Mary, c2)$
$enrolled(Bob, c3)$

(b) disjunctive Datalog program $\mathcal{P}$ (rules about students)

Fig. 1. Knowledge base $\mathcal{B} = (\mathcal{K}, \mathcal{P})$ of Example 1

$RICH \sqcap UNMARRIED \sqsubseteq \exists WANTS\text{-}TO\text{-}MARRY^-.\top$
$UNMARRIED(Mary)$
$UNMARRIED(Joe)$

(a) DL-KB $\mathcal{K}$

$happy(X) \leftarrow famous(X), WANTS\text{-}TO\text{-}MARRY(Y, X)\ [R1]$
$RICH(X) \leftarrow famous(X), not\ scientist(X)\ [R2]$
$famous(Mary)$
$famous(Paul)$
$famous(Joe)$
$scientist(Joe)$

(b) disjunctive Datalog program $\mathcal{P}$

Fig. 2. Knowledge base $\mathcal{B} = (\mathcal{K}, \mathcal{P})$ of Example 2

Example 2. Let $\mathcal{B} = (\mathcal{K}, \mathcal{P})$ be the knowledge base reported in Figure 2.

Again, DL predicates are denoted by uppercase names, while Datalog predicates are denoted by lowercase names. In this case, the rules in $\mathcal{P}$ (in particular, rule R1) do *not* satisfy the DL-safeness condition. ∎

5   A Brief State of the Art

In this section we briefly survey recent work in integrating ontologies and rules.[3]
We divide such studies in two main streams: (i) approaches dealing with forms
of DL-safe (and, more generally, loose) interaction between DL-KBs and rules;
(ii) approaches concerning forms of "non-DL-safe" (or tight) interaction.

5.1   Loose Integration

The first formal proposal for the integration of Description Logics and rules
is $\mathcal{AL}$-log [13]. $\mathcal{AL}$-log is a framework which integrates KBs expressed in the
description logic $\mathcal{ALC}$ and positive Datalog programs. Then, *disjunctive $\mathcal{AL}$-log*
was proposed in [35] as an extension of $\mathcal{AL}$-log, based on the use of Datalog$^{\neg\vee}$
instead of positive Datalog, and on the possibility of using binary predicates
(roles) besides unary predicates (concepts) in rules. Such approaches realize a
form of loose integration between DLs and Datalog that precisely corresponds
to the DL-safeness condition described in the previous section. Moreover, both
in $\mathcal{AL}$-log and in disjunctive $\mathcal{AL}$-log DL predicates can occur only in the bodies
of rules, which forces the information flow to be unidirectional.

The framework of $\mathcal{AL}$-log has been extended in a different way in [30]. There,
the problem of extending OWL-DL with positive Datalog programs is analyzed.
Again, the interaction between OWL-DL and rules is restricted through the DL-
safeness condition. With respect to disjunctive $\mathcal{AL}$-log, in [30] a more expressive
DL and a less expressive rule language (interpreted under first-order semantics)
are adopted: moreover, the information flow is bidirectional, i.e., DL predicates
may appear in the head of rules.

All the above approaches based on DL-safeness have been generalized in [36]
to the integration of arbitrary, decidable, first-order theories and disjunctive
Datalog rules. This paper establishes an important computational result, which
states that the DL-safe based integration preserves (under very general conditions) decidability of reasoning.

The work presented in [21] can also be seen as an approach based on a form of
safe interaction between the DL-KB and the rules: in particular, a rule language
is defined such that it is possible to encode a set of rules into a semantically
equivalent DL-KB. As a consequence, such a rule language is very restricted.

A different approach is presented in [23,22], which proposes Conceptual Logic
Programming (CLP), an extension of answer set programming (i.e., Datalog$^{\neg\vee}$)
towards infinite domains. In order to keep reasoning decidable, a syntactic restriction on CLP program rules is imposed. This approach is related to integrating DLs and rules, since the authors also show that CLPs can embed expressive
DL-KBs, which in turn implies decidability of adding CLP rules to such DLs.
However, the syntactic restriction on CLP rules, whose purpose is to impose a
"forest-like" structure to the models of the program, is different from the safeness
conditions analyzed so far, which makes it impossible to compare this approach
with the studies previously mentioned.

---

[3] For other surveys on this topic see, e.g., [5,15].

Another approach for extending DLs with Datalog⁻ rules is presented in [17,18]. Differently from the other approaches above described, this proposal allows for specifying, in rule bodies, *queries* to the DL component, where every query also allows for specifying an input from the rule component, and thus for an information flow from the rule component to the DL-KB. The meaning of such queries in rule bodies is given at the meta-level, through the notion of skeptical entailment in the DL-KB. Thus, from the semantic viewpoint, this form of interaction-via-entailment between the two components is more restricted than in the approaches previously mentioned; on the other hand, such an increased separation in principle allows for more modular reasoning methods, which are able to completely separate reasoning about the DL-KB and reasoning about the Datalog program. For a more detailed description of this approach see [15].

Finally, [3,2,4] present approaches for the combination of defeasible reasoning with Description Logics, under a safe interaction-via-entailment scheme which is semantically analogous to the one proposed in [17]. Besides the differences with the studies on nonmonotonic extensions of DL-KBs previously mentioned due to the semantics of nonmonotonic rules, a main characteristic of these proposals consists in the fact the information flow is unidirectional, i.e., it only goes from the DL-KB to the rules.

5.2   Tight Integration

Research in non-safe interaction of DLs and rules actually started with the work on CARIN [26,27,28], which established very important decidability and undecidability results concerning the integration of DL-KBs and rules. Roughly speaking, such results clearly indicate that, in case of unrestricted interaction between a DL-KB and a set of rules, decidability of reasoning holds only if at least one of the two components has very limited expressive power: e.g., in order to retain decidability of reasoning, allowing recursion in rules imposes very severe restrictions on the expressiveness of DL-KB.

Then, we remark that query answering over a knowledge base can be seen as a problem of reasoning in a DL-KB augmented with rules which encode the query. In this respect, an important undecidability result concerning query answering over databases with integrity constraints is reported in [10]. More precisely, it is shown that answering recursive Datalog queries over a database with simple integrity constraints (keys and foreign keys), interpreted as a knowledge base, i.e., under an open-world assumption, is undecidable. This setting also can be viewed as a DL-KB with non-DL-safe interaction between a knowledge base (database with integrity constraints) and a rule component (the query).

As already observed, it is difficult to provide a good semantic account for non-safe interaction between DL-KBs and nonmonotonic rules, due to the classical, open-world semantics of DL-KBs, and the closed-world assumption underlying nonmonotonic systems. For instance, [29] illustrates the problems in providing a semantic account for non-safe interaction of ontologies and Datalog$^{\neg\vee}$ programs.

Finally, another recent proposals in this field is SWRL [24], a non-safe approach to the integration of rules and DL-KBs in which rules are interpreted under the classical FOL semantics. The addition of this kind of rules to DLs leads to undecidability of reasoning.

5.3   Loose vs. Tight Integration

Summarizing, what emerges from the studies in the integration of DL-KBs and rules is that while, on the one hand, a safe form of interaction between DLs and rules generally allows for decidable reasoning and nice computational properties, on the other hand, the results concerning non-safe interaction indicate that a tight connection between the two components can only be obtained at the price of severely restricting the expressive power of either the DL-KB or the rules.

In the next section we present in detail $\mathcal{DL}+log$, which is currently one of the most expressive and decidable combinations of Description Logics and disjunctive Datalog. $\mathcal{DL}+log$ overcomes the DL-safeness condition to obtain a tighter form of interaction between DLs and rules.

6   The $\mathcal{DL}+log$ Approach

In this section we introduce $\mathcal{DL}+log$ (we refer to [38] for more details).

6.1   Syntax

We start from three mutually disjoint predicate alphabets:

- an alphabet of concept names Σ_C;
- an alphabet of role names Σ_R;
- an alphabet of Datalog predicates Σ_D.

We call a predicate p a *DL predicate* if either $p \in \Sigma_C$ or $p \in \Sigma_R$.[4] Then, we denote by $\mathcal{C}$ a countably infinite alphabet of constant names.

An *atom* is an expression of the form $p(X)$, where p is a predicate of arity n and X is a n-tuple of variables and constants.[5] If no variable symbol occurs in X, then $p(X)$ is called a *ground atom* (or *fact*). If $p \in \Sigma_C \cup \Sigma_R$, the atom is called a *DL-atom*, while if $p \in \Sigma_D$, it is called a *Datalog atom*.

To define a $\mathcal{DL}+log$ knowledge base, we can start from any description logic $\mathcal{DL}$: in other words, the construction defined in the following is parametric with respect to the description logic used to express the DL-KB.

Definition 1. *Given a description logic $\mathcal{DL}$, a $\mathcal{DL}+log$-knowledge base $\mathcal{B}$ is a pair $(\mathcal{K}, \mathcal{P})$, where:*

- *$\mathcal{K}$ is a $\mathcal{DL}$-KB, i.e., a pair $(\mathcal{T}, \mathcal{A})$ where $\mathcal{T}$ is the TBox and $\mathcal{A}$ is the ABox;*
- *$\mathcal{P}$ is a set of Datalog$^{\neg\vee}$ rules, where each rule R has the form*

---

[4] For DLs which allow for using equality, we assume that the equality predicate is a DL predicate.

[5] As usual, atoms involving equalities are written using the infix notation $t_1 = t_2$.

$$p_1(X_1) \lor \ldots \lor p_n(X_n) \leftarrow r_1(Y_1), \ldots, r_m(Y_m), s_1(Z_1), \ldots, s_k(Z_k),$$
$$not\, u_1(W_1), \ldots, not\, u_h(W_h)$$

such that $n \geq 0$, $m \geq 0$, $k \geq 0$, $h \geq 0$, each $p_i(X_i)$, $r_i(Y_i)$, $s_i(Z_i)$, $u_i(W_i)$ is an atom and:

- each p_i is either a DL predicate or a Datalog predicate;
- each r_i, u_i is a Datalog predicate;
- each s_i is a DL predicate;
- (Datalog safeness) every variable occurring in R must appear in at least one of the atoms $r_1(Y_1), \ldots, r_m(Y_m), s_1(Z_1), \ldots, s_k(Z_k)$;
- (weak safeness) every head variable of R must appear in at least one of the atoms $r_1(Y_1), \ldots, r_m(Y_m)$.

We remark that the above notion of weak safeness allows for the presence of variables that only occur in DL-atoms in the body of R. On the other hand, the notion of *DL-safeness* of variables adopted in previous approaches [35,31,36] can be expressed as follows: *every variable of R must appear in at least one of the atoms $r_1(Y_1), \ldots, r_m(Y_m)$*. Therefore, DL-safeness forces every variable of R to occur also in the Datalog atoms in the body of R, while weak safeness allows for the presence of variables that only occur in DL-atoms in the body of R.

Without loss of generality, in the rest of the paper we assume that in a $\mathcal{DL}+log$-KB $(\mathcal{K}, \mathcal{P})$ all constants occurring in $\mathcal{K}$ also occur in $\mathcal{P}$.

6.2   Semantics

We now define a semantics for $\mathcal{DL}+log$-KBs which is a "conservative extension" of both the open-world semantics of DLs and the closed-world semantics of disjunctive Datalog.

Given an interpretation $\mathcal{I}$ and a predicate alphabet Σ, we denote by $\mathcal{I}_\Sigma$ the projection of $\mathcal{I}$ to Σ, i.e., $\mathcal{I}_\Sigma$ is obtained from $\mathcal{I}$ by restricting it to the interpretation of the predicates in Σ.

Given a set of constants $\mathcal{C}$, the *ground instantiation of $\mathcal{P}$ with respect to $\mathcal{C}$*, denoted by $gr(\mathcal{P}, \mathcal{C})$, is the program obtained from $\mathcal{P}$ by replacing every rule R in $\mathcal{P}$ with the set of rules obtained by applying all possible substitutions of variables in R with constants in $\mathcal{C}$.

Given an interpretation $\mathcal{I}$ of an alphabet of predicates $\Sigma' \subset \Sigma$, and a ground program $\mathcal{P}_g$ over the predicates in Σ, the *projection of $\mathcal{P}_g$ with respect to $\mathcal{I}$*, denoted by $\Pi(\mathcal{P}_g, \mathcal{I})$, is the ground program obtained from $\mathcal{P}_g$ as follows. For each rule $R \in \mathcal{P}_g$:

- delete R if there exists an atom $r(t)$ in the head of R such that $r \in \Sigma'$ and $t^{\mathcal{I}} \in r^{\mathcal{I}}$;
- delete each atom $r(t)$ in the head of R such that $r \in \Sigma'$ and $t^{\mathcal{I}} \notin r^{\mathcal{I}}$;
- delete R if there exists an atom $r(t)$ in the body of R such that $r \in \Sigma'$ and $t^{\mathcal{I}} \notin r^{\mathcal{I}}$;
- delete each atom $r(t)$ in the body of R such that $r \in \Sigma'$ and $t^{\mathcal{I}} \in r^{\mathcal{I}}$;

Informally, the projection of $\mathcal{P}_g$ with respect to $\mathcal{I}$ corresponds to evaluating $\mathcal{P}_g$ with respect to $\mathcal{I}$, thus eliminating from $\mathcal{P}_g$ every atom whose predicate is interpreted in $\mathcal{I}$. Thus, when $\Sigma' = \Sigma_C \cup \Sigma_R$, all occurrences of DL predicates are eliminated in the projection of $\mathcal{P}_g$ with respect to $\mathcal{I}$, according to the evaluation in $\mathcal{I}$ of the atoms with DL predicates occurring in $\mathcal{P}_g$.

Then, we introduce the notions of minimal model and stable model for Datalog$^{\neg\vee}$ in the absence of the UNA.[6]

Given two interpretations $\mathcal{I}_1$, $\mathcal{I}_2$ of the set of predicates Σ and the set of constants $\mathcal{C}$, we write $\mathcal{I}_1 \subset_{\Sigma,\mathcal{C}} \mathcal{I}_2$ if (i) for each $p \in \Sigma$ and for each tuple t of constants from $\mathcal{C}$, if $t^{\mathcal{I}_1} \in p^{\mathcal{I}_1}$ then $t^{\mathcal{I}_2} \in p^{\mathcal{I}_2}$, and (ii) there exist $p \in \Sigma$ and tuple t of constants from $\mathcal{C}$ such that $t^{\mathcal{I}_1} \notin p^{\mathcal{I}_1}$ and $t^{\mathcal{I}_2} \in p^{\mathcal{I}_2}$.

Given a positive ground Datalog$^{\neg\vee}$ program $\mathcal{P}$ over an alphabet of predicates Σ and an interpretation $\mathcal{I}$, we say that $\mathcal{I}$ is a *minimal model* of $\mathcal{P}$ if: (i) $\mathcal{I}$ satisfies the first-order translation $FO(\mathcal{P})$ of $\mathcal{P}$ (defined in Section 4); (ii) there is no interpretation $\mathcal{I}'$ such that $\mathcal{I}'$ satisfies $FO(\mathcal{P})$ and $\mathcal{I}' \subset_{\Sigma,\mathcal{C}} \mathcal{I}$.

Given a ground Datalog$^{\neg\vee}$ program $\mathcal{P}$ and an interpretation $\mathcal{I}$ for $\mathcal{P}$, the *GL-reduct* [19] of $\mathcal{P}$ with respect to $\mathcal{I}$, denoted by $GL(\mathcal{P},\mathcal{I})$, is the positive ground program obtained from $\mathcal{P}$ as follows. For each rule $R \in \mathcal{P}$:

1. delete R if there exists a negated atom $not\, r(t)$ in the body of R such that $t^{\mathcal{I}} \in r^{\mathcal{I}}$;
2. delete each negated atom $not\, r(t)$ in the body of R such that $t^{\mathcal{I}} \notin r^{\mathcal{I}}$.

Given a ground Datalog$^{\neg\vee}$ program $\mathcal{P}$ and an interpretation $\mathcal{I}$, $\mathcal{I}$ is a *stable model* for $\mathcal{P}$ iff $\mathcal{I}$ is a minimal model of $GL(\mathcal{P},\mathcal{I})$.

Definition 2. *An interpretation $\mathcal{I}$ of $\Sigma_C \cup \Sigma_R \cup \Sigma_D$ is a model for $\mathcal{B} = (\mathcal{K},\mathcal{P})$ if the following conditions hold:*

1. $\mathcal{I}_{\Sigma_C \cup \Sigma_R}$ *satisfies* $\mathcal{K}$;
2. $\mathcal{I}_{\Sigma_D}$ *is a stable model for* $\Pi(gr(\mathcal{P},\mathcal{C}),\mathcal{I}_{\Sigma_C \cup \Sigma_R})$.

$\mathcal{B}$ *is called* satisfiable *if $\mathcal{B}$ has at least a model.*

We say that a ground atom $p(c)$ is entailed by $\mathcal{B}$ iff, for each model $\mathcal{I}$ of $\mathcal{B}$, $\mathcal{I}$ satisfies $p(c)$.

According to the above semantics, DL predicates are interpreted under the open-world assumption, while Datalog predicates are interpreted under the closed-world assumption of disjunctive Datalog (see [37] for a detailed discussion of this aspect).

Notice that, under the above semantics, entailment can be reduced to satisfiability, since it is possible to express constraints in the Datalog program. More precisely, it is immediate to verify that $(\mathcal{K},\mathcal{P})$ entails $p(c)$ iff $(\mathcal{K},\mathcal{P} \cup \{\leftarrow p(c)\})$

---

[6] Observe that the notions of minimal model and stable model presented here slightly differs from the standard ones for Datalog$^{\neg\vee}$ presented in Section 3, since they are expressed in a more general framework in which unique names are not assumed. Consequently, the interpretation of constants must be considered in the definition of minimal and stable model.

is unsatisfiable. In a similar way, it can be seen that *conjunctive query answering* can be reduced to satisfiability in $\mathcal{DL}+log$ (see [38]). Consequently, in the following we concentrate on the satisfiability problem in $\mathcal{DL}+log$-KBs.

Example 1.(contd.) Let us consider again the knowledge base $\mathcal{B} = (\mathcal{K}, \mathcal{P})$ reported in Figure 1, where the DL-KB $\mathcal{K}$ defines an ontology about persons, and the disjunctive Datalog program $\mathcal{P}$ defines nonmonotonic rules about students.

First, since all rules in $\mathcal{P}$ are DL-safe, the rules in $\mathcal{P}$ also satisfy the weak safeness condition of Definition 1: consequently, $\mathcal{B}$ is a $\mathcal{DL}+log$-KB.

Then, it can be easily verified that all models for $\mathcal{B}$ satisfy the following ground atoms:

- *boy(Paul)* (since rule R1 is always applicable for $X = Paul$ and R1 acts like a *default rule*, which can be read as follows: if X is a person enrolled in course *c1*, then X is a boy, unless we know for sure that X is a girl);
- *girl(Mary)* (since rule R2 is always applicable for $X = Mary$)
- *boy(Bob)* (since rule R3 is always applicable for $X = Bob$, and, by rule R4, the conclusion *girl(Bob)* is inconsistent with $\mathcal{K}$);
- *MALE(Paul)* (due to rule R5);
- *FEMALE(Mary)* (due to rule R4).

Notice that $\mathcal{B} \models FEMALE(Mary)$, while $\mathcal{K} \not\models FEMALE(Mary)$. In other words, adding rules has indeed an effect on the conclusions one can draw about DL predicates.   ∎

Example 2.(contd.) Let us consider again the knowledge base $\mathcal{B} = (\mathcal{K}, \mathcal{P})$ reported in Figure 2.

First, observe that $\mathcal{B}$ is a $\mathcal{DL}+log$-KB: in particular, the variable Y in rule R1 is weakly-safe according to Definition 1 (we also recall that rule R1 is *not* DL-safe, since Y does not occur in any Datalog predicate in rule R1).

Then, it can be easily verified that all models for $\mathcal{B}$ satisfy the following formulas:

- *RICH(Paul)* and *RICH(Mary)*, since the default rule R2 is always applicable for $X = Paul$ and $X = Mary$, but not for $X = Joe$, since the fact *scientist(Joe)* holds in every model for $\mathcal{B}$;
- $\exists WANTS\text{-}TO\text{-}MARRY^-.\top(Mary)$, due to the first axiom of the DL-KB and to the fact that both *RICH(Mary)* and *UNMARRIED(Mary)* hold in every model of the $\mathcal{DL}+log$-KB $\mathcal{B}$ (while $\exists WANTS\text{-}TO\text{-}MARRY^-.\top(Paul)$ is not forced by such axiom to hold in every model of $\mathcal{B}$, because *UNMARRIED(Paul)* is not forced to hold in every such model);
- *happy(Mary)*, due to the above conclusions and to the rule R1. Indeed, since $\exists WANTS\text{-}TO\text{-}MARRY^-.\top(Mary)$ holds in every model of $\mathcal{B}$, it follows that in every model there exists a constant x such that $WANTS\text{-}TO\text{-}MARRY$ $(x, Mary)$ holds in the model, consequently from rule R1 it follows that *happy(Mary)* also holds in the model.   ∎

6.3 Reasoning

In this section we study reasoning in $\mathcal{DL}+log$. In particular, we study satisfiability for finite $\mathcal{DL}+log$-KBs (as mentioned above, entailment can be easily reduced to satisfiability in $\mathcal{DL}+log$).

For ease of exposition, in the following we deal with the case when the DL is interpreted under the UNA: however, the algorithm can be easily extended to the case when unique names are not assumed in the DL (in a way analogous to the technique reported in [37] in the case of DL-safe rules).

We start by introducing Boolean conjunctive queries (CQs) and Boolean unions of conjunctive queries (UCQs), and the containment problem for such queries. A Boolean UCQ over a predicate alphabet Σ is a first-order sentence of the form $\exists \boldsymbol{x}.conj_1(\boldsymbol{x}) \vee \ldots \vee conj_n(\boldsymbol{x})$, where $\boldsymbol{x}$ is a tuple of variable symbols and each $conj_i(\boldsymbol{x})$ is a set of atoms whose predicates are in Σ and whose arguments are either constants or variables from $\boldsymbol{x}$. A Boolean CQ corresponds to a Boolean UCQ in the case when $n = 1$.

Given a $\mathcal{DL}$-TBox $\mathcal{T}$, a Boolean CQ Q_1 and a Boolean UCQ Q_2 over the alphabet $\Sigma_C \cup \Sigma_R$, Q_1 *is contained in* Q_2 *with respect to* $\mathcal{T}$, denoted by $\mathcal{T} \models Q_1 \subseteq Q_2$, iff, for every model $\mathcal{I}$ of $\mathcal{T}$, if Q_1 is satisfied in $\mathcal{I}$ then Q_2 is satisfied in $\mathcal{I}$. In the following, we call the problem of deciding $\mathcal{T} \models Q_1 \subseteq Q_2$ the *Boolean CQ/UCQ containment problem*.[7]

Algorithm. Given a program $\mathcal{P}$, we denote by $\mathcal{C}_\mathcal{P}$ the set of constants occurring in $\mathcal{P}$.

In the following definition, we assume that a rule R in $\mathcal{P}$ has the form $\alpha_R(\boldsymbol{x}) \leftarrow \beta_R(\boldsymbol{x}, \boldsymbol{y}, \boldsymbol{w}), \gamma_R(\boldsymbol{x}, \boldsymbol{y}, \boldsymbol{z})$, where $\gamma_R(\boldsymbol{x}, \boldsymbol{y}, \boldsymbol{z})$ is the set of DL-atoms occurring in the body of R (and, of course, $\beta_R(\boldsymbol{x}, \boldsymbol{y}, \boldsymbol{w})$ is the set of Datalog atoms in the body of R), $\boldsymbol{x}$ are the head variables in R, $\boldsymbol{y}$ are the existential variables occurring both in DL-atoms and in Datalog atoms in R, and $\boldsymbol{z}$ (respectively, $\boldsymbol{w}$) are the existential variables of R that only occur in DL-atoms (respectively, Datalog atoms) in R.

Definition 3. *Let* $\mathcal{B} = (\mathcal{K}, \mathcal{P})$ *be a* $\mathcal{DL}+log$-KB. *The DL-grounding of* $\mathcal{P}$, *denoted by* $gr_p(\mathcal{P})$, *is the following set of Boolean CQs:*

$$gr_p(\mathcal{P}) = \{\gamma_R(\boldsymbol{c_1}/\boldsymbol{x}, \boldsymbol{c_2}/\boldsymbol{y}, \boldsymbol{z}) \mid R \in \mathcal{P} \ and \ \boldsymbol{c_1}, \boldsymbol{c_2} \ are \ tuples \ of \ constants \ in \ \mathcal{C}_\mathcal{P}\}$$
$$\cup$$
$$\{p(\boldsymbol{c}/\boldsymbol{x}) \mid p \ is \ a \ DL \ predicate \ occurring \ in \ a \ rule \ head \ in \ \mathcal{P}$$
$$and \ \boldsymbol{c} \ is \ a \ tuple \ of \ constants \ in \ \mathcal{C}_\mathcal{P}\}$$

Notice that $gr_p(\mathcal{P})$ constitutes a *partial* grounding of the conjunctions of DL-atoms that occur in $\mathcal{P}$ with respect to the constants in $\mathcal{C}_\mathcal{P}$, since the variables that only occur in DL-atoms in the body of rules are not replaced by constants in $gr_p(\mathcal{P})$.

---

[7] This problem was called *existential entailment* in [28].

Let G be a set of Boolean CQs. Then, we denote by $CQ(G)$ the Boolean CQ corresponding to the conjunction of all the Boolean CQs in G, i.e., $CQ(G) = \bigwedge_{\gamma \in G} \gamma$. We also denote by $UCQ(G)$ the Boolean UCQ corresponding to the disjunction of all the Boolean CQs in G, namely $UCQ(G) = \bigvee_{\gamma \in G} \gamma$.[8]

Similarly to $gr(\mathcal{P}, \mathcal{C}_{\mathcal{P}})$, we define the *partial grounding of* $\mathcal{P}$ *on* $\mathcal{C}_{\mathcal{P}}$ (denoted by $pgr(\mathcal{P}, \mathcal{C}_{\mathcal{P}})$) as the program obtained from $\mathcal{P}$ by grounding with the constants in $\mathcal{C}_{\mathcal{P}}$ all variables *except the existential variables of* R *that only occur in DL-atoms*.

Finally, given a partition (G_P, G_N) of $gr_p(\mathcal{P})$, we denote by $\mathcal{P}(G_P, G_N)$ the ground Datalog$^{\neg\vee}$ program obtained from $pgr(\mathcal{P}, \mathcal{C}_{\mathcal{P}})$ by:

- deleting all occurrences of the conjunction γ from the body of the rules, for each $\gamma \in G_P$;
- deleting each rule in which γ occurs in the body, for each $\gamma \in G_N$;
- deleting each rule in which γ occurs in the head, for each $\gamma \in G_P$;
- deleting all occurrences of the conjunction γ from the head of the rules, for each $\gamma \in G_N$.

Notice that $\mathcal{P}(G_P, G_N)$ is a ground Datalog$^{\neg\vee}$ program over Σ_D, i.e., no DL predicate occurs in such a program.

We are now ready to present the algorithm $\mathcal{DL}+log$-SAT for deciding satisfiability of $\mathcal{DL}+log$-KBs. The algorithm is shown in Figure 3. The algorithm has a very simple structure, since it decides satisfiability by looking for a guess (G_P, G_N) of the Boolean CQs in $gr_p(\mathcal{P})$ that is consistent with the $\mathcal{DL}$-KB $\mathcal{K}$ and such that the Datalog$^{\neg\vee}$ program $\mathcal{P}(G_P, G_N)$ has a stable model.

Algorithm $\mathcal{DL}+log$-SAT$(\mathcal{B})$
Input: $\mathcal{DL}+log$-KB $\mathcal{B} = (\mathcal{K}, \mathcal{P})$ with $\mathcal{K} = (\mathcal{T}, \mathcal{A})$
Output: true if $\mathcal{B}$ is satisfiable, false otherwise
begin
    if there exists partition (G_P, G_N) of $gr_p(\mathcal{P})$
    such that
        (a) $\mathcal{P}(G_P, G_N)$ has a stable model **and**
        (b) $\mathcal{T} \not\models CQ(\mathcal{A} \cup G_P) \subseteq UCQ(G_N)$
    then return true
    else return false
end

Fig. 3. The algorithm $\mathcal{DL}+log$-SAT

Correctness of the algorithm is based on the following property, which relates consistency of a guess (G_P, G_N) of Boolean CQs with the problem of containment of a Boolean CQ in a Boolean UCQ with respect to a $\mathcal{DL}$-TBox.

---

[8] Without loss of generality, we assume that each γ in G uses different existential variable symbols, so that the expression $\bigwedge_{\gamma \in G} \gamma$ can be immediately turned into a Boolean CQ by factoring out all existential quantifications (an analogous simple transformation is needed for turning $UCQ(G)$ into a Boolean UCQ).

Lemma 1. *There exists a model $\mathcal{M}$ for $\mathcal{K} = (\mathcal{T}, \mathcal{A})$ such that every Boolean CQ in G_P is satisfied in $\mathcal{M}$ and every Boolean CQ in G_N is not satisfied in $\mathcal{M}$ if and only if $\mathcal{T} \not\models CQ(\mathcal{A} \cup G_P) \subseteq UCQ(G_N)$.*

Based on the above lemma, we are able to prove correctness of the algorthm $\mathcal{DL}+log$-SAT.

Theorem 1. *Let $\mathcal{B}$ be a $\mathcal{DL}+log$-KB. Then, $\mathcal{B}$ is satisfiable iff $\mathcal{DL}+log$-SAT($\mathcal{B}$) returns true.*

Decidability and complexity. First, from the analysis of the algorithm $\mathcal{DL}+log$-SAT presented above, we are able to prove a very general property that states decidability of reasoning in $\mathcal{DL}+log$ whenever the Boolean CQ/UCQ containment problem is decidable in $\mathcal{DL}$.

Theorem 2. *For every description logic $\mathcal{DL}$, satisfiability of $\mathcal{DL}+log$-KBs is decidable iff Boolean CQ/UCQ containment is decidable in $\mathcal{DL}$.*

From the above theorem and from previous results on query answering and query containment in DLs, we are able to state decidability of reasoning in $\mathcal{DL}+log$ in the case when $\mathcal{DL}$ corresponds to several known DLs. In particular, in the following we briefly analyze the description logics $\mathcal{ALCNR}$, $\mathcal{SHIQ}$, and *DL-Lite*.

First, we observe that, for the description logic $\mathcal{ALCNR}$ it is known that Boolean CQ/UCQ containment is decidable [28], hence reasoning in $\mathcal{ALCNR}+log$-KBs is decidable.

Theorem 3. *Satisfiability of $\mathcal{ALCNR}+log$-KBs is decidable.*

Of course, this result implies decidability of adding weakly-safe Datalog$^{\neg\vee}$ rules to all the DLs that are subsets of $\mathcal{ALCNR}$.

For (a large fragment of) the description logic $\mathcal{SHIQ}$ [25], it is known that answering conjunctive queries is decidable (see [32,20]), but decidability of Boolean CQ/UCQ containment in $\mathcal{SHIQ}$ has not been established yet, therefore satisfiability in $\mathcal{SHIQ}+log$ is still an open problem: however, we conjecture that Boolean CQ/UCQ containment in $\mathcal{SHIQ}$ is decidable as well, and hence that reasoning in $\mathcal{SHIQ}+log$ is decidable.

Finally, for the description logic *DL-Lite* [8], there are known results about the complexity of query answering, which allow us to establish the computational complexity of reasoning in *DL-Lite*$+log$ for different classes of Datalog programs. More precisely, the following theorem refers to *data complexity* of satisfiability, which in the framework of $\mathcal{DL}+log$ corresponds to the analysis of the computational complexity of the problem when we only consider the size of the ABox $\mathcal{A}$ and of the EDB of $\mathcal{P}$, i.e., the set of facts contained in $\mathcal{P}$. In other words, data complexity considers the TBox $\mathcal{T}$ and the rules not corresponding to facts (i.e., the IDB) in $\mathcal{P}$ as fixed, hence they are not part of the input. Data complexity is a very significant measure when the size of the data, i.e., the ABox and the EDB of $\mathcal{P}$, is much larger than the size of the intensional knowledge, i.e., the TBox and the IDB of $\mathcal{P}$.

The following results are based on the analysis of the previous algorithms and on the fact that conjunctive query answering in *DL-Lite* is in PTIME in data complexity (actually it is in LOGSPACE) [8].

Theorem 4. *Let* $\mathcal{B} = (\mathcal{K}, \mathcal{P})$ *be a DL-Lite+log-KB. Then:*

- *if* $\mathcal{P}$ *is a positive Datalog program, then deciding satisfiability of* $\mathcal{B}$ *is PTIME-complete with respect to data complexity;*
- *if* $\mathcal{P}$ *is a positive disjunctive Datalog program, then deciding satisfiability of* $\mathcal{B}$ *is NP-complete with respect to data complexity;*
- *if* $\mathcal{P}$ *is an arbitrary Datalog$^{\neg\vee}$ program, then deciding satisfiability of* $\mathcal{B}$ *is* Σ_2^p*-complete with respect to data complexity.*

Therefore, in DL-lite, under both semantics, the data complexity does not increase with respect to the data complexity of the Datalog program alone [11]. In other words, connecting a *DL-Lite*-KB to a Datalog program does not increase complexity of reasoning in the size of the data. We also point out that *DL-Lite* with arbitrary, non-weakly-safe recursive Datalog rules is undecidable (which follows from the results in [28,10]).

7 Open Problems

We conclude the paper by pointing out some of the most interesting open problems in the integration of DLs and rules.

Semantics. A first and crucial issue concerns the semantic account for logical systems integrating Description Logics and rules. In the paper, we have illustrated the technical problems due to the OWA of DLs and the CWA of non-monotonic Datalog. However, there is also an orthogonal problem which can be summarized as follows: what is the "intended" semantics of a system combining DLs and rules? Research in this field is still far from providing an ultimate answer to the above question. With respect to this issue, in this paper we have only claimed that a minimal requirement that an appropriate semantics for such systems should satisfy is to constitute a "conservative extension" of both the semantics of DLs and the semantics of disjunctive Datalog.

Expressiveness. Another important problem (which is directly related to the previous issue) concerns the expressiveness of a language integrating DLs and rules. In fact, the representational abilities that a system combining DLs and rules should provide to match "practical" needs are not completely clear.

In this respect, we believe that one of the most important expressive limitations of many of the current approaches to the integration of DLs and rules is the rigid separation between DL predicates and Datalog predicates. For instance, in $\mathcal{DL}+log$, since DL predicates have an open interpretation while Datalog predicates have a closed interpretation, it is not possible to express complex pieces of information in which the same predicate is interpreted in different ways (i.e., both under an open-world assumption and under a closed-world assumption) in different parts of the same knowledge base.

Reasoning. As we have explained in the paper, decidability (and complexity) of reasoning is a crucial issue in systems combining DLs and rules. In this respect, there are numerous computational open problems, and the results obtained so far can be seen as the first, preliminary results towards the identification of general computational properties for systems combining DLs and rules.

One important general goal in this direction concerns the identification of the frontier between decidability and undecidability of reasoning with respect to the semantics and the expressiveness (in particular, the "degree of integration") of the formalism combining DLs and rules. In more abstract terms, this corresponds to analyze the trade-off between the expressiveness and the computational properties of such formalism, as usual in Knowledge Representation.

With respect to the above general goal, examples of more specific open problems are the following: (i) it is possible to identify tighter forms of decidable interaction between DL-KBs and rules, which are able to overcome the limitations of $\mathcal{DL}+log$? (ii) within the interaction between DLs and rules imposed by the $\mathcal{DL}+log$ framework, is it possible to establish more general computational properties? for instance, is it possible to establish decidability of $\mathcal{DL}+log$ for very expressive DLs (like OWL-DL)?

Implementation. There is still a considerable distance between the current state of the art in the integration of DLs and rules and the implementation of effective systems. In many approaches, reasoning techniques have not been defined yet, and even in the approaches which have addressed the reasoning problem, the proposed techniques for reasoning in DLs combined with rules have the main goal of establishing general computational properties (decidability and worst-case complexity) of the combined language. Therefore, the problem of turning such techniques into effective and implementable algorithms is still open and mainly unexplored.

As we have explained in the introduction, an important property towards this goal is modularity, i.e., the possibility of reducing reasoning in a system combining a DL component and a rule component to reasoning as "locally" as possible in the single components. On the other hand, it is clear that this modularity is in contrast with the representational goal of increasing the interaction between the DL component and the rule component. So, again, it is necessary to identify suitable trade-offs between such desiderata.[9]

Relationship between Rules and Queries. Finally, the relationship between the integration of DLs and rules and query answering in DLs has not been fully explored yet. As described in the paper, the two problems are very strictly related, since queries can in principle be expressed in terms of rules. Therefore, the known results concerning query answering in DLs could be profitably used towards the design of an expressive and computationally attractive rule language for DLs (and vice versa). The $\mathcal{DL}+log$ approach presented above constitutes a first step in this direction.

---

[9] Modular techniques for dealing with the DL-safe integration of DLs and rules are described in [36,37].

Acknowledgments

The author is grateful to a lot of people for many stimulating discussions on the subject of this paper. In particular, the author wishes to warmly thank Enrico Franconi, Ian Horrocks, Boris Motik, Marie-Christine Rousset, and Sergio Tessaris. A special acknowledgment goes to some of the (present and former) members of the Artificial Intelligence research group and the Data and Knowledge Bases research group at the Dipartimento di Informatica e Sistemistica, Università di Roma "La Sapienza", for introducing the author to this research topic, for their continuous help and for their pioneering work in this topic: Diego Calvanese, Giuseppe De Giacomo, Francesco Donini, Maurizio Lenzerini, Daniele Nardi, Andrea Schaerf.

References

1. Rule interchange format working group charter. http://www.w3.org/2005/rules/wg/charter.
2. Grigoris Antoniou. A nonmonotonic rule system using ontologies. In *Proc. of the First International Workshop on Rules and Rule Markup Languages for the Semantic Web (RuleML 2002)*, volume 60 of *CEUR Workshop Proceedings*, 2002.
3. Grigoris Antoniou. Nonmonotonic rule systems on top of ontology layers. In *Proc. of the 2002 International Semantic Web Conference (ISWC 2002)*, pages 394–398, 2002.
4. Grigoris Antoniou, A. Bikakis, and Gerd Wagner. A system for nonmonotonic rules on the web. In *Proc. of the Third International Workshop on Rules and Rule Markup Languages for the Semantic Web (RuleML 2004)*, pages 23–36, 2004.
5. Grigoris Antoniou, Carlos Viegas Damsio, Benjamin Grosof, Ian Horrocks, Michael Kifer, Jan Maluszynski, and Peter F. Patel-Schneider. Combining rules and ontologies. A survey. REWERSE Deliverable, http://rewerse.net/publications#REWERSE-DEL-2005-I3-D3.
6. Franz Baader, Diego Calvanese, Deborah McGuinness, Daniele Nardi, and Peter F. Patel-Schneider, editors. *The Description Logic Handbook: Theory, Implementation and Applications*. Cambridge University Press, 2003.
7. Chitta Baral and Michael Gelfond. Logic programming and knowledge representation. *J. of Logic Programming*, 19–20:73–148, 1994.
8. Diego Calvanese, Giuseppe De Giacomo, Domenico Lembo, Maurizio Lenzerini, and Riccardo Rosati. DL-Lite: Tractable description logics for ontologies. In *Proc. of the 20th Nat. Conf. on Artificial Intelligence (AAAI 2005)*, pages 602–607, 2005.
9. Diego Calvanese, Giuseppe De Giacomo, and Maurizio Lenzerini. On the decidability of query containment under constraints. In *Proc. of the 17th ACM SIGACT SIGMOD SIGART Symp. on Principles of Database Systems (PODS'98)*, pages 149–158, 1998.
10. Diego Calvanese and Riccardo Rosati. Answering recursive queries under keys and foreign keys is undecidable. In *Proc. of the 10th Int. Workshop on Knowledge Representation meets Databases (KRDB 2003)*. CEUR Electronic Workshop Proceedings, http://ceur-ws.org/Vol-79/, 2003.
11. Evgeny Dantsin, Thomas Eiter, Georg Gottlob, and Andrei Voronkov. Complexity and expressive power of logic programming. *ACM Computing Surveys*, 33(3):374–425, 2001.

12. Jos de Bruijn, Ruben Lara, Axel Polleres, and Dieter Fensel. OWL DL vs. OWL flight: conceptual modeling and reasoning for the semantic web. In *Proc. of the 14th international conference on World Wide Web (WWW 2005)*, pages 623–632, 2005.

13. Francesco M. Donini, Maurizio Lenzerini, Daniele Nardi, and Andrea Schaerf. $\mathcal{AL}$-log: Integrating Datalog and description logics. *J. of Intelligent Information Systems*, 10(3):227–252, 1998.

14. Thomas Eiter, Georg Gottlob, and Heikki Mannilla. Disjunctive Datalog. *ACM Trans. on Database Systems*, 22(3):364–418, 1997.

15. Thomas Eiter, Giovambattista Ianni, Axel Polleres, Roman Schindlauer, and Hans Tompits. Reasoning with rules and ontologies. In Pedro Barahona, François Bry, Enrico Franconi, Ulrike Sattler, and Nicola Henze, editors, *Reasoning Web, Second International Summer School 2005, Tutorial Lectures*, Lecture Notes in Computer Science. Springer, 2006.

16. Thomas Eiter, Nicola Leone, Cristinel Mateis, Gerald Pfeifer, and Francesco Scarcello. The KR system dlv: Progress report, comparison and benchmarks. In *Proc. of the 6th Int. Conf. on Principles of Knowledge Representation and Reasoning (KR'98)*, pages 636–647, 1998.

17. Thomas Eiter, Thomas Lukasiewicz, Roman Schindlauer, and Hans Tompits. Combining answer set programming with description logics for the semantic web. In *Proc. of the 9th Int. Conf. on Principles of Knowledge Representation and Reasoning (KR 2004)*, pages 141–151, 2004.

18. Thomas Eiter, Thomas Lukasiewicz, Roman Schindlauer, and Hans Tompits. Well-founded semantics for description logic programs in the semantic web. In *Proc. of the Third International Workshop on Rules and Rule Markup Languages for the Semantic Web (RuleML 2004)*, pages 81–97, 2004.

19. Michael Gelfond and Vladimir Lifschitz. Classical negation in logic programs and disjunctive databases. *New Generation Computing*, 9:365–385, 1991.

20. Birte Glimm, Ian Horrocks, and Ulrike Sattler. Conjunctive query answering for description logics with transitive roles. In *Proc. of the 2006 Description Logic Workshop (DL 2006)*, 2006.

21. Benjamin N. Grosof, Ian Horrocks, Raphael Volz, and Stefan Decker. Description logic programs: Combining logic programs with description logic. In *Proc. of the 12th Int. World Wide Web Conf. (WWW 2003)*, pages 48–57, 2003.

22. Stijn Heymans, Davy Van Nieuwenborgh, and Dirk Vermeir. Semantic web reasoning with conceptual logic programs. In *Proc. of the Third International Workshop on Rules and Rule Markup Languages for the Semantic Web (RuleML 2004)*, pages 113–127, 2004.

23. Stijn Heymans and Dirk Vermeir. Integrating description logics and answer set programming. In *Proc. of the 2003 International Workshop on Principles and Practice of Semantic Web Reasoning (PPSWR 2003)*, pages 146–159, 2003.

24. Ian Horrocks and Peter F. Patel-Schneider. A proposal for an OWL rules language. In *Proc. of the 13th international conference on World Wide Web (WWW 2004)*, pages 723–731, 2004.

25. Ian Horrocks and Ulrike Sattler. Decidability of SHIQ with complex role inclusion axioms. *Artificial Intelligence*, 160(1–2):79–104, 2004.

26. Alon Y. Levy and Marie-Christine Rousset. CARIN: A representation language combining Horn rules and description logics. In *Proc. of the 12th Eur. Conf. on Artificial Intelligence (ECAI'96)*, pages 323–327, 1996.

27. Alon Y. Levy and Marie-Christine Rousset. The limits on combining recursive Horn rules with description logics. In *Proc. of the 13th Nat. Conf. on Artificial Intelligence (AAAI'96)*, pages 577–584, 1996.

28. Alon Y. Levy and Marie-Christine Rousset. Combining Horn rules and description logics in CARIN. *Artificial Intelligence*, 104(1–2):165–209, 1998.

29. Jing Mei, Shengping Liu, Anbu Yue, and Zuoquan Lin. An extension to OWL with general rules. In *Proc. of the Third International Workshop on Rules and Rule Markup Languages for the Semantic Web (RuleML 2004)*, pages 155–169, 2004.

30. Boris Motik, Ulrike Sattler, and Rudi Studer. Query answering for OWL-DL with rules. In *Proc. of the 2004 International Semantic Web Conference (ISWC 2004)*, pages 549–563, 2004.

31. Boris Motik, Ulrike Sattler, and Rudi Studer. Query answering for OWL-DL with rules. *Web Semantics*, 3(1):41–60, 2005.

32. Maria Magdalena Ortiz, Diego Calvanese, and Thomas Eiter. Characterizing data complexity for conjunctive query answering in expressive description logics. In *Proc. of the 21th Nat. Conf. on Artificial Intelligence (AAAI 2006)*, 2006.

33. Peter F. Patel-Schneider, Patrick J. Hayes, Ian Horrocks, and Frank van Harmelen. OWL web ontology language; semantics and abstract syntax. W3C candidate recommendation, http://www.w3.org/tr/owl-semantics/, november 2002.

34. Raymond Reiter. A logic for default reasoning. *Artificial Intelligence*, 13:81–132, 1980.

35. Riccardo Rosati. Towards expressive KR systems integrating Datalog and description logics: Preliminary report. In *Proc. of the 1999 Description Logic Workshop (DL'99)*, pages 160–164. CEUR Electronic Workshop Proceedings, http://ceur-ws.org/Vol-22/, 1999.

36. Riccardo Rosati. On the decidability and complexity of integrating ontologies and rules. *Web Semantics*, 3(1):61–73, 2005.

37. Riccardo Rosati. Semantic and computational advantages of the safe integration of ontologies and rules. In *Proc. of the 2005 International Workshop on Principles and Practice of Semantic Web Reasoning (PPSWR 2005)*, volume 3703 of *Lecture Notes in Computer Science*, pages 50–64. Springer, 2005.

38. Riccardo Rosati. $\mathcal{DL}$+log: Tight integration of description logics and disjunctive datalog. In *Proc. of the 10th International Conference on Principles of Knowledge Representation and Reasoning (KR 2006)*, 2006. To appear.

Business Rules in the Semantic Web, Are There Any or Are They Different?

Silvie Spreeuwenberg and Rik Gerrits

LibRT, Silodam 364,
1013 AW Amsterdam, Netherlands
{silvie@librt.com, Rik@LibRT.com}
http://www.librt.com

Abstract. The semantic web community and the business rules community have common roots. This article explores the differences and similarities between the two fields in order to encourage collaboration between the communities with respect to standardization efforts and research topics.

Keywords: Business rules, Semantic Web, SBVR, Rule standards, Reasoning languages, Specification languages.

1 Introduction

Research analysts are reporting more and more on the semantic web community (including the ontology research field and reasoning on the web) this last year. Their interest in this topic is triggered by the standardization efforts of the semantic web community at the W3C and the OMG.

In March of this year (2006) the OMG published the draft specification of "Semantics of Business Vocabulary and Business Rules" (SBVR) and the W3C Rule Interchange Format (RIF) working group published its first public working draft of RIF Use Cases and Requirements.

These are just two of several recent developments indicating that business rules are maturing, with standards emerging, clear positioning of rules in business and IT systems, and with regulatory compliance as a major driver.

My visits of several workgroups and conferences in the semantic web community, given my background as a practitioner in the business rules community, has let me to make the following observation: "*the business rules community and semantic web community talk about the same things, but by people with a different background; the business rules community is driven by the practical experiences of business people and business consultants while the semantic web community is a vision of scientists driven by (mostly) scientific publications*".

If this observation is correct, it is important that there is more understanding of each other's work so that we can end up with a 'semantic business' that supports a practical approach to business problems and is supported by a long-term vision.

If this observation is not correct, and the business rules community and the semantic web community do talk about different things, then we need to get a better understanding of the border between the two communities so that we can develop standard transformations or processes to cross these borders.

P. Barahona et al. (Eds.): Reasoning Web 2006, LNCS 4126, pp. 152–163, 2006.

The aim of this article is to get a better understanding of the differences and similarities between the semantic web and business rules community to encourage the collaboration between the two communities. The semantic web community is particularly driving the W3C standards, while the business rules community drives the OMG standards. Although there is no official collaboration between the W3C and the OMG on rules, there is quite strong informal interaction. For example: the OMG hosted the first W3C RIF meeting; 10 members of the RIF working group are also involved in related OMG specifications; the OMG's Ontology Definition Metamodel makes substantial use of the W3C's OWL Web Ontology Language.

Since these communities consist of individuals with private opinions, the choice for particular quotes and definitions influences the resulting conclusion in this article. Hopefully these form a basis for further, fruitful, discussions.

1.1 Organization

This article is organized as follows:

- Paragraph 2 gives a short overview of the semantic web, describing these topics that are needed for a comparison to business rules.
- Paragraph 3 gives a short overview of business rules, describing these topics that are needed for a comparison to semantic web.
- Paragraph 4 makes a comparison between similarities and differences of the ideas in the semantic web and business rules communities
- Paragraph 5 discusses the OMG specification of "Semantics of Business Vocabulary and Business Rules" (SBVR)
- Paragraph 6 makes some final conclusions.

2 Semantic Web

A business oriented description of the Semantic Web is: " … an extension of the current Web in which information is given well-defined meaning, better enabling computers and people to work in cooperation" [3]. A more technical description of the Semantic Web emphasizes the need to have interoperability between software programs on a semantic level, and not just at a precompiled-syntax level. When we look at the literature on and uses of the Semantic Web the support of the interaction between machines/software is very dominant as a goal. On a second place we find interactions between machines/software and humans.

The focus of the semantic web community on machine-machine interaction makes it a candidate to solve long existing integration problems in enterprise architecture. The semantic web should help in making more 'sense' out of software application data to improve interoperability between applications in an enterprise. Software analysts are already picking up this new trend by writing business oriented executive reports on this topic. See for example [1], [2].

The Semantic Web defines the semantics of data in an ontology. The word ontology has very distinct meanings. In the context of the semantic web an ontology structures data in a predefined way so that the semantics of the data can be derived from the relations between the data. An ontology description for a particular domain is referred to as an ontology model. An ontology model consists of concepts (also called classes) and relations between classes.

Typical relations in an ontology language are "sub class of", "class has property", "class is equivalent with". The semantics of the relations are defined in the ontology language specification and the expression power of the language is determined by the expression power of the pre-defined relations and, eventually, the other knowledge representation forms allowed by the language.

Software applications that share an ontology model can exchange information, even if they are not aware of each other's existence at compile time. These software applications are also called 'intelligent agents'. To model the behavior of intelligent agents they may have rules that are defined using the ontology model or in the ontology model (when the ontology language includes a rule language). Since a rule is always expressed in domain terms, any rule language needs to have a model of the domain and this model can be an ontology model.

The question whether the Semantic Web should be augmented to support behavior specification (with rules) is subject to debate (see debate "where are the rules" [4]). Question is if we should augment ontology languages with rules and what type of rules we would need. Take as an example the following rule that can not be expressed in OWL:

If a city code is associated with a state code, and an address uses that city code, then that address has the associated state code.

Current developments seem to point in the direction of augmenting ontology languages with rules. The first steps in this direction seem to restrict the expression power of the rule languages to particular rule types [5].

3 Business Rules

Business rules describe strategies that restrict or guide the behavior of enterprises [6]. An example is a statement that introduces an obligation:

A Customer who appears intoxicated or drugged must not be given possession of a Rental Car.

Such rule is called an operative business rule. These are rules that govern the conduct of business activity. In contrast to Structural Rules, Operative Rules are ones that can be *directly* violated by people involved in the affairs of the business.

A structural rule, like the following:

A Customer has at least one of the following:

- *a Rental Reservation.*
- *an in-progress Rental.*
- *a Rental completed in the past 5 years.*

introduces a necessity. These are rules about how the business chooses to organize (i.e., 'structure') the things it deals with.

A business rule is situated in the context of an enterprise, being *under business jurisdiction'*. 'Under business jurisdiction' is taken to mean that the business can enact, revise and discontinue business rules as it sees fit. If a rule is not under business jurisdiction in that sense, then it is not a business rule. For example, the 'law' of gravity is obviously not a business rule. Neither are the 'rules' of mathematics.

Business rules are described in a language that is natural to business people that are also responsible for the formulation and enforcement of the business rules.

Enforcement of business rules by software programs is a natural phenomenon in enterprises but is not the main goal of formulating and managing business rules. Business rules may be used directly in software programs if the business vocabulary can be mapped to an enterprise data model and a machine using the vocabulary can interpret the business rule expressions.

Rules should be unambiguous. There are several sources that give practitioners guidelines to write non-ambiguous business rules [7, 8]. They all share that all terms used in rules should be defined in a business vocabulary. The business vocabulary defines all the concepts and lists signifiers for those concepts (terms) relevant to describe the business rules of a domain (read: particular business area of interest) in a particular language. Besides the definitions of concepts a business vocabulary defines all the relations between concepts (needed for expression of all business rules). A structural definition defines a concept in terms of its relations to other concepts (similar to the way concepts are defined in an ontology model).

One or more concepts that are related are called 'fact types' and they form the basis for business rule expressions. Different type of relations may be predefined so that relations have consistent semantics in different vocabularies. Examples of those predefined relations are "is assorted to", "is a generalization of", "is a category of". There is an obvious overlap when we compare these relations with the relations we typical find in an ontology-model.

The examples in table 1 show that the synonyms 'car' and 'automobile' are not defined with a relation between the concepts 'car' and 'automobile', but that they are in fact different signifiers for the same concept in a particular language. The definition of the concept is considered part of the vocabulary, while such descriptions are not a required element of an ontology model. The simple relations between concepts (Fact Type 1 and 5) are defined in a similar way as in an ontology-model. Expression of the derived fact types (Fact type 2 and 3) and the rule may be very different in an ontology model, depending on the ontology language in use.

Current standardization efforts at the OMG are standardizing the semantics for business rules [9].

Table 1. Example of what you can find in a business vocabulary including business rules

Concept	Concept with definition 'a motorized vehicle' has signifier 'car' and 'automobile' for the English language
Fact type 1	A car has wheels
Fact type 2	A normal car is a category of an automobile where the car has exactly four wheels
Fact type 3	A car drives with a speed
Fact	A Mercedes is a 'normal car'
Rule	It is forbidden to drive with a speed greater than 100 km. per hour with a three-wheeled-car

4 Comparison Business Rules and Semantic Web

4.1 Common Roots

The semantic web and the business rules communities have their roots in Artificial Intelligence. However, the players in both communities like to decouple themselves from this ancestor. This seems to be due to the failure of AI technologies to deliver when the pioneers set high expectations. The idea to formalize and reason with domain knowledge using logic and logical inference is known in the field of AI as the study of knowledge representation. The offspring of this research are expert systems. Product vendors in this area are now positioning themselves as business rule management systems. Product vendors in the area of the semantic web position themselves more in the field of knowledge management where the challenge is to present the right information on the right time and in the right place.

4.2 Different Target Audience

Improvement of communication between humans is a goal of the business rules approach while improvement of the communication between machines is the goal of the semantic web. Both emphasize that improvement of the communication between humans and machines can be a happy side effect.

Given this difference in target audience the two approaches are also positioned differently in the Model Driven Architecture (MDA) of the Object Management Group [10]. An ontology-model is used in a run-time environment and should therefore be positioned at the PSM-level, while a vocabulary is used at the CIM level to improve human communication about a domain.

A survey under ontology tool builders [11, 12] shows a different trend. There focus is to decrease the complexity of building full-blown and full proof ontology's, especially for domain experts (business people without training in formal logics or computer programming) rather than professionals trained in formal logic and ontology design.

4.3 Same Goal

Both the business rules and semantic web techniques are supposed to capture semantics about real world domains (independent of a particular application or task). This distinguishes them (ontology models and vocabularies) from conceptual modeling approaches (like UML and ORM) that are both intended to describe the domain knowledge for one specific application.

The idea to be more independent of a particular application or task should encourage the reuse of business vocabularies and ontology models. There is an interesting friction here that is recognized in the business rules community [13] and the semantic web community [14] in that rules are affected by the nature of the problem (or business strategy) that they support and the inference strategy to be applied to the problem. Therefore the resulting rules that are captured in the context of a particular task will be less reusable and more specific to a particular (class of similar) task(s).

4.4 Similar Form

A business vocabulary and ontology both consist of interrelated concepts and rules (e.g. identity, cardinality, taxonomy etc.) that constrain and specify the intended meaning of concepts.

In an ontology-model only the structural relations between concepts define the semantics. In a business vocabulary the semantics can also be described by giving a definition for a concept. This definition may be informal and every concept needs to have a definition. In an ontology-model, concepts do not have a definition. You can just stop somewhere at the border of your domain with connecting a concept with other concepts.

The business rules approach focuses more on natural language / human readable descriptions, for example the expression of definitions and business rules is not restricted to a specific formal specification language. In the Semantic Web every element that is part of the ontology model should be compliant with a formal language because otherwise it cannot be used in a run-time environment.

4.5 Different Expression Power

The formal specification languages used by the semantic web and the business rules communities differ in expression power and assumption. The expression power that is requested in the business rules community is high, including the notion of higher order logic, deontic logic and predicate logic. The initiatives of rules in the Semantic Web are mostly based on horn clause logic or other descriptive logics and the expressiveness of these languages is questioned (see also the discussion in [4]). Another difference is that the business rules languages often work under a 'closed world assumption' while the semantic web languages uses an 'open-world assumption'.

The next paragraph gives an overview of the a business rules standard developed by the business rules community and provides more detail on the expression power available to the business rules community by this standard.

5 Semantics of Business Vocabulary and Rules (SBVR)[1]

The OMG has traditionally a strong technology focus, for example with a standard like CORBA. With the UML standard they entered the more conceptual side of IT. In recent years, its Business Modeling and Integration Domain Task Force has been widening the OMG's scope to include business modeling. SBVR (Semantics of Business Vocabulary and Rules) will be the first to emerge from this programme.

SBVR is a specification for building and interchanging business vocabulary and business rules at the business level, regardless of whether the rules will be automated in IT systems, or applied and enforced by people in the enterprise.

SBVR has a theoretical foundation of formal logic. The base is first-order predicate logic (with possible extensions into higher-order logics), with some limited extensions into modal logic – notably some deontic forms, for expressing obligation and prohibition, and alethic forms for expressing necessities.

5.1 Terminology Basis

The SVBR "Vocabulary for Describing Business Vocabularies" is based on the ISO terminology standards:

-   ISO 1087-1 (2000) "Terminology work — Vocabulary — Theory and application",
-   ISO 704 (2000) "Terminology work — Principles and methods", and
-   ISO 860 (1996) "Terminology work – Harmonization of concepts and terms".

These standards have been used for many decades for multilingual vocabularies in support of language translation work. An SBVR-based business vocabulary strengthens the semantics of ordinary business glossaries of terms and their definitions in several ways. It provides:

1. a multi-dimensional, hierarchical categorization capability to organize concepts from general to specific. This is often referred to as taxonomies or categorization schemes. The ability to define categories is also included.
2. the capabilities associated with Thesauri including synonyms, abbreviates, 'see also', multiple vocabularies for same set of meanings for different languages, etc.
3. the ability to specify definitions (both intensional and extensional) formally and unambiguously in terms of other definitions in the business vocabulary as a result of its formal logics and linguistic underpinning.
4. the ability to define connections between concepts that are of interest to the organization. These connections provide the business-level semantic structure required to find information about such relationships in text documents and relational databases, as well as providing the ability to specify business rules formally and unambiguously. The function in the ISO/IEC 13250:2000 "Topic Maps" standard is included in SBVR-based business vocabularies.

---

[1] SBVR is in the OMG's finalization process and is scheduled to become a released OMG specification in October 2006. The draft specification is available publicly for comment and issues (www.omg.org/technology/documents/bms_spec_catalog.htm) until 24 July 2006.

5. a semantically rich set of templates to facilitate capturing the full semantics of each concept and connection between concepts of interest to the business community owning the business vocabulary.
6. a basis for identification and/or definition of individual entities.
7. the basis for tools that can support powerful visualization and 'navigation' of business vocabulary based on business meaning.
8. business community ownership and management of their independent business vocabularies and business rules.
9. the ability to minimize the number of definitions an organization needs to create by providing powerful, pragmatic features for vocabulary adoption on a well-managed basis. The SBVR approach encourages (a) incorporation of ready-made 'outside' vocabularies and (b) communication between people in different communities.
10. a comprehensively integrated capability to support the specification of the meaning of all kinds of business rules.

5.2 Rules in SBVR

In SBVR, rules are always constructed by applying necessity or obligation to fact types. Informally, a fact type is an association[2] between two or more concepts; for example, the rule "A Rental must not have more than three Additional Drivers" is based on the fact type "Rental has Additional Driver".

By this means, SBVR realizes a core principle of the Business Rules Approach at the business level, which is that "Business rules build on fact types, and fact types build on concepts as expressed by terms." This notion is well-documented in published material by foremost industry experts over the past 10 years.

It is specifically *not* the intention of the BRT to mandate any particular notation(s) that must or should be used with the SBVR Metamodel. SBVR Structured English (presented in Appendix F of the specification) is just one of possibly many notations that can be used to express the SBVR Metamodel, and, as a notation, is non-normative in the SVBR standard.

Two styles of SBVR Structured English are documented in this submission:

- Prefixed Rule Keyword Style
- Embedded (mix-fix) Rule Keyword Style

The prefix style introduces rules by prefixing a statement with keywords that convey a modality. Examples of some of the prefixes are shown in the table below.

Operative	Structural
It is obligatory that	It is necessary that
It is prohibited that	It is impossible that
It is permitted that	It is possible that

The embedded style features the use of rule keywords embedded (usually in front of verbs) within rules statements of appropriate kinds. The table below shows a sample of embedded keywords used to form rules.

---

[2] "Association" is used here in its everyday, business sense - not the narrower, technical sense that would apply to a UML class model.

Operative	Structural
... must ...	... always ...
... must not ...	... never ...
... may ...	... sometimes ...

This style is an existing, documented notation[3] (RuleSpeak®, by Business Rule Solutions, LLC) that has been used with business people in actual practice for a number of years, as requested by the RFP.

5.3 Formal Logic

The SBVR initiative is intended to capture business facts and business rules that may be expressed either informally or formally. Business rule expressions are parsed, and are classified as formal only if they are expressed purely in terms of fact types in the pre-declared schema for the business domain, as well as certain logical/ mathematical operators, quantifiers etc. Formal rules are transformed into a logical formulation that is used for exchange with other rules-based software tools. Informal rules may be exchanged as un-interpreted comments.

All and only formal logic-based entries in SBVR will be able to be transformed into other standards based on formal logic like RDF(S) and/or OWL.

5.4 Open / Closed World

SBVR supports both open and closed world semantics. For any given domain, the business might have complete knowledge about some parts and incomplete knowledge about other parts. Therefore, a mixture of open and closed world assumptions is supported.

Adopting closed world semantics basically means that all relevant facts are known. So if a fact cannot be proved true, it is assumed to be false. This closed world assumption entails negation by failure, since failure to find a fact implies its negation. Open world semantics allows that some knowledge may be incomplete; so if a proposition and its negation are both absent, it is unknown whether the proposition is true.

In modeling any given business domain, SBVR restricts the facts in the vocabulary, to facts of interest to that domain. If a fact is not relevant to that domain, it is not included, but it is not assumed to be false, rather it is not considered. However, it is a practical issue whether one's knowledge pertaining to the population of a given fact type is complete or not, since this may impact how the business derives other facts (e.g. negations) or how it reacts to query results (e.g. whether to treat "not" as "not the case" or merely "not known to be the case"). Therefore SBVR regards the issue of open/closed world semantics to be relevant to the fact model itself, not just automated implementations of the fact model.

SBVR use the term "local closure" for the application of the closed world assumption to just some parts of the overall schema. One might assume open world semantics by default, and then apply local closure to specific parts as desired; or alternatively, assume closed world semantics by default and then apply "local openness".

---

[3] Principles of the Business Rule Approach, by Ronald G. Ross, Addison-Wesley, Boston, MA, 2003, Chapters 8-12.

Local closure may be explicitly asserted for any object type, on an individual basis, to declare that for each state the fact model population agrees with that of the object type's population in the actual business domain. The relevant meta-fact type is: "<u>concept</u> is closed in <u>conceptual schema</u>".

Closure may also be asserted for fact types. Semi-closure is with respect to the fact model population of the object types playing a role in the predicate. If closure has also been declared for the object types, then (full) closure also holds for the fact type (i.e. closure with respect to the domain population of the object types). The relevant meta-fact types are: "<u>fact type</u> is semi-closed in <u>conceptual schema</u>" and "<u>concept</u> is closed in <u>conceptual schema</u>", which applies to both object types and fact types.

Closure for a fact type is sometimes implied. A mandatory role with a frequency constraint, implies that the fact is semi-closed by implication. For example given the sentences:

- each employee has at most one employee name
- each employee must have an employee name
- employee is closed

The closed world assumption is implied for the employee name fact type (employee is closed, so we have all the employees; having a name is mandatory, so we have at least one name for each employee; the uniqueness constraint means that each employee has at most one name; so for all employees we now have all their names).

5.5 Higher Order Logic

SBVR allows both first-order logic and higher-order logic restricted to Henkin semantics. Henkin semantics restricts quantifiers to range over only individuals and those predicates that are specified in the universe of discourse (the business domain), where the n-ary predicates/functions (n > 0) range over a fixed set of n-ary relations/operations. By restricting the ranges of predicate, the Henkin interpretation retains certain desirable first-order properties (e.g. completeness, compactness, and the Skolem-Löwenheim theorems) that are lost in the standard interpretation of higher-order logic.

SBVR supports 'intentional roles' for sentences where a subject or object is really an intension, rather than a denotation. This results in sentences like:

*If the average of salaries of employees in a department **increases by** 10% in a given month then .*

This sentence is based on the fact:

*quantity [intensional] **increases by** percentage*

A logician may rewrite this rule to a first order statement:

If the average of salaries of employees in a department at a point in time in a given month is 10% less than the average of salaries of employees in that department at another point in time in that month and the other point in time follows the first point in time then ..

However, 'normal' people will not write such a statement. Support for higher order statements is motivated by the more 'natural' way of writing rules for business people.

In [15], some ways are suggested to avoid higher-order types, by treating types as intensional objects whose instances may sometimes be in 1:1 correspondence (but not identical) to subtypes, by requiring subtype definitions to be informative, by remodeling (including demotion of metadata to data), and by treating types as individuals in separate models.

The decision on whether to use higher-order types is left to the user of SBVR.

6 Conclusion

The similarities between the two approaches should encourage researchers and practitioners to work more closely together to explore fundamental issues at the level of capturing the semantics of real world domains. This collaboration is already started, for example with a W3C workshop on business rules (see http://www.w3.org/2005/rules). Tool builders that want to serve both communities to broaden their market drive these collaborations. Given the differences between the expression power and target audience of business rules and semantic web rules, they will need clearly defined transformations between business rules standards and semantic web standards. I see the most important challenge and research topic as the mapping from business rules that should be automated, written in a non technical language under a 'closed world assumption', to technical executable rules that can be used by IT systems with semantic web technology and an 'open world assumption'.

Acknowledgments. This research has been funded by the European Commission and by the Swiss State Secretariat for Education and Research within the 6th Framework Programme project REWERSE number 506779 (cf. http://rewerse.net).

References

1. Richard Edwards, Butler Group Review Journal Article: Impact of the Semantic Web October 2004
2. Diego Lo Giudice and Michael Guttman, Where Enterprise Architecture meets the Semantic Web, Enterprise Architecture, Vol. 8, No. 8 Cutter Consortium
3. Berners-Lee, Tim, James Hendler, and Ora Lassila. "The Semantic Web." *Scientific American*, May 2001.
4. IEEE Intelligent Systems, september - october 2003, Trends & Controversies, "Where are the rules?" p.76
5. Gerd Wagner Said Tabet, and Harold Boley, The Abstract Syntax of RuleML –Towards a General Web Rule Language Framework, IEEE/WIC/ACM International Conference on Web Intelligence (WI'04).
6. Business Rules Group, Defining business rules, what they really are, July 2000.
7. The BRS RuleSpeak® Practitioner Kit ,Software: PDF Reference Files. © 2001-2004 Business Rule Solutions, LLC

8. Silvie Spreeuwenberg, "Using Verification and Validation Techniques for High-quality Business Rules," Business Rules Journal, Vol. 4, No. 2, (February 2003), URL: http://www.BRCommunity.com/a2003/b132.html.
9. Object Management Group, Business Semantics of Business Rules RFP, OMG Document: br/2003-05-01
10. Joaquin Miller and Jishnu Mukerji., MDA Guide Version 1.0.1 OMG Document: omg/2003-06-01
11. OntoWeb, A survey on ontology tools, URL: http://www.aifb.unikarlsruhe.de/WBS/ysu/publications/OntoWeb_Del_1-3.pdf
12. Michael Denny, Ontology Tools Survey, Revisited, URL: http://www.xml.com/pub/a/2004/07/14/onto.html
13. Rik Gerrits, "Business Rules, Can They Be Re-used?" Business Rules Journal, Vol. 5, No. 9 (Sep. 2004), URL: http://www.BRCommunity.com/a2004/b203.html
14. Mustafa Jarrar, on using conceptual data modeling for ontology engineering, Journal on Data Semantics, Vol 1.1 Springer 2003
15. Halpin, T. 2004, 'Information Modeling and Higher-Order Types', Proc. CAiSE'04 Workshops, vol. 1, (eds Grundspenkis, J. & Kirkova, M.), Riga Tech. University, pp. 233-48. Available online at http://www.orm.net/pdf/EMMSAD2004.pdf.

Ontologies and Text Mining as a Basis for a Semantic Web for the Life Sciences

Andreas Doms[1], Vaida Jakonienė[2], Patrick Lambrix[2],
Michael Schroeder[1], and Thomas Wächter[1]

[1] Biotechnological Centre
Technische Universität Dresden, Germany
[2] Department of Computer and Information Science
Linköpings universitet, Sweden

Abstract. The life sciences are a promising application area for semantic web technologies as there are large online structured and unstructured data repositories and ontologies, which structure this knowledge.
We briefly give an overview over biomedical ontologies and show how
they can help to locate, retrieve, and integrate biomedical data. Annotating literature with ontology terms is an important problem to support
such ontology-based searches. We review the steps involved in this text
mining task and introduce the ontology-based search engine GoPubMed.
As the underlying data sources evolve, so do the ontologies. We give a
brief overview over different approaches supporting the semi-automatic
evolution of ontologies.

1 Introduction

Researchers in various areas, e.g. medicine, agriculture and environmental sciences, use biological data sources and tools to answer different research questions
or to solve various tasks [CGG03]. One of the main goals is to understand how
various organisms function as biological systems. To achieve this goal, it is important to explore functions and interactions of genome-encoded components.
This type of knowledge may be used for different purposes. For instance, it is
used to identify genes responsible for a disease, to develop drugs enabling treatment of diseases and to predict organisms' responses to a drug. Also, research
is conducted on how the genomes vary between species, how mutations affect
functioning of different components in organisms and what differences they cause
between organisms. Also, the influence of environmental factors on human health
and diseases is investigated.

During recent years an enormous amount of biological data, such as DNA
and protein sequences, gene regulatory and protein interaction networks, and
secondary together with tertiary structures of molecules, has been generated.
This data is spread in a large number of autonomous data sources that are often
publicly available on the Web. There are also numerous tools available on the
Web such as BLAST, a sequence alignment tool.

Researchers that need to use these databases and tools experience a number
of difficulties (e.g. [Lam05]). A first difficulty is to *locate the relevant data sources*

P. Barahona et al. (Eds.): Reasoning Web 2006, LNCS 4126, pp. 164–183, 2006.

and tools. There are many data sources and users need to have good knowledge about which data sources exist and what information they contain. Often data sources contain overlapping information and the required information can be obtained in a number of ways. Depending on which way is chosen, there may be a difference in the time it takes to obtain results as well as in the quality of the obtained results. Further, it is not easy to stay up to date as the environment is changing frequently. New data is added to the data sources on daily basis. For instance, in 1986 SWISS-PROT, a protein database, contained a few thousand data entries, while in 2006 the database contains over 200 000 entries. Further, new data sources appear frequently. For instance, the yearly database issue of the Nucleic Acids Research [NAR] journal and the NAR Molecular Biology Database Collection reported on 386 data sources in 2003, 548 in 2004, 719 in 2005 and 858 in 2006. Data sources may also disappear. A specific property of biological data sources is further that their structure is frequently modified. This happens, for instance, when new types of data are generated by novel tools and approaches.

A second difficulty is to, once the relevant data sources are identified, *retrieve the relevant information*. Current retrieval approaches are often syntax based and do not provide good precision and recall. This means that the query results often contain information that is not relevant for the user's query. One reason is that terms are often ambiguous. For instance, when looking for information about jaguars, the result will include documents about the animal as well as documents about the car. It is also the case that much relevant information may not be found. For instance, when looking for information about signal transducers also documents about receptors are interesting as receptors are a special kind of signal transducers. However, syntax-based retrieval systems will not return these documents unless signal transducer also occurs explicitly in these documents.

A third difficulty is that for most tasks data from different sources needs to be *integrated*. For instance, to find publications describing a given disease that relates to a certain type of sequences may require analysis of data sources for publications, diseases and sequences together with some other data sources combining these types of information [LMN04]. To predict properties of a new protein sequence, data sources containing information about protein sequences, protein families and protein structures may be needed. Because the data sources are developed and supported independently by different groups and organizations, the data sources are highly heterogeneous in various aspects [LJ03]. They differ in content, i.e. the type of information that they store, although data sources may also contain overlapping information. The quality of the data may differ. For instance, some data sources contain experimentally verified data while other data sources contain predicted data (e.g. generated by data mining programs). Different kinds of data models are used for the representation of the data such as the relational model, the object-oriented model, semi-structured data and flat files. The sources are also heterogeneous regarding their query languages and query capabilities. Further, there is a terminology discrepancy problem. Data sources can use different terminology to represent the same data or the same term may be used by different sources to refer to different data items.

In the remainder of the paper we introduce the vision of the Semantic Web and show how a first step towards this vision can be taken using ontologies and text mining. We show which efforts are being made to create bio-ontologies serving as source of a common vocabulary in a domain. Ontologies formulate biological knowledge. We show how ontologies are used to annotate biological databases like UniProt enabling the connection to other biological sources. We discuss cases in which overlapping ontologies are being aligned. A huge amount of biological knowledge is only accessible through texts. We show how text mining can be used the alleviate the access to large document sources. We present GoPubMed, an ontology-based literature search system. GoPubMed provides 33 million ontology annotations for articles in the literature database PubMed. This is a valuable source used for a bibliometrical analysis of all PubMed abstracts published since 1972. As scientific research develops, domain ontologies have to evolve. We give an overview over the design, maintenance and evolution of ontologies. Finally, we discuss how ontological knowledge can be used to support the querying of multiple biological data sources.

2   Semantic Web

The current Web is essentially a collection of documents that are interconnected by links and it is used as a portal to applications. For instance, the biological data sources available on the Web provide access through Web pages. To query the data sources often the users fill out forms. The results are again presented to the users as Web pages. The Web pages are presented to the users based on mark-up. This mark-up mainly represents rendering information, such as the font and color of the text, and links to other Web pages. Therefore, the current Web is mostly a medium of documents for people rather than for information that can be processed automatically by computers [BHL01].

The Semantic Web is a vision of a further development of the World Wide Web "in which information is given well-defined meaning, better enabling computers and people to work in cooperation" [BHL01]. The World Wide Web Consortium states it as follows [W3C-sw]: "The Web can reach its full potential only if it becomes a place where data can be shared and processed by automated tools as well as by people. ... The Semantic Web is a vision: the idea of having data on the Web defined and linked in a way that it can be used by machines not just for display purposes, but for automation, integration and reuse of data across various applications."

As a first step towards this vision of making the content of Web pages machine-understandable, people have started to use semantic annotation. One way to do this is to annotate the Web pages with 'meaningful' tags. In this case we annotate the Web pages with XML mark-up to distinguish the meaningful parts of the document. For instance, in a Web page about a protein we may distinguish between its name, coding DNA, three dimensional structure, family, function, source organism, etc. Then we use programs that recognize the mark-up and the different parts of the document can then be used in other programs based on the meaning represented by the mark-up. However, for this approach to be successful, there is a need for agreement on the annotation. A solution to this is to use ontologies to specify the meaning of the annotations. The ontologies define a vocabulary, specify the meaning of the terms and define how new terms can be formed by combining existing terms.

The use of ontology-based annotations will alleviate the problems discussed in section 1. An approach that would alleviate the difficulty of *locating the relevant data sources and tools* is to use Semantic Web services. In the current Web service [W3C-ws] approach, data sources and tools can be seen as service providers and announce their services. Data sources, for instance, can announce their content and query capabilities. Users can be seen as consumers that request services based on their task. User requests and services are matched by service matchers. When we semantically enable the Web service approach, service providers are able to use ontologies to describe their services and users can use ontologies when formulating their requests. The service matchers will then more easily find relevant services. By using ontologies during information retrieval, it is possible to *reduce the amount of non-relevant information* in the returned results. For instance, when looking for information about jaguars, the user may use an ontology to state that she is interested in the animal. The result will then only include documents about the animal. It is also possible to *find more relevant information*. For instance, when looking for information about signal transducers, we may take into account information from an ontology that states that receptors are a special kind of signal transducers. Therefore, also documents about receptors will be returned. Finally, semantic annotations can enhance the *integration* process. Entities in different data sources that are annotated with the same or related ontology terms are likely related. Relations between data items could be derived from relations (e.g. equivalent, is-a, part-of) between the ontology terms they are annotated with.

3   Ontologies in Bioinformatics

Intuitively, ontologies (e.g. [Lam04, Gom99]) can be seen as defining the basic terms and relations of a domain of interest, as well as the rules for combining these terms and relations. Ontologies are used for communication between people and organizations by providing a common terminology over a domain. They provide the basis for interoperability between systems. They can be used for making the content in information sources explicit and serve as an index to a repository of information. Further, they can be used as a basis for integration of information sources and as a query model for information sources. They also support a clear separation of domain knowledge from application-based knowledge as well as validation of data sources. The benefits of using ontologies include reuse, sharing and portability of knowledge across platforms, and improved documentation, maintenance, and reliability. Overall, ontologies lead to a better understanding of a field and to more effective and efficient handling of information in that field.

In the field of bioinformatics the work on ontologies is recognized as essential in some of the grand challenges of genomics research [CGG03] and there is much international research cooperation for the development of ontologies (e.g. the Gene Ontology (GO) [GO] and Open Biomedical Ontologies (OBO) [OBO] efforts) and the use of ontologies for the Semantic Web (e.g. the EU Network of Excellence REWERSE Working Group A2 [REWERSE]).

Many bio-ontologies exist. Many of the model organism databases such as Flybase and Mouse Genome database can be seen as simple ontologies. Further, there are ontologies focusing on things such as protein functions, organism development, anatomy and pathways. (For examples we refer to e.g. [Lam04, OBO, SOFG].) The use of ontologies in bioinformatics has grown drastically since database builders concerned with developing systems for different (model) organisms joined to create the Gene Ontology Consortium in 1998. The goal of GO is to produce a structured, precisely defined, common and dynamic controlled vocabulary that describes the roles of genes and proteins in all organisms. Currently, there are three independent ontologies publicly available: biological process, molecular function and cellular component. The GO ontologies have become a de facto standard and are used by many biological data sources for annotation.

Recently, Open Biomedical Ontologies was started as an umbrella Web address for ontologies for use within the genomics and proteomics domains. The member ontologies are required to be open, to be written in a common syntax, to be orthogonal to each other, to share a unique identifier space and to include textual definitions. Many bio-ontologies are already available via OBO.

The field has matured enough to start talking about standards. An example of this is the organization of the first conference on Standards and Ontologies for Functional Genomics (SOFG) in 2002 and the development of the SOFG resource on ontologies [SOFG].

4   Ontological Knowledge in Bioinformatics

The publicly available ontological knowledge in bioinformatics includes not only the actual ontologies, but there are also alignments between ontologies, ontological annotations of data sources, and mappings between data values and ontological terms. We briefly describe each of these.

Bio-ontologies. There is a large variety of bio-ontologies. They differ in the type of biological knowledge they describe, their intended use, the adopted level of abstraction and the knowledge representation language. For instance, via OBO we can access a number of ontologies having different biological focus and that are developed for different purposes. We have already mentioned the GO ontologies. MeSH is an ontology produced by the American National Library of Medicine and is used for indexing, cataloging, and searching for biomedical and health-related information and documents. Anatomical Dictionary for the Adult Mouse (MA) is an anatomy ontology covering part of the lifespan of the laboratory mouse. The TAMBIS ontology [GSN01] is an ontology covering a wide range of biological concepts and is used as a unified schema to support queries over multiple data sources in an information integration system. With respect to the described knowledge abstraction the ontologies may range from high level ontologies that define general biological knowledge to ontologies that describe selected biological aspects. For instance, some general biological knowledge is covered in the TAMBIS ontology, like protein and nucleic acid are biomolecules, and motif is-component-of protein. On the other hand, the GO molecular function ontology defines the space of possible biological functions, like signal transducer activity and the more specific function receptor activity. The ontologies can be represented in a spectrum of representation formalisms ranging from very informal to strictly formal. Depending on the types of knowledge that are represented the ontologies can be classified from controlled vocabularies, taxonomies, thesauri, data models, and frame-based ontologies to knowledge-based ontologies [Lam04]. Many ontologies in bioinformatics started as controlled vocabularies, which are essentially list of terms (e.g. MeSH). Nowadays, a number of ontologies are augmented to support more advanced representation. For instance, GO and MA can be classified as thesauri, as they organize terms in a graph where the arcs in the graph represent a fixed set of relations. For instance, MA organizes anatomical structures spatially and functionally, using is-a and part-of relations (e.g. brain is-a head organ and it is part-of central nervous system). In addition, GO ontologies support the exact_synonym and narrow_synonym relations. The TAMBIS ontology can be classified as a knowledge base which is based on description logics.

Ontology alignments. Several of the existing bio-ontologies contain overlapping information, provide different views on an area or may cover different but related areas. Often we would therefore want to be able to use multiple ontologies. For instance, companies may want to use community standard ontologies and use them together with company-specific ontologies. Applications may need to use ontologies from different areas or from different views on one area. Ontology builders may want to use already existing ontologies as the basis for the creation of new ontologies by extending the existing ontologies or by combining knowledge from different smaller ontologies. In each of these cases it is important to know the relationships between the terms in the different ontologies. We call these inter-ontology relationships alignments. These alignments may describe equivalence, specialization or other relations between the terms. It has been realized that this is a major issue and some organizations have started to deal with it. For instance, the organization for Standards and Ontologies for Functional Genomics (SOFG) [SOFG] developed the SOFG Anatomy Entry List which defines cross species anatomical terms relevant to functional genomics and which can be used as an entry point to anatomical ontologies. Currently, not so many inter-ontology alignments are available. In the near future we expect an increase of such knowledge as many ontology alignment tools are currently being developed to support the identification of such alignments. For instance, given the terms auditory bone (MA) and ear ossicle (MeSH), and knowing that incus is a kind of auditory bone (MA), an alignment system should be able to identify that auditory bone and ear ossicle represent the same thing and it should derive that incus is a kind of ear ossicle. The used matching techniques should also enable identifying relations between completely different terms, e.g. that inner ear (MA) is a synonym to labyrinth (MeSH). For an overview of ontology alignment systems see [LT06].

Annotations. To describe properties of biological objects in a uniform way, it becomes common in bioinformatics to annotate data entries in data sources with ontological terms. For instance, terms from the GO molecular function ontology are used to describe gene and protein functions. Annotations can be stored as separate mapping rules, included in an ontology or stored in a data source entry. For instance, different data source annotations by GO terms can be found on the web pages of the GO Consortium. In addition to other relations, GO ontologies support the xref_analog relation that allows to link ontological terms to biological objects having the described properties.

Mappings between data values and ontological terms. In a similar way as whole data entries are related to ontological terms, the allowed values for certain data properties can be indexed based on ontology terms. For instance, keywords used to describe data entries in UniProt, a data source of protein sequences and related data, are mapped to terms in GO ontologies. Similarly as for ontology alignments, different techniques could be used to support the identification of matching terms.

Not only biological databases like UniProt are use to collect biological knowledge. Most biological knowledge is still stored in texts. Text Mining is used to annotate large corpora of text in order to automatically extract knowledge from it. In a more advanced process text mining can even help discovering new knowledge by combining facts retrieved from different documents.

5   Biological Knowledge in Text

The amount of literature available online today is enormous. Ingenta (www.ingenta.com), an online index of 17,000 periodicals, has 7 million articles going back to 1988. Infotrieve (www.infotrieve.com) indexes over 20,000 journals with 15 million citations. CiteSeer (www.citeseer.com), a digital library, covers over 300,000 publications and over 4 million citations. Databases for scientific literature are growing at an astonishing rate. PubMed, a biomedical literature database, has grown by about half a million cited documents in the last year ([DDK04]) and covers now more than 14 million abstracts of scientific literature, although about half of them are retractions and corrections (www.PubMed.org, [SC03]).

Without effective access to the knowledge in the above literature repositories most of it will remain buried within the masses of text. Text mining addresses this dilemma by aiming to extract useful knowledge from unstructured or semi-structured text.

5.1   Text Mining

Text mining is the discovery of knowledge in natural language texts. The important difference between regular data mining and text mining is that text mining deals with natural language text. So the data is not structured and thus directly accessible for computer programs. We distinguish the discovery of new knowledge, which was not stated before, and information extraction, which reads in text and presents facts like author names, addresses or job skills from its content. In order to extract particular information hidden in text, one approach is called *computational linguistics* or *natural language processing*.

Natural language processing. Texts consist of sequences of sentences which themselves consist of words. A goal of natural language processing is to annotate the structure of sentences. The meaning of a sentence can be easier understood when the grammatical structure is known. [Bri93] uses learning algorithms to build a structural knowledge base which is then used to annotate sentences. Other approaches use manually created knowledge bases for their annotation. Such systems take sentences like "The children play." and assign the structural information that *children* stands for the plural of *child* that *play* is a verb, that the two words form a noun phrase and that all the words together form a sentence. This process is called *part of speech (POS) tagging*. The biggest available manually annotated corpus is the Penn Treebank corpus with one million annotated words.

Sentence splitting aims to find the boundaries of each sentence in a text. A simple approach is to search for periods followed by a space and an upper case letter. Problems occur with identifiers containing periods and abbreviations, which is frequently the case in the life sciences. For example, species are often abbreviated, such as the worm C. elegans.

Tokenizing is the operation of splitting up a string of characters into a set of tokens. The basic approach of splitting at each space character introduces problems with multi word tokens sometimes written as hyphenated compounds. Biological entities are often found in different spelling styles.

It is not trivial to decide how to tokenize GO terms. GO terms contain hyphens, commas, brackets, apostrophes and other special characters. If *"Interleukin-1"* is split to *interleukin* and *1*, it would become ambiguous. The word *low-density* in **low-density lipoprotein receptor binding** (GO:0050750), however, keeps the same meaning when written *"low density"*. Even the authors of GO use this phrase inconsistently. In the definition of the GO term, they write: *"Interacting selectively with a low density lipoprotein receptor."*

Stemming transforms words of different morphological variants into their stem, e.g. *trees* is transformed into *tree*. One well known algorithm is the Porter-Stemmer. It applies rules to strings in order to transform them into their stem. Other approaches use dictionaries of word stems.

PMID 7744799: *"The protein products of this gene contain the basic-helix-loop-helix motif characteristic of a large family of **transcription factors** that **bind** to the canonical DNA sequence CANNTG as protein heterodimers."*
is mentioning the GO term **transcription factor binding** (GO:0008134), but stemming is needed here to identify *bind* as *binding*.

Term extraction systems take a text document and return a list of potential terms, one-word units or multi-word units, which characterize the content of the document. Two approaches can be distinguished: The linguistic approach uses morphological, syntactic and semantic information, such as known suffixes of verbs, to find relevant terms. Statistical approaches on the other side try to examine statistical properties of lexical units. One assumption is that terms characterizing a document's content occur very frequently in this document but infrequently in other documents.

Extracting terms is difficult as the following examples illustrate:

The text *"Primed monocytes transcribed TNF mRNA at a higher rate than freshly isolated **monocytes** upon **activation** with LPS."* contains the ontology term **monocyte activation** (GO:0042117). Another example with even longer gaps is: *"Although all nm23 **proteins** contain nucleoside diphosphate (NDP) **kinase activity**, it has not been established that the enzyme activity mediated the various functions of nm23 proteins."* (**protein kinase activity** (GO:0004672)).

The use of hyphenated compounds and spaced words is not always consistent: Terms like **thioredoxin-disulfide reductase activity** (GO:0004791) occur with and without the hyphen between the first two words. **Endonuclease activity, active with either ribo- or deoxyribonucleic acids and producing 5'-phosphomonoesters** (GO:0016893) most likely will be used without the complementary subclause after the comma, although omitting it without reference to the context can make it ambiguous. 1,239 terms (7.3%) contain one or more commas.

Terms have brackets in their names like: **[methionine synthase] reductase activity** (GO:0030586).

1,101 of the GO terms (6.4%) contain expressions within parentheses. Complementary expressions, as in **glutathione dehydrogenase (ascorbate) activity** (GO:0045174), explanatory expressions, as in **NAD synthase (AMP-forming) activity** (GO:0008795), differentiating expressions, as in **poly(beta-D-mannuronate) lyase activity** (GO:0045135) as well as restricting expressions, as in **hydrolase activity, acting on carbon-nitrogen (but not peptide) bonds** (GO:0016810) are frequently used.

Once we have a system able to annotate biological meaningful terms in text we can use ontological information to assign semantic to those annotations. For example a text mentioning car manufacturers is likely to talk about luxury cars whereas texts mentioning the fauna of Guyana are more likely to talk about the mammal *Panthera onca*.

5.2   Extracting Ontological Terms from Text

Semantic meta-information is useful for large collections of documents in order to search them efficiently, identify document subsets of similar relevance or characterize (or summarize) a document collection to abstract from the content of concrete documents. Meta-information is found in private music collections (title, artist, genre) as well as public databases of biological entities, e.g. protein sequences in PDB (3D structure, side chains, experimental methods).

Meta-information found for text documents is often very general (keyword list) or still too complex for an automated evaluation (article abstract). Literature abstracts are very useful for human readers in order to summarize the documents content. Computer systems are necessary for handling millions of documents but have difficulties understanding literature abstracts. Keyword lists are often very short and abstract too much from the documents content. Better meta-information than keyword lists are formal logical statements reflecting the statement in the text. They are difficult to extract in an automated post-processing step. A fine-grained list of domain terms characterizing the text is shown to be useful ([DS05]). Domain ontologies can serve as a pool of useful domain terms. They often contain vocabulary which a large number of experts can agree on, e.g. most PubMed abstracts contain several terms of the Gene Ontology.

Structural problems identifying ontology terms. Scientific texts are often partitioned into sections like Introduction, Background, Methods and Conclusion. The sections about methods and conclusion contain new information contributed by the authors in solving an open problem. Whereas the background section summarizes the current research state for the topic and even might state contrary statements from other researchers. The abstract section often contains a summary of high level statements made in the text and is therefore a good source for such information.

The abstract section of a text is often published separately and therefore easy to identify. Other section of a document can only be identified when the document is transformed into a structured representation.

5.3 GoPubMed - Ontology-Based Literature Mining

Finding relevant literature is an important and difficult problem. GoPubMed is a web server which allows users to explore PubMed search results with the Gene Ontology, a hierarchically structured vocabulary for molecular biology. The system provides the following benefits:

1. It gives an overview over literature abstracts by categorizing abstracts according to the Gene Ontology and thus allowing users to quickly navigate through the abstracts by category.
2. It automatically shows general ontology terms related to the original query, which often do not even appear directly in the abstract.
3. It enables users to verify its classification because Gene Ontology terms are highlighted in the abstracts and as each term is labeled with an accuracy percentage.
4. Exploring PubMed abstracts with GoPubMed is useful as it shows definitions of Gene Ontology terms without the need for further look up.

The annotation database of GoPubMed contains 33 million Gene Ontology annotations. This information can be used to analyse research interest over time. Combining this data with spatial information about research institutes enables a large scale analysis across countries.

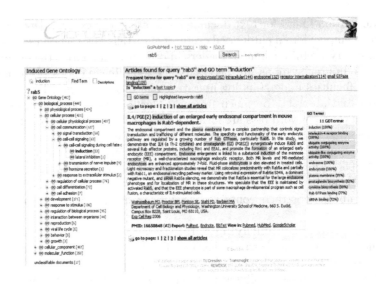

Fig. 1. GoPubMed is a web server which allows users to explore PubMed search results with the Gene Ontology, a hierarchically structured vocabulary for molecular biology

Bibliometrical analysis. GoPubMed's association of GO terms with PubMed abstracts is a valuable resource to understand how a research topic - represented by a GO term - develops. It shows how many articles were published over time, which authors are most prolific for the topic, which journals cover the topic best, and which countries publish most on the topic. The use of an ontology for these analysis is very important as it includes synonyms and subterms. As an example, [GM97] point out that during the 60s and 70s researchers in the US used "programmed cell death" while their European colleagues used "apoptosis". In our analysis, these are treated as equivalent with the help of the underlying ontology. Also it is important to consider subterms as some papers may mention GTPases in general, while others refer to specific GTPases such as Ran, Rac, Rho, etc. Again, the use of the ontology ensures that an analysis of GTPases will include all specific GTPases.

Term extraction in GoPubMed. GoPubMed evaluates only the abstract section of a biomedical publication in PubMed. Thus only the substantial high level statements of a text are considered. The abstract is split into sentences using a simple heuristic looking for common sentence endings. The tokenization is optimized for a sensible tokenization of Gene Ontology terms, e.g. hyphenated chemical names or typical biological terms containing apostrophes and parentheses within words like *N-1-naphthylphthalamic acid binding*, *poly(A) binding* or *mRNA 3-UTR binding* are split appropriately. A modified version of the Porter-Stemmer is then used to transform the tokens into there stems. Again the stemmer avoids the modification of abbreviations or words with hyphens, primes or parentheses.

The matchvalue for each potential term is then calculated by the sum of the information value of each Gene Ontology word found in a sentence. High frequent words in the ontology, e.g. *activity* have a low information value single occurring words of an information value of 1. The matchvalue is ratio of identified words vs. term words.

The literature database PubMed is growing by 500.000 abstracts each year. The scientific vocabulary constantly grows with the number of research fields being discussed. As a research field becomes more mature the vocabulary converges on a set of terms commonly used. There is the need to keep the domain ontologies up to date with those changes.

6 Ontology Evolution

Ontology evolution can be defined as the adaption of an ontology which is based on a consistent propagation of changes to the dependent artefacts [MBS03]. In other words, it is a process of changing an ontology while maintaining its consistency. Given the case, that a concept needs to be deleted, it has to be decided which actions have to be performed to reach a consistent state. One could decide to remove all the subclass relationships, followed by removing all the concepts which are not participating in a subclass relations after the first step. Another strategy would be to ensure that all the concepts which were in subclass relationship to the deleted concept become re-linked to other concepts. The chosen strategy depends on the application. To ensure transparency and a deterministic nature in ontology evolution, the tools used need to support the decision process and give the ontology engineer the freedom to configure his tools accordingly.

As the complexity in ontology evolution increases with the size of the ontology, the process has to be highly structured. The task can be compared with the development of complex software. During the last decades a huge effort has been undertaken to unify the software development process (e.g. [JBR99]) and pass on the experiences of generations of software developers (e.g. [TH99]). This knowledge is valuable in the context of ontology evolution and only a highly structured and controlled development process will lead to well designed ontologies. Many features own to software development tools can directly be used. Automatic consistency test are as important as a complete documentation. Collaborative tools and versioning will enable users to work at the same ontology simultaneously. As reality changes, ontologies need to change as well. Knowledge might change due to latest research results and terms need to be added, reclassified or even deleted. Additionally, relations between terms and properties of terms need to be revised. Despite some advances in semi-automatic ontology design and evolution, most ontologies are created and maintained manually. In these cases, the ontology editor plays a crucial role, as it provides support to the ontology engineer for browsing, checking and modifying ontologies. Editors will be discussed in section 7. An example of ontology evolution is described in [AS05]. The authors analysed the Medical Subject Headings (MeSH) focusing on syntactical and semantical consitency.

Ontology Learning

Ontology learning is the automatization of the ontology building process aiming for lower development costs and faster construction of ontologies. For automatic learning information sources like the ontology itself or a text corpus of relevant documents are needed.

Ontology-based approaches to ontology learning are using the ontology itself as source of information. In [OCA04] the compositional structure of Gene Ontology (GO) terms was analysed. The authors found that many GO terms contain each other and many GO terms are derived from each other. For example, the term *membrane* [GO:0016020] has *inner membrane* [GO:0019866] as a direct subconcept. This and similar knowledge can be used to automatically generate new candidate terms following the observed patterns. In a second step, a filtering is necessary to select candidates based on a broad text base which can then be propagated to the ontology. Additionally, the authors analysed the relationships between terms. They calculated the percentage of cases with explicit substring relationships between terms, where approximately 65% of all GO terms contain another GO term. A deeper analysis revealed, that complements occur very frequently. Examples are negative/positive, binding/biosynthesis, or female/male. These finding can be utilised for candidate generation.

Learning from text corpora is based on methods which try to extend ontologies by applying natural language processing techniques to text [GM03]. Early publications focus on pattern-based concept and relation extraction, where a concept or relation will be added to the ontology if it is found to match a predefined pattern [Mor99]. As in classical shopping cart analysis, association rules can also be used for corpus-based learning of ontologies [MS00]. Association rules evaluate the co-occurrence of items within an item set and use the likelihood of an item A being member of a set, if B is already a member. A different technique called conceptual clustering was proposed in [FP00]. After the acquisition of syntactic frames in a text, the learning method relies on the observation of syntactic regularities in the context of words. Concepts found are grouped according to their semantic distance and become this way ordered in a hierarchy. For this, no annotation is needed beforehand, but the validation of the result is performed manually and is therefore time-consuming. A pattern-based learning approach instead would use labeled examples for extracting instances from texts. While the annotation of the learning examples is time-consuming, the quality of the learning results would be predictable and could be validated automatically.

Beside text corpora and ontologies other sources for semantic concepts can be explored for ontology evolution. In [KMV00], a method named ontology pruning uses GermaNet, the German counterpart to WordNet, natural language texts and semi-structured domain-specific dictionaries. In this work the authors acquire general concepts by measuring term frequencies in texts. A term occurring more frequently in a domain-specific text corpus than in a general corpus becomes a candidate to be included in the ontology. The ontologies subclass relationships are constructed following [Hea92], where a hypernym relations between words are induced according to patterns found in the text.

7 Ontology Editors

Current ontology editors use knowledge models of varying complexity and differ in scalability and usability. Numerous editors are available to the ontology engineer, e.g. Protégé[1], OntoStudio from Ontoprise[2], OilEd[3], pOWL[4], and DIP D2.8: Ontology Editing and Browsing tool. Protégé, OntoEdit (now OntoStudio) and OilEd are stand-alone applications for managing standard ontologies and were compared in [SM02]. A recent development is pOWL, a web-based editor and development platform for the semantic web that supports RDFS/OWL ontologies of arbitrary size, and DIP D2.8 with support for ontologies specified using the Web Service Modelling Language (WSML)[5].

Functionalities

Features of the editor are features of the underlying ontology model. Most editor include standard editing capabilities for concepts, properties, instances as well as standard relations, namely concept inheritance based on *part-of* and *is-a* relationships. For all these entities the operations add, remove and modify are supported. All listed operations can be regarded as simple changes [SM02] and are implemented in nearly every editor. On the other side there exist composite changes. An examples for a composite change is moving a concept from one parent to another one. Here the concept's subclass relationships are deleted and new subclass relationships to the new parent concept are created.

The identifiers of the subclass relationship will therefore change. Instance data and/or properties of the relation might get lost. The operation of moving concept or relation as a composite change will preserve the identifiers and the associated data. Generally it can be said: moving concepts as a task cannot be replaced by a sequence of deletions and additions, because the identity of the subject of change itself gets changed.

Beside the described actions, certain constraints have to be maintained by the editors. All changes performed within one encapsulated action need to transform the ontology from one consistent and valid state to another one. Accordingly, the constraints *consistency* and *validity* need to be ensured. The constraints which have to be met in particular depend strongly on the actual type and application of the ontology. In general it can be stated that an ontology is inconsistent if one part of the ontology does not agree with another one. The language specification, e.g. for OWL [PH04], is a source for consistency constraints. If an ontology is consistent with its language specification it is regarded as *well-formed*. If an ontology

---

[1] http://protege.stanford.edu
[2] http://ontoedit.com/
[3] http://oiled.man.ac.uk/
[4] http://powl.sourceforge.net/
[5] http://www.wsmo.org/TR/d16/d16.1/v0.2/

is consistent with its language specification it is regarded as *well-formed*. Validity ranges from syntactical, are all concepts and relations declared when used, to semantical validity, are all concepts or relations use as declared for the ontology.

Some editors include support for collaborative editing. Here, most of the necessary features will regard usability aspects, but also the possibility to reverse changes and a general versioning support is needed.

Features of an ideal ontology editor would adapt capabilities of software development tools used today. It would support automatic consistency testing, include learning components, support logging of changes, implement a variety of composite changes and always make the user aware of side effects of his actions. Furthermore it would support the specification of a predefined workflow for ontology evolution and allow the user to document his changes.

8   Ontology-Based Querying Over Multiple Data Sources

In this section we first discuss and exemplify how the ontological knowledge identified in section 4 can be used to support the querying of multiple biological data sources. Then, we present an approach for ontology-based support for access to multiple biological data sources [JL05]. We focus on how knowledge should be set up to support query processing.

8.1   Query Support

Some of the important steps in querying over multiple data sources are user query formulation (important for *locating and retrieving the relevant data*), data source selection (important for *locating the relevant data*) together with the query rewriting into subqueries over the selected data sources, and identification of relevant data items on which results from different subqueries can be joined (important for *integration of data*). The ontological knowledge identified in section 4 can be used to support these steps.

Query formulation. Ontologies can be used for guiding users through query formulation. The ontology itself can be used as a query model or the inclusion of ontology terms into a query may be allowed. High level ontologies enable the selection of relevant types of biological knowledge, while specialized ontologies (e.g. GO molecular function ontology) can be useful for the precise specification of properties for data items. Different ontologies support querying from different points of view, e.g. query for genes involved in a biological process or genes expressed in a particular cellular component. As the user query may cover different types of biological knowledge that is spread over a number of ontologies, ontology alignments are important. This enables ontological reasoning over different domains. For instance, such alignments would allow reasoning based on relationships between protein function and diseases. An important use of ontologies is for query expansion. This leads to better query results. When queries are expanded using terms equivalent to the query terms, the terminology discrepancy problem is reduced. When is-a relationships are used, more relevant results are retrieved.

For instance, knowing that receptor is-a signal transducer, a query asking for specific signal transducers can be expanded to retrieve receptors having the same properties. Also, checking query validity can be performed with respect to the domain knowledge.

Data source selection and query rewriting. The ontological knowledge is important for describing data sources uniformly from the domain perspective. When user queries include ontological terms, such data source descriptions provide support for data source selection and the user query rewriting into subqueries over data sources. Terms from high level ontologies can specify types of biological data stored in data sources such as, for instance, that sequences stored in UniProt represent protein sequences. At the same time relations between data items in a data source could be derived by the available relations between ontological terms (e.g. domain is a part-of sequence). Specialized ontologies could be used to specify the range of possible values for a data type (e.g. which organisms are covered in a data source). Also, ontological terms can be used to refine the description of the content of a data source. Often, not all data is stored explicitly in a biological data source. For instance, in a data source containing mouse-related data, mouse will not be mentioned explicitly in the data entries. In addition, the knowledge about existing ontological annotations of data sources and mapping rules between data source and ontology terms should be used to specify the data source schema. Ontological annotations are useful for fast and focused searches on a certain type of data (e.g. search UniProt on GO terms describing protein function). The annotations directly lead to relevant data entries in data sources. Mapping rules between data source and ontology terms provide a basis for translating query constraints expressed over ontologies to data source specific terms.

Data integration. When results for the subqueries are retrieved from different data sources, the next step is to identify which data entries can be joined. A straightforward approach is to require equality between the joined data items. As there is no agreed terminology and there are no unique identifiers for terms in bioinformatics, often this approach is not suitable. The joined data items may have different but synonymous data values, they can be described at different levels of granularity or use different lexical variations. For instance, a gene can be referred to by different identifiers, like insulin promoter factor, a gene activating transcription of insulin genes, is named IPF1, IDX-1, STF-1, PDX-1, PDX1 and MODY4. For an organism its scientific or common name can be used, e.g. mus or mice. In some data sources the type of organism could be specified more precisely, e.g mus famulus. Also, B Cell Leukemia can be written as Leukemia, B Cell. Ontological knowledge provides a range of possibilities on how to handle these issues. Joins could be performed on the basis of ontological terms. Mapping rules between data source and ontology terms could be used to translate values into a uniform representation. Also, data can be joined on the available ontological annotations. Further, ontological knowledge about synonyms can be used to locate alternative data item representations. To cover different granularity of data items, is-a relationships in ontologies should be explored. Mapping

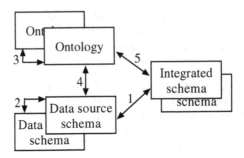

Fig. 2. Types of supported knowledge and mapping rules between them

rules between ontologies should be used to combine data items retrieved from different domains.

8.2   Framework

Figure 2 represents the main types of knowledge that should be maintained for ontology-based querying as well as the mapping rules (MR) between them. The main types of knowledge in traditional information integration systems are data source schemas and integrated schemas. An integrated schema combines the relevant domain knowledge with data structures in the integrated data sources. Such systems enable data source integration through e.g. global-as-view or local-as-view rules (MR 1). Also, for joining data existing cross-references between data entries at different data sources are used (MR 2). Ontological knowledge may provide extra information and we suggest that in addition to the traditionally used knowledge, also domain ontologies, ontological alignments (MR 3) and ontology-based data source descriptions (MR 4) should be used. Ontology-based data source descriptions use ontological annotations, mappings between data values and ontological terms together with ontology-based data source schema descriptions. To reuse the existing ontological knowledge and to uniformly specify the integrated data, also ontology-based integrated schema descriptions should be maintained (MR 5).

There are several information integration systems for integrating biological data sources (for an overview see [Jak05]). Some of these information integration systems use ontology-based technologies to support querying (e.g. BACIIS [MWL03], KIND [LGM03], SEMEDA [KPL03] and TAMBIS [GSN01]), but not so much ontological knowledge is used yet. A common feature in these systems is that the integrated schemas are seen as ontologies. In contrast, we expect ontologies to be agreed upon and shared by many users [Lam04]. The integrated schemas include domain knowledge and information on data structures at the data sources. All the systems use the maintained ontology to describe the content of data sources (MR 1). Though it is not explicitly stated, cross-references between data sources are probably used to join the retrieved data items (MR 2). KIND uses two ontologies describing static and process knowledge, respectively. The ontologies combine domain knowledge from neuroanatomy and neurophysiology (MR 3). In SEMEDA controlled vocabularies can be used to specify semantics of data type values, which covers part of MR 4 in our framework. Also, data source content descriptions can be refined with integrated schema terms. Ontological annotations and ontology alignments are not taken into account in any of the systems.

Acknowledgments

We acknowledge the financial support of the Swedish Research Council (Vetenskapsrådet), the Center for Industrial Information Technology (CENIIT), the Swedish national graduate school of computer science (CUGS), the EU Project Sealife (027269), and the European Commission and the Swiss State Secretariat for Education and Research within the 6th Framework Programme project REWERSE number 506779 (cf. `http://rewerse.net`).

References

[AS05]   Abecker A, Stojanovic L (2005) Ontology evolution: Medline case study.

[BHL01]   Berners-Lee T, Hendler J, Lassila O (2001) The Semantic Web. *Scientific American*, May issue.

[BAB05]   Bodenreider O, Aubry M, Burgun A (2005) Non-lexical approaches to identifying associative relations in the gene ontology. *Pacific Symposium on Biocomputing*, 10:91–102.

[Bri93]   Brill E (1993) A corpus-based approach to language learning. *Univeristy of Pennsylvania*.

[CFP06]   Cohen-Boulakia S, Froidevaux C, Pietriga E (2006) Selecting biological data sources and tools with xpr, a path language for rdf. *Pacific Symposium on Biocomputing*, 11:116–127.

[CGG03]   Collins F, Green E, Guttmacher A, Guyer M (2003) A vision for the future of genomics research. *Nature*, 422:835-847.

[DDK04]   Delfs R, Doms A, Kozlenkov A, Schroeder M (2004) GoPubMed: ontology-based literature search applied to Gene Ontology and PubMed. *German Conference on Bioinformatics*.

[DS05]   Doms A, Schroeder M (2005) GoPubMed: exploring PubMed with the Gene Ontology. *Nucleic Acids Res*, 33:W783 -W786.

[FP00]   Faure D, Poibeau T (2000) First experiments of using semantic knowledge learned by asium for information extraction task using intex. *Proceedings of the ECAI Workshop on Ontology Learning*.

[GM97]   Garfield E, Melino G (1997) The growth of the cell death field: an analysis from the isi science citation index. *Cell Death and Differentiation*, 4:352–61.

[GM03]   Gómez-Pérez A, Manzano-Macho D, editors (2003) *A survey of ontology learning methods and techniques*. Universidad Politecnica de Madrid.

[GO]   The Gene Ontology Consortium (2000) Gene Ontology: tool for the unification of biology. *Nature Genetics*, 25(1):25-29. http://www.geneontology.org/.

[Gom99]   Gómez-Pérez A (1999) Ontological Engineering: A state of the Art. *Expert Update*, 2(3):33-43.

182   A. Doms et al.

[GSN01]   Goble CA, Stevens R, Ng G, Bechhofer S, Paton N, Baker P, Peim M,
               Brass A (2001) Transparent access to multiple bioinformatics informa-
               tion sources. *IBM Systems Journal* 40(2).
[GTT06]   Good B, Tranfield E, Tan P, Shehata M, Singhera G, Gosselink J, Okon
               E, Wilkinson M (2006) Fast, cheap and out of control: A zero curation
               model for ontology development. *Pacific Symposium on Biocomputing*,
               11:128–139.
[Hea92]   Hearst M (1992) Automatic acquisition of hyponyms from large text
               corpora. *In Proceedings of the Fourteenth International Conference on
               Computational Linguistic.*
[Jak05]   Jakonienė V (2005) *A Study in Integrating Multiple Biological Data
               Sources.* Licentiate thesis No 1149, Linköpings universitet, Sweden.
[JBR99]   Jacobson I, Booch G, Rumbaugh J (1999) *The unified software devel-
               opment process.* Addison-Wesley Longman Publishing Co., Inc. Boston,
               MA, USA.
[JL05]   Jakoniene V, Lambrix P (2005) Ontology-based Integration for Bioin-
               formatics. *Proceedings of the VLDB Workshop on Ontologies-based
               techniques for DataBases and Information Systems - ODBIS 2005,*
               pp 55-58.
[KMV00]   Kietz J, Maedche A, Volz R (2000) A method for semi-automatic
               ontology acquisition from a corporate intranet. *EKAW00 Workshop
               on Ontologies and Texts,* volume 51, page 4.14.14. CEUR Workshop
               Proceedings.
[KPL03]   Köhler J, Philippi S, Lange M (2003) SEMEDA: ontology based seman-
               tic integration of biological databases. *Bioinformatics* 19(18):2420-2427.
[KS05]   Kalfoglou Y, Schorlemmer M (2005) Ontology mapping: The
               state of the art. *Semantic Interoperability and Integration,* number
               04391 in Dagstuhl Seminar Proceedings. Internationales Begegnungs-
               und Forschungszentrum (IBFI), Schloss Dagstuhl, Germany, 2005.
               <http://drops.dagstuhl.de/opus/volltexte/2005/40> [date of citation:
               2005-01-01].
[Lam04]   Lambrix P (2004) Ontologies in Bioinformatics and Systems Biology.
               Chapter 8 in Dubitzky W, Azuaje F (eds) *Artificial Intelligence Methods
               and Tools for Systems Biology,* pp 129-146, Springer. ISBN: 1-4020-
               2859-8.
[Lam05]   Lambrix P (2005) Towards a Semantic Web for Bioinformatics using
               Ontology-based Annotation. *Proceedings of the 14th IEEE International
               Workshops on Enabling Technologies: Infrastructures for Collaborative
               Enterprises,* pp 3-7. Invited talk.
[LGM03]   Ludäscher B, Gupta A, Martone ME (2003) A Model-Based Media-
               tor System for Scientific Data Management. Chapter 12 in Lacroix Z,
               Critchlow T (eds) *Bioinformatics: Managing Scientific Data,* pp 335-
               370, Morgan Kaufmann Publishers.
[LJ03]   Lambrix P, Jakonienė V (2003) Towards Transparent Access to Multiple
               Biological Databanks. *Proceedings of the Asia-Pacific Bioinformatics
               Conference,* pp 53-60.
[LMN04]   Lacroix Z, Murthy H, Naumann F, Raschid L (2004) Links and Paths
               through Life Science Data Sources. *Proceedings of International Work-
               shop on Data Integration in the Life Sciences,* LNCS 2994, pp 203-211.
[LT06]   Lambrix P, Tan H (2006) SAMBO - A System for Aligning and Merging
               Biomedical Ontologies. *Journal of Web Semantics,* to appear.

[MBS03]   Maedche A, Motik B, Stojanovic L (2003) Managing multiple and distributed ontologies on the semantic web. *VLDB*, 12:286–302.

[Mor99]   Morin E (1999) Automatic acquisition of semantic relations between terms from technical corpora. *Proc. Of the Fifth Int. Congress on Terminology and Knowledge Engineering (TKE-99)*, Vienna. TermNet-Verlag.

[MS00]   Maedche A, Staab S. Discovering conceptual relations from text. *Proceedings of the 14th European Conference on Artificial Intelligence, ECAI 2000*, pp 21–25.

[MWL03]   Miled ZB, Webster YW, Liu Y, Li N (2003) An Ontology for Semantic Integration of Life Science Web Databases. *International Journal of Cooperative Information Systems* 12(2):275-294.

[NAR]   Nucleic Acids Research. http://nar.oupjournals.org

[NM00]   Noy N, Musen M (2000) PROMPT: Algorithm and tool for automated ontology merging and alignment. *AAAI/IAAI*, pp 450–455.

[OBO]   Open Biomedical Ontologies. http://obo.sourceforge.net/

[OCA04]   Ogren P, Cohen K, Acquaah-Mensah G, Eberlein J, Hunter L (2004) The compositional structure of gene ontology terms. *Pac Symp Biocomput*, pp 214–225.

[PH04]   Patel-Schneider P, Horrocks I (2004) Owl web ontology language semantics and abstract syntax.

[PM]   PubMed. http://www.ncbi.nlm.nih.gov/entrez/query.fcgi

[REWERSE]   REWERSE. http://www.rewerse.net

[SC03]   Smith T, Cleary J (2003) Automatically linking MEDLINE abstracts to the GeneOntology. *Proc. of the Sixth Annual Bio-Ontologies Meeting.*

[SM01]   Stumme G, Maedche A (2001) FCA-MERGE: Bottom-up merging of ontologies. *IJCAI*, pp 225–234.

[SM02]   Stojanovic L, Motik B (2002) Ontology evolution within ontology editors. *In Proceedings of the OntoWeb-SIG3 Workshop at the 13th International Conference 22 on Knowledge Engineering and Knowledge Management (EKAW)*, pp 53–62.

[SOFG]   Standards and Ontologies for Functional Genomics. http://www.sofg.org/

[Swa86]   Swanson DR (1986) Fish oil, Raynaud's syndrome, and undiscovered public knowledge. *Perspectives in Biology and Medicine.*

[TH99]   Thomas D, Hunt A (1999) *The Pragmatic Progarmmer: From Journeyman to Master.* Addison-Wesley.

[UG96]   Uschold M, Grüninger M (1996) Ontologies: principles, methods, and applications. *Knowledge Engineering Review*, 11(2):93–155.

[VOS03]   Volz R, Oberle D, Staab S, Motik B (2003) Kaon server - a semantic web management system. *Proceedings of the Twelfth International World Wide Web Conference.*

[W3C-sw]   World Wide Web Consortium. Semantic Web. http://www.w3.org/2001/sw/

[W3C-ws]   World Wide Web Consortium. Web Services. http://www.w3.org/2002/ws/

Integrating Web Resources to Model Protein Structure and Function

Ludwig Krippahl

Dep. de Informática, Universidade Nova de Lisboa, 2825 Monte de Caparica, Portugal
`ludi@di.fct.unl.pt`

Abstract. In this paper we address computational aspects of protein structure and function, including prediction of secondary structure, folding, structure determination from Nuclear Magnetic Resonance data, modelling of protein interactions, and metabolic pathways. The subject is introduced with an overview of protein structure and chemistry and the algorithms and representations used to model protein structures. The main focus of the paper is the integration of information from sources relevant to protein structure modelling, such as structure databases and modelling servers, a task made difficult by the heterogeneity of formats, the diversity of data sources, and the sheer volume of information available, making evident the need for a standard framework for data sharing, i.e. the Semantic Web. To help solve this problem, we present tools being developed according to the concept of a Semantic Web. These include the UniProtRDF project and tools currently implemented on the Chemera molecular modelling software which can facilitate the search and application of information available from Internet servers and databases.

1 Introduction

Proteins are ubiquitous in living organisms, mediating all life processes from growth to thought. They catalyse chemical reactions and are involved in the movements of our muscles and in the structure of our bodies, and are the direct expression of the genome. The study of proteins ranges from molecular genetics, as a gene is the recipe for a protein, to protein structure, function, interactions, and metabolic pathways. The techniques involved are many and diverse, from gene sequencing to activity assays, kinetics, spectroscopy, cloning and over-expression, among others.

There are four features of protein studies that make the semantic web such an attractive concept in this field:

1. The importance of understanding how proteins are regulated and how they operate makes this a major research field in biochemistry, and such a research effort leads to a large output of data, both as databases and publications.
2. The computational demands of gene database searches, structural analysis, and interaction modelling led to the availability of a variety of services on the internet.
3. Research in this area often requires the integration of many information sources, models, and experimental data.
4. The large throughput of the research community.

The following sections outline different elements of protein structure, from primary to quaternary structure, and provide some examples of databases and services available

P. Barahona et al. (Eds.): Reasoning Web 2006, LNCS 4126, pp. 184–196, 2006.

on the internet. Some familiarity with these concepts is necessary for anyone wishing to enter this field, but a detailed description of protein structure is outside the scope of this paper, so I refer the interested reader to introductory textbooks on protein structure (*e.g.* 1, 2).

Genes and amino acid sequence

Proteins consist of amino acid residues bound together in long chains, with a sequence determined by the sequence of nucleotides in the gene encoding for the protein. Figure 1 shows a segment of an amino acid chain. The repeating sequence of Nitrogen, Carbon, Carbon atoms forms the backbone, or main chain. Branching out from the main chain we can see the amino acid side chains, which are unique to each amino acid.

The amino acid side chains have important properties that affect both the structure and the function of the protein, such as their interaction with solvent molecules, charge distribution, and chemical reactivity. Some side chains bind covalently forming cross-links between different parts of a protein chain, different protein chains, or even to non-proteic groups.

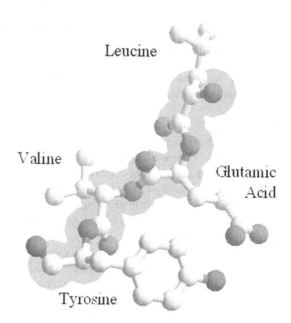

Fig. 1. A short segment of four amino acid residues. The backbone is outlined in grey, and the atoms are represented in different colours (nitrogen and oxygen in grey, carbon in white). Each amino acid residue has a unique side chain and a common sequence of Nitrogen-Carbon-Carbon in the main chain.

The direct relation between gene sequence and protein sequence allows the determination of protein sequences with gene sequencing techniques, a great advantage because gene sequencing is currently fast, inexpensive, and often fully automated. For example, while the UniProtKB/Swiss-Prot database contains approximately two hundred thousand annotated protein sequences (as of April 2006), the UniProtKB/TrEMBL database of protein sequences automatically generated from gene sequence data contains nearly three million different sequences (as of April 2006) (3, 4), and most of the protein sequences in the annotated database have been obtained by gene sequencing too.

The relationship between gene (and thus protein) sequences resulting from evolution is an important aspect of these data. The change in lineages over time by the gradual accumulation of random mutations results in similar sequences being closely related, descending from a more recent ancestor than more differing sequences. Sequence similarity is thus highly correlated with structural and functional similarity, making sequence similarity searches and clustering important computational tools in this field. The BLAST algorithm and derivatives (4) is currently available in all major gene databases for searching and aligning gene and protein sequences.

Also important are the annotations of the protein and gene sequences, and the associations with other databases. The UniProtKB/Swiss-Prot database (5), for example, provides links to literature references, annotated comments regarding function, activity and regulation, and cross references to approximately twenty other databases, ranging from protein structure, family classifications and interactions to genome mappings and metabolic pathways databases. The Gene Ontology Annotation project at the European Bioinformatics Institute (6, 7) currently provides manual annotations for seventy thousand UniProtKB entries and electronic (automatic) annotations for nearly two million UniProtKB entries.

Secondary Structure

Protein chains form several characteristic local structures due to hydrogen bonds between main chain atoms of different amino acids. Some examples are the alpha-helix, the beta strand, and the beta turn. The important aspects of these structures, for our purposes in this paper, is that they are usually stabilized by the interaction of amino acid residues that are proximate in the sequence, and that they are stable structures that can be seen as building blocks for the tertiary structure of the protein, the large scale three dimensional folding.

These are very important for structural modelling for several reasons. One reason is predictability; from sequence data alone it is possible to predict secondary structure motifs with 70-75% accuracy. Another reason is the conservation of secondary structure within protein families, both because of its strong correlation with local amino acid sequences and because evolution seems to favour the conservation of local structures in general. Finally, secondary structure elements are often easier to identify from experimental data, which even allows automated assignment procedures in multidimensional NMR spectroscopy. Figure 2 shows two common secondary structure elements, a beta sheet and alpha helices. A beta sheet is formed by a set of beta strands, parts of the protein chain in an extended conformation and oriented parallel or anti-parallel to each other. Alpha helices are segments of protein chain that are rolled in a spiral conformation. Though the structures may vary slightly, as the three helix examples illustrate, these structural motifs are quite characteristic and well defined.

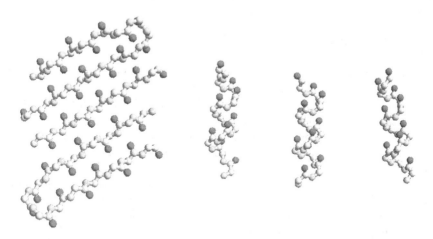

Fig. 2. Two common secondary structure motifs. A beta sheet formed by five beta strands on the left, and three alpha helices on the right.

Domains and tertiary structure

Each protein chain folds over itself to form a three-dimensional structure, called the tertiary structure of the protein. The tertiary structure is organized at a larger scale than secondary structure, more dependent on interactions between amino acid residues distant in the sequence of the protein chain. It is this overall structure that determines most properties of the protein and how it interacts with other molecules, so knowledge of the tertiary structure is crucial for understanding and manipulating reaction pathways and for drug design.

Except for the smallest proteins, the tertiary structure is generally organized in distinct structural elements, protein domains, which do not span the whole protein chain. These domains often have different functions and distinctive structures, and evolution often splits these regions apart into different genes, or splices genes together to form multi-domain proteins, as if they were several different proteins kept together by peptide linkers.

The semi-independence of protein domains makes these structural features the natural unit of protein structure and function. When comparing different proteins, or even protein systems, it is often necessary to take into account the modular nature of protein chains.

Protein Interactions

Most proteins interact with other proteins. These interactions range from transient contacts, in which the partners meet briefly to perform some chemical reaction, to life-long partnerships, with each protein chain specifically adapted to be permanently associated to its partners. The structure of such assemblies of protein chains is the quaternary structure, and one such assembly often referred to as a protein complex. Protein interactions play a central role in all living organisms, hence the importance of understanding the mechanisms and structure of protein complexes.

2 Algorithms and Methods

There are many different problems and solutions related to protein structure, ranging from finding a good model for a known sequence from known structures of similar proteins to modelling a protein complex or determining a protein structure from X-Ray diffraction patterns. Though not in themselves the focus of this paper, it is useful to have an idea of these problems to better understand the usefulness of a Semantic Web approach to integrating knowledge in protein structural studies.

In this section we will look at four cases. The first two, homology modelling and structure prediction with the Rosetta algorithm (8), illustrate two approaches to the general problem of modelling protein structures, and these tools are nowadays widely used by the community. The other two examples, protein structure determination using constraint processing with PSICO (9, 10) and constrained protein docking with BiGGER (11, 12) illustrate an ongoing effort at automating the integration of structural information from a wide range of sources.

Homology modelling
Homology modelling is based on the structural similarity of proteins with similar sequences. This similarity is a consequence of the evolutionary processes that connect genes, and their corresponding proteins, to common ancestors. Gene lineages spawned from a common ancestor will diverge by the accumulation of mutations, and given the huge number of possible gene sequences, sequence similarity indicates close kinship and proximity to the common ancestor. Furthermore, a mutation that results in a large change in the protein structure will most likely be deleterious and eliminated by natural selection, since a large random change on a highly complex and adapted mechanism will tend to reduce its performance. The consequence is that proteins that have similar sequences are most likely to have diverged from a recent ancestor gene by the accumulation of mutations that have a small impact on protein structure.

The SWISS-MODEL server (16, 17, 18, 19) illustrates how easy it is to use this technique using current technology, even for non-experts. The server can select templates for different parts of the structure based on sequence homology, or use user defined templates, assemble the structure by threading the new sequence into the templates, and even optimise side chain conformations, all automatically. However, there is a cost to this convenient approach: the dependence on a centralised database and automation do not allow for the integration of different data sources, or for more flexible approaches to modelling when there are no good homologous templates for parts of the structure.

Ab-initio protein structure prediction

The Rosetta algorithm was developed by the Baker group (8) and was very successful at several of the Critical Assessment of Structure Prediction (CASP) trials (14, 15). Rosetta is essentially a minimization by simulated annealing, but the algorithm assumes that local, smaller, structures to form and change rapidly until stabilized by a low-energy configuration that brings them together at a larger scale. This assumption is quite reasonable based on current knowledge of protein folding dynamics, and is probably the main reason for the success of this algorithm.

Integrating structural information

The previous two examples illustrate well-established approaches that are publicly available on the Internet. While easy to use and widely used, they are not meant to allow for flexible integration of structural data, relying on internal databases for all the information required for computation. The next two examples are the opposite in these respects, as one goal is flexible integration of information using the Semantic Web concepts and, like the Semantic Web, they are still in a development and testing stage.

The PSICO (Processing Structural Information with Constraint propagation and Optimization) algorithm is primarily intended to help in the determination of protein structures from NMR data (10), but goes beyond that by using generic structural information that can be derived from databases, prediction servers, experimental data, or other sources (9).

PSICO builds an approximate structural model by processing a set of structural constraints. These can include simple binary distance constraints (10) or global constraints on rigid groups of atoms (9), or even more complex constraints such as bond and dihedral angles. From the approximate model constructed by constraint processing, PSICO then refines the structure by local search and optimization, minimizing residual constraint violations. This is an efficient approach to incorporating a variety of structural information data into the modelling process, and can thus benefit greatly from the Semantic Web goal of data integration and reasoning over decentralized data sources.

The BiGGER (12) algorithm (Bimolecular Complex Generation with Global Evaluation and Ranking) models protein-protein interactions by geometrically matching the shapes of the proteins and then evaluating physical properties of the interaction, such as solvation effects, electrostatics, side chain contacts. In this approach to modelling protein interactions without additional information, BiGGER is similar to other protein docking algorithms (see 13 for a review). However, using an approach similar to that used in PSICO, BiGGER is meant to incorporate any available data (11), and it is generally the case that experimental data is obtained before researchers attempt to model a protein complex.

3 Web Resources

There are many internet resources available on proteins structure and molecular biology in general, ranging from structure databases to software repositories and prediction or computation servers. This section will show some examples that illustrate this diversity, some of which already provide structured access either as web services or in XML.

UniProtKB

The UniProt Knowledgebase is a large repository for annotated protein sequence data. It includes entries for sequences translated from gene sequencing data or direct protein sequences, annotations regarding organism, literature references, and cross-references to other databases.

The UniProtKB databases are available in XML format and the XML schema and document type definitions are available from the UniProt site. An independent project at the Swiss Institute of Bioinformatics also supplies the UniProtKB data in RDF format (21). Currently, the European Bioinformatics Institute (EBI) supports Simple Object Access Protocol (SOAP) access to web services for homology searches, multiple sequence alignment, data retrieval, and sequence analysis (22, 23, 24). Most of the data and the most used tools for sequence retrieval, alignment, and analysis are now available in structured formats or as web services.

The UniProt databases are also connected to the Gene Ontology (GO) through the Gene Ontology Annotation project (6) at the European Bioinformatics Institute, aimed at assigning GO terms to gene and protein sequences.

Secondary structure

There are several free servers for secondary structure prediction, such as the Advanced Protein Secondary Structure Prediction Server (25), or the PHDSec or PROFsec services (26, 27) at the PredictProtein site (28). Though easy to use, these services are designed mainly for direct interaction with human users and not for machine access.

Protein Data Bank

The Protein Data Bank (PDB) is a repository of protein structures hosted at the Research Collaboratory for Structural Bioinformatics (29, 30). This is the most important database on protein structures at present, storing over 36,000 structures linked to the SCOP and CATH structural classification databases and the Gene Ontology. The PDB site provides browsers for accessing the data according to different classifications, such as GO terms for biological processes, cellular components, or molecular function, or structural classification according to the SCOP or CATH systems.

More important for our purpose is the PDBML/XML format, an XML file format encoding the information that was until recently stored in the flat text file format of the original PDB files. This format structures complex information on amino acid residues, sequence, atomic composition, atomic coordinates, and annotations such as literature references and experimental techniques.

Finally, the PDB website implements web services methods using SOAP and XML for querying entries by sequence homology, keywords, for obtaining literature references for a structure, for determining if the structure is obsolete, among others. This is a very important feature of the PDB site, already in use by some other bioinformatics services, such as the Protein Mutant Resource Database.

Domain classification: CATH, SCOP, and Pfam

The Class, Architecture, Topology, and Homologous superfamily (CATH) protein domain database provides a hierarchical classification of protein domains from known structures (31, 32, 33). The identification of domains is an important part of protein structure modelling because genes can fuse together and split apart, and so domains are effectively the basic structural units of proteins, more so than amino acid chains, which can contain more than one domain. Though individual CATH query results can be retrieved in XML format, the CATH dataset is in a flat file format.

The Structural Classification of Proteins (SCOP) database is another hierarchical classification of structural domains (34, 35), also widely used by the community, but SCOP only supplies the data as flat text files.

The Pfam database, at the Sanger Institute (36, 37, 38), classifies protein domains using the SCOP domain definitions but extends protein families and domains to sequences of unknown structure, using multiple alignment techniques to find homologous region. This allows a tentative identification of domains in a protein before determining the structure. The full database is available from the Pfam website, but in a flat text format. Related to Pfam is the iPfam database of interactions between protein domains, also built from the SCOP domain definitions in known structures and extended by sequence comparison to proteins of unknown structure (39).

4 Integration of Resources: A Work in Progress

One of the main goals of the Semantic Web is the automated integration of data from multiple sources. In the previous sections we outlined the problem of studying protein structure and interactions, and the relevant data sources and services available. In this section we take a more detailed look at two examples of how queries to these services and databases could be composed in order to help model protein structures and interactions in a way that is consistent with the idea of the Semantic Web, taking advantage of decentralised data sources.

For the first example we can consider the determination of a protein structure from a known sequence, using PSICO to combine any available experimental data and information from prediction models. The first step could be the identification of domains in the sequences using the Pfam database, obtaining the PDB code for the structure of any likely domains. The structures would then be retrieved from the PDB database, and used to provide rigid group constraints to be used by PSICO. PSICO would then process these constraints along with the experimental data constraints, possibly leading to the rejection of some domain models and to the search for alternate structure candidates for those regions. The whole process would have to take into account the reliability of the models and the coverage of the experimental data, and the plan would be quantitatively different depending on these factors.

This simple example of structure determination could be part of a problem of interaction modelling. It is often the case that experimentally determined structures are not available for the docking simulations, and the modelling of the missing structures could be linked to the prediction of the interactions. Using the SCOP domain classifications of each partner, either directly from the structures or models or from the sequences by querying the Pfam database, one could look for similar domain interactions in known structures (using the iPfam database, for example). This could lead to revising the domains attributed to a modelled structure, if this interaction was found to be less likely than the confidence in the domain assignment. It would also provide examples of similar interactions that should give similar results in a docking simulation, allowing a better evaluation of the quality of the results (see Figure 3).

Additional considerations could increase the complexity of this plan. Identifying likely surface interaction sites would involve examining the co-evolution of surface patches, requiring multi-sequence alignments and phylogenetic tree computations. More detailed computations of physical and chemical properties that may help select good models for the interaction would require the use of specialized servers. Thus even a simple example of trying to model how two proteins interact can require a complex plan for identifying missing information, retrieving and integrating data, and evaluating the models, both at a final stage or at intermediate stages.

Even more challenging would be the automatic generation of these plans by reasoning on the goals and available data. That would be truly in the spirit of a Semantic Web, wherein computers could compose complex sequences of steps towards the declared goal, and could adapt these plans according to the data and services available.

Current technology is still a long way from that ideal, but there is constant progress in that direction. Conceptually, we can divide this technology in two levels. At the lower level we can consider data interchange, data and service descriptions, and standardization of formats; in other words, technology such as SOAP and XML. This technology is available today. For the researcher interested in a good scripting language to help process and access bioinformatics data and web services, Python would be a good starting point. Python is a widely used language in bioinformatics, being freely available and portable, and there are many code libraries for bioinformatics, such as those distributed by the BioPython project (41), and SOAP and XML tools, for example from the Python Web Services project (40).

Figure 3 is a schematic representation of one such process. On the left side we can see a hierarchy of different tasks. At the lowest level, we have the task of mediating the communication with the different services. Currently this is a necessary inconvenience, due to the different formats and protocols for querying these services, but one that will tend to diminish as the application of Semantic Web principles and practice result in a more standardized service landscape.

On the next level of the hierarchy we have one form of reasoning over a set of rules modelling a plan. This requires an interaction with the services because the rules may include conditional steps, or reactivity to updates. For example, a homologous structure may be used to set up constraints for the determination of part of an unknown structure, but conditioned on acceptance criteria to ensure that the known structure is a reliable template. Reactivity is also important because databases can be revised, or additions may provide better models for homology, more potential partners for docking, or new experimental data. The engine reasoning over the plan would have to determine which steps have to be recalculated and which results to use in these cases.

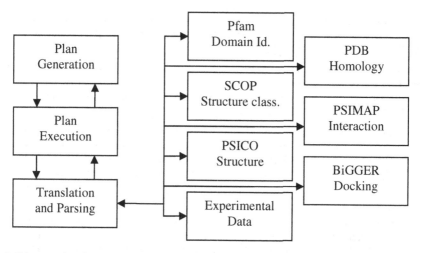

Fig. 3. Diagram for the determination of protein interactions. On the right side the services, local or remote, from where the relevant information can be obtained. The queries and results are handled by a translation and parsing service (bottom left) that mediates between the structured (XML-based) representation used by the rules engines and the diverse formats of the services. The rules engines can execute a fixed plan (center left) or reason over the goals and results of previous plans to generate new plans (top left).

At this level the technological requirements include a language that would allow users to specify these plans, expressive enough to encode the necessary conditional steps and reactivity. A natural candidate would be a language like RuleML (42), or the rule markup formalisms and tools being developed by the REWERSE (43) group I1. The advantage of such a system would be to decouple the gathering and integration of data from the details of each particular service, allowing the bioinformatics researcher to focus on the issues of what information is relevant and how to combine it. Thus the user would not specify the exact services to use, but rather model the plan using more general concepts like sequence homology, structure, contact interface, and so forth.

As part of our participation in the REWERSE Bioinformatics group we are currently implementing this technology in Chemera, our molecular modelling package. One goal is to enable the application to link to remote bioinformatics services and databases in a seamless manner, so that the user has access to all information from the same interface, and in a coherent format. Current features already include secondary structure assignment, domain identification and multi-alignment of sequences, and we are expanding the range of services. The next step is to tackle the more interesting problem of reasoning over the data, responding to information that is constantly updating, and inferring the sequence of services and databases to use in order to obtain specific information, such as a structure model or a set of potential interaction partners. This is the broader goal involving other working groups in the REWERSE project, as it requires intelligent querying languages such as Xcerpt (44) to perform complex queries combining different data sources, reactivity languages such as Xchange (45) to respond to events such as updates in databases, model design technologies to better specify complex plans for data integration, and in general places high demands automated reasoning and planning capabilities.

The long term challenge is to increase the abstraction level by automatically inferring the details of the plan needed to reach some goal. Ultimately, the user would be able to specify some high-level objective, like modelling the interaction between two proteins, and the system would devise the necessary plans to achieve such goal. This could be a gradual extension to simple plan execution, but one of increasing complexity as the system is expected to infer more complex plans from more abstract goals. For example, the problem of finding the best homology model would require a few steps, whereas the goal of finding the most likely interaction partner and respective complex could require obtaining multiple structures, combining these data with interaction information, screening likely candidates, running docking simulations, and so forth. This higher level of reasoning, represented in Figure 3 by the Plan Generation box at the top left, will require technology developed by several REWERSE groups, such as Rule Markup (I1), Composition and Typing (I3), Query (I4) and Reactivity (I5). Though hard to achieve in the near future, this would be a worthy objective that would allow the bioinformatics researcher to represent methods for data integration that based on goals instead of on procedural details.

5 Conclusion

The study of protein structure and function presents an important challenge to web reasoning. It is a large field within bioinformatics, with complex problems to solve; it has an abundance of freely available information and services, unlike many business-oriented areas where information tends to be proprietary; it involves a large number of researchers all over the world, generating a great interest in web reasoning technologies; and finally it is a field where the rewards of optimizing information use can be high, given the impact on important fields like medicine, drug design, and genetics.

The Semantic Web would help address the problem of integrating information, a problem that is becoming a limiting factor in the progress of bioinformatics. The technology being developed for data interchange and automated reasoning over data and services would greatly increase the effective use of research data, which we can expect would boost all areas of bioinformatics research.

Acknowledgements

This work has been funded by the European Commission and by the Swiss Federal Office for Education and Science within the 6th Framework Program project REWERSE number 506779 (cf. http://rewerse.net).

References

1. Darby NJ, Creighton TE, 1993, Protein Structure: In Focus, Oxford University Press
2. Branden C, Tooze J, 1999, Introduction to Protein Structure, 2nd Ed. Garland

3. http://www.expasy.org/sprot/
4. Stephen F. Altschul, Warren Gish, Webb Miller, Eugene W. Myers and David J. Lipman J. Mol. Biol. 215:403-410 (1990)
5. Bairoch A., Apweiler R., Wu C.H., Barker W.C., Boeckmann B., Ferro S., Gasteiger E., Huang H., Lopez R., Magrane M., Martin M.J., Natale D.A., O'Donovan C., Redaschi N., Yeh L.S., The Universal Protein Resource (UniProt), Nucleic Acids Res. 33: D154-D159 (2005).
6. http://www.ebi.ac.uk/GOA/
7. Gene Ontology Consortium (2006). The Gene Ontology (GO) project in 2006. Nucleic Acids Research 34: D322-D326 (2006).
8. Simons KT, Kooperberg C, Huang E, Baker D Assembly of protein tertiary structures from fragments with similar local sequences using simulated annealing and Bayesian scoring functions. J Mol Biol. 1997 Apr 25;268(1):209-25.
9. Krippahl, L, Barahona P, Propagating N-ary Rigid-Body Constraints, 2003. Principles and Practice of Constraint Programming, Springer Verlag. Principles and Practice of Constraint Programming, Springer Verlag, 2003: 452-465
10. Krippahl,   L., Barahona, P., PSICO: Solving Protein Structures with Constraint Programming and Optimisation, Constraints 2002, 7, 317-331
11. Krippahl, L, Barahona P. Applying Constraint Programming to Rigid Body Protein Docking (2005), Lecture Notes in Computer Science CP 2005: 373-387.
12. Krippahl, L., Moura, J.J., Palma, P.N., Modeling Protein Complexes with BiGGER (2003). Proteins. 2003 Jul 1;52(1):19-23
13. Inbal Halperin, Buyong Ma, HaimWolfson, and Ruth Nussinov. Principles of Docking: An Overview of Search Algorithms and a Guide to Scoring Functions. PROTEINS: Structure, Function, and Genetics 47:409–443 (2002)
14. Lattman, E. E. Protein-structure prediction -- a special issue. Proteins: Struct., Funct., Genet. 1995 23, 1.
15. Bonneau, R., Strauss, C., Rohl, C., Chivian, D., Bradley, P., Malmstrom, L., Robertson, T., Baker, D. De Novo Prediction of Three-dimensional Structures for Major Protein Families. J Mol Biol 322: (1) 65 Sep 6 2002
16. Schwede T, Kopp J, Guex N, and Peitsch MC (2003) SWISS-MODEL: an automated protein homology-modeling server. Nucleic Acids Research 31: 3381-3385.
17. Guex, N. and Peitsch, M. C. (1997) SWISS-MODEL and the Swiss-PdbViewer: An environment for comparative protein modelling. Electrophoresis 18: 2714-2723.
18. Peitsch, M. C. (1995) Protein modeling by E-mail Bio/Technology 13: 658-660.
19. http://swissmodel.expasy.org//SWISS-MODEL.html
20. Guex, N. and Peitsch M.C. (1997) SWISS-MODEL and the Swiss-PdbViewer: An environment for comparative protein modelling. Electrophoresis 18:2714-2723.
21. http://expasy3.isb-sib.ch/~ejain//rdf/
22. http://www.ebi.ac.uk/Tools/webservices/index.html
23. Labarga, A. et al. Web services at EBI EMBnet.news, 11(4) 18-23 (2005)
24. Pillai S., Silventoinen V., Kallio K., Senger M., Sobhany S., Tate J., Velankar S., Golovin A., Henrick K., Rice P., Stoehr P., Lopez R. SOAP-based services provided by the European Bioinformatics Institute.Nucleic Acids Res. 33(1):W25-W28 (2005)
25. Raghava, G. P. S. (2002) APSSP2 : A combination method for protein secondary structure prediction based on neural network and example based learning. CASP5. A-132
26. B Rost & C Sander (1993) J. of Molecular Biology, 232:584-599
27. B Rost: PROF: predicting one-dimensional protein structure by profile based neural networks. unpublished, 2000

28. B Rost, G Yachdav and J Liu (2003) The PredictProtein Server. Nucleic Acids Research 32(Web Server issue):W321-W326.

29. http://www.rcsb.org/pdb/Welcome.do

30. H.M. Berman, J. Westbrook, Z. Feng, G. Gilliland, T.N. Bhat, H. Weissig, I.N. Shindyalov, P.E. Bourne: The Protein Data Bank. Nucleic Acids Research, 28 pp. 235-242 (2000).

31. Orengo, C.A., Michie, A.D., Jones, S., Jones, D.T., Swindells, M.B., and Thornton, J.M. (1997) CATH- A Hierarchic Classification of Protein Domain Structures. Structure. Vol 5. No 8. p.1093-1108.

32. Pearl, F.M.G, Lee, D., Bray, J.E, Sillitoe, I., Todd, A.E., Harrison, A.P., Thornton, J.M. and Orengo, C.A. (2000) Assigning genomic sequences to CATH Nucleic Acids Research. Vol 28. No 1. 277-282

33. http://www.biochem.ucl.ac.uk/bsm/cath/cath.html

34. Murzin A. G., Brenner S. E., Hubbard T., Chothia C. (1995). SCOP: a structural classification of proteins database for the investigation of sequences and structures. J. Mol. Biol. 247, 536-540

35. http://scop.mrc-lmb.cam.ac.uk/scop/

36. A Bateman, L Coin, R Durbin, R Finn, V Hollich, S Griffiths-Jones, A Khanna, M Marshall, S Moxon, E Sonnhammer, D Studholme, C Yeats and S Eddy. The Pfam Protein Families Database. Nucleic Acids Research(2004) Database Issue 32:D138-D141

37. Sonnhammer ELL, Eddy SR, Birney E, Bateman A, Durbin R (1998) Pfam: multiple sequence alignments and HMM-profiles of protein domains Nucleic Acids Research 26:320-322

38. http://www.sanger.ac.uk/Software/Pfam/

39. Finn RD, Marshall M, Bateman A. iPfam: visualization of protein-protein interactions in PDB at domain and amino acid resolutions. Bioinformatics. 2005;21:410-2

40. http://pywebsvcs.sourceforge.net/

41. http://www.biopython.org/

42. http://www.ruleml.org/

43. http://rewerse.net/

44. Berger, S., Bry, F., Bolzer, O., Furche, T., Schaffert, S. and Wieser, C. (2004). Xcerpt and visXcerpt: Twin Query Languages for the Semantic Web. In Proc. Int. Semantic Web Conf.

45. Pătrânjan, P.L. The Language XChange: A Declarative Approach to Reactivity on the Web. PhD Thesis, Institute for Informatics, University of Munich, July 2005

Ontological and Practical Issues in Using a Description Logic to Represent Medical Concept Systems: Experience from GALEN

Alan Rector and Jeremy Rogers

School of Computer Science, University of Manchester, Manchester M13 9PL, UK
rector@cs.man.ac.uk, rogers@cs.man.ac.uk

Abstract. GALEN seeks to provide re-usable terminology resources for clinical systems. The heart of GALEN is the Common Reference Model (CRM) formulated in a specialised description logic. The CRM is based on a set of principles that have evolved over the period of the project and illustrate key issues to be addressed by any large medical ontology. The principles on which the CRM is based are discussed followed by a more detailed look at the actual mechanisms employed. Finally the structure is compared with other biomedical ontologies in use or proposed.

1 Introduction

1.1 Background

GALEN seeks to provide re-usable terminology resources for clinical systems. The heart of GALEN is the use of an "ontology", the Common Reference Model (CRM), formulated in a specialised description Logic, GRAIL [46] . Since GALEN's inception there have been several other major efforts at medical "ontologies", the most important being SNOMED-CT[1] which has been made widely available in the United States via licensing by the National Library of Medicine and in the UK via licensing to the National Health Service [75].

Likewise, since GALEN's inception, "ontologies" have come to be much more widely studied in relation both to information systems theoretically (*e.g.* [20] [69]), practically (*e.g.* [5, 18, 81]) , in biomedical applications generally (*e.g.* [23, 70]) and in specific areas such as anatomy [32, 63]. Indeed, a track on "ontologies" is a feature of many conferences on the Semantic Web and database design in biohealth informatics. GALEN itself drew heavily on the pioneering work of the CANON group [11, 16, 79] and on ideas from early phases of the Cyc project [31].

GALEN has been used, amongst other activities, for the development of the French national classification of surgical procedures CCAM [57], as part of the procedure for revising the Dutch classification of procedures, in the development of a drug ontology in the UK [72, 87] and in associated work "untangling" forms and routes of drug administration as part of a collaboration with HL7 [86]. Two independent studies have examined the issues in reconciling GALEN's modelling of anatomy with that of

---

[1] http:/www.snomed.org

P. Barahona et al. (Eds.): Reasoning Web 2006, LNCS 4126, pp. 197–231, 2006.

the Digital Anatomist Foundational Model of Anatomy [35, 36, 88-90]. GALEN has also given rise to a methodology for normalising ontologies to promote modularisation [44].

This paper presents a unified approach to the principles and details of the GALEN Common Reference Model (CRM), previously partly described in [26, 58, 59]. GALEN's CRM is one of four models at the core of an overall architecture for use, and re-use, of clinical terminology [49, 51, 56]. A discussion of broader issues and the relation to Cimino's desiderata for clinical terminologies [12] can be found in [52]. A discussion of the use of the ontology in representing pharmaceutical information can be found in [72, 87]. The discussion section of this paper reassesses some of the decisions in the GALEN CRM in terms of developments since its inception in the early 1990s and includes a brief comparison with Welty and Guarino's Ontoclean/Dolce [18, 19, 83] and Smith's Basic Formal Ontology (BFO) [69, 70].

1.2 GALEN's Aims and Criteria for Success

The overall aim of the GALEN terminology resources is to support clinical information systems. For individual patients, it aims to allow clinical information to be recorded faithfully in their electronic record, and then abstracted from it. Such abstraction supports re-organisation or filtering to provide a clearer view of the patient, and linkage to knowledge resources such as decision support, bibliographic, and general web-based information systems. For populations of such patients it supports aggregation for secondary re-use in management, research, and administrative contexts. Abstraction, re-organisation, and re-use are fundamentally dependent on classification, and therefore the primary technical criterion for the GALEN ontology is: *correct and complete classification of its definitions and descriptions.*

More generally, we can describe any ontology in terms of:

1. *Expressiveness* – the ability to represent formally the notions required by its users; for medical ontologies this means all relevant symptoms, diseases, procedures, etc.
2. *Classification* – the ability to infer the correct classification (indexing) of the expressions represented, a) soundly, and b) completely, where by "soundness" we mean that all inferences made are correct, and by "completeness" that all possible sound inferences are made.
3. *Parsimony* – GALEN was specifically designed for use as a "post-coordinated system", in which the classification of new expressions is inferred and dynamically maintained *post hoc*. This avoids the combinatorial explosion inevitable with pre-coordinated systems, in which all legitimate expressions must be pre-enumerated and classified *pre hoc*. An explicit goal of post-coordinated systems is to obtain maximum expressiveness from a finite and limited range of basic notions.

Achieving these goals, however, still requires greater complexity than clinical authors can be expected to cope with. The GALEN ontology is, therefore, designed as an internal 'assembly language', rarely to be seen directly by users or even by most software developers. Intuitive, user-oriented presentation is handled separately through 'intermediate representations' described elsewhere [56, 60].

2 Rationale for the GALEN Common Reference Model

2.1 Basic Principles

2.1.1 'Logical Approximations'

Any logical model for knowledge representation is at best an approximation of the relevant concepts as used in human language and thought. A "logical approximation" may seem an oxymoron, but logical models of any kind behave very differently from language or our internal conceptualisation. Thought and language are typically dependent on context in a fluid manner that eludes the rigidity of logical representation for at least three reasons:

1. Logic, at least standard first order logic and description logics, are "two-valued" – they deal only in truth and falsehood. 'Shades of grey', or probabilities, are not supported.
2. There are well known trade-offs between expressiveness and computational tractability in computational logical systems [6, 14].
3. Reality is fractal – no matter how much detail a model represents, it is always possible to represent more. Hence every formal representation must make choices of what to represent.

2.1.2 'Linguistic Approximations'

Since any ontology is an approximation, the labels attached to representations internally in the ontology are necessarily also at best approximations. Arguments such as "Is the hand still a division of the upper extremity if it has been amputated?" or "Is there a difference between an 'act' and a 'deed'?" rarely affect the utility of the ontology for the intended applications. When arguments over the labelling of representations occur, the GALEN team asks two questions:

1. Does the representation represent *some* entity that most users or authors agree to be useful and clearly defined, even if they cannot agree on what it should be called?
2. Is the label seriously misleading? Ambiguous? Does it mean different things to different groups?

With respect to 1), GALEN has usually found agreement on substance to be easier than agreement on the words to describe that substance. Once the two issues are separated, agreement is possible. For example, whether "neoplasm" should mean any new growth or only any specifically malignant new growth was a matter for great debate. There was no debate, however, regarding whether or not separate representations could and should exist for each of "new growth, whether benign or malignant" and "malignant new growth", merely about how they should be named.

With respect to 2), GALEN has found non-understanding to be better than misunderstanding. Internal labels are often deliberately awkward, *e.g.* "*PathologicalPhenomenon*" rather than "disease" or "disorder".

2.1.3 Canonical Forms and "canonization"

Most notions can be represented in more than one logically and/or semantically equivalent form. Although humans recognise such equivalences easily, one such form must be selected as 'canonical' [16] if logical computational systems are to be able to manipulate representations and data consistently. GALEN recognises two distinct levels of transformation ("canonization") between equivalent forms to be dealt with:

1. Logical – *e.g.* to transform "fracture of a long bone located in the femur" to "Fracture of femur". This is a purely logical operation dependent on the representations of "Fracture", "Long bone" and "Femur", where "Femur" is a more specific subclass of 'Long bone'.
2. Ontological – *e.g.* to transform variants such as "Fixation of femur by means of insertion of pins" and "Insertion of pins to fixate femur" to their preferred form [39]. Such variant forms are not logically equivalent – "Fixations" are not kinds of "Insertions" nor *vice versa*   [56]). Such alternatives can be resolved only by metamodel conventions embodying ontological commitments. (See 0.)

2.2 Ontological Issues

2.2.1 Categories, Instances and Natural Kinds

The GALEN Common Reference Model (CRM) contains only "categories" ("classes")[2] and not "instances".

Categories can be abstract, such as "phenomenon" or "disease", general such as "blood dyscrasia" or very specific such as "sugar-free syrup" or "foot". In principle, however, all categories can be specialised to define new categories which can in turn be further specialised, indefinitely – *e.g.* "sugar-free syrup" to "flavoured sugar-free aspirin syrup"; "foot" to "left foot", "deformed foot", "deformed left foot", etc.

Statements in real world medical records represent statements about "instances"[3] of these categories and, by contrast to categories, can not have kinds or subclasses (can not be "specialised"). It makes no sense to say "a sugar-free kind of *this* tablet of Aspirin" or "a kind of *Alan's* left foot.".

Some authors on ontologies identify instances as being entities specialised to the level of detail required for a particular application, e.g Brachman *et al.*'s "Living with Classic" [7]. This approach is fatal to re-use, since, as Brachman *et al.* so elegantly demonstrate, the appropriate level of detail for different applications will almost certainly be different. It is for this reason that the GALEN Common Reference Model contains only categories and no instances.

However, even though it deals only with categories, GALEN must still decide which categories should be "elementary" ("primitive")[4] and which "composite" ("defined")[5], *i.e.* defined by expressions made up of other categories. GALEN considers two issues in deciding whether to represent a given entity as elementary or composite:

---

[2] GALEN categories are known variously in other systems as "types", "classes", or in Welty & Guarino's writing "predicates". The status of what many call "concept" is controversial; we use the word "entity" throughout this paper as a neutral term for either an instance or a category although - since GALEN does not represent instances - "entity" and "category" are for most purposes synonymous.

[3] In some other systems known variously as "individuals"

[4] Also known as "primitive"

[5] Also known as "defined"

1. Whether it is possible to define the category. A definition must give the complete set of all necessary and sufficient criteria for recognising that category. Many important categories defy complete definition by sufficient criteria. Such categories are related to concepts that are often termed "natural kinds" and include most simple notions such as "leg", "tree", "process", "flow", etc. Natural kinds can also occur at a more abstract level. For example, one might be tempted to define "Heart valve" as equivalent to "valve in the heart", and "valve" as a "structure that controls flow". However, this definition results in the "foramen ovale" being classified as a "heart valve", since it undoubtedly is located in the heart and functions as a valve (to switch between the foetal and post-natal patterns of circulation). Such experiences led GALEN to the rule that, in general, named body parts would be treated as natural kinds and represented as "elementary". Exceptions include cases of generic parts that can be selected, e.g. "lobe of liver" (see 4.1.3) and "named" entities (see 3.1.4).

2. Whether it is useful to define the category, with respect to the needs of the applications expected to be supported within the scope of the model. Some categories are simply not worth the trouble to define, even though definition might be possible. This is particularly true if constructing the definition would necessarily involve the creation and modelling of new categories otherwise very much outside the scope of the ontology and applications. For example, although a sufficient definition of "stroboscope" might be possible in a much broader ontology, within the scope of GALEN it suffices to leave it as elementary.

2.2.2 Explicitness and Orthogonal Taxonomies: "Normalising" the Ontology

Potentially, it should be possible to re-arrange the ontology along any axis. In a description logic, this corresponds to saying that it should be possible to classify any entity according to each of its stated properties. Therefore, all properties must be represented explicitly and independently, even at the cost of apparent redundancy. For example, GALEN maintains that the indications for a drug should be represented separately from its actions even though one can often be inferred from the other, *e.g.* that an indication of "relief of bronchoconstriction" should be represented separately from the action of "bronchodilatation".

GALEN formulates this as the "principle of orthogonal taxonomies" [43, 45], and it has since been elaborated into a general rationale and methodology for "normalising" ontologies [44]. Interestingly, there is a close analogy between the "principle of orthogonal taxonomies" and Smith's advocacy of single inheritance for the "is-a" relation [70], based on entirely different considerations.

2.2.3 Self-standing Entities and Modifiers

The entities in the GALEN ontology can be divided into two kinds:

1. Those that represent things that can exist on their own, *e.g.* physical objects, processes, ideas, etc. Sowa [73] after Pierce terms these "first class objects, whilst Welty and Guarino term them "sortals" [20, 83]. In more recent work the authors of this manuscript have termed them "self-standing entities" [44].

2. Those that only make sense when linked to some other object *e.g.* modifier, modalities, or notions such as "collection of". "Modifiers" are notions such as

"severe", "soft" or "short" that describe other entities and specialise them further. "Modalities" are notions such as "presence", "uncertainty", "family history" etc. that take their meaning from the kernel entity. Sowa [73] after Pierce terms such entities "seconds" and "thirds"

The most important principled differences between self-standing entities and modifiers in GALEN's Common Reference Model are that:

1. Lists of self-standing entities are almost always 'open', *i.e.* they cannot be assumed to be complete, so that it is not legitimate to infer from the negation of some that one of the others is present, even in formalisms supporting such inferences.
2. Lists of modifiers may be 'closed', *i.e.* may be assumed to be complete so that inferences of the form "not raised or normal, therefore depressed" can be justified logically, although they must be used with care clinically.

For both technical and clinical reasons, GALEN treats all lists of categories as 'open'. It never makes inferences such as "not absent implies present" on the grounds that this risks imputing a degree of logical rigour to clinicians' statements which is rarely intended. Nonetheless, it maintains the distinction between self-standing entities and modifiers as a top level dichotomy in the model.

2.2.4   Reified Relations[6] or "Features"
The choice of what should be represented as an "Attribute" or "semantic link"[7] is less simple than it seems, since any attribute can be reified (or "nominalised") into a category, *e.g.* in GRAIL notation:

> Disease <u>which</u> hasSeverity severe

might also be expressed as

> Disease which hasFeature (Severity which hasState severe)

In the second form, the attribute *hasSeverity* has been 'reified' to the category *Severity* plus two subsidiary attributes, *hasFeature* and *hasState*. Such reified attributes, such as *"Severity"*, are known in GALEN as *Features*.

Given that this transformation is always possible formally, in the extreme a system could be built with just two attributes (semantic links) for modifiers – *hasFeature* and *hasState*. How, then, should the decision be made as to which attributes to reify? GALEN offers two criteria

1. Need for further description of the attribute – In most formalisms including GRAIL, attributes cannot themselves be described except in predefined ways in the formalism, such as being transitive or having a parent super-attribute in the kind-of hierarchy. Therefore, if the 'fact of being linked' may need to be described, even if only in a few cases, then the attribute representing the link must be reified to a *Feature*.

---

[6] Note that the word "reify" is used differently with different technical meanings in each of the RDF and Topic Map communities.

[7] Known variously as a "semantic link" (CEN TC251/ISO 215), "property" (OWL), "role" (most other description logics) and slots (frame systems).

2. Consistency of representation – If there are a series of properties that appear analogous, it is almost impossible for authors to maintain a system in which some are represented as an attribute and some as a *Feature*. Therefore, if any must be described as in a) and therefore reified, then all similar attributes should be reified.

In practice, GALEN reifies all modifiers such as severity, height, body temperature, etc. but not 'selectors' such as right in "right hand" about which nothing more can be said. *Features* in GALEN correspond closely to what Welty and Guarino term "qualities" [83], and GALEN's values and *States* to what they call "quale".[8]

2.2.5 Dualities
Many medical concepts come naturally in dualities, and it is not always obvious which should be represented as primary. For example, the "process of ulceration" has as its outcome "ulcer lesions". Should the process be defined in terms of the lesion or *vice versa*? Or should both be treated as elementary and related by necessary but not sufficient conditions? The choice is unclear and possibly arbitrary, but it needs to be made consistently if classification is to work consistently, since "lesions", "processes" and "situations" are different kinds of categories and one will never be inferred to be a subclass of another. GALEN represents the process as elementary and defines the lesion in terms of the process in virtually all cases, even when this requires some linguistic awkwardness (*e.g.* what is the name of the process by which a bullous lesion is formed?).

2.2.6 Top Level Ontologies
The original belief of those developing the GALEN ontology was that it would be built from the bottom up. The top level, domain independent, categories were seen as making little difference to classification and inference, since most inferences depended more on consistency of expression locally than on top level constraints. Experience has largely confirmed this view technically but, paradoxically, refuted it pragmatically with respect to the development process. An agreed and understandable top level ontology has proved essential to allow groups to co-operate effectively.

However, just as all ontologies are approximations, so all high level ontologies are to some degree arbitrary. There were several candidate starting points early in GALEN's development – PENMAN[3], Cyc [21, 31], traditional schemes from Artificial Intelligence and linguistics such as those deriving from Shank [64] and Sowa [73]. GALEN's top level categories were originally adapted from those in early versions of Cyc [31]. Of recent developments, they are closely related to those in Guarino and Welty's DOLCE [33] and conform to most of the precepts advocated in their OntoClean methodology [19].

In addition, it seems that each major field such as medicine requires one or two very high level abstractions which are broad disjunctions cutting across the traditional boundaries of top level categories. In GALEN, the category *Phenomenon* and the attribute *involves* are designed to range over anything that is, or might become, pathological – in common parlance anything that might be or become a disease, disorder or condition.

---

[8] For a recent discussion of these issues in the context of OWL, see the Semantic Web Best Practice Committee's note on "n-ary relations", http://www.w3.org/TR/swbp-n-aryRelations/.

2.2.7 Normative Statements, Congenital Malformations, and Imputed Intentions

Many of the descriptive axioms used in terminology models are actually 'normative' rather than absolute, *i.e.* they really pertain to our view of 'normal' anatomy, physiology, etc. This gives rise to problems when describing congenital malformations and mutilations. There are at least three complementary approaches to this problem:

1. To adjust the interpretation of the attributes and categories. For example, GALEN interprets the *has Division* attribute in such a way that the *"Hand isDivisionOf Arm"* is true even if the hand is severed from the arm. Since we may still wish to represent information about the missing hand relating it to its original owner, this is the best 'logical approximation'.
2. To model both normal and abnormal, but use the interface and related mechanisms to limit the initial display view only to the normal conformation. The PEN&PAD/Clinergy systems based on GALEN[30, 38] used this approach in many places.
3. To model anatomical normality explicitly, so that almost all statements become statements about "normal hand", "normal body", etc. Although elegant, and discussed at greater length in [47, 53], the additional complexity in both modelling and computation combined with the large size of the GALEN ontology made this approach impractical.

Normative statements give more difficulty when applied to procedures and treatments. Consider O'Neil's classic example, "Insertion of pins in the Femur" [39], which is almost always performed only in order to fixate a broken femur. If a classifier is to infer that it should be classified under "Operations to fixate long bones", then the information about the goal of the procedure must be added to the description of the method. However, to do so risks imputing unstated intentions to the clinicians using the terminology. GALEN is cautious about adding such unstated normative descriptors, but has found that some cannot be avoided if the classification expected and intended by users is to be maintained.

2.3 Logical Issues

2.3.1 Negation and Uncertainty

Negation and uncertainty lead to difficulties for at least four reasons:

1. The meaning of negation and uncertainty in clinical observations is unclear. For example, where no mention of diabetes exists in a medical record, what should be the answer to a query "Does the patient have diabetes?" Most database systems would answer "no" on the basis of a 'closed world assumption' and 'negation as failure' – the assumption that all relevant information about the domain of discourse is contained in the database and that therefore failure to find a fact can be taken as equivalent to its negation. In many clinical applications, neither assumption seems safe. Furthermore, if uncertainty is catered for, should it be included with negation or be a separate dimension? *e.g.* what are the comparative

meanings of "possibly present" and "possibly absent"? Whatever choice is made, can we count on doctors to use it consistently? Dare we therefore support or depend on it?

2. The scope of negation is often unclear. At least three cases must be distinguished: a) "It is not the case that the patient has X"; b) "The patient has non-X" *e.g.* apyrexia (no fever), atonia (no muscle tone), amastia (no breast); and c) "The patient has X but not some specific kinds of X", *e.g.* "idiopathic hypertension" (hypertension but not any of a list of recognised kinds), "Non-toxic goitre", (goitre but not any of the toxic varieties") or "non-A non-B hepatitis" (hepatitis but not that caused by either the hepatitis A or B virus).

3. Adding negation and uncertainty to formalisms increases their computational complexity and makes canonization difficult. Even ontologies based on underlying formalisms that support negation may choose not to use it.

4. Negation and uncertainty are often represented in information systems models *e.g.* the HL7 Reference Information Model (RIM)[9]. If negation can be represented both in the information system and in the ontology, then the meaning of all possible combinations of negations in the two systems must be defined. (See[50, 54, 55].)

GALEN's GRAIL formalism does not support negation, but the GALEN Common Reference Model includes constructs such as "presence" and "absence" which provide a limited 'work around' and that can be qualified by an uncertainty.

2.3.2 Defaults and Indexing

The definition of "B is a kind of A" in formal logical representations is that "All Bs are As". Hence, all of the properties in the definition and description of 'As' must also apply to 'Bs' without exception. Adding exceptions to such logical patterns has had little success [15], although it remains an area of ongoing research. This contrasts with most, although not all, frame systems in which default values for a 'slot' (equivalent to a GRAIL attribute) can be both inherited and overridden.

However, if additional facts are indexed by an ontology that conforms to this logical definition of 'is kind of', then it is still possible to use the ontology in conjunction with other inference mechanisms to reason about defaults and exceptions. For example, a logical subsumption hierarchy from an ontology of drug classes can be used to index potential side effects, even though some side effects are subject to exceptions [71] The scaffold provided by the subsumption hierarchy can be used to select the most specific candidate side effects using the standard "Touretzky distance measure" [78].

GALEN refers to such indexing statements as "extrinsic" because they do not affect the classification and are therefore not part of the ontology proper but rather use the ontology as, in Wood's [85] phrase, a "conceptual coat rack" on which to hang other information.

GALEN's experience is that if the taxonomies are properly orthogonal – *i.e.* if the ontology is normalised – the set of candidate values usually has exactly one member.

---

[9] http://www.hl7.org.

If it does have more than one member, then GALEN treats this as a signal that other reasoning methods and knowledge are required.

2.3.3 Definitions and General Inclusion Axioms

Unlike most DLs of its generation including that used in SNOMED-CT, GRAIL allows defined categories ("classes") to be further described by "necessary statements". This means that GALEN's authors do not have to choose between making all of the characteristics of an entity part of its definition (*i.e.* necessary *and* sufficient) or all merely necessary. For example, consider the notion that "severing of an artery" causes "haemorrhage". One would not want "causing haemorrhage" as part of the definition of the severing of an artery – *e.g. Severing which actsOn Artery* – because then we should have to state explicitly that "severing the aorta" had caused a haemorrhage before a machine could classify it as a "severing of an artery". On the other hand, we would want the ontology to include the information that all such injuries are kinds of injuries that cause haemorrhage. Such additional necessary but not sufficient conditions are known in description logic as "general inclusion axioms".

2.3.4 Embedded Expressions

If a category's representation depends on its use, then this limits its re-use. Categories such as "lobe of the liver" or "fluid in cyst in the kidney" should appear the same regardless of context – whether as aspects of disease, targets of surgery, substances to be injected or drained, or specimens in a pathology examination. Since many of these categories are themselves composite, a primary requirement on the GRAIL language was that it allow definitions to be recursively embedded within other definitions to any degree required. For example, GRAIL supports expressions such as "upper part *of* third segment *of* middle lobe *of* right lung". Such embedding is impossible in most frame languages and has not been used in SNOMED-CT, beyond the mechanism of "role grouping" for a single level of embedding.

2.3.5 Transitive Attributes and Inheritance Across Transitive Attributes

Part-whole relations, causal links, and connections are all transitive. Some other attributes, though not themselves transitive, are 'inherited' across these transitive attributes. Establishing the pattern of transitive relations and the inheritance along them is a key part of any ontology of medicine [46].

GALEN's original primary use for transitive attributes was for part-whole relations; its original use case of inheritance across transitive attributes was for representing the patterns "The disease of the part is a disease of the whole" and "The procedure on the part is a procedure on the whole". These two specific cases might now be implemented instead by SEP triples [24, 25] or one of their variants [42]. However, GALEN also uses inheritance across transitive attributes to support several other clinically important inferences in an otherwise relatively 'weak' description logic. For example:

1. 1)In the representation of syndromes, to represent the fact that the presence of a syndrome implies the presence of each disease in the syndrome.

2. 2)In the representation of procedures, to represent that a global procedure acts on all of the structures acted on by its subprocedures.

3. In the representation of anatomy, to represent that where a subbranch of a larger vessel supplies blood to a particular structure, then this implies that the larger vessel also supplies blood to that structure

In GALEN, such axioms are implemented by the use of the *specialisedBy* construct, equivalent to "right identities" in SNOMED-CT's representation.

In addition, GRAIL supports a construct for 'single valued' transitive attributes, which is interpreted as indicating that the transitive attribute must form a tree. This avoids the need to provide non-transitive "direct" subattributes of transitive attributes.[10]

2.3.6 Issues Minimally or Poorly Represented

1. *Adjacency and spatial/temporal reasoning.* A "fracture of the tibia and fibula" makes sense; a "fracture of the tibia and humerus" does not. GALEN provides very limited support for this type of reasoning, although there have been experiments with several work arounds. Likewise for more complex relations involving spatiotemporal reasoning and its interaction with plausible mechanisms of injury or pathophysiology. It is assumed that these will be dealt with either by the information model or by separate reasoners outside the central terminology/ontology.

GRAIL	OWL	DL	Paraphrase
(C which prop C_1) name CN-	CN class C complete restriction (*prop_* someValuesFrom C_1)	CN $\cong$ C $\sqcap$ $\exists$ *prop.* C_1	CNs are defined as any C which *prop* some C_1
C topicNecessarily prop C_1	subclassOf(C, restriction(*prop_* someValuesFrom C_1))	C $\sqsubseteq$ $\exists$ *prop.* C_1	All Cs prop some C_1
<prop$_1$ C_1 prop$_2$ C_2 ... prop$_n$C$_n$>	intersectionOf(restriction(*prop$_1$* someValuesFrom C_1), restriction(*prop$_2$* someValuesFrom C_2) ... restriction(*prop$_n$* someValuesFrom C_n))	$\exists$ *prop$_1$.C$_1$* $\sqcap$ $\exists$ *prop$_2$.C$_2$* $\sqcap$ ... $\sqcap$ $\exists$ *prop$_n$.C$_n$*	*prop$_1$* some C_1 and *prop$_2$* some C_2 and .... and *prop$_n$* some C_n
prop$_1$ specialisedBy prop$_2$; prop$_1$ refinedBy inverse prop$_2$	-------------------------------------	*prop$_1$* $\circ$ *prop$_2$* $\sqsubseteq$ *prop$_1$* equivalent to *prop$_2$*$^{-1}$ $\circ$ *prop$_1$*$^{-1}$ $\sqsubseteq$ *prop$_1$*$^{-1}$	Any C_1 that *prop$_1$* some C_2 that *prop$_2$* some C_3= also *prop$_1$* some C_3, or equivalently: Any C_1 that inverse *prop$_2$* some C_2 that inverse *prop$_1$* some C_3 also inverse *prop$_1$* some C_3.

Fig. 1. Grail modeling **constructs**

---

[10]   See Simple Part-Whole Relations in OWL ontologies, Rector & Welty (eds.) http://www.w3.org/2001/sw/BestPractices/OEP/SimplePartWhole/

GRAIL	OWL	DLs (FaCT/Racer)	OntoClean/ Dolce	Logic
Category	Class	Class	(unary) Predicate	unary predicate / Type
Attribute	Property	Role	Relation	Binary predicate/ Relation
necessary statement *topicNecessarily*	subclassOf() axiom	"General inclusion axiom" *implies* ($\sqsubseteq$)	$\rightarrow$	$\rightarrow$

Fig. 2. Comparsion of Grail and other vocabularies

2. *Numerical conversions, calculations and other 'non-terminological' reasoning.* There are numerous services that users might naturally expect to be packaged with a terminology but which require entirely different types of reasoning from logical classification based on definitions, descriptions and first order logic. The most obvious of these are conversion between different unit and coordinate systems. GALEN's intention has always been to package these services separately within the 'terminology server', and the architecture provides for them although, in practice, none have been implemented. However, they are strictly excluded from the "ontology" or Common Reference Model (CRM).

3 The GALEN Upper Domain Ontology

The GALEN Common Reference Model is presented here using the notation of GALEN's GRAIL language. However, the presentation is intended to be sufficiently general to allow comparison and potential harmonisation with other clinical ontologies such as that of SNOMED-CT[11], the Digital Anatomist Project [34, 63], where appropriate with the Gene Ontology and other ontologies from the Open Biomedical Ontologies (OBO) group [76, 77][12], with more language oriented work such as that of Zweigenbaum [91] or Hahn [23], or with more general upper ontologies such as DOLCE/OntoClean from Guarino and Welty [33, 74, 83], SUMO[13] or Smith's Basic Formal Ontology and its biological adaptations [13, 70]. The full ontology is available from the *Open*GALEN web site, http://www.opengalen.org, and a detailed description of the GRAIL language is available in [46]. A short summary of GRAIL notation as used in this paper and its equivalents in OWL and standard German DL notation along with notes on unusual features is given in Figure 1, and additional vocabulary comparisons are given in Figure 2. The GALEN vocabulary is explained in the text.

This paper focuses on the issues raised and is not intended as a guide to the current implementation. In some cases, the constructs and language used reflect more recent developments not fully implemented in the existing resources available from *Open*GALEN. Where there are significant departures from the actual implementation, they are noted in the text.

---

[11] http://www.snomed.org
[12] http://http://obo.sourceforge.net/
[13] http://suo.ieee.org/

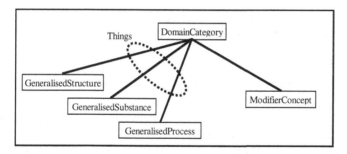

Fig. 3. Primary structure of Galen's Toplevel Categories

The ontological patterns described in this paper are for the raw, underlying ontology. GALEN treats this ontology as an 'assembly language' that few users ever see. The goal of this underlying ontology is to be unambiguous and result in correct classification. Intuitive presentations to users are dealt with via intermediate representations and tools [48, 56, 60] which are outside the scope of this paper.

3.1 The Top Level Categories

3.1.1 Top Level Distinctions
The primary structure of GALEN's top level categories is shown in Figure 3. GALEN's top level distinction is between self-standing entities, or *Things*, and everything else, termed *Modifier Categories*. *Things* are roughly equivalent to 'sortals' in DOLCE and are further divided into

GeneralisedStructure	abstract or physical discrete *Things* with parts that exist at particular times, e.g. bodies, organs, cells,...
GeneralisedSubstance	abstract or physical continuous *Things* with parts which exist at particular times, e.g. tissues, fluids,...
GeneralisedProcess	changes which occur over time, e.g. metabolic processes, procedures, ...

These distinctions are now common currency although under different names. *GeneralisedStructure* and *GeneralisedProcess* together are approximately equivalent to "endurants" in DOLCE , or "continuants" in the BFO and many other ontologies. *GeneralisedProcess* is equivalent to "occurents" in the BFO and "perdurants" in DOLCE. *GeneralisedSubstance* corresponds to "Amount of matter" in DOLCE but has no equivalent in BFO. The structure was originally adapted from Lenat and Guha [31], but where they maintain a distinction for processes analogous to that between *GeneralisedStructure* and *GeneralisedSubstance* – e.g. between "the digestion of a meal" and "the activity of digestion"– GALEN does not, because knowledge engineers and users found it to be confusing and difficult to maintain reliably. Neither DOLCE nor BFO support this distinction nor, it appears, does the current version of OpenCYC.[14] For different reasons, the notion of *"Thing"* as the common parent of *GeneralisedStructure* and *GeneralisedProcess* was left implicit, as its labelling led to arguments about language. GALEN does not make the distinction between "function"

---

[14] http://www.cyc.com/doc/

and "process", i.e. between the potential for a process to occur and an occurrence of the process, as made in BFO and DOLCE.

3.1.2 Modifiers

The first level break down of *ModifierCategory* falls into:

- **Aspect and Modality**[15]

Aspect	'modifiers proper' that refine a category, e.g. size, shape, age, laterality, etc[16].
Modality	Separate notions that take part of their meaning from the primary things, e.g. family history of, risk of, history of, etc.

- **Other categories that are dependent on self-standing entities for their full meaning**

Role	sometimes arbitrary categories used to make elementary taxonomies orthogonal, e.g. *DoctorRole*, HormoneRole, *DrugRole*, etc.
Collection	set, system, multiple, etc. GALEN's collections are not mathematical sets but rather various forms of general collection such as vertebrae, the cells in the liver, etc. GRAIL supports no special operations on collections.

- **Miscellaneous categories with special significance or behaviour**

Unit	units of measure, *e.g.* mg, ml, day, ...

Of the above, the most complex is *Aspect,* which is further subdivided into:

Feature	reified attributes (see 0) representing mutable properties *e.g.* severity, duration, etc. To have meaning, *Features* must be further refined either by one or more *States* in a "Feature-state pair" (*e.g. Temperature which hasState hot*) or by the entity that it is a property of (e.g. *Length which isLengthOf Bone*).
State	(usually) closed sets of qualitative 'value's that may be assigned to *Features*, e.g. *mild, moderate, severe.*
Quantity	used to refine *Features* with quantitative values, including numerical magnitudes and units or levels
Selector	immutable properties *e.g.* laterality (left/right) and position (upper/middle/lower) etc. of anatomical parts. Selectors identify a specific entity rather than modifying it[17].
Status	Modifiers other than selectors that are not reified; many are used to support special inference in the model or in applications using the model, *e.g. normal/nonNormal, countable/indefinitely Divisible/mass,* and various topological indicators[18].

---

[15] The labels "Aspect" and "Modality" were arrived at after much internal discussion. "Modality" corresponds roughly to what SNOMED-CT refers to as "Axis modifying qualifiers" and "Aspect" to "Non-axis modifying qualifiers".

[16] Corresponds approximately in SNOMED-CT to "non-axis changing qualifiers".

[17] In terms of OntoClean, selectors are part of what gives an individual an identity. A left hand cannot cease to be of laterality left without becoming something different.

[18] Also used as a ragbag for qualitative values not currently represented as feature-state pairs.

Most mutable properties except *Status*es are reified in GALEN to *feature-state*-pairs, *e.g. Disease <u>which</u> hasFeature (Severity <u>which</u> hasState severe)*. By contrast, *Selector*s are immutable and always linked directly to the entity they modify by a single attribute, *e.g. Hand <u>which</u> hasLeftRightSelector rightSelection. Status* in GALEN is defined by engineering rather than ontological principles; it includes primarily immutable properties such as an organs topology but also the sometimes mutable property of whether or not a given entity is *nonNormal* and/or *pathological*.

The special Quantity[19] *Level* is used amongst other things to represent the recurrent pattern in departures from expected values first pointed out by Shahar [68]. *Level* takes a series of subattributes of *hasState – hasAbsoluteState, hasChangeInState, hasTrendInState, hasRelativeLevelState,* and *hasExpectedLevelState.* This allows the expression of complex notions such as "temperature with an absolute state of 39°C, which is falling, but which is still elevated (*i.e.* higher than expected)".

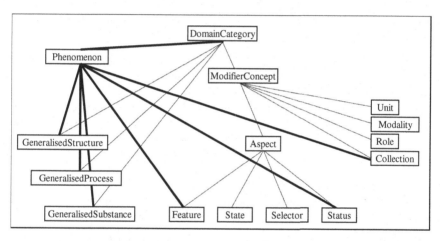

Fig. 4. Secondary structure of Galen's top level categories

3.1.3 *Phenomenon* – Secondary Structure for Top Level Categories

As with many ontologies oriented to a particular domain, GALEN requires a very high level disjunctive category to allow representation of key clinical generalisations. In GALEN this category is labelled *Phenomenon*, the common ancestor of anything that can be, or can be modified to be, worth noting clinically as either *nonNormal* or *pathological*. GALEN lacks an operator for disjunction, so Phenomenon is added manually, as shown in Figure 4, as the common parent of the subsidiary categories. As defined, this is clearly too inclusive to meet GALEN's original goal of representing all and *only* what is clinically sensible. However, the effort to tighten the constraints whilst avoiding arguments over issues such as whether or not an infected prosthesis can be *pathological* has not so far been warranted.

---

[19] Whether "*Level*" should be a *Quantity* or a *Feature* has been a matter of some controversy but is without obvious consequences for the inferences to be made.

3.1.4 Breaking Up Long Lists: The NAMED... Convention

The principle of orthogonal taxonomies combined with the principle that all anatomical entities be treated as natural kinds, results in a broad flat hierarchy of elementary categories that is difficult to work with. For convenience, GALEN breaks this hierarchy up by introducing categories such as *NAMEDArtery*, *NAMEDJoint*, NAMEDSensoryPart etc.

3.2 Top Level Attributes[20]

3.2.1 Primary Distinctions

In GRAIL, as in many but not all other description logics, one attribute ("role", "property") can be a kind of one or more others, just as one category can be a kind of another. *DomainAttribute* is the root of the attribute polyhierarchy, and it breaks down into three major branches, each of which will be discussed in turn. (Note that all attributes in GRAIL have inverses that have been omitted in this paper for clarity. By convention, attributes and their inverses are named by analogy to *isPartOf* and *hasPart*.)

ConstructiveAttribute	Relations between self-standing entities (Things), ie. GeneralisedStructures, GeneralisedSubstances, and GeneralisedProcesses
ModifierAttribute	Relations between Things and ModifierCategories
TemporalAttribute	Relations between Statuses involving time (deliberately weak, see 2.3.6)
WrapperAttribute	Used in ClinicalSituations (see 5)

3.2.2 ConstructiveAttribute

ConstructiveAttribute further breaks down into three primary subattributes plus the domain specific secondary attribute, *LocativeAttribute* (alias *involves*).

PartitiveAttribute	Part-whole relations –e.g. *isDivisionOf* - see **4.1.1**
StructuralAttribute	Non-partitive relations e.g. *isServedBy*, *isBranchOf*, *isSpaceDefinedBy*, etc.
FunctionalAttribute	Functional relations such as *isFunctionOf*, *actsOn* etc.
LocativeAttribute (*involves*)	A heterogeneous disjunction of locative, purposive, functional and causal relations, e.g. *isConsequenceOf*, *isFeatureOf*
- *hasLocation*	The relation between a disease and the anatomical or physiological entity in which it is localised. NB does not imply physical location.[21]

---

[20] "Properties" in OWL; "Roles" in standard DLs; "relations" in standard mathematical terms; "semantic link types" in CEN TC251/ISO TC215.

[21] Because the naming of the attribute "hasLocation" has led to confusion in alignment with other ontologies, for conversions and other external uses it has been renamed to "hasLocus". Approximately equivalent to the SNOMED-CT "site".

The key construction in most medical entities is to localise a disease or procedure to an anatomical or functional entity or to one of its parts. Correspondingly, the most common pattern in GALEN for disease or procedure entities is:

Disease/Procedure <u>*which*</u> *LocativeAttribute BodyStructure/Process*

specialisedBy		Example
hasLocation	isDivisionOf	Disease hasLocation (Part <u>which</u> isDivisionOf Whole) → Disease hasLocation Whole
isComponentOf	isSubdivisionOf	Bone isComponent of (Finger <u>which</u> isDivisionOf RightHand) → Bone isComponentOf RightHand
isLayerOf	isSubdivisionOf	Skin isLayerOf (Hand <u>which</u> isSubdivisionOf UpperExtremity) → Skin isLayer of UpperExtremity.
isBranchOf	isLinearDivision Of	CoronaryArtery isBranchOf (AscendingAorta isLinearDivisionOf ThoracicAorta) → Vessel isBranchOf ThoracicAorta
serves	isDivisionOf	BloodVessel serves (Part which isDivisionOf Whole) → BloodVessel serves Whole
contains	isLocationOf	Abdomen contains (Liver isLocationOf Tumour) → Abdomen contains Tumour
actsOn	isFunctionOf	Drug actsOn (PathologicalProcess isFunctionOf Organ) → Drug actsOn Organ
actsOn	makesUp	Process actsOn (Tissue makesUp Liver) → Process actsOn Liver
contains	isLocationOf	BodySpace contains (Organ isLocationOf Lesion) → BodySpace contains Lesion

Fig. 5. Important uses of the specialisedBy construct indicating inheritance along a transitive role and equivalent to SNOMED-CT right identities

3.2.3 ModifierAttribute

The modifier attributes and modifier categories are intimately tied, one main branch of the attribute hierarchy for each branch of the *ModifierCategory* hierarchy: *modalityAttribute, RoleDesignatingAttribute, CollectionAttribute, UnitAttribute* and the attributes related to *Aspect – isFeatureOf, isStateOf, QuantityAttribute, SelectorAttribute,* and *StatusAttribute.*

Two limitations of GRAIL lead to a proliferation of subattributes that are of no ontological significance but can obscure the overall structure.

1. Cardinality can be controlled only at the level of attributes – in modern parlance "qualified cardinality restrictions" are not supported. GRAIL shares this feature with OWL (in all its flavours) and SNOMED-CT, although not with most modern DLs. Therefore, separate subattributes must be used for single valued variants of attributes.

2. The GRAIL category hierarchy represents most modifiers by reifying the relation to a kind of *Feature*. Since each individual can have many *Features*, but only one of each kind of *Feature*, a separate subattribute of *hasFeature* is required for each *Feature – hasTemperatureFeature, hasHeightFeature*, etc.

3.2.4 Structure of Inheritance Across Transitive Attributes

In addition to the attribute hierarchy as described above, GALEN provides the *specialisedBy* construct as described in 0 for inheritance of attributes across transitive roles. Some of the most important *specialisedBy* axioms are given in Figure 5.

3.2.5 Additional Uses of the Attribute Hierarchy

Two further uses of the attribute hierarchy deserve special mention. The first two are logical; the third is ontological.

1. To allow single-valued and multi-valued variants of an attribute. Logically, the single-valued variant must be a descendent of the multi-valued variant, and its purpose is signalled by the infix "specific" or "specifically", *e.g. hasSpecificConsequence* or *actsOnSpecifically*. Such "specific" attributes are often used to indicate a main, or primary action, cause, etc.

2. As a workaround for the lack of 'shared variables' in GRAIL (as in other description logics). GRAIL provides no mechanism to represent 'X *containedIn* Y ← X *part of* Y'. GALEN achieves an approximation to this inference by the attribute *isPartitivelyContainedIn*, which a descendant of both *IsDivisionOf* and *Contains*.

3. To allow very general queries, such as "disorders of the heart". *LocativeAttribute* (also known as *involves*) has been steadily generalised in the course of the project until it has become the analogue of *phenomenon*, a domain specific disjunction of the attributes needed for high level generalisations and queries. It is worth noting that, in this very general form, *LocativeAttribute* subsumes causal relations since, for example, classifying "spider angiomata" under "phenomena involving liver disorder" is appropriate. Similarly, rheumatic heart disease *involves* bacterial disease as well as a heart disease since the lesions located in heart are in response to an infection caused by bacterium.

4   The GALEN Common Reference Model

4.1 Anatomy

One of the key aspects of any biomedical ontology is its representation of anatomy. Because GALEN has been used most extensively for developing terminologies of surgical procedures, its anatomy representation is considered the best developed and tested and is presented in detail below.

4.1.1 Physical Part Whole Relations and Physical Connection

There has been much study of parts and wholes – in GALEN's parlance "partitive relations"– in AI generally, *e.g.* [40, 84], and in description logics more specifically [1, 2, 41]. An entire subfield of philosophy and linguistics - "mereology" - is devoted to their study [4, 9, 82]. Technical details of how GALEN's mechanism for inheritance across transitive properties is applied to parts and wholes, and how this relates to other formalisms, can be found in [42]. Since GALEN's ontology was established, variants on Schulz and Hahn's SEP triples formalism have been widely used as a means to implement related ideas [24, 25, 65-67]; these will be further considered in the discussion section.

As anatomy is physical, we deal here only with partonomy as it relates to physical things[22]. The basic axioms of the GALEN model of partonomy are as follows:

Rule 1) All primary partitive attributes between discrete objects are transitive. This includes isLayerOf on the grounds that anatomical layers are always concentric [56].

Rule 2) Diseases/disorders/procedures of/on a part pertain also to the whole

Rule 3) "Connection" is transitive23 but not always partitive. A combined attribute, isPartitiveConnectionOf, is provided for cases where it is partitive;

Rule 4) "Branching" is neither partitive nor transitive, although because isBranchOf is refined along isLinearDivisionOf (See

Rule 5) and Section 2.3.5 above), branches of linear divisions are branches of the whole, e.g. branches of the infrarenal aorta are classified under branches of the abdominal aorta.

Rule 6) Connected physical sets such as the "digestive tract" are distinct from functional systems such as "the digestive system"

Rule 7) Membership in collections is not partitive, contrary to [40, 84].

GALEN then classifies the range of possible part-whole relationships between discrete physical parts along several axes, with strong constraints based on the topology of the arguments and whether they are *Structures* (discrete) or *SubstanceOrTissues* (continuous/mass).

isDivisionOf	The most general partitive attribute
- *isLinearDivisionOf*	Relates any two topologically linear structures, *e.g.* between an arterial segment and the artery
- *isSurfaceRegionOf*	Relates a two-dimensional structure to a three-dimensional structure, such as between an organ and its surface
- *isSolidRegionOf*	Most general relationship between any two three-dimensional structures.
- - *isLayerOf*	Relates things like skin or muscle or periosteum that occur in all divisions of an entity to that entity.
- - *isSolidDivisionOf*	Relates all other three-dimensional entities, ie wherever the relationship is not 'layer-of'
- *isComponentOf*	Relates discrete things like joints, ligaments and organs that occur only in one or more divisions of an object
- - *isFunctionalComponentOf*	Participates in a specialisedBy axiom such that functions of the part are also functions of the whole.

---

[22] Physical endurants/continuants in DOLCE/BFO's parlance.

[23] Other authors take connection as only symmetric, and not transitive. GRAIL does not support symmetric relations, while GALEN's "connection" corresponds to the transitive closure of all direct and indirect connectivity, where a true 'directly connected to" relation would indeed not be transitive.

These partitive attributes are further related by the following rules:

Rule 8) Components of any discrete part are components of the whole, *e.g.* the chordae *of* the leaflets *of* the valves *of* the ventricles are components of the heart.

Rule 9) Layers of divisions are layers of the whole, *e.g.* the skin of the hand is a kind of skin of the upper extremity.

Rule 8) above is a pragmatic approximation and the one case in GALEN where part-hood and subsumption are deliberately conflated. The rule should be: "Layers of divisions *are divisions of* the corresponding layer of the whole", *e.g.* "The hand is a division of the upper extremity; therefore the skin of the hand is a division of the skin of the upper extremity." Unfortunately, this rule is outside the expressivity of description logics[24] [42]. In practice, we have not discovered any errors due to this subsumption at the gross level of anatomy needed for GALEN's focus on diseases and procedures, although it would not be adequate for some parts of developmental anatomy.

Rules 2,4,7 & 8 are implemented by the use of the *specialisedBy*[25] construct for propagation along transitive roles (see 2.3.5).

One rule was not properly implemented in GALEN although it appears in various places in the documentation, because the distinction between discrete components and subdivisions was not fully implemented.

Rule 10) Layers of discrete components should not be layers of the whole (e.g. the cartilage layer of the tibial plateau should not be a kind of layer of the knee joint)

One further rule would be required in most other formalisms that - unlike GRAIL - do not support restrictions of transitive attributes *e.g.* to strict trees.

Rule 11) All transitive attributes have a direct non-transitive subproperty.

4.1.2 Regions

The problem of describing what clinicians refer to as regions of the body poses significant headaches for a logic based ontology, not least because regions have borders that are either ill defined or defined differently by different experts and even different text books. In addition to these difficulties, the following challenges were encountered:

1. Regions named identically with the primary structure that they contain, *e.g.* 'knee' may refer either to the knee joint or the knee region. GALEN treats both "regions" and associated primary structures as primitives, with the structure being necessarily *isStructuralComponentOf* the region. (Note that GALEN's naming convention assigns the 'simple' name to the surface region, *e.g.* "Chest" or "Knee", whereas the FMA assigns it to the associated structure. GALEN's *Knee* corresponds to FMA's "Region of the knee"; GALEN's *KneeJoint* is FMA's "Knee")

2. Regions defined as those areas of (unspecified) tissue that have a particular, though often loosely bounded, spatial relationship to some named structure (*e.g.* paracolic

---

[24] It requires at least three variables to express the rule in formal logic. It is therefore is outside F2, first order logic with two variables. All DLs are subsets of F2.

[25] Often expressed in the actual source files by its converse, *refinedAlong* – see Fig 1.

gutter) or are simply 'near' them (*e.g.* perianal abscess). GALEN defines such structures using the special attributes *hasProximity* (*e.g.* perianus), *isParallelTo* (*e.g.* paramedian line), *isColinearWith* (transurethral route) and *passesThrough* (*e.g.* percutaneous route).

3. Regions named according to their clinical significance and whose boundaries cannot be inferred on the basis of purely anatomical relations: *e.g.* the "precordium" is the region of the chest specifically associated with observation and auscultation of the heart. GALEN represents such structures as primitives, though these may be further described using one or more of the partitive, spatial and proximity attributes.

4.1.3 Generic Bits and Pieces

Notions such as "capsule", "spine", or "edge" are widely used in anatomy to identify elements of anatomical structure – *e.g.* "capsule of kidney", "spine of 5th lumbar vertebra", "edge of liver" etc. In modelling such generic notions there are two choices:

1. To represent the generic notions as elementary and the real anatomic structures as defined compositions, *e.g.* "*Angle which isSubdivisionOf Mandible*", "*Pole which isDivisionOf Kidney*", etc.

2. To represent each occurrence of the substructure individually as elementary, *e.g. AngleOfMandble, PoleOfKidney,* etc.

In general, GALEN has chosen 1) because a) there seems to be sufficient commonality in notions such as "lobe" or "pole" that some are used for classification, *e.g.* "Lobulated organ" *e.g.* in the FMA, and b) the partitive relationship between such substructures (*e.g.* renal pole) and the anatomical entities of which they are part (e.g. kidney) appears to be defining in nature, rather than only incidentally true[26].

4.1.4 Tissues, Cells and Substances: *Mass*, *Discrete*, and *IndefinitelyDivisible*[27]

Most western languages make a distinction between a) "mass nouns" and "count nouns". Mass nouns such as "water" and "sand" are normally used in the singular; count nouns may be either singular or plural. Lenat and Guha make a corresponding semantic distinction between mass "stuff" and discrete "things" [31]. DOLCE makes the corresponding distinction between "Amount of matter" and "Physical object"; the realist stance of the BFO[28] [4] does not support this distinction.

In GALEN, structures and substances have a countability that is one of:

discrete	Bones, organs, membranes, etc.("countable")
mass	Substances and tissues
- *indefinitelyDivisible*	Cells, grains of sand, etc.
- *indefinitelyMultiple*	(present but not used in existing model)

---

[26] In terms of other philosophical constructs, the notion of "renal pole" can be considered as "analytic".

[27] Actually termed "infinitelyDivisible" etc. in the implemented version.

[28] http://ontology.buffalo.edu/bfo/BFO.htm

The *indefinitelyDivisible* category covers things like cells that are usually treated en masse, as in their count-concentration in a body fluid, but which can have discrete parts. A general mechanism for dealing with granularity has been developed from the GALEN experience, though the issue was never extensively explored in GALEN itself.

4.1.5 Topologies, Cavities, Spaces, Lines and Anatomical Landmarks

All solid structures in GALEN have a topology that may be *topologicalyHollow* or *topologicalySolid*. Being solid is simple; GALEN recognises the following kinds of being hollow:

surfaceHollow	Surface regions such as the "abdomen" which overlie a cavity and are often seen as having things in them
trulyHollow	Properly hollow structures,
- *actuallyHollow*	Not bilayered
- - *closedHollow*	No openings
- - *tubularHollow*	One or two openings. The cavity defined is a *Lumen*.
- *bilayered*	Membranes such as the pericardium and pleura, where the layers are normally in apposition such that the space between them is abolished for all clinical purposes (a potential space)

TrulyHollow body structures define a *Cavity*, which is related to the object that defines it by the attribute *definesSpace*, which is not partitive in the current implementation. The more general notion of a *Space* may be defined or only partly described using the attribute *boundsSpace* to refer one or more objects that are coterminus with any part of the boundary of the space e.g the dura mater and the subarachnoid membrane *boundsSpace* the subdural space.

Clinical anatomy also recognises a large number of points, lines and surfaces. These may be related to other anatomical structures (*e.g.* the pectineal line is the attachment of the pectineus muscle on the femur), while others such as the McBurney's point, the midclavicular line, inguinal triangle and parasagittal planes are treated as structures by fiat. Surgical procedures may reference routes of approach (*e.g.* transoesophageal and percutaneous) that are conceptually linear in nature, though not strictly one dimensional. Furthermore, other notions such as the quadrants of the abdomen have uncertain dimensionality: though they may be defined as planar sections of a planar structure (*e.g.* the anterior abdominal wall) they may also be spoken of as either containing or having as part those structures lying directly below them. Similarly, tubular body structures (however highly convoluted in space they may be) are often referred to as having linear properties – they can have segments.

Therefore, all *PhysicalStructures* are assigned (or inherit) a *Topology*[29] value: *linear*, *laminar* or *solid*. In addition, to deal with cases such as the intestine and quadrants of the abdomen they may be given an *AnalogousTopology*[30] value. The *Topology* governs constraints such as that only a *SolidStructure* may *contain* another

---

[29] Actually "*Shape*" in *Open*GALEN for historical reasons
[30] Actually "*AnalogousShapeValue*" in *Open*GALEN for historical reasons

PhysicalStructure, and that a *LinearStructure* can only have another *LinearStructure* or a *Point* as a subpart. The *AnalogousTopology* governs constraints such as whether a topologically hollow structure is elongated to be *Tubular* and can therefore have linear divisions.

GALEN recognises two further generic anatomical notions: *SurfaceVisibility* – whether a structure is internal or external – and *PairedOrUnpaired* – whether a structure comes in paired variants (left/right, medial/lateral etc.) and if so, whether they are mirror images of each other (*e.g.* hands) or not (*e.g.* cardiac ventricles).

Finally, whilst GALEN has avoided many of the difficulties inherent in representing non-normative anatomy such as arises through disease (see 2.2.7), even 'normative' human anatomy is inherently sexually dimorphic. GALEN's approach to sexual dimorphism is as follows: all primitive anatomical structures that are specific to one sex only (*e.g.* uterus, testis) are assigned a male or female phenotype value. Structures present in both sexes and with no sexual dimorphism have no phenotype value. Structures with dimorphic variant subforms (*e.g.* breast) carry no phenotype value, but their male- and female-specific variant subforms are instead defined (e.g. *Breast which hasPhenotype male*). Part-whole relations are asserted so that e.g. the sex unspecific *PelvicCavity* is asserted to contain the *Rectum*, but only the *FemalePelvicCavity* contains the *Uterus* (and also, by inheritance from its ancestor *PelvicCavity*, the *Rectum*).

4.1.6 Arbitrary Portions

Clinical descriptions of practical interactions with real anatomy (as opposed to descriptions purely of idealised canonical anatomy) often involve the notion of an arbitrary portion of a named anatomical structure. For example: removal of a *segment* of artery; excision of a *piece* of liver; tumour in the distal third of the humerus. The particular term chosen to denote the portion – *e.g.* segment, chunk or slice – may imply a particular topology of both the target structure and the referenced portion, as well as a particular partitive relationship holding between them.

Building on its strong typing of topology and partonomy as already described, GALEN represents arbitrary portions by means of a single primitive entity: *SolidRegion*. Individual arbitrary portions may then be described as a *SolidRegion* that has a particular partitive relationship with some structure. The topological properties of the portion itself may then be inferred from the topology of the structure of which it is part, and the nature of the partitive relation. Thus, a *Segment* can be defined as a *SolidRegion which isLinearDivisionOf LinearStructure* and must itself have *LinearAnalagousShape*.

4.1.7 Reciprocal Expressions

Unlike most representations of anatomy based on description logic, GALEN contains both statements of the form *B is_part_of A*, equivalent to "All Bs are part of some A" and *A has_part B*, equivalent to "All As have part some B". For example, both "*(All) Hand isDivisionOf (some) Arm*" and "*(All) Arm hasDivision (some)Hand*" can be represented. Such statements are terms "reciprocals". Neither separately implies the other even though *is_part_of* and *has_part* are mutual inverses. Modern "Tableaux reasoners" such as FaCT [27, 28] and Racer [22] are intrinsically exponentially explosive in the face of even small numbers of reciprocal statements. This does not occur in GALEN because the structural algorithms used by GALEN's GRAIL classifiers while incomplete, are efficient even for very highly connected ontologies containing many reciprocals.

This allows GALEN to be much more precise about normative anatomy than systems, such as SNOMED-CT, which confine themselves to "*isPartOf*". However, strictly speaking, it is not true to say that all arms have hands as parts, but only that normatively arms have hands as parts. However, the advantages of being able to express both sides of such relationships outweigh the disadvantages. For purposes of expressing clinical information, the normative interpretation is almost always appropriate, provided notions such as "missing" supplement it.

4.2 Processes and Functions

GALEN uses a relatively simple model of processes and functions. No distinction is made between mass and discrete processes or between processes and events. There are a few primary attributes linking the structure together

actsOn	Processes act on other phenomena: processes, structures, or substances.
hasConsequence	The primary causal attribute – see 4.3.2 below
– hasUniqueAssociatedProcess	Links processes to their outcomes. Used in process-outcome duals such as *UlcerProcess* and *UlcerLesion* – see 2.2.5 above
isFunctionOf	Links processes to their actor or the organs or organ system which carry them out
isSubprocessOf	The single primary partitive attribute for processes.
hasGoal	Links processes to their intention (either another process, or a state or a structure)

All of the above functions except *isSubprocessOf* are locative – *i.e.* all are subsumed by *involves* – so that any pathological process linked to an anatomical structure or process by any chain of these attributes will be considered localised to that structure.

Unusually, GALEN has no notion analogous to "agent" in other systems. Agency is a primary concern of most models of medical record and other information systems in which the GALEN Common Reference Model (CRM) is likely to be used. Therefore it is explicitly left to those systems and excluded from the CRM. There is, however, the notion of "intention" which is required to describe surgical procedures, and of a *VolitionalAct* – a process that has a voluntary intention. However, within the terminology resources, there is no need for a means to identify the actor who will, almost by definition, not be known to it.

Despite its relatively simple structure, this pattern has proved sufficient for extensive modelling both diseases and surgical procedures, including the development of the complete French national surgical procedure classification CCAM [57].

4.3 Diseases

4.3.1 What is a "disease"?

What is a "disease" or "disorder"? What does it mean to say that something is "normal", "abnormal", "pathological" or "physiological"? There are many philosophical definitions[31]. GALEN based its decisions on the pragmatic outcomes required: a sufficient logical approximation that would achieve classifications acceptable to our experts. Required consequences include being able to:

1. Distinguish normal from abnormal anatomy and to list normal anatomical parts, connections, etc. for any structure.
2. Identify entities whose presence was potentially noteworthy in a medical record - *i.e.* "abnormal"
3. Identify entities as in potential need of medical management – *i.e.* as "pathological"
4. Represent the notion of being "abnormal but not pathological" – defined pragmatically as "note-worthy but not in need of medical management"
5. Represent that the presence of some entities is always pathological, *e.g.* a malignant tumour or fracture.

GALEN provides two separate status distinctions intended to address these specific requirements: *normal* vs *nonNormal* and *pathological* vs *physiological* with associated status attributes *hasNormalityStatus* and *hasPathologicalStatus*. In addition it provides stronger versions of *nonNormal* and *pathological*, *intrinsicallyNonNormal* and *intrinsicallyPathological* for those cases in which a category's presence is always *nonNormal* or *pathological*. Using GRAIL's necessary statement mechanism, it is possible to express the following rules:

1. intrinsicallyPathological → pathological → nonNormal
2. intrinsicallyNonNormal → nonNormal

Note that *intrinsicallyNormal* does not imply *normal* nor does *instrinsicallyPhysiological* imply *physiological*. These categories are provided for symmetry and convenience only.

The closest logical approximation to "disease" or "disorder" in GALEN is *PathologicalPhenomenon*, defined as:

> Phenomenon <u>which</u> hasPathologicalStatus pathological.

Combining this notion with the general locative attribute *involves* allows broad disease categories to be defined, *e.g.* "cardiovascular disease" is represented as *CardiovascularPathology* defined as:

> Pathologica Phenomenon <u>which</u> involves CardiovascularSystem

The label *PathologicalPhenomenon* has been explicitly chosen to avoid implying too close a mapping to any natural language phrase such as "disease", "disorder", or

---

[31] Internal debate within GALEN revealed a surprising diversity of opinion regarding the meaning of both "normal" and "pathological"; the current solution is a pragmatic compromise intended to achieve specific functional goals. Others may prefer alternative labels.

"condition". It has so far proved impossible to reach any consensus on reliable distinctions between such terms.

4.3.2 Causation

Causation, or aetiology, is a critical notion to medical knowledge but surprisingly slippery. GALEN recognises at least two dimensions around causation:

1. Strength of association – from statistical association to physiological cause
2. Timing – temporal relationship between cause and effect (motivated by rheumatic aortitis as a consequence of streptococcal infection but occurring many years later)

Attributes indicating close causal connections are transitive – e.g. isImmediateConsequenceOf – whereas attributes indicating loose connections are not – e.g. isLateConsequenceOf or isAssociatedWith. This is a coarse grained logical approximation for the probabilistic attenuation of causal connection with the length of the causal chain.

Multiple causation gives rise to still more complex issues. Many conditions are defined by their cause, e.g. "viral pneumonia", "bacterial meningitis", etc. What is to be done about conditions in which there is more than one cause? Clinicians do not accept the logical inference that "mixed pneumonia" is a kind of "bacterial pneumonia" because they have different implications for management; for the same reason clinicians require the ability to distinguish between a "mixed pneumonia" and a "viral pneumonia complicated by bacterial infection".

GALEN addresses this issue by providing special single-valued child attributes of each causal attribute marked by the naming convention "Specific", e.g. isSpecificImmediateConsequenceOf. Using this convention, ViralPneumonia is defined as:

Pneumonia <u>which</u> *isSpecificImmediateConsequenceOf ViralInfection.*

Other dimensions that have been encount   ered but not modelled in detail include: a) which of multiple simultaneous effects is considered primary from a clinical point of view; and b) whether an effect is pathophysiologically a direct or indirect consequence of its cause.

5 Application Constructs: Medical Records and Coding Schemes

Two of GALEN's specific objectives are to encapsulate categories so that they can be incorporated into medical records and to provide means of mapping to existing coding and classification schemes. A prerequisite for achieving these objectives is deciding what it is that must be entered into a record, and what should be mapped to a coding scheme. The answers to both questions require additional constructs.

In many electronic medical records, all information must be in the coded expression [8, 10], e.g. a code from the Read Clinical Terms [39], SNOMED-CT [75] or earlier schemes such as ICD and its clinical variants [80].

These terminologies have characteristics that are not easy to represent directly in GRAIL or similar formalisms:

1. They include negative as well as positive terms, for example "apyrexia" or "absent pedal pulse". Many systems that include such terms have no other means of expressing negation.
2. They include complexes of several conditions – *e.g.* A with B without C

To cope with these characteristics, GALEN supports 'wrapping' one or more clinical entities in two outer modalities:

Existentiality	presence or absence
ClinicalSituation	A collection of several clinical entities to be recorded together as one "chunk" of clinical information

For example, the expression for "Stomach ulcer with penetration but without haemorrhage" would be:

ClinicalSituation which isCharacterisedBy <
(presence which isExistenceOf StomachUlcer)
(presence which isExistenceOf Stomach Penetration)
(absence which isExistenceOf Haemorrhage)>

For consistency, the wrapping with *ClinicalSituation* and *presence* must be used even when the notion to be represented is just the presence of a single entity, *e.g.*

ClinicalSituation which isCharacterisedBy (presence which isExistenceOf StomachUlcer)

Note that *presence/absence* are not a proper substitute for negation. In the above what is stated logically is the absence of *some Haemorrhage* rather than *any Haemorrhage*. The difference between the semantics of *presence/absence* and true negation must be taken into account when retrieving information from medical records.

However, *presence/absence* works well for mapping to ICD whose "broader than"/ "narrower than" notions work similarly. *ClinicalSituation* therefore provides the basis for mappings to traditonal coding and classification systems such as ICD9/10. The details are beyond the scope of this paper, but key considerations include:

1. The categories in the GALEN Common Reference Model (CRM) do not represent codes directly, rather they are mapped to codes using the indexing methods described in Section 2.3.2. Each ICD, or similar, code is mapped to the most specific corresponding GALEN entity or entities.
2. An ICD, or similar, code may be mapped to more than one GALEN category. Typically this occurs if there is an "includes" or disjunctive clause in the code rubric. In this case it is treated as the disjunction of the GALEN categories to which it is mapped.
3. "Excluding ..." clauses in ICD – *e.g.* "hypertension excluding pregnancy" – indicate that a more specific code exists elsewhere in ICD. The indexing method in 1) deals with this automatically. No exceptions to this rule have so far been reported.
4. Any code whose rubric includes "Not otherwise specified" ("NOS") is mapped to the parent entity with a suitable annotation in the mapping. Likewise for "Not elsewhere classified" ("NEC") and "Other"
5. All consideration of the rules for handling multiple codes (volume 2 of ICD) are left to external reasoners.

6 Discussion

6.1 Evaluation Against Criteria

In terms of the original criteria of expressiveness, classification and parsimony, GALEN has been sufficiently used in real projects of significant scale to be confident of its expressiveness with respect to either surgical procedures or the clinical information needed to describe the effects and uses of drugs. Surgical procedures were the primary focus of the GALEN-In-USE project, and the tools developed there were subsequently used for the development of the French national surgical classification CCAM [57] and The UK Drug Ontology project [72, 86, 87]. The original use case in clinical information systems has been tested within a limited commercial deployment of a clinical user interface, PEN&PAD/Clinergy [30, 38], based in UK Primary Care.

With respect to classification, cross comparisons have been undertaken with specific subsections of the Clinical Terms Version 3 [62] whilst the entire GALEN ontology has undergone extensive but *ad hoc* manual validation in the course of both GALEN-IN-USE and the Drug Ontology development. These comparisons and quality assurance mechanisms identified errors, but none that led to reconsideration of the basic structure of the ontology.

With respect to parsimony, assessment is more difficult. Constructing an ontology by parsimonious re-use of a deliberately limited set of building blocks inevitably results in increased representational complexity in the way the building blocks are assembled. The question most often raised about GALEN is nearly the converse of parsimony, *i.e.* "Isn't it over engineered?" Would a simpler starting point have been more effective? How much complexity is it worth accepting in return for parsimony? No definitive answer is available. GALEN's response has been to hide the complexity wherever possible.   It treats the underlying representation suitable for logical classification as described in this paper as a low level "assembly language" and provides higher level "Intermediate Representations" for authors and users [56, 61].

6.2 Issues with the GRAIL Formalism

Many of the specific details of the Common Reference Model (CRM) follow from limitations of the GRAIL formalism; others are possible because of GRAIL's non-standard features.

The most obvious easily remedied shortcoming is that cardinalities are assigned only to attributes and cannot be specialised when those attributes are used. This results in a proliferation of subattributes that obscure the basic structure. Similarly, disjunction and conjunction of primitives would have helped to clarify the structure and made the intention of notions such as "Phenomenon" clearer. The absence of true negation has not proved a serious problem; its inclusion would bring a major increase in complexity.

That the structural algorithms in the GRAIL classifier are sound but incomplete is well known but has caused little difficulty. The main area of incompleteness can be dealt with relatively easily. Most concern variants on expressions of the form *C1 which attr1 (C2 which invAttr1 C1)* – *e.g.* "a fracture in a limb which is the site of trauma". Such expressions – with cycles of whatever length – have been pragmatically banned from the Common Reference Model. Although legal in modern tableaux algorithm based reasoners, they often cause exponential explosions in classification time.

As described in 2.3.5 and detailed in 3.2.4, GALEN's constructs for inheritance across transitive attributes were originally designed for dealing with part-whole relations, but they have since proved valuable in other contexts. The range of possibilities for achieving the same functionality is much greater today than when GALEN was devised. SEP triples [25, 67] might replace GALEN's constructs in part-whole relations, whilst many of their other functions might also be replaced by constructs in more expressive languages such as OWL.   Experimental reasoners supporting "role inclusion axioms" – of which GALEN's *specialisedBy* construct is a subset – have been implemented although they are not yet widely available [29]. An evaluation of the alternatives against defined criteria – both human factors and computational tractability – would be a valuable piece of research. For a preliminary investigation see [42].

Almost uniquely amongst DL based ontologies, GALEN uses both "is part of" and its inverse "has part" (and their subattributes).   Both the NCI thesaurus and SNOMED-CT support only "is part of", which is the form required to answer questions such as "What diseases affect the liver or anything that is part of the liver?" Including both "is part of" and "has part" makes classification computationally intractable using now standard tableaux based inference engines, *e.g.* FaCT or Racer. Both "is part of" and "has part" are present in the FMA, but it does not, currently, use DL reasoners. A solution to this limitation in description logic reasoners is urgently required before large biomedical ontologies can be satisfactorily managed using description logics based languages including OWL.[32]

GRAIL is unusual in supporting general inclusion axioms (see Section 2.3.3), but they have proved essential for the ontology.   Serendipitously, a side effect of GRAIL's restrictions and GALEN's method of orthogonal taxonomies is that all such axioms are "absorbable" so that they do not have a global impact on the performance of tableaux reasoners [28].

Finally, GRAIL's notation makes it natural to form 'normalised' ontologies with orthogonal taxonomies [44], although the language does not quite force this choice.

6.2.1 Comparison with Other Ontologies

In order to get meaningful comparisons between ontologies, it is first necessary to overcome superficial differences in naming conventions and organisations. For upper ontologies and their modelled extensions this requires careful examination. The most obvious high level comparisons are to DOLCE [17] and BFO [69, 70]. A detailed comparison is beyond the scope of the paper, but some general points follow. GALEN's *Thing* maps very closely to DOLCE's "sortals"; GALEN's disjunction of *GeneralisedStructure* and *GeneralisedSubstance* maps to "Continuant" (BFO) or "Endurant" (DOLCE); *GeneralisedProcess* maps to "Occurrent" (BFO) and "Perdurant" (DOLCE). The major items map smoothly, but there are differences in

---

[32] The computational issues are independent of philosophical discussions about the comparative status of the two statements, *e.g.* that "normal hands" have five fingers.

the placement of *Collection* and *Feature* that both other ontologies treat as "Continuants". GALEN is intended for use within medical record systems where temporal relations and reasoning are handled external to the ontology; therefore it has only weak notions of time. By contrast, temporal constructs are central to the BFO.

GALEN's *Features* are a reasonable match to DOLCE's "Qualities" and GALEN's *States* to DOLCE's "quale", but neither DOLCE nor BFO have made the distinction between "selectors" and "features" as made in GALEN.

The major difference between the DOLCE and BFO is that DOLCE takes a "cognitivist" view whereas the BFO takes a "realist" view. GALEN's representation is broadly cognitivist. DOLCE makes a distinction between "physical object" and "amount of matter" analogous to GALEN's distinction between *GeneralisedStructure* and *GeneralisedSubstance*. Correspondingly, DOLCE has a role "constitutes" representing the relation between substances and the things made of those substances. GALEN has an equivalent attribute *makesUp/isMadeOf*. "Realists" reject the "constitutes" relation, maintaining that the "physical object" is identical to the "amount of matter" rather than being made of it.

The other obvious comparison is with the anatomy modelling in the Digital Anatomist Foundational Model of Anatomy (FMA) [34, 37, 63]. The FMA, like GALEN, is a domain ontology but confined purely to structural relations. Two groups have independently attempted to reconcile the two ontologies [35, 36, 88-90]. Both met with only limited success, the greatest problem being systematic differences including a) naming conventions; b) the choice of whether or not to reify relations; and c) that GALEN does not enumerate all sanctioned variants, *e.g.* it does not pre-enumerate all possible left and right handed variants of anatomical structures, instead it allows them to be created and classified (post-coordinated) dynamically. A more collaborative attempt at reconciliation dealing with these three issues remains to be performed.

6.3 Outstanding Issues

There are a series of issues that remain outstanding:

- Normative statements, congenital disease, and imputed intentions (See 2.2.7)
- Spatial temporal reasoning and numerical calculations (See 2.3.6)
- Improved handling of the pattern exemplified in "the skin of the hand is a division of the skin of the upper extremity". (See 4.1.1)
- Testing of the consequences of use of SEP triples rather than GALEN's *specialisedBy* axioms (See 6.2)
- How best to take advantage of improvements in description logic and ontology technology now becoming available (See 6.2)

6.4 Summary

GALEN has pioneered the construction of large-scale biomedical ontologies based on description logic. Its experiences illustrate both the advantages and disadvantages of the approach in principle and the limitations of the current state of the art. It provides a set of modelling conventions and patterns that have proved sufficiently robust to be used in practical developments – surgical terminologies, drug information, and data entry systems – which it hopes will continue to provide a useful resource both to developers of biomedical ontologies and as a test corpus for those developing description logic reasoners.

GALEN's pursuit of its combined goals of expressivity, logical classification, and parsimony have led to a complex ontology. However, this complexity can be mitigated for users by intermediate representations and tools. Given adequate support, it has proved accessible and usable. Whether a simpler approach would suffice for future applications, or whether a still more complex approach will be required, remains to be seen.

Acknowledgements

This work supported in part by the European Healthcare Telematics programme in the GALEN, GALEN-IN-USE and SemanticMining projects, by the UK Department of Health Drug Ontology subproject of the Prodigy Project, and by the EPSRC funded HyOntUse project (GR/S44686/01) and the UK JISC funded CO-ODE project, www.co-ode.org. The partners in the GALEN and GALEN-IN-USE projects have contributed extensively. Particular mention is due to Anthony Nowlan who first formulated key parts of what has become the GALEN ontology.

References

1. Artale, A., E. Franconi, and N. Guarino. *Open problems for part-whole relations.* in *International Workshop on Descripition Logics.* 1996. Boston, MA.
2. Artale, A., E. Franconi, and L. Pazzi, *Part-whole relations in object-centered systems: An overview.* Data and Knowledge Engineering, 1996. **20**: p. 347-383.
3. Bateman, J.A., *Upper modelling: a general organization of knowledge for natural language processing.* 1989, USC/Information Sciences Institute.
4. Bittner, T., M. Donnelly, and B. Smith. *Individuals, Universals, collections: On the foundational relations of ontology.* in *International Conference on Formal Ontology and Information Systems (FOIS 2004).* 2004. Turin, Italy.
5. Borgida, A., *Description logics in data management.* IEEE Transactions on Knowledge and Data Engineering, 1995. **7**(5): p. 671-682.
6. Brachman, R. and H. Levesque. *The tractability of subsumption in frame-based description languages.* in *AAAI-84.* 1984: Morgan Kaufman.
7. Brachman, R.J., et al., *Living with Classic: When and how to use a KL-ONE-like language,* in *Principles of Semantic Networks: Explorations in the representation of knowledge,* J. Sowa, Editor. 1991, Morgan Kaufmann: San Mateo, CA. p. 401-456.
8. Brown, P., M. O'Neil, and C. Price, *Semantic definition of disorders in Version 3 of the Read Codes.* Methods of Information in Medicine, 1998. **37**: p. 415-419.
9. Casati, R. and A.C. Varzi, *Parts and Places.* Parts and Places: The Structurres of Spatial Representation. 1999, Oxford: Clarendon Press.
10. Chute, C., *Clinical classification and terminology: Some history and current observations.* Journal of the American Medical Informatics Association, 2000. **7**(3): p. 293-303.
11. Cimino, J., *Controlled Medical Vocabulary Construction: Methods from the Canon Group.* Journal of the American Medical Informatics Association, 1994. **1**(3): p. 296-197.
12. Cimino, J., *Desiderata for controlled medical vocabularies in the twenty-first century.* Methods of Information in Medicine, 1998. **37**(4-5): p. 394-403.

13. Degen, W., et al. *Formal Ontology in Information Systems (FOIS 2001).* 2001.

14. Doyle, J. and R. Patil, *Two theses of knowledge representation: Language restrictions, taxonomic classification and the utility of representation services.* Artificial Intelligence, 1991. **48**: p. 261-297.

15. Etherington, D., *Formalising nonmonotonic reasoning systems.* Artificial Intelligence, 1987. **31**: p. 41-85.

16. Evans, D.A., et al., *Position statement: Towards a medical concept representation language.* Journal of the American Medical Informatics Association, 1994. **1**(3): p. 207-217.

17. Gangemi, A., et al. *Sweetening ontologies with DOLCE.* in *European Knowledge Aquisition Workshop (EKAW-2002).* 2002. Siguenza, Spain: Spring Verlag.

18. Gruber, T.R., *Toward Principles for the Design of Ontologies Used for Knowledge Sharing.* 1993, Knowledge Systems Laboratory, Stanford University.

19. Guarino, N. and C. Welty, *An overview of OntoClean,* in *Handbook of Ontologies,* S. Staab and R. Studer, Editors. 2004, Springer Verlag. p. 151-159.

20. Guarino, N. and C. Welty. *Towards a methodology for ontology-based model engineering.* in *ECOOP-2000 Workshop on Model Engineering.* 2000. Cannes, France.

21. Guha, R. and D. Lenat, *Enabling agents to work together.* Communications of the ACM, 1994. **37**: p. 127-142.

22. Haarslev, V. and R. Moeller. *Expresive ABox reasoning with number restrictions, role hierarchies, and transitively closed roes.* in *Proceedings of the Seventh International Conference on Knowledge Representation and Reasoning (KR2000).* 2000. San Francisco, CA: Morgan Kaufmann.

23. Hahn, U., M. Romacker, and S. Schulz, *How knowledge drives understanding - matching medical ontologies with the needs of medical language processing.* Artificial Intelligence in Medicine, 1999. **15**(1): p. 25-52.

24. Hahn, U., S. Schulz, and M. Romacker, *Part-whole reasoning: a case study in medical ontology engineering.* IEEE Intelligent Systems and their Applications, 1999. **14**(5): p. 59-67.

25. Hahn, U., S. Schulz, and M. Romacker. *Partonomic reasoning as taxonomic reasoning in medicine.* in *Proc. of the 16th National Conf. on Artificial Intelligence & 11th Innovative Applications of Artificial Intelligence (AAAI-99/IAAI-99).* 1999. Orlando FL: AAAI Press/MIT Press.

26. Hardiker, N.R. and A.L. Rector, *Modeling nursing terminology using the GRAIL representation language.* Journal of the American Medical Informatics Association, 1998. **5**: p. 120-128.

27. Horrocks, I., *Optimising Tableaux Decision Procedures for Description Logics,* in *Computer Science.* 1997, University of Manchester: Manchester. p. 176.

28. Horrocks, I. *Using an expressive description logic: FaCT or Fiction.* in *Principles of Knowledge Representation and Reasoning: Proceedings of the Sixth International Conference on Knowledge Representation (KR 98).* 1998. San Francisco, CA: Morgan Kaufmann.

29. Horrocks, I. and U. Sattler., *The decidability of SHIQ with complex role inclusion axioms.* Artificial Intelligence, 2004. **160**(102): p. 79-104.

30. Kirby, J. and A.L. Rector. *The PEN&PAD Data Entry System: From prototype to practical system.* in *AMIA Fall Symposium.* 1996. Washington DC: Hanley and Belfus, Inc.

31. Lenat, D.B. and R.V. Guha, *Building Large Knowledge-Based Systems: Representation and inference in the Cyc Project.* 1989, Reading, MA: Addison-Wesley. 372.

32. Martin, R.F., et al. *Foundational Model of Neuroanatomy:Implications for the Human Brain Project.* in *AMIA Fall Symposium.* 2001. Washington DC.

33. Masolo, C., et al., *WonderWeb Deliveable 18.* 2003, WonderWeb consortium.

34. Mejino, J.L.V. and C. Rosse, *Conceptualization of anatomical spatial entities in the Digital Anatomist Foundational Model.* Journal of the American Medical Informatics Association, 1999(1999 Annual Symposium Special Issue): p. 112-116.

35. Mork, P. and P. Bernstein. *Adapting a generic match algorithm to align ontologies of human anatomy.* in *20th International Conference on Data Engineering.* 2004. Boston: IEEE.

36. Mork, P., R. Pottinger, and P. Bernstein. *Challenges in precisely aligning models of human anatomy.* in *Proceedings of Medinfo 2004.* 2004. San Francisco, CA: IMIA.

37. Neal, P.J., L.G. Shapiro, and C. Rosse, *The Digital Anatomist structural abstraction: a scheme for the spatial description lf anatomical entities.* Journal of the American Medical Informatics Association, 1998((Fall Symposium Special Issue)): p. 423-427.

38. Nowlan, W.A., *Clinical workstation: Identifying clinical requirements and understanding clinical information.* International Journal of Bio-Medical Computing, 1994. **34**: p. 85-94.

39. O'Neil, M., C. Payne, and J. Read, *Read Codes Version 3: A user led terminology.* Methods of Information in Medicine, 1995. **34**: p. 187-192.

40. Odell, J.J., *Six different kinds of composition.* Journal of Object Oriented Programming, 1994. **5**(8): p. 10-15.

41. Padgham, L. and P. Lambrix. *A framework for part-of hierarchies in terminological logics.* in *KR-94.* 1994.

42. Rector, A. *Analysis of propagation along transitive roles: Formalisation of the GALEN experience with medical ontologies.* in *2002 International Workshop on Description Logics (DL2002).* 2002. Toulouse France: CEUR-Proceedings 53.

43. Rector, A. *Coordinating taxonomies: Key to re-usable concept representations.* in *Fifth conference on Artificial Intelligence in Medicine Europe (AIME '95).* 1995. Pavia, Italy: Springer.

44. Rector, A. *Modularisation of domain ontologies Implemented in description logics and related formalisms including OWL.* in *Knowledge Capture 2003.* 2003. Sanibel Island, FL: ACM.

45. Rector, A., *Thesauri and formal classifications: Terminologies for people and machines.* Methods of Information in Medicine, 1998. **37**(4-5): p. 501-509.

46. Rector, A., et al., *The GRAIL concept modelling language for medical terminology.* Artificial Intelligence in Medicine, 1997. **9**: p. 139-171.

47. Rector, A., et al. *Scale and Context: Issues in ontologies to link health- and bio-Informatics.* in *AMIA Fall Symposium.* 2002. Austin Texas: Hanley and Belfus, Philadelphia.

48. Rector, A., et al. *Making sound re-usable terminology practical: The GALEN approach.* in *Towards and Electronic Health Care Record, Europe.* 1998. London: Medical Records Institute, Newton Mass.

49. Rector, A., et al., *A Terminology Server for Medical Language and Medical Information Systems.* Methods of Information in Medicine, 1995. **34**: p. 147-157.

50. Rector, A., A. Taweel, and J. Rogers. *Models and inference methods for clinical systems: A principled approach.* in *Medinfo.* 2004. San Francisco: North Holland.

51. Rector, A., et al., *GALEN: Terminology Services for Clinical Information Systems,* in *Health in the New Communications Age,* M. Laires, M. Ladeira, and J. Christensen, Editors. 1995, IOS Press: Amsterdam. p. 90-100.

52. Rector, A.L., *Clinical Terminology: Why is it so hard?* Methods of Information in Medicine, 1999. **38**: p. 239-252.

53. Rector, A.L. *Defaults, context and knowledge: Alternatives for OWL-Indexed Knowledge bases.* in *Pacific Symposium on Biocomputing (PSB-2004).* 2004. Kona, Hawaii: World Scientific.

54. Rector, A.L. *The Interface between Information, Terminology, and Inference Models.* in *Tenth World Conference on Medical and Health Informatics: Medinfo-2001.* 2001. London, England.

55. Rector, A.L., et al. *Interface of inference models with concept and medical record models.* in *Artificial Intelligence in Medicine Europe (AIME).* 2001. Cascais, Portugal: Springer Verlag.

56. Rector, A.L., et al., *Reconciling users' needs and formal requirements: Issues in developing a re-usable ontology for medicine.* IEEE Transactions on Information Technology in BioMedicine, 1999. **2**(4): p. 229-242.

57. Rodrigues, J.M., et al. *Galen-In-Use: An EU Project applied to the development of a new national coding system for surgical procedures: NCAM.* in *Medical Informatics Europe '97.* 1997. Porto Carras, Greece: IOS Press.

58. Rogers, J. and A. Rector. *The GALEN ontology.* in *Medical Informatics Europe (MIE 96).* 1996. Copenhagen: IOS Press.

59. Rogers, J. and A. Rector, *GALEN's model of parts and wholes: Experience and comparisons.* Journal of the American Medical Informatics Association, 2000((Fall symposium special issue)): p. 819-823.

60. Rogers, J., et al. *From rubrics to dissections to GRAIL to classifications.* in *Medical Informatics Europe (MIE-97).* 1997. Thesalonika, Greece: IOS Press.

61. Rogers, J.E., *Development of a methodology and an ontological schema for medical terminology,* in *School of Medicine, Dentistry, Nursing and Pharmacy.* 2004, University of Manchester. p. 185.

62. Rogers, J.E., et al., *Validating clinical terminology structures: Integration and cross-validation of Read Thesaurus and GALEN.* Journal of the American Medical Informatics Association, 1998(Fall Symposium Special Issue): p. 845-849.

63. Rosse, C., I.G. Shapiro, and J.F. Brinkley, *The Digital Anatomist foundational model: Principles for defining and structuring its concept domain.* Journal of the American Medical Informatics Association, 1998(1998 Fall Symposium Special issue): p. 820-824.

64. Schank, R.C. and R. Abelson, P, *Scripts, Plans, Goals, and Understanding.* 1977, Hilsdale, NJ: Lawrence Erlbaum Associates.

65. Schulz, S. and U. Hahn. *Mereotopological reasoning about parts and (w)holes in bio-ontologies.* in *Formal Ontology in Information Systems (FOIS-2001).* 2001. Ogunquit, ME: ACM.

66. Schulz, S. and U. Hahn. *Parts, locations, and holes - Formal reasoning about anatomical structures.* in *Artificial Intelligence in Medicine Europe (AIME-2001).* 2001. Cascais, Portubal: Springer.

67. Schulz, S., U. Hahn, and M. Romacker. *Modeling anatomical spatial relations with description logics.* in *AMIA Fall Symposium (AMIA-2000).* 2000. Los Angeles, CA: Hanly & Belfus.

68. Shahar, Y., et al. *A problem-solving architecture for managing temporal data and their abstractions.* in *Workshop on Implementing Temporal Reasoning, AAAI-92.* 1992. San Jose, CA.

69. Smith, B. *The basic tools of formal ontology.* in *Formal Ontology in Information Systems (FOIS).* 1998. Amsterdam: IOS Press (Frontiers in Artificial Intelligence and Applications).

70. Smith, B. *The logic of biological classification and the foundations of biomedical ontology*. in *10th International Conference in Logic Methodology and Philosophy of Science*. 2004. Oviedo Spain: Elsevier-North-Holland.

71. Solomon, W. and H. Heathfield. *Conceptual modelling used to represent drug interactions*. in *Twelfth International Congress of the European Federation for Medical Informatics, MIE-94*. 1994. Lisbon, Portugal.

72. Solomon, W., et al., *A reference terminology for drugs*. Journal of the American Medical Informatics Association, 1999((Fall Symposium Special Issue)): p. 152-155.

73. Sowa, J., *Knowledge Representation*. 1999: Morgan Kaufmann.

74. Staab, S. and A. Maedche. *Ontology engineering beyond the modeling of concepts and relations*. in *ECAI 2000. 14th European Conference on Artificial Intelligence; Workshop on Applications of Ontologies and Problem-Solving Methods*. 2000.

75. Stearns, M., et al. *SNOMED clinical terms: overview of the development process and project status*. in *AMIA Fall Symposium (AMIA-2001)*. 2001: Henley & Belfus.

76. The Gene Ontology Consortium, *Creating the gene ontology resource: design and implementation*. Genome Research, 2001. **11**: p. 1425-1433.

77. The Gene Ontology Consortium, *Gene Ontology: tool for the unification of biology*. Nature Genetics, 2000. **25**: p. 25-29.

78. Touretzky, D., *The Mathematics of Inheritance Systems*. 1986, Los Altos, CA: Morgan Kaufmann.

79. Tuttle, M.S., *The position of the canon group: A reality check*. Journal of the American Medical Informatics Association, 1994. **1**(3): p. 298-299.

80. United States Center for Health Statistics, *International Classification of Diseases, Ninth Revision with Clinical Modifications*. 1980, Washington, DC: The Center.

81. Uschold, M. and M. Gruninger, *Ontologies: principles, methods and applications*. Knowledge Engineering Review, 1996. **11**(2).

82. Varzi, A.C., *Mereological commitments*. Dialectica, 2000. **54**: p. 283-305.

83. Welty, C. and N. Guarino, *Supporting ontological analysis of taxonomic relationships*. Data and Knowledge Engineering, 2001. **39**(1): p. 51-74.

84. Winston, M., R. Chaffin, and D. Hermann, *A taxonomy of part-whole relations*. Cognitive Science, 1987. **11**: p. 417-444.

85. Woods, W., *What's important about knowledge representation?* IEEE Computer, 1983. **16**: p. 22-29.

86. Wroe, C. and J. Cimino. *Using openGALEN techniques to develop the HL7 drug formulation vocabulary*. in *American Medical Informatics Association Fall Symposium(AMIA-2001)*. 2001.

87. Wroe, C., et al., *Inheritance of drug information*. Journal of the American Medical Informatics Association, 2000(Annual Symposium Special Issue): p. 1158.

88. Zhang, S. and O. Bodenreider. *Comparing associative concepts among equivalent concepts across ontologies*. in *Medinfo-2004*. 2004. San Francisco, CA: IMIA, IOS Press.

89. Zhang, S. and O. Bodenreider. *Investigating implicit knowledge in ontologies with application to the anatomical domain*. in *Pacific Symposium on Bioinformatics*. 2004: Bioinformatics.

90. Zhang, S., P. Mork, and O. bodenreider. *Lessons learnned from aligning two represen- tations of Anatomy*. in *First international workshop on formal biomedical knowledge representation*. 2004. Whistler, Canada.

91. Zweigenbaum, P., et al., *Issues in the structuring and acquisition of an ontology for medical language understanding*. Methods of Information in Medicine, 1995. **34**(1/2): p. 15-24.

The Semantic Web from an Industry Perspective

Alain Léger[1], Johannes Heinecke[1], Lyndon J.B. Nixon[2],
Pavel Shvaiko[3], Jean Charlet[4], Paola Hobson[5],
and François Goasdoué[6]

[1] France Telecom R&D - Rennes, 4 rue du clos courtel,
35512 Cesson-Sévigné, France
{alain.leger, johannes.heinecke} @rd.francetelecom.com
[2] Freie Universität Berlin, Takustrasse 9,
14195 Berlin, Germany
nixon@inf.fu-berlin.de
[3] University of Trento, Via Sommarive 14,
38050 Trento, Italy
pavel@dit.unitn.it
[4] STIM, DPA/AP-Hopitaux Paris & Université Paris 6,
75006 Paris, France
charlet@biomath.jussieu.fr
[5] Motorola Labs, Centre for Applications, Content and Services, Hants, UK
Paola.hobson@motorola.com
[6] LRI, CNRS et Université Paris Sud XI, Bâtiment 490,
91405 Orsay Cedex, France
fg@lti.fr

Abstract. Semantic Web technology is being increasingly applied in a large spectrum of applications in which domain knowledge is conceptualized and formalized (e.g., by means of an ontology) in order to support diversified and automated knowledge processing (e.g., reasoning) performed by a machine. Moreover, through an optimal combination of (cognitive) human reasoning and (automated) machine reasoning and processing, it is possible for humans and machines to share complementary tasks. The spectrum of applications is extremely large and to name a few: corporate portals and knowledge management, e-commerce, e-work, e-business, healthcare, e-government, natural language understanding and automated translation, information search, data and services integration, social networks and collaborative filtering, knowledge mining, business intelligence and so on. From a social and economic perspective, this emerging technology should contribute to growth in economic wealth, but it must also show clear cut value for everyday activities through technological transparency and efficiency. The penetration of Semantic Web technology in industry and in services is progressing slowly but accelerating as new success stories are reported. In this paper and lecture we present ongoing work in the cross-fertilization between industry and academia. In particular, we present a collection of application fields and use cases from enterprises which are interested in the promises of Semantic Web technology. The use cases are detailed and focused on the key knowledge processing components that will unlock the deployment of the technology in the selected application field. The paper ends with the presentation of the current technology roadmap designed by a team of Academic and Industry researchers.

P. Barahona et al. (Eds.): Reasoning Web 2006, LNCS 4126, pp. 232–268, 2006.

1 Industry Perspective

1.1 Introduction

As a result of the pervasive and user-friendly digital technologies emerging within our information society, Web content availability is increasing at an incredible rate but at the cost of being extremely multiform, inconsistent and very dynamic. Such content is totally unsuitable for machine processing, and so necessitates too much human interpretation and its respective costs in time and effort for both individuals and companies. To remedy this, approaches aim at abstracting from this complexity (i.e., by using ontologies) and offering new and enriched services able to process those abstractions (i.e., by mechanized reasoning) in a fully automated way. This abstraction layer is the subject of a very dynamic activity in research, industry and standardization which is usually called "Semantic Web" (see, for example, DARPA, European IST Research Framework Program, W3C initiative). The initial application of Semantic Web technology has focused on Information Retrieval (IR) where access through semantically annotated content, instead of classical (even sophisticated) statistical analysis, aimed to give far better results (in terms of precision and recall indicators). The next natural extension was to apply IR in the integration of enterprise legacy databases in order to leverage existing company information in new ways. Present research has turned to focusing on the seamless integration of heterogeneous and distributed applications and services (both intra- and inter-enterprise) through Semantic Web Services, with the expectation of a fast return on investment (ROI) and improved efficiency in e-work and e-business.

This new technology takes its roots in the cognitive sciences, machine learning, natural language processing, multi-agents systems, knowledge acquisition, automated reasoning, logics and decision theory. It can be separated into two distinct – but cooperating fields - one adopting a formal and algorithmic approach for common sense automated reasoning (automated Web), and the other one "keeping the human being in the loop" for a socio-cognitive semantic web (automated social Web) which is gaining momentum today with the Web 2.0 paradigm[1].

On a large scale, industry awareness of Semantic Web technology has started only recently, e.g., at the EC level with the IST-FP5 thematic network Ontoweb[2] [2001-2004] which brought together around 50 motivated companies worldwide. Based on this experience, within IST-FP6, the Network of Excellence Knowledge Web[3] [2004-2008] is making an in-depth analysis of the concrete industry needs in key economic sectors, and in a complementary way the IST-FP6 Network of Excellence Rewerse[4] is tasked with providing Europe with leadership in reasoning languages, also in view of a successful technology transfer and awareness activities targeted at the European industry for advanced Web systems and applications.

The rest of the paper is organized as follows. Four prototypical application fields are presented in Section 2, namely (i) healthcare and biotechnologies, (ii) knowledge

---

[1] http://www.web2con.com
[2] http://www.ontoweb.org
[3] http://knowledgeweb.semanticweb.org
[4] http://rewerse.net

management (KM), (iii) e-commerce and e-business, and finally (iv) multimedia and audiovisual services. Then key knowledge processing tasks and components are presented in detail in Section 3. Finally, Section 4 reports on a current vision of the achievements and some perspectives are given.

1.2 Overall Business Needs and Key Knowledge Processing Requirements

1.2.1 Use Case Collection and Analysis

In order to support a large spectrum of application fields, the EU FP6 Networks of Excellence Knowledge Web and Rewerse are tasked with promoting transfer of best-of-the-art knowledge-based technology from academia to industry. The networks are made up of leading European Semantic Web research institutions and co-ordinate their research efforts while parallel efforts are made in Semantic Web education and transfer to Industry.

In the Industry Area activities of Knowledge Web, we have formed a group of companies interested in Semantic Web technology. By the end of 2005, this group consisted of about 45 members (e.g., France Telecom, British Telecom, Institut Français du Pétrole, Illy Caffe, Trenitalia, Daimler Chrysler, Thalès, EADS, ...) from across 14 nations and 13 economic sectors (e.g., telecoms, energy, food, logistics, automotive).

The companies were requested to provide illustrative examples of actual or hypothetical deployment of Semantic Web technology in their business settings. This was followed up with face-to-face meetings between researchers and industry experts from the companies to gain additional information about the provided use cases. Thus, in 2004, we collected a total of 16 use cases from 12 companies as shown in Figure 1.

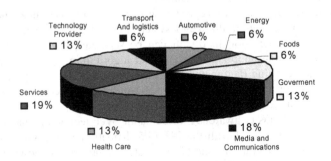

Fig. 1. Breakdown of use cases by industry sector

In particular, it represents (the most active) 9 sectors, with the highest number of the use cases coming from the service industry (19%) and media & communications (18%) respectively. This initial collection of use cases can be found in [11], while a constantly growing and updated selection are available on the Knowledge Web Industry portal[5].

1.2.2 Analysis of Use Cases by Expert Estimations

A preliminary analysis of the use cases has been carried out in order to obtain a first vision of the current industrial needs and to estimate the expectations from

---

[5] http://knowledgeweb.semanticweb.org/o2i/

knowledge-based technology with respect to those needs. The industry experts were asked to indicate the existing legacy solutions in their use cases, the service functionalities they would be offered and the technological locks they encountered, and eventually how they expected that Semantic Web technology could resolve those locks. As a result, we have gained an overview of:

- Types of business or service problems where the knowledge-based technology is considered to bring a plausible solution;
- Types of technological issues (and the corresponding research challenges) which knowledge based technology is expected to overcome.

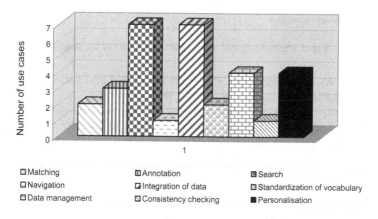

Fig. 2. Preliminary vision for solutions sought in use cases

Figure 2 shows a breakdown of the areas in which the industry experts thought Semantic Web technology could provide a solution. For example, for nearly half of the collected use cases, data integration and semantic search were areas where industry was looking for knowledge-based solutions. Other areas mentioned, in a quarter of use cases, were solutions to data management and personalization.

Figure 3 shows a breakdown of the technology locks identified in the use cases. There are three technology locks which occur the most often in the collected use cases. These are: ontology development, i.e., modeling of a business domain, authoring, reusing existing ontologies; knowledge extraction, i.e., populating ontologies by extracting data from legacy systems; and ontology matching, i.e., resolving semantic heterogeneity among multiple ontologies.

Below, we illustrate, with the help of a use case from our collection, how a concrete business problem can be used to indicate the technology locks for which knowledge-based solutions potentially might be useful. This use case addresses the problem of an intelligent search of documents in the corporate data of a coffee company.

The company generates a large amount of internal data and its employees encounter difficulties in finding the data they need for the research and development of new solutions. The aim is to improve the quality of the document retrieval and to enable personalization services for individual users when searching or viewing the

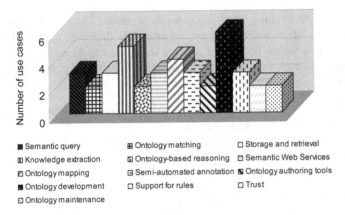

Fig. 3. Preliminary vision of technology locks in use cases

corporate data. As technology locks, the expert mentioned here the corporate domain *ontology development* and *maintenance*, and *semantic querying*.

Eventually, this analysis (by experts estimations) provides us with a preliminary understanding of scope of the current industrial needs and concrete technology locks where knowledge-based technology is expected to provide a plausible solution. However, to be able to answer specific industrial requirements, we need to conduct further a detailed technical analysis of the use cases, thereby associating to each technology lock a concrete knowledge processing task and a component realizing its functionalities.

1.2.3 Knowledge Processing Tasks and Components
Based on the knowledge processing needs identified during the technical use cases analysis [12], we built a typology of knowledge processing tasks and a library of high level components for realizing those tasks, see Table 1. Our first tentative typology includes 12 knowledge processing tasks. Let us discuss knowledge processing tasks and components of Table 1 in more detail.

Table 1. Typology of knowledge processing tasks & components

N°	Knowledge processing tasks	Components
1	Ontology Management	Ontology Manager
2	Ontology Matching	Match Manager
3	Ontology Matching results Analysis	Match Manager
4	Data Translation	Wrapper
5	Results Reconciliation	Results Reconciler
6	Composition of Web Services	Planner
7	Content Annotation	Annotation manager
8	Reasoning	Reasoner
9	Semantic Query Processing	Query Processor
10	Ontology Merging	Ontology Manager
11	Producing explanations	Match Manager
12	Personalization	Profiler

<u>Ontology Management, Ontology Merging and Ontology Manager</u>. These tasks and component are in charge of ontology maintenance (e.g., reorganizing taxonomies, resolving name conflicts, browsing ontologies, editing concepts) and merging multiple ontologies (e.g., by taking the union of the axioms) with respect to evolving business case requirements, see [13, 14, 15].

<u>Matching, Matching Results Analysis, Producing Explanations and Match Manager</u>. These tasks and component are in charge of (on-the-fly and semi-automatic) determining semantic mappings between the entities of multiple schemas, classifications, and ontologies, see [16, 17]. Mappings are typically specified with the help of a similarity relation which can be either in the form of a coefficient rating match quality in the (0,1] range (i.e., the higher the coefficient, the higher the similarity between the entities, see [18,19,20,21,22]) or in the form of a logical relation (e.g., equivalence, subsumption), see [23, 24]. The mappings might need to be ordered according to some criteria, see [25, 21].

Finally, explanations of the mappings might be also required, see [26, 27]. Matching systems may produce mappings that may not be intuitively obvious to human users. In order for users to trust the mappings (and thus use them), they need information about them. They need access to the sources that were used to determine semantic correspondences between terms and potentially they need to understand how deductions and manipulations are performed. The issue here is to present explanations in a simple and clear way to the user.

<u>Data Translation and Wrapper</u>. This task and component is in charge of automatic manipulation (e.g., translation, exchange) of instances between heterogeneous information sources storing their data in different formats (e.g., RDF, SQL DDL, XML ...), see [28, 29]. Here, mappings are taken as input (for example, from the match manager component) and are analyzed in order to generate query expressions that perform the required manipulations with data instances.

Results Reconciliation and Results Reconciler. This task and component is in charge of determining an optimal solution, in terms of contents (no information duplication, etc.) and routing performance, for returning results from the queried information sources, see [30].

<u>Composition of Web Services and Planner</u>. This task and component is in charge of automated composition of web services into executable processes, see [31]. Composed web services perform new functionalities by interacting with pre-existing services that are published on the Web.

<u>Content Annotation and Annotation Manager</u>. This task and component is in charge of automatic production of metadata for the contents, see [32]. Annotation manager takes as input the (pre-processed) contents and domain knowledge and produces as output a database of content annotations. In addition to the automatic production of content metadata, prompt mechanisms should enable the user with a possibility to enrich the content annotation by adding some extra information (e.g., title, name of a location, title of an event, names of people) that could not be automatically detected.

<u>Automated Reasoning</u>. This task and component is in charge of providing logical reasoning services (e.g., subsumption, concept satisfiability, instance checking tests),

see [33]. For example, when dealing with multimedia annotations, logical reasoning can be exploited in order to check consistency of the annotations against the set of spatial (e.g., left, right, above, adjacent, overlaps) and temporal (e.g., before, after, during, co-start, co-end) constraints. Thus, this must certify that the objects detected in the multimedia content correspond semantically to the concepts defined in the domain ontology. For example, in the racing domain, the automated analyzer should check whether a car is located above a road or whether the grass and sand are adjacent to the road.

Semantic Query Processing and Query Processor. This task and component is in charge of rewriting a query by using terms which are explicitly specified in the model of domain knowledge in order to provide a semantics preserving query answering, see [32, 34]. Examples of queries are "Give me all the games played on grass" or "Give me all the games of double players", in the tennis domain. Finally, users should be able to query by a sample image. In this case, the system should perform an intelligent search of images and videos (e.g., by using semantic annotations) where, for example, the same event or type of activity takes place.

Personalization and Profiler. This task and component is in charge of tailoring services available from the system to the specificity of each user, see [35]. For example, generation and updating of user profiles, recommendation generation, inferring user preferences, and so on. For example users might want to share annotations within trusted user networks, thus having services of personal metadata management and contacts recommendation. Also, a particular form of personalization, which is media adaptation, requires knowledge-based technology for a suitable delivery of the contents to the user's terminal (e.g., palm, mobile phone, portable PC).

2 Key Application Sectors and Problematic

2.1 Healthcare and Biotechnologies

The medical domain is a favourite target for Semantic Web applications just as the expert system was for Artificial Intelligence applications 20 years ago. The medical domain is very complex: medical knowledge is difficult to represent in a computer format, making the sharing of information even more difficult. Semantic Web solutions become very promising in this context.

One of the main mechanisms of the Semantic Web - resource description using annotation principles - is of major importance in the medical informatics (or sometimes called bioinformatics) domain, especially as regards the sharing of these resources (e.g. medical knowledge in the Web or genomic database). Through the years, the IR area has been developed by medicine: medical thesauri are enormous (e.g., 1,000,000 terms in Unified Medical Language System, UMLS) and are principally used for bibliographic indexation. Nevertheless, the MeSh thesaurus (Medical Subject Heading) or UMLS[6] have been used to provide data semantics with varying degrees of difficulty. Finally, the web services technology allows us to

---

[6] http://www.nlm.nih.gov/research/umls/umlsmain.html

imagine some solutions to the interoperability problem, which is substantial in medical informatics. Below, we will describe current research, results and expected perspectives in these biomedical informatics topics in the context of Semantic Web.

2.1.1 Biosciences Resources Sharing

In the functional genomics domain, it is necessary to have access to several data bases and knowledge bases which are accessible separately on the Web but are heterogeneous in their structure as well as in their terminology. Among such resources, we can mention SWISSPROT[7] where the gene products are annotated by the Gene Ontology[8], Gen-Bank[9], etc. When comparing these resources it is easy to see that they propose the same information in different formats. The XML language, which acts as a common data structure for the different knowledge bases, provides at most a syntactic Document Type Definition (DTD) which does not resolve the semantic interoperability problem.

One of the solutions comes from the Semantic Web with a mediator approach [7] which allows for the accessing of different resources with an ontology used as the Interlingua pivot. For example and in another domain than that of genomics, the NEUROBASE project [8] attempts to federate different neuro-imagery information bases situated in different clinical or research areas. The proposal consists of defining an architecture that allows the access to and the sharing of experimental results or data treatment methodologies. It would be possible to search in the various data bases for similar results or for images with peculiarities or to perform data mining analysis between several data bases. The mediator of NEUROBASE has been tested on decision support systems in epilepsy surgery.

2.1.2 Web Services for Interoperability

The web services technology can propose some solutions to the interoperability problematic. We describe now a new approach based on a "patient envelope" and we conclude with the implementation of this envelope based on the web services technology.

The patient envelope is a proposition of the Electronic Data Interchange for Healthcare group (EDI-Santé[10]) with an active contribution from the ETIAM society[11]. The objective of the work is on filling the gap between "free" communication, using standard and generic Internet tools, and "totally structured" communication as promoted by CEN[12] or HL7[13]. After the worldwide analysis of existing standards, the proposal consists of an "intermediate" structure of information, related to one patient, and storing the minimum amount of data (i.e. exclusively useful data) to facilitate the interoperability between communicating peers. The "free" or the "structured" information is grouped into a folder and transmitted in a secure way over the existing communication networks [9]. This proposal has reached widespread

---

[7] http://us.expasy.org/sprot/
[8] http://obo.sourceforge.net/main.html
[9] http://www.ncbi.nlm.nih.gov/Genbank/index.html
[10] http://www.edisante.org/
[11] http://www.etiam.com/
[12] http://www.centc251.org/
[13] http://www.hl7.org/

adoption with the distribution by Cegetel.rss of a new medical messaging service, called "Sentinelle", fully supporting the patient envelope protocol and adapted tools.

After this milestone, EDI-Santé is promoting further developments based on ebXML and SOAP (Simple Object Access Protocol) in specifying exchange (see, items 1 and 2 below) and medical (see, items 3 and 4 below) properties:

1. Separate what is mandatory to the transport and the good management of the message (e.g., patient identification from what constitutes the "job" part of the message.
2. Provide a "container" for the message, collecting the different elements, texts, pictures, videos, etc.
3. Consider the patient as the unique object of the transaction. Such an exchange cannot be anonymous. It concerns a sender and an addressee who are involved in the exchange and who are responsible. A patient can demand to know the content of the exchange in which (s)he is the object, which implies a data structure which is unique in the form of a triple {sender, addressee, patient}.
4. The conservation of the exchange semantics. The information about a patient is multiple in the sense that it comes from multiple sources and has multiple forms and supporting data (e.g., data base, free textual document, semi-structured textual document, pictures). It can be fundamental to maintain the existing links between elements, to transmit them together, e.g., a scanner and the associated report, and to be able to prove it.

The interest of such an approach is that it prepares the evolution of the transmitted document from a free form document (from proprietary ones to normalized ones as XML) to elements respecting HL7v3 or EHRCOM data types.

2.1.3 What Is Next in the Healthcare Domain?
These different projects and applications highlight the main consequence of the Semantic Web being expected by the medical communities: the sharing and integration of heterogeneous information or knowledge. The answers to the different issues are the use of mediators, a knowledge-based system, and ontologies, which are all based on normalized languages such as RDF, OWL, and so on. The work of the Semantic Web community must take into account these expectations, see for example the FP6 projects[14,15,16]. Finally, it is interesting to note that the Semantic Web is an integrated vision of the medical community's problems (thesauri, ontologies, indexation, inference) and provides a real opportunity to synthesize and reactivate some research [10].

2.2 Knowledge Management

2.2.1 Leveraging Knowledge Assets in Companies
Knowledge is one of the key success factors for enterprises, both today and in the future. Therefore, company knowledge management has been identified as a strategic

[14] http://www.cocoon-health.com
[15] http://www.srdc.metu.edu.tr/webpage/projects/artemis/index.html
[16] http://www.simdat.org

tool. However, if information technology is one of the foundational elements of KM; KM, in turn, is also interdisciplinary by its nature. In particular, it includes human resource management as well as enterprise organization and culture[17].We view KM as the management of the knowledge arising from business activities, aiming at leveraging both the use and the creation of that knowledge for two main objectives: capitalization of corporate knowledge and durable innovation fully aligned with the strategic objectives of the organization.

Conscious of this key factor of productivity in a faster and faster changing ecosystem, the European KM Framework (CEN/ISSS[18], KnowledgeBoard[19]) has been designed to support a common European understanding of KM, to show the value of this emerging approach and help organizations towards its successful implementation. The Framework is based on empirical research and practical experience in this field from all over Europe and the rest of the world. The European KM Framework addresses all of the relevant elements of a KM solution and serves as a reference basis for all types of organizations, which aim to improve their performance by handling knowledge in a better way.

2.2.1 Knowledge-Based KM Benefits

The knowledge backbone is made up of ontologies that define a shared conceptualization of an application domain and provide the basis for defining metadata that have precisely defined semantics, and are therefore machine-interpretable. Although the first KM approaches and solutions have shown the benefits of ontologies and related methods, a large number of open research issues still exist that have to be addressed in order to make Semantic Web technology a complete success for KM solutions:

– Industrial KM applications have to avoid any kind of overhead as far as possible. A *seamless integration* of knowledge creation (i.e., content and metadata specification) and knowledge access (i.e., querying or browsing) into the working environment is required. Strategies and methods are needed to support the creation of knowledge, as side effects of activities that are carried out anyway. These requirements mean *emergent semantics* that can be supported through *ontology learning*, which should reduce the current time consuming task of building-up and maintaining ontologies.

– Access to as well as presentation of knowledge has to be *context-dependent*. Since the context is setup by the current business task, and thus by the business process

---

[17] Some of the well-known definitions of KM include:

(Wiig 1997) " Knowledge management is the systematic, explicit, and deliberate building, renewal and application of knowledge to maximize an enterprise's knowledge related effectiveness and returns from its knowledge assets" [1].

(Hibbard 1997) "Knowledge management is the process of capturing a company's collective expertise wherever it resides in databases, on paper, or in people's heads and distributing it to wherever it can help produce the biggest payoff" [2].

(Pettrash 1996) "KM is getting the right knowledge to the right people at the right time so they can make the best decision" [3].

[18] http://www.cenorm.be/cenorm/index.htm

[19] http://www.knowledgeboard.com

being handled, a tight integration of business process management and knowledge management is required. KM approaches can provide a promising starting point for *smart push services* that will proactively *deliver relevant knowledge* for carrying out the task at hand more effectively.

– *Conceptualization* has to be supplemented by *personalization*. On the one hand, taking into account the experience of the user and his/her personal needs is a prerequisite in order to avoid information overload, and on the other hand, *to deliver knowledge at the right level of granularity and from the right perspective*.

The development of knowledge portals serving the needs of companies or communities is still a manual process. Ontologies and related metadata provide a promising conceptual basis for generating parts of such knowledge portals. Obviously, among others, conceptual models of the domain, of the users and of the tasks are needed. The *generation of knowledge portals* has to be supplemented with the (semi-) automated evolution of portals. As business environments and strategies change rather rapidly, *KM portals have to be kept up-to-date in this fast changing environment*. Evolution of portals should also include some mechanisms *to 'forget' outdated knowledge*.

KM solutions will be based on a combination of intranet-based functionalities and mobile functionalities in the very near future. Semantic Web technology is a promising approach to meet the needs of mobile environments, like location-aware personalization and adaptation of the presentation to the specific needs of mobile devices, i.e., the presentation of the required information at an appropriate level of granularity. In essence, employees should have access to the KM application *anywhere* and *anytime*.

Peer-to-Peer computing (P2P), combined with Semantic Web technology, will be a strong move towards getting rid of the more centralized KM approaches that are currently used in ontology-based solutions. P2P scenarios open up the way to derive consensual conceptualizations among employees within an enterprise in a bottom-up manner.

Virtual organizations are becoming more and more important in business scenarios, mainly due to decentralization and globalization. Obviously, semantic interoperability between different knowledge sources, as well as trust, is necessary in inter-organizational KM applications.

The integration of KM applications (e.g., skill management) with *e-learning* is an important field that enables a lot of synergy between these two areas. KM solutions and e-learning must be integrated from both an organizational and an IT point of view. Clearly, interoperability and integration of (metadata) standards are needed to realize such integration.

Knowledge Management is obviously a very promising area for exploiting Semantic Web technology. Document-based KM solutions have already reached their limits, whereas semantic technology opens the way to meet KM requirements in the future.

2.2.2 Knowledge-Based KM Applications

In the context of geographical team dispersion, multilingualism and business unit autonomy, usually a company wants a solution allowing for the identification of strategic information, the secured distribution of this information and the creation of transverse working groups. Some applicative solutions allowed for the deployment of an Intranet intended for all the marketing departments of the company worldwide, allowing for a better division of and a greater accessibility to information, but also capitalisation on the total knowledge. There are three crucial points that aim at easing the work of the various marketing teams in a company: (i) Business intelligence, (ii) Skill and team management[20], (iii) Process management and (iv) Rich document access and management.

Thus, a system connects the "strategic ontologies" of the company group (brands, competitors, geographical areas, etc.) with the users, via the automation of related processes (research, classification, distribution, knowledge representation). The result is a dynamic Semantic Web system of navigation (research, classification) and collaborative features.

At the end from a functional point of view, a KM system organises skill and knowledge management within a company, in order to improve interactivity, collaboration and information sharing. This constitutes a virtual workspace which facilitates work between employees that speak different languages, automates the creation of work groups, organises and capitalises structured and unstructured, explicit or tacit data of the company, and offers advanced features of capitalisation [36, 37, 38].

Finally, the semantic backbone makes possible to cross a qualitative gap by providing cross-lingual data.

2.3 E-Commerce and E-Business

Electronic commerce is mainly based on the exchange of information between involved stakeholders using a telecommunication infrastructure. There are two main scenarios: Business-to-Customer (B2C) and Business-to-Business (B2B).

B2C applications enable service providers to promote their offers, and for customers to find offers which match their demands. By providing unified access to a large collection of frequently updated offers and customers, an electronic marketplace can match the demand and supply processes within a commercial mediation environment.

B2B applications have a long history of using electronic messaging to exchange information related to services previously agreed among two or more businesses. Early plain-text telex communication systems were followed by electronic data interchange (EDI) systems based on terse, highly codified, well structured, messages. A new generation of B2B systems is being developed under the ebXML (electronic business in XML) heading. These will use classification schemes to identify the context in which messages have been, or should be, exchanged. They will also introduce new techniques for the formal recording of business processes, and for the linking of business processes through the exchange of well-structured business messages. ebXML will also develop techniques that will allow businesses to identify new suppliers through the use of registries that allow users to identify which services a supplier can offer. ebXML needs to include well managed multilingual ontologies

---

[20] Semantic Web, Use Cases and Challenges at EADS, http://www.eswc2006.org Industry Forum.

that can be used to help users to match needs expressed in their own language with those expressed in the service providers language(s).

2.3.1 Knowledge-Based E-Commerce and E-Business Value

At present, ontology and more generally knowledge-based systems, appear as a *central issue* for the development of *efficient and profitable* e-commerce and e-business solutions. However, because of an actual partial standardization for business models, processes, and knowledge architectures, it is currently difficult for companies to achieve the promised ROI from knowledge-based e-commerce and e-business.

Moreover, a technical barrier exists that is delaying the emergence of e-commerce, lying in the need for applications to *meaningfully share information*, taking into account the lack of reliability, security and eventually trust in the Internet. This fact may be explained by the variety of e-commerce and e-business systems employed by businesses and the various ways these systems are configured and used. As an important remark, such *interoperability problems* become particularly severe when a large number of trading partners attempt to agree and define the standards for interoperation, which is precisely a main condition for maximizing the ROI indicator.

Although it is useful to strive for the adoption of a single common domain-specific standard for content and transactions, such a task is often difficult to achieve, particularly in cross-industry initiatives, where companies co-operate and compete with one another. Some examples of the difficulties are:

- *Commercial practices* may vary widely, and consequently, cannot always be aligned for a variety of technical, practical, organizational and political reasons.
- *The complexity of a global description* of the organizations themselves: their products and services (independently or in combination), and the *interactions* between them remain a formidable task.
- It is not always possible to establish a priori rules (technical or procedural) governing participation in an electronic marketplace.
- Adoption of *a single common standard may limit business models* which could be adopted by trading partners, and therefore, potentially reduce their ability to fully participate in e-commerce.

A knowledge-based approach has the potential to significantly accelerate the penetration of electronic commerce within vertical industry sectors, by *enabling interoperability at the business level*, and reducing the need for standardisation at the technical level. This will enable services to adapt to the rapidly changing online environment.

2.3.2 Knowledge-Based E-Commerce and E-Business Applications

The Semantic Web brings opportunities to industry to create new services[21], extend markets, and even develop new businesses since it enables the inherent meaning of the data available in the Internet to be accessible to systems and devices able to interpret and reason on the knowledge. This in turn leads to new revenue opportunities, since information becomes more readily accessible and usable. For

---

[21] DIP Data, Information, and Process Integration with Semantic Web Services, http://dip.semanticweb.org/

example, a catering company whose web site simply lists the menus available is less likely to achieve orders compared to one whose menus are associated with related metadata about the contents of the dishes, their origin (e.g., organic, non-genetically modified, made with local produce), links to alternative dishes for special diets, personalised ordering where a user profile can be established which automatically proposes certain menu combinations depending on the occasion (e.g., wedding banquet, business lunch). The latter case assumes that both provider-side knowledge generation and knowledge management tools are available, such that the asset owner can readily enhance their data with semantic meaning, and client-side tools are available to enable machine interpretation of the semantic descriptions related to the products being offered, such that the end user can benefit from the available and mined knowledge. Examples of some possible application areas were studied by the Agent Cities project[22].

In the e-business area Semantic Web technology can improve standard business process management tools. One prototypical case is in the area of logistics. The application of knowledge technology on top of today's business management tools enables the automation of major tasks of business process management[23] [39].

2.4 Multimedia and Audiovisual Services

2.4.1 Multimedia and Semantic Technology

Practical realisation of the Semantic Web vision is actively being researched by a number of experts, some of them within European collaborative projects such as SEKT[24] and DIP, but these mainly focus on enhancing text based applications from a knowledge engineering perspective. Although significant benefits in unlocking access to valuable knowledge assets are anticipated via these projects, in various do-mains such as digital libraries, enterprise applications, and financial services, less attention has been given to the challenging and potentially highly profitable area of integration of multimedia and Semantic Web technologies for multimedia content based applications.

Users express dissatisfaction at not being able to find what they want, and content owners are unable to make full use of their assets. Service providers seek means to differentiate their offerings by making them more targeted toward the individual needs of their customers. Semantic Web technology can address these issues. It has the potential to reduce complexity, enhance choice, and put the user at the center of the application or service, and with future expected advances in mobile communication protocols, such benefits can be enjoyed by consumers and professional users in all environments using all their personal devices, in the home, at work, in the car and on the go.

Semantic Web technologies can enhance multimedia based products to increase the value of multimedia assets such as content items which are themselves the articles for sale (songs, music videos, sports clips, news summaries, etc) or where they are used as supporting sales of other goods (e.g. promotional images, movie trailers etc).

---

[22] Agentcities RTD project http://www.agentcities.org/EURTD/
[23] Semantic Business Automation, SAP, Germany http://www.eswc2006.org Industry Forum
[24] Semantically Enabled Knowledge Technologies http://www.sekt-project.com/

Value is added in search applications, such that returned items more closely match the user's context, interests, tasks, preference history etc, as well as in proactive push applications such as personalised content delivery and recommendation systems, and even personalised advertising. However, applications such as content personalisation, where a system matches available content to the user's stated and learned preferences, thereby enabling content offerings to be closely targeted to the user's wishes, rely on the availability of semantic metadata describing the content in order to make the match. Currently, metadata generation is mostly manual, which is costly and time consuming. Multimedia analysis techniques which go beyond the signal level approach to a semantic analysis have the potential to create automatic annotation of content, thereby opening up new applications which can unlock the commercial value of content archives.

Automated multimedia analysis tools are important enablers in making a wider range of information more accessible to intelligent search engines, real-time personalisation tools, and user-friendly content delivery systems. Such automated multimedia analysis tools, which add the semantic information to the content, are critical in realising the value of commercial assets e.g. sports, music and film clip services, where manual annotation of multimedia content would not be economically viable, and are also applicable to users' personal content (e.g. acquired from video camera or mobile phone) where the user does not have time, or a suitable user interface, to annotate all their content.

Multimedia ontologies are needed to structure and make accessible the knowledge inherent in the multimedia content, and reasoning tools are needed to assist with identification of relevant content in an automated fashion. Although textual analysis and reasoning tools have been well researched, fewer tools are available for semantic multimedia analysis, since the problem domain is very challenging. However, automated multimedia content analysis tools such as those being studied within aceMedia[25] are a first step in making a wider range of information more accessible to intelligent search engines, real-time personalisation tools, and user-friendly content delivery systems. Such tools will be described later in this paper.

Furthermore, interoperability of multimedia tools is important in enabling a wide variety of applications and services on multiple platforms for diverse domains. The W3C Multimedia Task Force recently published a review of image annotation on the semantic web[26] in which the advantages of using Semantic Web languages and technologies for the creation, storage, manipulation, interchange and processing of image metadata were presented, along with some illustrative use cases. In parallel, a multimedia ontology harmonisation effort has proceeded to the requirements stage[27], in which requirements for multimedia ontologies for many applications (including authoring, annotation, search, personalisation, and simulation) are considered. Contributions from more than 16 organisations demonstrated the importance of harmonisation in ontologies as a key precursor to interoperability. Interoperability is essential in achieving commercial success with semantic multimedia applications,

---

[25] http://www.acemedia.com

[26] http://www.w3.org/2001/sw/BestPractices/MM/image_annotation.html

[27] http://www.acemedia.org/aceMedia/files/multimedia_ontology/cfr/
MM-Ontologies-Reqs-v1.3.pdf

since it enables multiple manufacturers, content providers and service providers to participate in the market. This in turn enables consumer confidence to be achieved, and a viable ecosystem to be developed.

2.4.2 Knowledge Enhanced Multimedia Services

In aceMedia the main technological objectives are to discover and exploit knowledge inherent in multimedia content in order to make content more relevant to the user; to automate annotation at all levels; and to add functionality to ease content creation, transmission, search, access, consumption and re-use.

Users in the future will access multimedia content using a variety of devices, such as mobile phones and set-top-boxes, as well as via broadband cable or wireless to their PC. aceMedia research outcomes will assist users interacting with their multimedia content through innovative search technologies, automated indexing and cataloguing methods, and content adaptation to best match the user's available device and environment. aceMedia technologies will be supported by innovative user interfaces enabling advanced functionality, such as intelligent search and retrieval, self-organising content, and self-adapting content to be enjoyed by both professional content providers and end consumers.

Another interesting reported experiment is MediaCaddy[28] aiming at providing movie or music recommendations based on published online critics, user experience and social networks. Indeed, for the entertainment industry, traditional approaches to delivering meta-content about movies, music, TV shows, etc. were through reviews and articles that were done and published in traditional media such as newspapers, magazines and TV shows. With the introduction of the Internet, non-traditional forms of delivering entertainment started surfacing. The third quarter of 2003 in the U.S was the best ever for broadband penetration bringing such services as content on-demand and mobile multimedia. As of today more than 5000 movies and 2,500,000 songs are available on line. In the next couple of years this figure is expected to grow in leaps and bounds. With such a phenomenal rise in content over IP, a new need for secondary metacontent related to the movies/music emerged. Initially this was through movie reviews or music reviews published on web portals such as Yahoo, MSN and online magazine portals as well as entertainment sales sites such as Netflix.com and Amazon.com.

Most consumers today get information about media content primarily from reviews/articles in entertainment/news magazines, their social network of friends (one user recommends a song or movie to a friend), acquaintances and advertisements. In most of the cases, one or all of the above influence user's opinion about any content (s)he chooses to consume. In addition, a new breed of customizable meta-content portal has emerged, which specifically targets the entertainment industry. Examples of such portals include Rotten Tomatoes and IMDB. However, these services today are typically accessed via portals thereby limiting the interactions and access to the information to exchanges between a user and the source for non-PC environment.

---

[28] MediaCaddy - Semantic Web based On-Demand Content Navigation System for Entertainment. Shishir Garg et al. ISWC 2005.

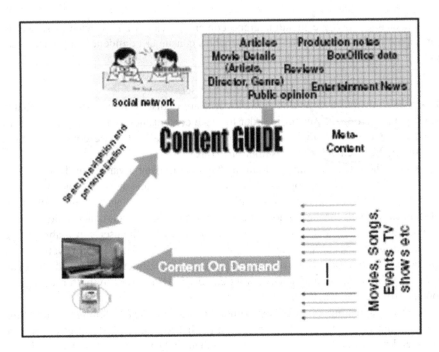

Fig. 4. Conceptual Model of Content Navigation System

MediaCaddy is a recommendation and aggregation service built around a self-learning engine, which analyzes a click stream generated by user's interaction and actions with meta-content displayed through a UI. This meta-content (Music /Movies/ TV reviews/ article/ synopsis/ production notes) is accessed from multiple Internet sources and structured as an ontology using a semantic inferencing platform.

This provides multiple benefits, both allowing for a uniform mechanism for aggregating disparate sources of content, and on the other hand, also allowing for complex queries to be executed in a timely and accurate manner. The platform allows this information to be accessed via Web Services APIs, making integration simpler with multiple devices and UI formats. Another feature that sets MediaCaddy apart is its ability to achieve a high level of personalization by analyzing content consumption behavior in the user's personal Movie/Music Domain and his or her social network and using this information to generate music and movie recommendations. Fig 4 illustrates the conceptual model of MediaCaddy.

2.5   Other Prominent Applications

Here are listed some excellent illustrations of the applications of Semantic Web technology, as they have been selected from a worldwide competition[29] offering participants the opportunity to show the best of the art.

---

[29] Annual Semantic Web applications challenge: http://challenge.semanticweb.org

CONFOTO, Essen, Germany. CONFOTO is an online service which facilitates browsing, annotating and re-purposing of photo, conference, and people descriptions. 1st Prize 2005: http://www.confoto.org/

FungalWeb, Concordia University, Canada.
"Ontology, the Semantic Web, Intelligent Systems for Fungal Genomics"
2nd Prize 2005: http://www.cs.concordia.ca/FungalWeb/

Personal Publication Reader, Uni Hannover, TU Vienna and Lixto Software GmbH –
3rd Prize 2005: http://www.personal-reader.de/semwebchallenge/sw-challenge.html

Bibster – A semantics-based Bibliographic P2P system
http://bibster.semanticweb.org
CS AKTive space – Semantic data integration
http://cs.aktivespace.org (Winner 2003 Semantic Web challenge)
Flink: SemWeb for analysis of Social Networks
http://www.cs.vu.nl/~pmika (Winner 2004 Semantic Web challenge)
Museum Finland: Sem Web for cultural portal
http://museosuomi.cs.helsinki.fi (2nd prize 2004 Semantic Web challenge)
ScienceDesk: collaborative knowledge management system in NASA
http://sciencedesk.arc.nasa.gov/ (3rd prize 2004 Semantic Web challenge)
Also see Applications and Demos at W3C SWG BPD
http://esw.w3.org/mt/esw/archives/cat_applications_and_demos.html

3 Analysis of Some Knowledge Reasoning Tasks

3.1 Multilingual Interface for QUERYING E-SERVICES

One of the challenging problems that web service technology faces is the ability to effectively discover services based on their capabilities. An approach to tackle this problem in the context is to use description logics (DL) to describe their capabilities. Service discovery can be considered as a new instance of the problem of rewriting concepts using terminologies.

The matchmaking algorithm that takes as input a service request (or query) Q and an ontology T of services, and find a set of services is called a "best cover" of Q whose descriptions contain as much as possible of common information with Q and as less as possible of extra information with respect to Q.

The proposed discovery technique has been implemented and used in the context of Multilingual e-Commerce where it is supposed that the user is expressing his or her needs in his or her own language. This has been tested for Spanish, French and English successfully for the Multilingual Knowledge Based European Electronic Marketplace (MKBEEM[30]) project.

3.1.1 Technical Architecture

In MKBEEM, ontologies are used to provide a consensual representation of the electronic commerce field in two domains (tourism with both transportation and

---

[30] http://www.mkbeem.com

accommodations as well as mail order of clothing) allowing the exchanges independently of the language of the end user, the service, or the content provider. Ontologies are used for classifying and indexing catalogues, for filtering user queries, for facilitating man-machine dialogues between users and software agents, and for inferring information that is relevant to the user requests. The ontologies are structured in three layers, as shown in Figure 5.

The global ontology describes the common terms used in the given application domain. This ontology represents the general knowledge in different domains (e.g., date, time) while each domain ontology contains specific concepts (e.g., trip) corresponding to vertical domains such as transports and accommodations. The service ontology describes all the offers available in the MKBEEM platform in terms of classes of services, i.e., service capabilities, non-functional attributes. Service classes are generic in the sense that they are described independently from a specific provider (e.g., trains services offers from Italy or Portugal are conceptually equivalent). The source descriptions (views in the Database terminology) described in terms of the Domain ontology, specify concrete instances that can be retrieved from the sources (i.e., reservation on trains). A further ontology is the linguistic domain ontology which assures an unambiguous interpretation of the user requests (see below in section 3.1.2).

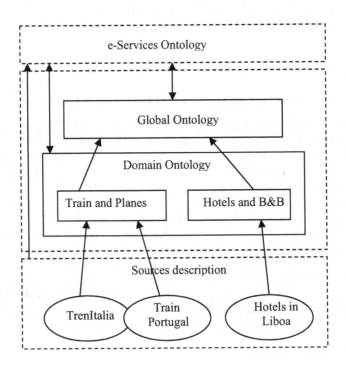

Fig. 5. Knowledge Base architecture

The MKBEEM-system allows to fill the gap between customer queries and diverse concrete providers offers. In a typical scenario, an end user submits to the MKBEEM-system a natural language query. The query is processed by a Human Language Processing Server (HLP Server) which is in charge of meaning extraction: it analyses the input string and converts the query into an ontological formula (OF) which is a language-independent formula containing the semantic information of the corresponding phrase in human language in terms of the service ontology. The OF is then sent to the Domain Ontology server (DO server). The DO server is responsible of storing, accessing and maintaining the ontologies used by the MKBEEM-system. It also provides the core reasoning mechanisms needed to support the mediation services. The DO server achieves a contextual interpretation of the formula using its knowledge about the application domain. This task consists mainly in the identification of the offers (services) delivered by the MKBEEM-system that best match the ontological formula. The aim here is to allow the users/applications to automatically discover the available services that best meet their needs, to examine their capabilities and to possibly complete missing information. The set of solutions computed by the DO server is sent back to the user to choose one solution and to complete the parameters, if any of that are missing. After this dialogue phase, the retained solution is sent back to the DO server to generate the query plans. A query plan contains information about the real services that are able to answer the user query. Then, by using the information provided in the source descriptions, a query plan is translated into specific provider requests which are executed on the remote provider platforms (e.g., train reservation systems, hotel booking, car rentals).

Thus, the user poses queries in terms of the integrated knowledge (services and domain ontology) rather than directly querying specific provider information data-bases. This enables users to focus on what they want, rather than worrying about how and from where to obtain the answers.

3.1.2 Human Language Request Analysis

Within MKBEEM, we currently cover three basic services of the tourism domain, i.e., train reservation, accommodation reservation, car rental as well as mail order of clothing. In all of these cases, human languages allow a wide range of expressions and the related linguistic ontology therefore contains all the necessary information. Another benefit of this is that it helps the user to specify as much parameters as needed in a single request, in natural language, thus avoiding tiresome form-filling. The combination of several requests (e.g., "I want to visit Lisbon and reserve an hotel next weekend") is also possible. To ensure that the generated, language neutral ontological formulas will contain all relevant information given by the user, the user request is treated in several interdependent steps [40].

Since the MKBEEM-prototype is multilingual, the first step is to identify the language of the user request. In the next step, it is analysed and a language independent semantic graph is created. The linguistic analysis is based on dependency syntax, a set of language dependent rules comparable to the Semantic Interpretation Rules of Discourse Representation Theory [41] and a set of language independent predicates. To ensure the ontological appropriateness of the generated semantic graph, it is checked by the linguistic domain ontology developed for this purpose[31]. Any inappropriate semantic graph is deleted from the set of possible solutions. Finally, in order to deal with e.g., travel dates (especially in the tourism domain), temporal expressions which are relative to the time of utterance (deictic elements like now, today, in two hours, in five days, next Monday, at ten to eleven pm) or incomplete or varying dates (the 12th of April, on Good Friday are transformed into the corresponding absolute temporal expression (if no exact time is specified, it is not generated):

temporal expression	transformation
now	*17.06.2003 13:56*
today	*17.06.2003*
next Monday	*21.06.2003*
at ten to eleven pm	*17.06.2003 22:50*
the 12th of April	*12.04.2004*
on Good Friday	*9.04.2004*

The next step is the transformation of the internal semantic representation into the ontological formula, which works as a KR interlingua for the other processing components. The concepts (and roles) differ considerably from the linguistic ontology due to the fact that linguistic expressions and semantic nuances are present in the semantic representation, which are not needed in the ontological formula. So for instance temporal or modal information (I want to/I would like to/we will/we have to) must be eliminated by the transformation. Further, different lexemes expressing a move (go/arrive/depart/travel/be in/visit) need to be mapped on the concept "trip", which is the only move-concept of the service ontology (see Fig. 6) As an example we take a typical user request, as follows:

Example1. *"I'll arrive in Lisboa on Monday evening and I look for an accommodation with swimming pool."*

The request inquires information on public transport to Lisbon on (next) Monday evening (uttered on Tuesday, 17th June). After analysing the sentence and processing the relative temporal information, we obtain an internal, language independent, semantic representation:

Semantic representation 2 (simplified)

```
coord(coord1=x3005, coord2=x3006) &
arrival(destination=x3009, origin=u3010, situation=x3005, agent=x3013) &
speaker(theme=x3013) &
Lisboa(town=u3015, location=x3009) &
weekday~monday(date=x3005, wday=u3014) &
monthday~23(date=x3005, day=u3069) &
month~june(date=x3005, month=u3070) &
year~2003(date=x3005, year=u3071) &
hour~18(time=x3005, hour=u3072) &
```

---

[31] See PICSEL http://www.lri.fr/~sais/picsel3 (1999-2006)

minute~0(time=x3005, minute=u3073) &
staying(agent=x3021, situation=x3006, place=x3022, means=x3023,
          leisure=x3024) &
speaker(theme=x3021) &
accomodationorg(city=x3022, theme=x3023, leisure=x3024) &
swimmingPool(type=x3024).

As users are not directly concerned by the organisation of data provided by information systems (in our case train, car rental, tourism), the main difficulty is to map efficiently the user concepts (go, arrive, depart, take a train, etc.), identified by the HLP, onto the domain concepts (ontologies). Since some user requests are complex utterances, mixing motion verbs with absolute or relative time and space representation, the linguistic ontology is first used to constrain the parser during the construction of the linguistic formulas and to reduce the ambiguity ([42], cf. also [43]). In a next step irrelevant information (from an application point of view) must be pruned to produce a new formula compliant to the DO server (cf. Fig. 7), devoted identify the service and to plan the data-base queries.

The linguistic ontology has been designed using the experience and knowledge gained in a previous project (Picsel[32]) using Description Logics language (DL), and which tools have been enriched to fit the needs of the linguistic analyser.

Usually, ontologies are organised as directed graphs and use multiple inheritance. In consequence the more general concepts subsume the more specific. In contrast to superordinates which are less specific concepts, the greatest common subsumee (GCS) are more complete. Our experience, however, shows that domain concepts are rather GCS than superordinates. As outlined in [42] we use a common formalism for information representation (ontology). The ontologies are represented in Carin-$\mathcal{ALN}$[33], where concepts are unary predicates and roles binary predicates joining two concepts or a concept and a constant. The common inter-module communication language is Carin-$\mathcal{ALN}$ which is in the framework of DL. As a consequence the HLP must transform utterances into formulas (using the inter-module communication language).

Picsel[34] ontologies are organised as directed graphs and use multiple inheritance. Thus in Carin-$\mathcal{ALN}$ (and other DLs) the more generic concepts subsume the more specific ones. In natural languages, however, more general concepts combine features of more specific ones. In consequence, the greatest common subsumees (GCS) are the

---

[32] The Use of CARIN Language and Algorithms for Information Integration: The PICSEL Project by F. Goasdoué, V. Lattes, and M.C. Rousset. International Journal of Cooperative Information Systems (IJCIS) World Scientific Publishing Company, Volume 9, Number 4, pages 383-401.

[33] Carin is a family of theoretical languages for knowledge representation, Carin-$\mathcal{ALN}$ is the most expressive description logic for which subsumption and satisfiability are polynomial.

[34] "Picsel is an information integration system over sources that are distributed and possibly heterogeneous. The approach which has been chosen in Picsel is to define an information server as a knowledge-based mediator in which Carin is used as the core logical formalism to represent both the domain of application and the contents of information sources relevant to that domain." See http://www.lri.fr/~sais/picsel3/

best candidates to represent these more general concepts. Our experience shows that applications should rather use GCS than concepts of the linguistic sub-ontology (LSO) in order to keep the power of inheritance and to manage a more generic notion at the same time.

Discrepancies between the semantic representation (of the user request) and the main ontology must thus be bridged: The semantic representations (graphs) are using the LSO (i.e. concepts and roles defined in the LSO). To obtain the ontological formula, we need to rewrite this representation in service ontology (SO) terms. In order to achieve this, the principal rewriting rule is to replace the LSO concept (as found during the syntactical-semantic analysis) by the GCS concept of the SO.

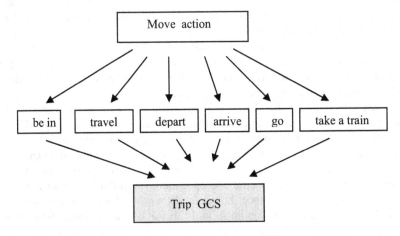

Fig. 6. Links between linguistic ontology and service ontology

As figure 6 shows, the service ontology concept trip GCS is a more complete and less generic concept than the (linguistic) concepts "go", "arrive" etc., which express the meanings of the verbs in question. The motion verb is rewritten using the GCS (in this case trip GCS). The resulting formula can be correctly interpreted within the service ontology. Taking our example 1, the semantic representation 2 is thus transformed into the corresponding ontological formula 3 in service ontology terms.

Ontological formula 3

```
(trip)(V5609),
      (arrPlace)(V5609, properName Paris),
(date)(C63),
      (weekday)(C63, monday),
      (day)(C63, 23),
      (month)(C63, june),
      (year)(C63, 2003),
      (arrDate)(V5609, C63),
```

(time)(C64),

    (hour)(C64, 18),

    (minute)(C64, 0),

    (arrTime)(V5609, C64),

(accommodation)(V5610),

    (leisure)(V5610, swimmingPool)

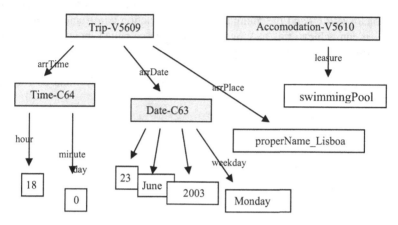

Fig. 7. Visualisation of the ontological formula used for the service identification

3.1.3 Service Identification

In MKBEEM, service identification is achieved by means of a dynamic service discovery reasoning mechanism. Dynamic service discovery is used in association with the Picsel system to achieve the reasoning tasks in the DO Server. The complementary roles of these two complex logical reasoning constitutes the description logic core for query processing in the MKBEEM-system. They are in fact two different instances of the problem of rewriting concepts using terminologies [44].

The following example illustrates the interest of the service discovery reasoning mechanism.

Let us consider an e-commerce platform that delivers the following four offers:
– hotel, which allows to consult a list of hotels.
– apartment, which allows to consult a list of apartments.
– timetable1, which allows to consult a journey given the departure place, the arrival place, the departure date and the departure time.
– timetable2, which allows to consult a journey given the departure place, the arrival place, the arrival date and the arrival time.

Let us assume that, according to architecture of the MKBEEM-ontology, these offers are formally described in a given service ontology. Consider now, the example 1 and the ontological formula 3 created by HLP-Server. Now the service discovery is used by the DO Server to identify the corresponding relevant service(s) in the service ontology. This task is achieved in two steps:

1. Converting an ontological formula F into a concept description Q_F:

   This task depends on the structure of the ontological formula and on the expressive power of the target language. The current ontological formulas generated by the HLP-Server have relatively simple structures that can be described using the small description logic $\mathcal{FL}o \cup \{(\geq nR)\}$. This logic contains the concept conjunction constructor ($\sqcap$), the universal role quantification constructor ($\forall R.C$) and the minimal number restriction constructor ($\geq nR$). In this case, we can achieve this task by computing the so-called most specific concept [45] corresponding to the ontological formula.

The concept description Q_{OF1} corresponding to the ontological formula $OF1$ given in the previous example is:

$$
\begin{aligned}
Q_{OF1} \doteq \; & \text{accommodation} \\
& \sqcap (\geq 1 \text{ leisure}) \\
& \sqcap (\forall \text{ leisure string}) \\
& \sqcap \text{trip} \\
& \sqcap (\geq 1 \text{ arrPlace}) \\
& \sqcap (\forall \text{ arrPlace string}) \\
& \sqcap (\geq 1 \text{ arrDate}) \\
& \sqcap (\forall \text{ arrDate (date} \sqcap (\geq 1 \text{ day}) \sqcap (\forall \text{ day integer}) \\
& \qquad\qquad\qquad\quad \sqcap (\geq 1 \text{ year}) \sqcap (\forall \text{ year integer}) \\
& \qquad\qquad\qquad\quad \sqcap (\geq 1 \text{ month}) \sqcap (\forall \text{ month string}) \\
& \qquad\qquad\qquad\quad \sqcap (\geq 1 \text{ weekday}) \sqcap (\forall \text{ weekday string)})) \\
& \sqcap (\geq 1 \text{ arrTime}) \\
& \sqcap (\forall \text{ arrTime (time} \sqcap (\geq 1 \text{ hour}) \sqcap (\forall \text{ hour integer}) \\
& \qquad\qquad\qquad\quad \sqcap (\geq 1 \text{ minute}) \sqcap (\forall \text{ minute integer)}))
\end{aligned}
$$

2. Selecting the relevant services:

   This problem can be stated as follows: given a user query Q_F and an ontology of services T, find a description E, built using (some) of the names defined in T, such that E contains as much as possible of common information with Q_F and as less as possible of extra information with respect to Q_F. We call such a rewriting E a *best cover* of Q_F using T. Therefore, our goal is to rewrite a description Q_F into the closest description expressed as a conjunction of (some) concept names in T.

A best cover E of a concept Q using T is defined as being any conjunction of concept names occurring in T which shares some common information with Q, is consistent with Q and minimizes, in this order, the extra information in Q and not in E and the extra information in E and not in Q. Once the notion of a best cover has been formally defined, the second issue to be addressed is how to find a set of services that best covers a given query. This problem, called best covering problem, can be stated as follows: given an ontology T and a query description Q, find all the best covers of Q using T.

More technical details about the best covering problem can be found in [46, 47]. To sum up, the main results that have been reached are:

– The precise formalisation of the best covering problem in the framework of languages where the difference operation is semantically unique (e.g., the description logic $\mathcal{FL}o \cup \{(\geq nR))\}$.

– A study of complexity showed that this problem is NP-Hard.
– A reduction of the best covering problem to the problem of computing the minimal transversals with minimum cost of a weighted hypergraph.
– Based on hypergraph theory, a sound and complete algorithm that solves the best covering problem was designed and implemented.

Continuing with the example, we obtain the following result from the DO Server:

Table 2. Results from the Domain Ontology Server

	Identified services	Rest	Missing information
Solution 1	Timetable2, apartment	leisure	depPlace, numberOfRooms, apartmentCategory
Solution 2	Timetable2, hotel	leisure	depPlace numberOfBeds, hotelCategory

These solutions correspond to the combinations of services that best match the ontological formula *OF1*. For each solution, the DO Server computes the extra information (column missing information) brought by the services but not contained in the user query. The column rest contains the extra information (leisure) contained in the user query and not provided by any services. This means that, in the proposed solutions the requirement concerning the leisure is not taken into account.

To continue with the example, assume that the user chooses the first solution (timetable2, apartment). Then, he is asked to complete the missing information: the departure place, the apartment category and the number of rooms the user wants in the apartment. The result is a global query *Q*, expressed as a service formula that will be sent to the Query plan generation (Picsel) to identify the providers which are able to answer to this query.

3.1.4 Summary

In this key technology components presentation we have described the successful implementation of a multilingual interface to semantically enabled services, based on knowledge which is coded in ontologies. It shows, how after the identification of the language, a user request is analysed and transformed into a language independent ontological representation. This representation is used to identify the service (or product in an e-commerce environment) the user wants to consult/buy with the help of service ontologies. Existing parameters are extracted and missing ones might be requested to the user in a subsequent step. Finally, to get the instances (e.g., the travel ticket, the room reservation) the selected content providers are contacted to present the user the results of his or her initial requests.

3.2 Knowledge-Based Multimedia Services

3.2.4 Multimedia Reasoning

Several methods for extracting the meaning of image regions were introduced. All these methods share the characteristic that they mainly work on low-level features of the image, e.g. on comparing colours or the direction of edges. While this type of algorithm provides good results for very specific problems, e.g. person detection, they do not work as well when used on more generic problems, such as labelling of an image. Labelling of an image refers to finding the correct concept depicted in a region of the image. In Figure 9 and Figure 10, one can see the different stages of the image analysis procedure. In the upper right the image was divided into different regions, where each region is depicted in a different grey tone. Apparently, the sea was divided into different regions. Now, if one wants to find out what is depicted in these regions and just starts to compare the colours, one will have problems to distinguish e.g. between sea and sky. Both are blue in colour, so it is hard to tell what is depicted. Also other objects can be blue, such as cars, towels or clothes. In the multimedia reasoning step we try to overcome this problem.

It is well known that correctly interpreting a scene does not only take typical low level features such as colours or textures into account, but that also higher level knowledge is of great importance. One very important type of such knowledge is the spatial context, i.e. how certain concepts are usually related in terms of their spatial arrangement. An example is that you will nearly always find the sky depicted above the sea. Also, an aeroplane will be usually depicted within the sky and not within the sea, and so on. This type of knowledge is of course not always true, but it is true with a high probability. Therefore we are implementing algorithms in order to refine the output of the knowledge assisted analysis (KAA) using such spatial knowledge, which is specified beforehand by a domain expert. Based on this we can exclude certain concepts, e.g. if we encounter a region that is completely surrounded by sky, and this region is supposed to be sea or sky (result of the knowledge assisted analysis), we can safely discard the sea label, as we know that sea is never depicted within the sky, but only below, and keep the sky one. After discarding false labels we also try to use this kind of spatial knowledge to further refine the regions, e.g. merging regions that all depict sky into one big sky region.

3.2.1 Knowledge-Assisted Image/Video Analysis

A knowledge-assisted analysis (KAA) platform has been developed, in the context of the aceMedia project[35]. The interaction between the analysis algorithms and the knowledge base is continuous and tightly integrated, instead of being just a pre- or post-processing step in the overall architecture (see Figure 8). To achieve this, a region adjacency graph for image representation is used, that can interact dynamically (i.e., save, update, create new information) with the analysis processes.

---

[35] IST-aceMedia http://www.acemedia.org

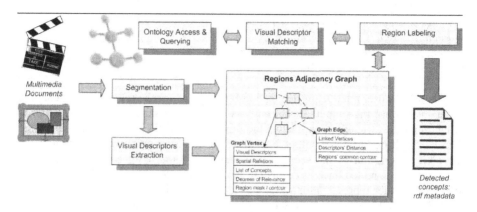

Fig. 8. Overall architecture

Whenever new multimedia content is provided as input for analysis, an initial segmentation algorithm generates a number of connected regions and then MPEG-7 visual descriptors are extracted for each region. A matching process queries the knowledge base and assigns to each region a list of possible concepts along with a degree of confidence. Those concepts are used (along with the degrees and spatial information of the regions) for the construction of an RDF description that is the actual system output: a semantic interpretation of the multimedia content.

Fig. 9. Knowledge Assisted Analysis

The objective of this ontology-supported analysis, is to extract high-level, human comprehensible features and automatically create semantic metadata describing the multimedia content itself. For each image/video shot, an RDF description is generated, which is a set of triples for each region/graph vertex. For example:

- *Image X decomposed-into region Y*
- *Region Y depicts concept-instance Z*
- *Concept-instance Z has-degree-of-confidence d*
- *Region Y is-left-of Region W*

The KAA's user interface is depicted in Figure 9, where the four panels display the input image and the output of the analysis in different steps. This visualisation is much more user friendly than reading the produced RDF file. As illustrated in Figure 10, the resulting system's output includes also a segmentation mask outlining the semantic description of the scene. The different colours assigned to the generated regions correspond to concepts defined in the domain ontology. This labelled mask is, in effect, another representation of the concepts detected, without the strict format of RDF, but with the major advantage of being very easily interpreted by humans.

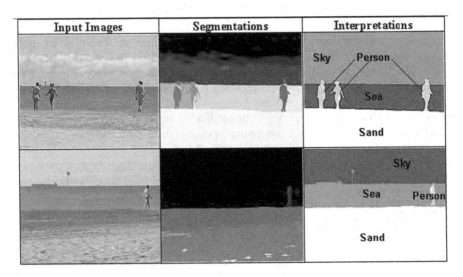

Fig. 10. Analysis carried out by KAA

3.2.2 Person Detection and Identification

Human body forms are usually what a person notices first in audiovisual content. The aceMedia person detection and identification module can detect persons, as well as identify them. Furthermore, human faces are detected.

With the help of aceMedia KAA (Knowledge Assisted Analysis) and content classification modules, the person detection and identification module further extends the capabilities of aceMedia high-level intelligent modules. Figure 11 shows examples of person detection. It also shows how a combination of different aceMedia modules can form a very powerful search tool. Person detection detects people, face detection detects faces, and content classification detects image background – allowing high-level user queries such as *"find all images with people playing football"*.

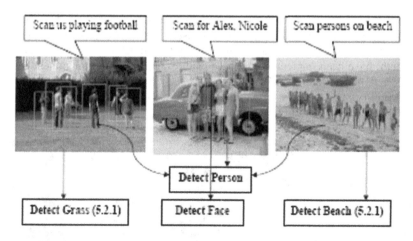

Fig. 11. Person detection

The aceMedia person detector represents the current state-of-the-art in person detection. The detector performs as much as 50 times better than previous state of the art detectors in our evaluation experiments [48]. The module uses a new paradigm by mapping images in a very high dimensional feature space – a feature space specially designed to reliably detect people irrespective of their clothing, poses, appearance, image background, and image illumination. Besides person detection, the detector is known to work well for other image classes also, such as detecting cars, motorbikes, etc.

Another version of the aceMedia person detection module, which is work in progress, combines motion information, i.e., how people move. This module further improves the accuracy of person detection, enabling the new detector to reliably detect people in videos. This module also provides person part detection capabilities, allowing automatic labelling of body parts, such as arms, torso, legs. This will allow even more powerful search applications such as activity recognition.

An efficient face detection technology based on convolutional neural network architecture has also been integrated and tested, within the aceMedia system. This detector is able to robustly detect, in real time, multiple highly variable face patterns, of minimal size 30x30 pixels, rotated up to±20 degrees in the image plane and turned by up to ±60 degrees.

The robustness of the face detector to varying poses and facial expressions as well as lighting variations and noise was evaluated by considering its sensitivity with respect to various transformations of the face patterns and using real sets of difficult images. Experiments have shown high detection rates with a particularly low number of false positives, on difficult test sets. For instance, a good detection rate of 90.3 % with 8 false positives have been reported on the CMU test set2, which are the best results published so far on this test set. Figure 12 shows some examples of detected faces. We have also been working on how to automatically identify the detected faces. The idea is to attach an identity to each of the detected faces using a reference database of digital face images. An off-line processing step is performed to learn the faces in the reference database. A recognition model is then computed and used to identify newly detected faces online. Statistical approaches for face recognition have been investigated and a novel method called Bilinear Discriminant Analysis has been developed [49]. This method achieves better results than state of the art technologies. Furthermore, facial feature extraction techniques (positions of the eyes, the nose and the mouth) have been implemented. These features enable a better alignment of facial images and hence significantly improve the face recognition performance. Other classification issues of faces in feature space are also being investigated in order to provide a rejection possibility of unknown people.

Fig. 12. Face detection

3.2.3 Onological Text Analysis in Acemedia

For natural language processing within aceMedia, the domain ontology and their mapping onto a semantic thesaurus has been stabilized. This is essential, since the natural language processing tool needs to know the meaning of the ontological classes and relations in order to assign lexical or syntactical meanings onto the ontological entities. This work is an extension of the ontological text analysis presented for MKBEEM (see 3.1.2).

During 2005, the linguistic data provided for aceMedia have been enhanced. This meant revising the lexicon for domain specific expressions not yet in the lexicon (words such as "jet-ski") and adding robust rules to the dependency grammar analysis in order to be able to parse ungrammatical textual input (the content annotation corpus provided for the prototype contained phrases such as "child at bottom of mountain", which normally would have passed the syntactic analysis). Secondly the natural language processing application module (NLP AM) has been developed integrating FTRD's natural language toolbox ©Tilt.

Another important achievement is the first implementation of the ontological correction. This means that the ontological representations created from natural languages (textual annotations or user queries) have to be coherent with aceMedia's (domain) ontologies. Finally, the RDF produced by the NLP AM goes directly into the semantic metadata. It is thus available for intelligent search and retrieval.

4 Conclusions: Where We Are and Perspectives

In 2000, three prominent authors in the Semantic Web activity expounded in a seminal Scientific American paper [50] the Semantic Web vision. In the time since then, the Semantic Web has become real. Currently, there are hundreds of millions of RDF triples, on tens of thousands of Web pages, and thousands of ontology pages have been published using RDF schema and OWL, with a growing level of industrial support. This very active support from industry was recently witnessed at a worldwide key conference[36] very focused on the applications of the Semantic Web Technology. Indeed, about 100 talks on industry experience in testing and deploying the technology and about 30 technology showcases were actively followed by 700 attendees mostly from the industry.

However, the Semantic Web is still in its early days and there are many exciting innovations on the horizon.

A keynote speech[37] foresaw a "re-birth of AI" (or the end of the AI-winter) thanks to big-AI applications (Deep Blue, Mars Rover, Deep Space 1, Sachem-Usinor) and Web AI (IR, NLP, Machine Learning, Services, Grid, Agents, social nets) needed due to the tremendous amount of data continuously available on the Web and the emergence of new ways of doing things (loose coupling of distributed applications or services, new business models, etc.).

From 2000 to 2005, we can mention three strong endeavours: DARPA, W3C and EU IST where DARPA and EU IST funded projects particularly were clearly forces towards production of recommendations to W3C (RDF-S, OWL, Rules, ...), for fast adoption in industry. In the meantime, 2003 saw early government adoption and emerging corporate interest, in 2005 the emergence of commercial tools, lots of open source software and even good progress in the problem of scalability (tractable reasoning over 10 million triples has already been claimed!).

So, a significant corporate activity is clearly noticeable today compared to 5 years ago:

– Semantic (Web) technology companies are starting and growing: Cerebra, Siderean, SandPiper, SiberLogic, Ontology Works, Intellidimension, Intellisophic, TopQuadrant, Data Grid, Software AG, OntoText, SAP AG, etc.
– Bigger players are buying in: Adobe, Cisco, HP, IBM, Nokia, Oracle, Sun, Vodaphone etc. for use in 2006.
– Government projects are in and across agencies: US, EU, Japan, Korea, China etc.

---

[36] Semantic Technology Conference 2006 http://www.semantic-conference.com/
[37] SemWeb@5: Current status and Future Promise of the Semantic Web, James Hendler, Ora Lassila, STC 2006, 7 March 2006, San José, USA

– Life sciences/pharma is an increasingly important market, e.g. the Health Care and Life Sciences Interest Group at W3C[38]
– Many open source tools are available: Kowari, RDFLib, Jena, Sesame, Protégé, SWOOP, Wilbur etc. see the W3C SWAD inititiative[39]

Then, it is also witnessed that adding a few semantics to current web applications - meaning "not harnessing the full picture at once but step by step" – gives a significant push in todays applications: richer metadata, data harvesting and visualization, web-based social network, digital asset management, scientific portals, tools for developers, and so gradually closing the semantic gap.

Semantic Web lessons: What has been learned from AI?
– Cross-breeding with AI succeeded, stand-alone AI did not
– Tools are hard to sell (needed too much skill and education)
– Reasoners are a means, not an end (a key component but not the end)
– Knowledge engineering bottleneck (Ontology development and management)

Semantic Web lessons: What has been learned from the Web?
– Web needed high value sites: Internet and Intranet
  – As these linked up, new functionality emerged: Yahoo, Google, and in companies extranet etc.
– New business models followed
  – Netscape, Amazon, GDS, eBay, Yahoo, Google, Apple etc.
– The magic word: Sharing!
  – Internet (Web 1.0), Companies' internal portals ….
  – And now Social Networks (Web 2.0), corporate Knowledge Management

– Key technology locks are still:
  – Development of ontologies i.e. modelling of business domains, authoring, best practices and guidelines, re-use of existing ontologies and simple tools!
  – Knowledge Extraction i.e. the population of ontologies by finding knowledge within legacy data
  – Mapping i.e. overcoming heterogeneity
  – Scalability: approximation, modularization, distribution
  – Reasoners and KR: performance(!) and acceptable heuristics in real world applications
  – Web services: discovery, composition, choreography, execution frameworks, .
  – Language extensions: what aspects are missing? e.g. data types, fuziness, rules

In summary, the performance of semantic technologies clearly shows efficiency gain, effectiveness gain and strategic edge. Those facts are based on a survey of about 200 business entities engaged in semantic technology R&D for development of products and services to deliver solutions. More than 70 have announced and launched semantic technology based products or services. Most things that have been predicted have happened - the semantic chasm is closing. Some things happened

---

[38] http://www.w3.org/2001/sw/hcls/
[39] Semantic Web Advanced Development for Europe http://www.w3.org/2001/sw/Europe/

faster than anticipated like – triple store scaling – and others still need to be realized: ontologies are there (but very little interlinking and the need is huge especially in the healthcare domain), public information sources and public re-usable ontologies (as RDF, OWL etc.), technology transparency for the final user and the practitioners, pervasive computing is just emerging.

Acknowledgements

This work has been possible thanks to the three large European consortia REWERSE, KnowledgeWeb and aceMedia. Acknowledgements are also for the large gathering of international conferences mixing research results and prospects from academia and industry: ESWC, ISWC, ASWC, ICWS, WWW, STC etc. Lastly, credits go also directly to the numerous people, in research labs in academia and in industry who are contributing so strongly to make semantic technology a real momentum in industry.

IST-REWERSE is a NoE supported by the European Commission under contract FP6-506779 http://rewerse.net
IST-Knowledge Web is a NoE supported by the European Commission under contract FP6-507482 http://knowledgeweb.semanticweb.org
IST-aceMedia is an Integrated Project supported by the European Commission under contract FP6-001765. http://www.acemedia.org

References

[1] K.Wiig, Knowledge management: where did it come from and where will it go? Journal of Expert Systems with Applications, 13(1), 1–14, 1997.

[2] J. Hibbard, Knowledge management—knowing what we know. Information Week, 20 October 1997.

[3] G. Petrash, Managing knowledge assets for value. In Proceedings of the Knowledge-Based Leadership Conference,Boston, MA, October 1996. Boston, MA: Linkage.

[4] Zyl J. Corbett D. (2000), A framework for Comparing the use of a Linguistic Ontology in an Application, Workshop Applications of Ontologies and Problem-solving Methods, ECAI'2000, Berlin Germany, August, 2000

[5] Guarino N., Masolo C., Vetere G., OntoSeek: (1999) Content-Based Access to the Web, IEEE Intelligent System.

[6] MKBEEM (2002) Multilingual Knowledge-Based E-Commerce http://www. mkbeem.com

[7] Wiederhold G. (1992). Mediators in the architecture of future information systems, Computer, Vol. 25(3). p.38-49

[8] Barillot C., Amsaleg L., Aubry F., Bazin J-P., Benali H., Cointepas Y., Corouge I., Dameron O., Dojat M., Garbay C., Gibaud B., Gros P., Inkingnehun S., Malandain G., Matsumoto J., Papadopoulos D., Pélégrini M., Richard N., Simon E., Neurobase: Management of distributed knowledge and data bases in neuroimaging . In Human Brain Mapping, Volume 19, Pages 726-726, New-York, NY, 2003.

[9] Cordonnier E., Croci S., Laurent J.-F., Gibaud B. (2003) Interoperability and Medical Communication Using "Patient Envelope"-Based Secure Messaging Proceedings of the Medical Informatics Europe Congress.

[10] Charlet J., Cordonnier E., Gibaud B. (2002) Interopérabilité en médecine: quand le contenu interroge le contenant et l'organisation. Revue Information, interaction, intelligence 2(2).

[11] L. Nixon, M. Mochol, A. Léger, F. Paulus, L. Rocuet, M. Bonifacio, R. Cuel, M. Jarrar, P. Verheyden, Y. Kompatsiaris, V. Papastathis, S. Dasiopoulou, and A. Gomez Pérez. D1.1.2 Prototypical Business Use Cases. Technical report, Knowledge Web NoE, 2004.

[12] P. Shvaiko, A. Léger, F. Paulus, L. Rocuet, L. Nixon, M. Mochol, Y. Kompatsiaris, V. Papastathis, and S. Dasiopoulou. D1.1.3 Knowledge Processing Requirements Analysis. Technical report, Knowledge Web NoE, 2004.

[13] D. Dou, D. McDermott, and P. Qi. Ontology translation on the Semantic Web. Journal on Data Semantics, pages 35–57, 2005.

[14] Stanford Medical Informatics. Protégé ontology editor and knowldege aquisition system. http://protege.stanford.edu/index.html.

[15] D. L. McGuinness, R. Fikes, J. Rice, and S.Wilder. An environment for merging and testing large ontologies. In Proceedings of KR, pages 483–493, 2000.

[16] E. Rahm and P. Bernstein. A survey of approaches to automatic schema matching. VLDB Journal, (10(4)):334–350, 2001.

[17] P. Shvaiko and J. Euzenat. A survey of schema-based macthing approaches. Journal on Data Semantics (IV):146-171, 2005.

[18] A. Billig and K. Sandkuhl. Match-making based on semantic nets: The xml-based approach of baseweb. In Proceedings of the 1st workshop on XML-Technologien fr das Semantic Web, pages 39–51, 2002.

[19] M. Ehrig and S. Staab. QOM: Quick ontology mapping. In Proceedings of ISWC, pages 683–697, 2004.

[20] J. Euzenat and P.Valtchev. Similarity-based ontology alignment in OWL-lite. In Proceedings of ECAI, pages 333–337, 2004.

[21] H.H.Do and E. Rahm. COMA - a system for flexible combination of schema matching approaches. In Proceedings of VLDB, pages 610–621, 2002.

[22] J. Zhong, H. Zhu, J. Li, and Y. Yu. Conceptual graph matching for semantic search. In Proceedings of the 2002 International Conference on Computational Science, 2002.

[23] F. Giunchiglia and P. Shvaiko. Semantic matching. Knowledge Engineering Review Journal, (18(3)):265–280, 2003.

[24] F. Giunchiglia, P. Shvaiko, and M. Yatskevich. S-Match: an algorithm and an implementation of semantic matching. In Proceedings of ESWS, pages 61–75, 2004.

[25] T. Di Noia, E. Di Sciascio, F. M. Donini, and M. Mongiello. A system for principled mat-chmaking in an electronic marketplace. In Proceedings of WWW, pages 321–330, 2003.

[26] R. Dhamankar, Y. Lee, A. Doan, A. Halevy, and P. Domingos. iMAP: Discovering complex semantic matches between database schemas. In Proceedings of SIGMOD, pages 383 – 394, 2004.

[27] P. Shvaiko, F. Giunchiglia, P. Pinheiro da Silva, and D. L. McGuinness. Web explanations for semantic heterogeneity discovery. In Proceedings of ESWC, pages 303-317, 2005.

[28] J. Petrini and T. Risch. Processing queries over rdf views of wrapped relational databases. In Proceedings of the 1st International workshop on Wrapper Techniques for Legacy Systems, Delft, Holland, 2004.

[29] Y. Velegrakis, R. J. Miller, and J. Mylopoulos. Representing and querying data transforma-tions. In Proceedings of ICDE, 2005.

[30] N. Preguica, M. Shapiro, and C. Matheson. Semantics-based reconciliation for collaborative and mobile environments. In Procced ings of CoopIS, 2003.

[31] P. Traverso and M. Pistore. Automated composition of semantic web services into executable processes. In Proceedings of ISWC, pages 380–394, 2004.

[32]   aceMedia project. Integrating knowledge, semantics and content for user centred intelligent media services. http://www.acemedia.org

[33]   V. Haarslev, R. Moller, and M. Wessel. RACER: Semantic middleware for industrial projects based on RDF/OWL, a W3C Standard. http://www.sts.tu-harburg.de/˜r.f.moeller/racer/

[34]   E. Mena, V. Kashyap, A. Sheth, and A. Illarramendi. Observer: An approach for query processing in global information systems based on interoperability between pre-existing on-tologies. In Proceedings of CoopIS, pages 14–25, 1996.

[35]   G. Antoniou, M. Baldoni, C. Baroglio, R. Baumgartner, F. Bry, T. Eiter, N. Henze, M. Herzog, W. May, V. Patti, R. Schindlauer, H. Tompits, and S. Schaffert. Reasoning Methods for Personalization on the Semantic Web. Annals of Mathematics, Computing & Teleinformatics,

[36]   M. Bonifacio, A. Molani. Managing Knowledge needs at Trenitalia. ESWC 2005, Industry Forum proceedings. ESWC 2005 Industry Forum http://www.eswc2005.org/industryforum_presentschedule.html

[37]   B. Brunschweig, J.F. Rainaud. Semantic Web applications for the Petroleum industry. ESWC 2005 Industry Forum http://www.eswc2005.org/industryforum_presentschedule.html

[38]   D. Norheim, R. Fjellheim. Computas AS Norway. Knowledge management in the petroleum industry. ESWC 2006 Industry Forum. http://www.eswc2006.org/

[39]   Semantic Web Case Studies and Best Practices for eBusiness (SWCASE) at ISWC 2005 on line version http://sunsite.informatik.rwth-aachen.de/Publications/CEUR-WS/Vol-155/

[40]   Lehtola, A., Heinecke, J., Bounsaythip, C.: Intelligent Human Language Query Processing in mkbeem. In: Proceedings of the Workshop on Ontologies and Multilinguality in User Interface. HCII 2003, Creta, Greece. (forth)

[41]   Kamp, H., Reyle, U.: From Discourse to Logic. Introduction to Modeltheoretic Semantics of Natural Language, Formal Logic and Discourse Representation Theory. Studies in Linguistics and Philosophy 42. Kluwer, Dordrecht (1993)

[42]   Heinecke, J., Cozannet, A.: Ontology-Driven Information Retrieval. a proposal for multilingual user requests (2003) Paper given at the Workshop on Ontological Knowledge and Linguistic Coding at the 25th annual meeting of the German Linguistics, Feb. 26-28. 2003.

[43]   Guarino, N.: Towards a common ontology for multilingual information access and integration. Paper held at the Third Meeting of SIG on Intelligent Information Agents. Barcelona (1999)

[44]   Baader, F., Kusters, R., Molitor, R.: Rewriting Concepts Using Terminologies. In: Proceedings of the Seventh International Conference on Knowledge Representation and Reasoning, Colorado, USA. (2000) 297–308

[45]   Donini, F., M. Lenzerini, D. Nardi, A.S.: Reasoning in description logics. In Brewka, G., ed.: Foundation of Knowledge Representation, CSLI-Publications (1996) 191–236

[46]   Hacid, M., Léger, A., Rey, C., Toumani, F.: Computing concept covers: A preliminary report. In: International Workshop on Description Logics (DL 2002).Toulouse, France. (2002)

[47]   Hacid, M., Léger, A., Rey, C., Toumani, F.: Dynamic discovery of e-services: A description logics based approach. In: Proceedings of the 18th French conference on advanced databases (BDA), Paris. (2002) 21–25

[48]   Navneet Dalal and Bill Triggs, Generalized SIFT based Human Detection, IEEE Computer Society International Conference on Computer Vision and Pattern Recognition, June 2005.

[49]   Muriel Visani, Christophe Garcia and Jean-Michel Jolion, Face Recognition using Modular Bilinear Discriminant Analysis, 8th International Conference on Visual Information and Information Systems, VISUAL 2005, Amsterdam, The Netherlands, July 5, 2005

[50]   Berners-Lee, T., Hendler, J., Lassila, O.: The semantic web. Scientific American (2001)

And a Few Selected Main References

- The Semantic Web: research and Applications LNCS series:
  - LNCS 2342 (ISWC 2002), LNCS 2870 (ISWC 2003), LNCS 3053 (ESWS 2004), LNCS 3298 (ISWC 2004), LNCS 3532 (ESWS 2005)
- Journal of Web semantics (Elsevier)
- Thematic portal: http://www.semanticweb.org
- Annual Semantic Web applications challenge: http://challenge.semanticweb.org
- W3C http://www.w3.org/2001/sw/ (Best Practices, Rules, Web Services, SWAD)

Author Index

Lecture Notes in Computer Science

For information about Vols. 1–4055

please contact your bookseller or Springer